In this book Jonathan Hall seeks to demonstrate that the ethnic groups of ancient Greece, like many ethnic groups throughout the world today, were not ultimately racial, linguistic, religious or cultural groups, but social groups whose 'origins' in extraneous territories were just as often imagined as they were real. Adopting an explicitly anthropological point of view, he examines the evidence of literature, archaeology and linguistics to elucidate the nature of ethnic identity in ancient Greece. Rather than treating Greek ethnic groups as 'natural' or 'essential' – let alone 'racial' – entities, he emphasises the active, constructive and dynamic role of ethnography, genealogy, material culture and language in shaping ethnic consciousness. An introductory chapter outlines the history of the study of ethnicity in Greek antiquity.

Ethnic identity in Greek antiquity

Ethnic identity in Greek antiquity

JONATHAN M. HALL

Assistant Professor in the Departments
of History and Classics,
University of Chicago

CAMBRIDGE
UNIVERSITY PRESS

DF
135
.H33
1997

PUBLISHED BY THE PRESS SYNDICATE OF THE UNIVERSITY OF CAMBRIDGE
The Pitt Building, Trumpington Street, Cambridge CB2 1RP, United Kingdom

CAMBRIDGE UNIVERSITY PRESS
The Edinburgh Building, Cambridge CB2 2RU, UK http://www.cup.cam.ac.uk
40 West 20th Street, New York, NY 10011-41211, USA http://www.cup.org
10 Stamford Road, Oakleigh, Melbourne 3166, Australia

© Jonathan M. Hall 1997

First published 1997
Reprinted 1998
First paperback edition 2000

Printed in Great Britain at the University Press, Cambridge

Typeset in Monotype Baskerville 10/12 pt

A catalogue record for this book is available from the British Library

Library of Congress cataloguing in publication data

Hall, Jonathan M.
Ethnic identity in Greek antiquity / Jonathan M. Hall.
p.   cm.
Includes bibliographical references and index.
ISBN 0 521 58017 X (hardback)
1. Greece – Ethnic relations.   2. Minorities – Greece – Ethnic
identity.   3. Greece – Civilization – To 146 BC.   I. Title.
DE135.H33   1997
305.8'00938–dc20   96–9563 CIP

ISBN 0 521 58017 X hardback
ISBN 0 521 78999 0 paperback

To Ilaria

Contents

Figures

Preface and acknowledgements

I hope it will not seem too perverse to establish, at the outset, what this book is *not* about. In the first place, its object of study is not a *collective* Hellenic identity, but rather the plurality of 'intrahellenic' identities, of which the Ionians, Dorians, Aiolians and Akhaians are simply the best-known examples. It might be argued that this distinction is simply one of degree and that what we have in Greek antiquity is a situation that is sometimes termed 'nested ethnicity', whereby a citizen of a city such as Sparta could subscribe not only to a Dorian ethnicity but also to a Greek identity that was itself constituted by ethnic subdivisions such as the Dorians and Aiolians. That is certainly one way of explaining why Greek myth regarded ethnic eponyms such as Doros and Aiolos as the sons of the Hellenic *Urvater*, Hellen, though I believe that there is a case to be made for keeping the two levels of identity distinct. Firstly, it is clear that some of these intrahellenic ethnic identities may have existed prior to the emergence of a fully blown Hellenic consciousness which sought to subsume them. Secondly, while the identity of groups such as the Dorians or the Ionians could undoubtedly become politicised, it generally tended to retain (with varying degrees of salience) its ethnic definition. Conversely, although Hellenic identity was clearly envisaged in the sixth century BC as being ethnic in character, there is some evidence that by the fourth century it was conceived more in cultural terms. The clearest enunciation of this comes in Isokrates' comment (*Panegyrikos* 50) that 'the name of Hellene should be applied to persons sharing in the culture rather than the ancestry of the Greeks', and reaches its apogee in the Hellenistic world when cities from Spain to Afghanistan could participate equally within a cultural-linguistic (though not ethnic) paradigm of Hellenism.

In the second place, this book does not seek to serve as a gazetteer of all the numerous ethnic groups which inhabited Greece in antiquity. Its aim is rather to establish some methodological principles governing the possibilities (and, more importantly, limitations) of studying in the distant past a topic of contemporary anthropological interest. Thus, the core chapters of the book (chapters 3, 5 and 6) examine the three principal areas of evidence available to the student of antiquity - literature and myth; archaeology; and linguistics - and the examples that are included are intended to be illustrative or cautionary rather than exhaustive. Since the work is intended to be a methodological exercise rather than a systematic survey, there are no strictly defined chronological limits to its scope, though in prac-

xiii

tice the period with which it is largely concerned falls between 1200 and 400 BC. Within this broad chronological sweep, examples are drawn from various parts of the Greek world from South Italy to Cyprus, though there is a noticeable emphasis on the Argolid region of the northeast Peloponnese. The reason why the Argolid provides such a fertile area for ethnic analysis is partly due to the quality of its literary, archaeological and linguistic material which is (arguably) second only to that of Attika, but more importantly because - unlike Attika - the region was continually characterised by literary sources as being multi-ethnic.

At the time of writing, the topic of ethnicity is beginning to figure increasingly within research proposals in classical studies and particularly in classical archaeology - a discipline which has, in the last few decades, become far more receptive (albeit belatedly) to the theories and trends being elaborated within the wider field of world archaeology. The distant origins of this book are not, however, situated within this fashionable pedigree. They are instead rooted in a field trip that I made as an undergraduate to Troizen, in the Eastern Argolid, in the summer of 1986. My primary intention was to study the archaeology and history of the site, but in the course of this I became increasingly interested in the notion, recited in much of the modern literature (though, oddly enough, less explicit in literary sources), that an Ionian population had been overlaid by Dorian migrants during the Early Iron Age. Although the terms 'Dorian' and 'Ionian' were familiar ones, I began to wonder exactly how this rather mechanistic view of settlement history might have been negotiated 'on the ground'. My curiosity led to doctoral research, undertaken between 1989 and 1993 at the University of Cambridge, in which I examined the evidence for ethnic identity in the Argolid region in the years 900 to 600 BC. It is that study which has provided the springboard for the current work.

My principal debts of gratitude are to Anthony Snodgrass, who supervised my doctoral dissertation, and to Paul Cartledge and Robin Osborne who examined it. Their continued support and interest have been crucial in nurturing the post-doctoral development of this book. I should also like to acknowledge the inspiration I derived from George Forrest, Lin Foxhall and Nicholas Purcell in the early and formative days of my research. A number of friends, colleagues and mentors have at various times over the last six years read and commented upon drafts of certain sections - in particular, Tamsyn Barton, Robert Coleman, Eric Hamp, Valérie Huet, Martin Maiden, Paul Millett, Catherine Morgan, Colin Renfrew, Todd Whitelaw and Greg Woolf, as well as the readers of Cambridge University Press. While they should not be held responsible for the views expressed here, I have considered their opinions carefully and would like to extend to them my sincere gratitude.

Every study which adopts an explicitly interdisciplinary approach also risks the charge of superficiality. If this criticism has been mitigated in any small way, it is largely due to all those friends and colleagues who have given so freely of their time and expertise to discuss various issues arising from my research. In this connection, I wish to thank Padma Anagol-McGinn, Tjeerd van Andel, Carla Antonaccio,

Anton Bensen, Neil Brodie, Keith Brown, Stephen Colvin, Catherine Dyer, Nic Fields, Jonathan Fletcher, Lisa French, David Good, Adrian Gregory, Robin Hägg, Michael Jameson, Nancy Klein, John Lavery, Patrick McGinn, Anne Pariente, Marcel Piérart, Wolf Rudolph, Guy Sanders, Ingrid Strøm, Andrea Swinton, Sofia Voutsaki, Berit Wells and James Whitley. I should also like to acknowledge the helpful information communicated to me by the late Paul Courbin and Ernest Gellner, as well as the assistance afforded me by the *dimarkhio* of Argos.

My research would have quickly ground to a halt without the financial assistance of the British Academy, the Managing Committee of the British School at Athens, and both the Faculty of Classics and King's College, Cambridge. The book was largely written up during my tenure of a Research Fellowship at Downing College, Cambridge and I should like to thank the Master and Fellows of the college for providing me with such a congenial environment in which to work. In addition, certain sections were researched and written in warmer climes, and I am grateful to the British School at Athens and the Deutsches Archäologisches Institut in Rome for permission to use their excellent library facilities. I should also like to acknowledge the warm but professional assistance that I have received from Pauline Hire and Susan Beer for Cambridge University Press.

Finally, I should like to thank my parents for their long-standing encouragement and above all my wife, Ilaria Romeo. Apart from acting as the most patient of sounding-boards, her critical judgement and wide knowledge of the classical world have proved indispensable, and it is to her that I gratefully dedicate this book.

Note on the spelling of Greek names

In general, I have tried to resist the Latinisation of Greek words: I thus write Aitolia for Aetolia; Akhilleus for Achilles; 'akropolis' for 'acropolis'; Herodotos for Herodotus; 'synoikism' for 'synoecism', etc. I freely admit, however, to a certain amount of inconsistency for which I apologise in advance. Firstly, I retain the convention of rendering Greek *upsilon* by English *y* - thus, Thoukydides (Thucydides) instead of Thoukudides, and Aiskhylos (Aeschylus) instead of Aiskhulos. Secondly, I often preserve familiar English forms of Greek proper nouns, but with Greek orthography - e.g. Korinth, Tiryns and Attika instead of the more technically correct Korinthos, Tirynthos and Attike. Finally, there are certain names such as Strabo, Plato and Plutarch, which I have never been able to bring myself to transliterate strictly as Strabon, Platon and Ploutarkhos.

There is, however, one area in which my inconsistency is more rational. In the case of Mykenai (Mycenae), I use the Greek form of the adjective (Mykenaian) to refer to the site and its occupants in the historical period, but the Latin form of the adjective (Mycenaean) to refer to the chronological phase of the Late Bronze Age to which the site gave its name.

Abbreviations used in the text and bibliography

AA	*Archäologischer Anzeiger des Deutschen Archäologischen Instituts,* Berlin.
AAA	*Athens Annals of Archaeology,* Athens.
Act.Arch	*Acta Archaeologica,* Copenhagen.
Act.Hyp	*Acta Hyperborea,* Copenhagen.
Africa	*Africa: Journal of the International African Institute,* London.
AION (ASA)	*Annali, Istituto Universitario Orientale, Dipartimento di Studi del Mondo Classico e del Mediterraneo: sezione di archeologia e storia antica,* Naples.
AION (L)	*Annali, Istituto Universitario Orientale, Dipartimento di Studi del Mondo Classico e del Mediterraneo: sezione linguistica,* Naples.
AJA	*American Journal of Archaeology,* New York.
AJPA	*American Journal of Physical Anthropology,* Washington.
AK	*Antike Kunst: herausgegeben von der Vereinigung der Freunde antiker Kunst in Basel,* Olten.
AM	*Mitteilungen des Deutschen Archäologischen Instituts, Athenische Abteilung,* Berlin.
Am.Ant	*American Antiquity,* Menasha.
Am.Anth	*American Anthropologist,* New York.
Am.Eth	*American Ethnologist,* Washington.
AN	*Archaeological News,* Tallahassee.
Ann.ESC	*Annales (Économies, Sociétés, Civilisations),* Paris.
Ant	*Antiquity: a Quarterly Review of Archaeology,* Newbury.
ARC	*Archaeological Review from Cambridge,* Cambridge.
Archaiognosia	Ἀρχαιογνωσία, Athens.
Arch.Eph	Ἀρχαιολογική Ἐφημερίς, Athens.
Areth	*Arethusa: a Journal of the Wellsprings of Western Man,* Buffalo.
Arion	*Arion: a Journal of Humanities and the Classics,* Boston.
A.S.Atene	*Annuario della Scuola Archeologica di Atene,* Rome.
ASNSP	*Annali della Scuola Normale Superiore di Pisa,* Pisa.
AT	*Anthropology Today (Royal Anthropological Institute),* London.
Athenaeum	*Athenaeum: Studi di Letteratura e Storia dell' Antichità,* Pavia.
BAR	*British Archaeological Reports,* Oxford.
BCH	*Bulletin de Correspondance Hellénique,* Paris.
BICS	*Bulletin of the Institute of Classical Studies,* London.
BSA	*Annual of the British School at Athens,* London.

CAH	*Cambridge Ancient History*, Cambridge.
Cl.Ant	*Classical Antiquity*, Berkeley.
CP	*Classical Philology*, Chicago.
CQ	*Classical Quarterly*, Oxford.
Cret.Stud	*Cretan Studies*, Amsterdam.
CSCA	*Californian Studies in Classical Antiquity*, Berkeley.
CSSH	*Comparative Studies in Society and History*, Cambridge.
Deltion	Ἀρχαιολογικόν Δελτίον, Athens.
EAC	*Entretiens sur l'Antiquité Classique*, Geneva.
Emerita	*Emerita: Revista de Lingüística y Filologia Clásica*, Madrid.
Eth	*Ethnicity*, New York.
FGrH	F. Jacoby, *Die Fragmente der griechischen Historiker*. Berlin and Leiden.
Glotta	*Glotta: Zeitschrift für griechische und latineische Sprache*, Göttingen.
Hermes	*Hermes: Zeitschrift für klassische Philologie*, Wiesbaden.
Hesperia	*Hesperia: Journal of the American School of Classical Studies at Athens*, Princeton.
Historia	*Historia: Zeitschrift für alte Geschichte*, Wiesbaden.
IF	*Indogermanische Forschungen*, Berlin.
IG	*Inscriptiones Graecae*, Berlin.
JAA	*Journal of Anthropological Archaeology*, New York.
JDAI	*Jahrbuch des (kaiserlich) Deutschen Archäologischen Instituts*, Berlin.
JFA	*Journal of Field Archaeology*, Boston.
JHE	*Journal of Human Evolution*, London.
JHS	*Journal of Hellenic Studies*, London.
JMA	*Journal of Mediterranean Archaeology*, Sheffield.
JMS	*Journal of Mediterranean Studies*, Msida.
JRS	*Journal of Roman Studies*, London.
JSP	*Journal of Social Psychology*, Worcester MA.
Kadmos	*Kadmos: Zeitschrift für vor- und frühgriechische Epigraphik*, Berlin.
Kernos	*Kernos: Revue Internationale et Pluridisciplinaire de Religion Grecque Antique*, Liège.
Klio	*Klio: Beiträge zur alten Geschichte*, Berlin.
Kratylos	*Kratylos: kritisches Berichts- und Rezensionorgan für indogermanische und allgemeine Sprachwissenschaft*, Wiesbaden.
Latomus	*Latomus: Revue d' Études Latines*, Brussels.
LSJ	H.G. Liddell and R. Scott, *A Greek-English Lexicon*, revised by H.S. Jones, Oxford (1968).
MAAP	*University of Michigan, Museum of Anthropology: Anthropological Papers*, Ann Arbor.
MAGW	*Mitteilungen der anthropologischen Gesellschaft in Wien*, Vienna.
Man	*Man (Royal Anthropological Institute)*, London.
Mnem	*Mnemosyne: Bibliotheca Classica Batava*, Leiden.

Morph.Unt	*Morphologische Untersuchungen auf dem Gebiete der indogermanischen Sprachen*, Leipzig.
Mus.Helv	*Museum Helveticum*, Basel.
Op.Ath	*Opuscula Atheniensia*, Lund.
PAPS	*Proceedings of the American Philosophical Society*, Philadelphia.
PCPS	*Proceedings of the Cambridge Philological Society*, Cambridge.
PDIA	*Proceedings of the Danish Institute at Athens*, Copenhagen.
Peloponnesiaka	Τα Πελοποννησιακά τῆς ἐν Ἀθήναις Ἑταιρείας Πελοποννησιακῶν Σπουδῶν, Athens.
PP	*La Parola del Passato: Rivista di Studi Antichi*, Naples.
P.Pres	*Past and Present: a Journal of Historical Studies*, Oxford.
PPS	*Proceedings of the Prehistoric Society*, Cambridge.
Praktika	Πρακτικά τῆς ἐν Ἀθήναις Ἀρχαιολογικῆς Ἑταιρείας, Athens.
QUCC	*Quaderni Urbinati di Cultura Classica*, Rome.
RAALBA	*Rendiconti della Accademia di Archeologia Lettere e Belle Arti*, Naples.
RANL	*Rendiconti della Accademia Nazionale dei Lincei*, Rome.
REG	*Revue des Études Grecques*, Paris.
Rev.Arch	*Revue Archéologique*, Paris.
RGZM	*Jahrbuch des Römisch-Germanischen Zentralmuseums in Mainz*, Bonn.
Rh.M	*Rheinisches Museum für Philologie*, Frankfurt.
SEG	*Supplementum Epigraphicum Graecum*, Leiden.
SMEA	*Studi Micenei ed Egeo-Anatolici*, Rome.
TAPA	*Transactions of the American Philological Association*, Boston.
TPS	*Transactions of the Philological Society*, Oxford.
Verbum	*Verbum: Revue de Linguistique*, Nancy.
WA	*World Archaeology*, London.
ZE	*Zeitschrift für Ethnologie*, Berlin.
Zephyrus	*Zephyrus: Crónica del Seminario de Arqueología y de la Sección Arqueológica del Centro de Estudios Salmantinos*, Salamanca.
ZPE	*Zeitschrift für Papyrologie und Epigraphik*, Bonn.

1

Phrasing the problem

Introduction

We live in a world surrounded by ethnic conflict. Since the 1960s, ethnic resurgences have occurred between Walloons and Flemings in Belgium; Serbs, Croats and Muslims in Bosnia; Hutu and Tutsi in Burundi and Rwanda; Greeks and Turks in Cyprus; Sikhs, Hindus and Muslims in India; Catholics and Protestants in Ireland; Chinese and Malay in Malaysia; Ibo, Hausa and Yoruba in Nigeria; English and French in Québec; Christian Armenians and Muslim Azerbaijanis in the south of the former Soviet Union; and Sinhs and Tamils in Sri Lanka, to name just a few.[1] At first sight, the appearance of a book on ancient ethnicity might seem like a gratuitous and anachronistic exercise, attempting to impose upon antiquity a subject whose true relevance is more topical. Nothing could be further from the truth. Quite apart from the fact that the separation of past and present tends to be dissolved in the proclamation of ethnic claims and counterclaims (consider the dispute that arose between Greece and the Former Yugoslav Republic of Macedonia over the so-called 'Star of Vergina'),[2] the study of ethnic identity in antiquity is nothing new as the remainder of this chapter will demonstrate.

Indeed, from as early as the eighteenth century, classical scholars were interested in examining the fields of art, architecture, music, dress, philosophy, customs and political forms in order to identify the specific 'character' of the various ethnic groups which inhabited Greece in antiquity. The construction of this discourse on ancient ethnicity was influenced primarily by contemporary romantic beliefs which attributed ethnic specificity to environmental and racial determinants, yet it is precisely the assumed immutability of these determinants which allowed romantic theorists such as Johann Herder and the Comte de Gobineau to lay the foundation stone for the racial philosophy of Nazism. In the wake of the Second World War – and more particularly the Holocaust – the motives for treating ethnic identity as a valid area of research were discredited. The subject of ancient Greek ethnicity was no exception, and scholars either practised a studied circumspection in this regard or else attempted to recast the ethnic groups of antiquity in a more

---

[1] For a fuller list, see Tambiah 1989, 337.
[2] See Borza 1981, 87 n. 60; Adams 1983, 6 n. 16; Green 1982; 1989, 160–64; Faklaris 1994; Brown 1994; Danforth 1995.

I

sanitised role by substituting lexical terms such as 'linguistic groups' or 'cultural groups'.

The anthropological response to the crisis of scholarship occasioned by the Second World War was the 'instrumentalist' approach to ethnicity which proclaimed that ethnic identity was a guise adopted by interest groups to conceal aims that were more properly political or economic. Yet the ethnic resurgences of the 1970s and 1980s presented a clear challenge to the validity of the instrumentalist approach; this prompted a renewed anthropological interest in the subject of ethnic identity which is examined in chapter 2. Current research tends to grant at least an intersubjective reality to ethnic identity, though it differs from pre-war scholarship on a number of important points. Firstly, it stresses that the ethnic group is not a biological group but a social group, distinguished from other collectivities by its subscription to a putative myth of shared descent and kinship and by its association with a 'primordial' territory. Secondly, it rejects the nineteenth-century view of ethnic groups as static, monolithic categories with impermeable boundaries for a less restrictive model which recognises the dynamic, negotiable and situationally constructed nature of ethnicity. Finally, it questions the notion that ethnic identity is primarily constituted by either genetic traits, language, religion or even common cultural forms. While all of these attributes may act as important symbols of ethnic identity, they really only serve to bolster an identity that is ultimately constructed through written and spoken discourse.

If the construction of ethnic identity is considered to be primarily discursive, then it is literary evidence that should represent our first point of departure. In chapter 3, I begin by examining ancient terminology and conclude that although the use of the word *ethnos* is not restricted to ethnic groups, it is often coupled with the terms *genos* and *syngeneia* which do explicitly introduce the notions of descent and kinship which are so central to ethnic consciousness. I then turn to consider myths of ethnic origin. These have often been taken to be the remnants of a genuine historical memory of migrations at the end of the Bronze Age, though I suggest that they are better viewed as the means by which ethnic communities 'thought themselves' in the historical period. Indeed, a close examination of the constitutive myths of the Athenians, the Dorians and the Herakleidai shows how these groups used and manipulated ethnographic and genealogical traditions not only to carve out distinct identities but also to effect assimilation with (and differentiation from) other ethnic groups. The fact that these myths exist in so many (sometimes contradictory) variants is testimony not to the confused debility of human memory but to the varying functions which they served through time and across different regions.

The role of ethnography and genealogy in the construction of ethnic identity is examined in further detail in chapter 4 by means of an extended case-study dealing with the Argolid region of Greece. The demographic composition of the Argolid is consistently envisaged as multi-ethnic in character by a number of literary sources ranging from the sixth century BC to the second century AD. Nevertheless, although the ethnographic picture provides a useful point of departure (and lends justification) for the analysis of ethnicity in the ancient Argolid, it is a rather blunt tool for capturing the subtle and dynamic operation of ethnic strategies. From this point of view, the genealogies which served to express the changing relations between ethnic groups over time are more helpful. By understanding the internal logic of these genealogies and thus identifying the contradictions which challenge that logic, it is possible to distinguish at least two originally independent genealogical assemblages which structured group identity. The first is concerned with exogenous origins and conquest and was eventually incorporated within the ethnic pedigree of the Dorians. The second stresses ancestral hereditary rights and is explicitly associated with the myth of the Return of the Herakleidai. Furthermore, the areas in which this second genealogical tradition is attested are those where particular accord was paid to the cult of Hera – a goddess who was not only thought of as the primeval patron of the Argive plain but whose name is etymologically connected (via Herakles) with that of the Herakleidai.

The emphasis on the discursive construction of ethnic identity and on the fact that ethnic groups are not primarily defined by language or culture obviously has important implications for the role of archaeology and linguistics in the study of ancient ethnicity. In chapter 5, I summarise the arguments that have been proposed for and against the historicity of the Dorian invasion on the basis of material culture and suggest that the *impasse* which has resulted is due to a misunderstanding of how material culture functions within strategies of ethnic self-definition. With the help of some ethnographic examples, I conclude that while material symbols can certainly be selected as active emblems of a consciously proclaimed ethnic identity, it is a mistake to assume that material cultural patterning can serve as an objective or passive indication of ethnic groups.

A similar conclusion is reached in the case of language (chapter 6). Traditionally, the distribution of the dialect groups in ancient Greece has been explained by (and used to justify) the literary tradition of ethnic migrations. More recently – no doubt as part of the post-war reaction to ethnic studies already observed – some historians have sought to reduce the ethnic groups of the literary tradition to the status of linguistic groups. In fact, a close analysis of these dialects reveals that linguistic boundaries are not entirely coterminous with ethnic boundaries, that the Greeks themselves could not have relied upon linguistic cues only in assigning dialect-speakers to ethnic groups and that linguistic development in ancient Greece may operate independently of ethnic factors. Again, however, linguistic symbols may be actively employed at certain times as part of an ethnic strategy, and I consider some examples where ethnic groups consciously sought to bolster their distinctiveness through the medium of language. The intention is not to deny the self-evident contribution of archaeology and language but to define more closely the role which they play in the study of ethnic identity in Greek antiquity.

The Dorians in a 'sociology of knowledge'

It is then that we are recalled to the life immediately before us, at our feet; the hundreds of workmen with marked Southern features, in varied and picturesque costumes; the small native horses drawing numerous carts with their rumbling noise, through which the shouts of the drivers pierce, – and all these men speaking the language of ancient Greece, changed and attenuated and abused, but still the tongue of ancient Hellas. Dotted among them are foreign-looking young men, different in feature and garb and tongue, watching over the work. And we ask, Who are these new men, *these new Dorians,* who speak the foreign tongue? and whence come they, and wherefore? And the answer is, They come from afar, from the land of the setting sun, thousands of miles over the salt sea. But they come not to destroy and conquer, but to restore to the light of day the life that has been buried under that soil for countless ages. And we are overcome by the sense of the great poetic justice, the rightness of things, – that the youngest inheritors of Hellenic culture among the nations should restore to the light of day the oldest sanctuary of ancient Hellas.[3] (my italics)

The above description of the American excavations at the Argive Heraion between 1892 and 1895 by Charles Waldstein (later Sir Charles Walston) is a perfect example of what Annie Schnapp-Gourbeillon has described as the 'spectre' of the Dorians which haunts the historians of ancient Greece.[4] In this unashamedly colonialist pastiche, the role of the latter-day Dorian intruders 'from the land of the setting sun' (i.e. the American trench supervisors) is contrasted with that of the indigenous 'colourful' labourers with their 'abused' language. Unlike their forebears, however, the conquest of these 'new Dorians' is cultural rather than territorial. The task of bringing to light 'the oldest sanctuary of ancient Hellas' (actually a good deal less ancient than Waldstein believed) appropriately falls to those whose neonate national identity was so bound up with classical ideals, exemplified by Thomas Jefferson's foundation of the University of Virginia, or the practice of endowing new cities with classical names – for instance, Athens, Georgia; Troy, New Hampshire; Olympia, Washington; or Ithaca, New York.[5]

Throughout history, the Dorians have commanded interest as an *explanans.* For the ancients, the migrations of the Dorians southwards from central and north-west Greece served to explain the manner in which the last dynasties of Homer's Akhaians were ousted, thus putting an end to the Heroic Age. In more recent scholarship, their role as an *explanans* has been rather to account for the widespread destructions which put an end to the Mycenaean palaces (chapter 5) and for the historical distribution of dialects belonging to the Doric dialect group (chapter 6). They have also, however, been treated as an *explanandum* – as a phenomenon worth studying in their own right. In this field, the concern has been to determine what characterised the Dorians as a collective entity and what it was that distinguished them from other groups such as the Ionians or the Aiolians.

---

[3] Waldstein 1902, 88.   [4] Schnapp-Gourbeillon 1986, 43.   [5] Highet 1949, 399–400.

One of the most famous (though by no means earliest) attempts to re-enrol the Dorians in the historical imagination of modern scholarship was the publication in 1824 of Karl Otfried Müller's *Die Dorier* (translated into English in 1830). Müller's position within intellectual history may best be understood through an extract from his preface to the second edition of *Die Dorier*, regrettably omitted from the English translation:

> ... das wir uns einerseits schon einen Begriff von dem geistigen Wesen eines Volkes gebildet haben müssen, ehe wir dasselbe in dem äussern Handeln der Einzelnen, in denen sich die Sinnesart der Gesamtheit mehr oder minder darstellt, zu erkennen und nachzuweisen vermögen, und das uns anderseits doch nichts Anders als die unbefangenste Betrachtung des Letztern zur richtigen Erkenntniss des Erstern führen kann . . .[6]

> On the one hand, we must have already formed a concept of the spiritual nature of a people, before we are able to recognise and demonstrate it in the external behaviour of individuals, in which the spirit of the community is more or less represented. On the other hand, nothing other than the most impartial examination of the latter can lead us to the correct recognition of the former.

This apparent contradiction between comprehending the *a priori* existence of the 'spiritual nature of the people' and the necessity of resorting to a rigorous and impartial examination of ancient behavioural patterns to recognise it more accurately is perhaps symptomatic of what Martin Bernal has termed Müller's 'romantic positivism'.[7]

Positivism may be defined as the philosophical belief in an objective knowledge, governed by laws akin to those postulated for the natural sciences, that can be arrived at through empirical induction.[8] In historical terms, positivism proclaims both the existence of a real, objective past that is external to the historical analyst, and the possibility of describing it in its most accurate details. For R.G. Collingwood, such ideas were symbolised by the *Cambridge Ancient History* which, apart from setting itself up as an authoritative and comprehensive account of antiquity, subscribed to a positivist vision of history as an assemblage of isolated and easily ascertainable facts through its practice of farming out chapters (or sometimes even subdivisions of chapters) to different authors. The compilation of contributions by authors from varying cultural, social, political and intellectual backgrounds, working in disciplines with their own unique methodologies and goals, was not viewed as problematic precisely because the past that they were describing was deemed real, objective and unitary.[9]

Strictly speaking, it is a little anachronistic to refer to Müller's work as positivist, especially since the term (first formulated in its current sense by the sociologist Auguste Comte) was not applied widely outside the social sciences until the second half of the nineteenth century. Nonetheless, there is a certain positivist flavour in

---

[6] Müller 1844, vii. [7] Bernal 1987, 309. [8] Collingwood 1946, 127; Lloyd 1986, 42.
[9] Collingwood 1946, 147.

5

Müller's emphasis on the 'most impartial examination' of past behaviour. This was a dictate of *Quellenkritik*, or 'source criticism', which was developed during the eighteenth century at the University of Göttingen where Müller held a chair. By espousing a more systematic and 'scientific' approach to literary sources, which attempted to distinguish authorial bias from more reliable literary testimony, the aim of *Quellenkritik* was research that was 'historical and critical not of *things* to be hoped for, but for *facts*'.[10]

A good example of the positivist method in *Die Dorier* is the way Müller traces the migration of the Dorians. For Müller, Apollo was the principal Dorian deity – the 'totem of the tribe' – fulfilling much the same role as Poseidon did for the Ionians. The prevalence of cults to Apollo in Dorian cities, and especially Sparta, could be contrasted with the fact that the Akhaians and Arkadians possessed few Apollo temples, and that those that did exist generally commanded little importance. One had, therefore, only to trace the transmission of the cult of Apollo (widely regarded as a newcomer to the Greek pantheon) to track the migrations of the Dorians. In the first phase, the cult was diffused from the Tempe valley in northeast Thessaly towards Delphi, Delos and Knossos. The second phase involved a radiation from Krete both westwards to mainland Greece and eastwards towards the coast of Asia Minor. Finally, the cult of Apollo arrived in the Peloponnese as a consequence of the Dorian migrations described in the literary texts.[11] This reconstruction of the diffusion of Apollo cults was no mean achievement, not least because it predated the excavation of most of the major sanctuaries of Greece. In fact, Müller plumbed the murky depths of aetiological poetry such as the *Homeric Hymn to Apollo*, which purported to account for the origins of Apollo sanctuaries and which Müller took as a hazy reflection of a 'real', objective past.

It is, however, the decision to focus on the *Volksgeist* or 'spirit of the community' which reveals the more important contextual influence on Müller's work. The emphasis on the community as an organic whole, rather than a collection of individuals, is very much a product of romantic opposition to the Enlightenment. *Die Dorier* cannot be fully comprehended without reference to a German romantic paradigm, in which the two themes of environmental determinism and consanguinity ('the Dark Gods, Blood and Earth')[12] are dominant.

Environmental determinism is not a concept that is fundamentally novel to the student of classical antiquity. Herodotos attributes to the Persian king Kyros the Great the maxim that 'soft regions breed soft men', and the doctrine is elaborated further by the author of a fifth-century Hippokratic treatise, who argues that geography, local water-supplies and prevailing winds determine not only the health of a population, but also its collective character.[13] Where German romanticism differed from the classical picture was in its greater emphasis on the rootedness of the

---

[10] This citation of Friedrich August Wolf is quoted in Bernal 1987, 286. See also Collingwood 1946, 127–31.   [11] See especially Müller 1830, 227, 266, 271, 276–77.
[12] The phrase is that of Gellner (1987, 87).
[13] Herodotos 9.122.3; Pseudo-Hippokrates, *Airs, Waters, Places* 24.

6

Volk in its native soil. The theme of migration is recurrent in Greek literature, whether pertaining to a genuine historical memory or an aetiological construct, but the important distinction is that the migrating population could change its collective character along with its homeland: Kyros' utterance is designed to act as a warning against the Persians moving to a more hospitable land where they would lose their rugged temperament and cease to be rulers. In the romantic imagination, on the other hand, the character of the *Volk* was moulded more by its original homeland than by its current location. This is why the Dorians, even after their migration south from a homeland that romantic scholars were eventually to locate in Germany, could still be seen as representing the purer, more ideal model of Indogermanism (a term used in nineteenth- and twentieth-century German scholarship to denote what would now be called Indo-Europeanism).[14]

Consanguinity refers to a notion of kinship that uses blood as a metaphor. Again, this is to be found in antiquity: Homer uses the word 'blood' (*haima*) to express kin relationships, and Herodotos enumerates blood as one of the criteria of Hellenic identity.[15] For the romantics, blood symbolised the 'natural essence' of life; but it is this image of an essence that has led to some dangerous associations, because one of the qualities of an essence is its purity. Pure, 'unsullied' blood is blood that has been 'uncontaminated' by another type of blood – that is, blood of a different ethnic origin. Before the construction of a field of genetics, it was the image of blood as essence that lay behind the concept of 'racial purity' and permeated so much of nineteenth-century thought not only in Germany, but also in Britain in the work of people like Carlyle or Matthew Arnold.[16]

Elements of these two themes had already coalesced within the romantic paradigm in the few decades prior to the publication of *Die Dorier*. In the 1790s, Friedrich von Schlegel had studied the character of the Greek *Stämme*, as expressed through art, customs and political forms. Since, however, these *Stämme* were largely defined on the basis of literary genres, whereby epic poetry was categorised as Ionian, lyric poetry as Dorian and drama as Athenian, Schlegel did not envisage the boundaries between the groups as being necessarily impermeable.[17]

Müller was probably influenced also by the Norwegian natural philosopher Henrik Steffens, who argued for an indissoluble link between the natural environment, human nature and the history of humanity, and whose lectures Müller apparently attended.[18] By far the most important figure, however, in the genealogy of romantic thinking that Müller inherited was Johann Herder (1744–1803). Accredited today as the founder of *both* cultural pluralism as a good *and* racism, he proposed that humankind was divided into various races, each having its primal physical and mental characteristics shaped by its original environment. By adopting a supposedly scientific, multilineal evolutionary view (which in some respects

---

[14] This notion of a Teutonic homeland for the Indo-Europeans was later to receive support from archaeologists, especially Gustav Kossinna: see further chapter 5.
[15] Homer, *Odyssey* 8.583; Herodotos 8.144.2.   [16] Bell 1975, 155.   [17] Rawson 1991, 318–20.
[18] Wittenburg 1984, 1037.

prefigured Darwin's theory of natural selection) Herder argued not only that humankind represented the highest organism in its development from animal life, but that within this humankind there emerged an even higher type of human organism, the historical human, who arose (hardly surprisingly) in Europe and was therefore moulded by the geography and climate of that continent.[19]

With the development of comparative philology, language also came to reinforce 'blood' in defining ethnic groups. Herder maintained that for a people to retain its specific character (which he defined in terms of its creativity, spirit, individuality and genius), it had to preserve its linguistic and ethnic authenticity.[20] Schlegel drew a distinction between the 'animal' non-inflected languages and the 'noble and spiritual' inflected ones, by which he was referring primarily to German and Greek – languages linked in the German imagination by the fact that they both used definite articles, a plethora of particles and prepositions, and were the languages of religious protest after the Reformation.[21] Müller's pupil Ernst Curtius was later to argue that a language as beautiful as Greek could not have developed in the Mediterranean, but must have originated further north.[22] In a similar vein, Karl Wilhelm von Humboldt claimed German and Greek to be 'pure' and 'uncontaminated':[23] the metaphorical allusions to the 'blood essence' are clear.

It would be wrong to suggest that Karl Otfried Müller was purely a 'man of his time' – an ineffectual actor in a socially determined world. In fact, many of his influences derived from closer to home. In a work of 1817, entitled *De arte Aeginetica* ('On the art of Aigina'), he attributed to the Dorians characteristics such as moderation, simplicity, frugality and steadfastness – all traits which, as Andreas Wittenburg has pointed out, assume a greater relevance when one learns that Müller's father was a Protestant military chaplain in Silesia.[24] In other words, the character of Müller's Dorians is uncannily Protestant.

Nevertheless, *Die Dorier* clearly does find its niche within the romantic paradigm. Shades of Schlegel resurface in Müller's stress on the 'nordic character' of the Doric dialect, particularly in the use of masculine endings in *-r*, and the presence of intervocalic aspirates in word roots.[25] Just as Greek was a 'noble and spiritual' language, Doric was held to be the 'true Greek' dialect, of which the Ionic dialect could only be an enervated and degenerated form resulting from Asiatic influence.[26] The themes so dear to Steffens also show through in Müller's attention to geographical determinants.[27] It is, for example, the destiny of Illyrian blood and earth which assigns to the Thessalians their 'impetuous and passionate character, and the low and degraded state of their mental facilities'.[28]

---

[19] See Collingwood 1946, 89–90.   [20] See Fishman 1983, 135.

[21] Schlegel 1808, 60–70. See Bernal 1987, 193, 231.

[22] Curtius 1857, 19–20; Bernal 1987, 335.   [23] Humboldt 1903, 266; Bernal 1987, 288.

[24] Wittenburg 1984, 1031–34.   [25] Müller 1830, 18.   [26] Müller 1830, 18–19.

[27] E.g. Müller 1830, 75–76.

[28] Müller 1830, 5. That said, the destiny of blood was not always immutable for Müller. In the case of the Dorians of Phokis, it was the number of non-Dorian strangers flocking to Delphi which led to 'a lazy, ignorant, superstitious, and sensual people...[which]...cast a shade over the few traces of a nobler character': Müller 1830, 422.

Müller approached the question of the Dorian *Volksgeist* by considering art, music, dress, architecture, philosophy but more especially the oppositions articulated in the literature of the Peloponnesian War period – particularly by Thoukydides – between Sparta, the archetypal Dorian *polis*, and Athens, its Ionian equivalent. For Müller, the Dorian character represented the polar opposite of the Ionian character in seven respects: (i) the Dorians are represented as defending a sense of freedom while the Ionians are enslaved to the ambitions of the state; (ii) the Dorians fight, in the time-honoured tradition, on land while the Ionians take the cowardly option of fighting on the sea; (iii) the Dorians place their faith in the integrity of their manpower while the Ionians use their wealth to buy support; (iv) the Dorians value tradition while the Ionians welcome innovation; (v) the Dorians act cautiously and after due deliberation while the Ionians act rashly and impetuously; (vi) the Dorians predicate their collective consciousness on ancestry while the Ionians resort to *ad hoc* contingencies; and (vii) the Dorians prefer aristocratic forms of government while the Ionians opt for democracy.[29] Above all else, the Dorian spirit was characterised by a tendency to subordinate individual elements to the whole and to preserve unity, from which obedience and self-restraint sprang.[30]

Much maligned and seldom read today, *Die Dorier* did, nonetheless, set the stage for the way in which the Dorians have been viewed by historians even up to the present day. In the second half of the nineteenth century, however, two new themes became entwined with this essentially romantic vision of the Dorians: the first was social evolutionism, the second the rise of true historical positivism.

The populations of many Classical *poleis* were distributed among *phylai* (singular, *phyle*) – a word that is generally, although not entirely adequately, translated as 'tribe'. In describing the attempts on the part of Kleisthenes, the sixth-century tyrant of Sikyon, to humiliate his Dorian opponents, Herodotos recounts how he changed the names of the Dorian *phylai*:

> And in this he ridiculed greatly the Sikyonians, because he altered the *phyle* names by adding endings to the words for swine, donkey and piglet, with the exception of his own *phyle*, to which he gave a name deriving from his own rule. These then were called the Arkhelaoi ('leaders of people'), but the others were called Hyatoi ('swinemen'), Oneatoi ('assmen') and Khoireatoi ('pigletmen'). The Sikyonians used these names for the *phylai* during Kleisthenes' reign and for sixty years after his death, but then, after consultation, they changed them to those of the Hylleis, Pamphyloi and Dymanes.[31]

It is debatable how seriously we should take this story, though the increasing number of inscriptions which were coming to light in the nineteenth century did reveal that the names of the Hylleis, Pamphyloi and Dymanes recurred throughout many of the cities which called themselves Dorian in the historical period. At Megara and Sparta only these three *phylai* are attested until the Roman period.[32]

9

In other cities a fourth (supposedly non-Dorian) *phyle* appears: for instance, the Hyrnathioi at Argos or the Skheliadai at Troizen.[33] At Epidauros, the two otherwise unknown *phylai* of Azantiaoi and Hysminates appear alongside those of the Hylleis and the Dymanes.[34] The distribution of the same *phyle* names throughout the Dorian cities was considered important for two reasons. Firstly, it seemed to lend support to the literary tradition's view that the Dorians had formed a cohesive unit, divided into three sub-units, prior to their migration southwards. Secondly, it appeared to imply a more 'primitive' stage of social organisation prior to the rise of the *polis* – something that was completely in tune with contemporary ideas about social evolution.

Social evolutionism concerns the growth, progressive specialisation or increased unity of societal forms. Like environmental determinism and consanguinity, it too is an idea that is not totally alien to classical thought. In accounting for the formation of the state, Aristotle proposed an evolutionary conglomeration of discrete cells. In the first stage man unites with woman, and the free master with his slave, to form the household. Driven by the necessity of satisfying more than daily needs, households then come together to form the village. Finally, the state emerges from an association of villages.[35]

A teleological confidence in the idea of 'progress' during the nineteenth century dictated that the past was to be viewed as an earlier evolutionary stage along the same axis as the present. The development of a society was represented metaphorically by the life of a human, so that as early as the 1730s Thomas Blackwell could see the Greeks as the childhood of Europe – in other words, they represented an earlier stage along a European axis that claimed unconditionally the Greek heritage for itself.[36] In the 1860s, Fustel de Coulanges was similarly to suggest that the evolutionary development of a society mirrors that of a young man.[37] Furthermore, the contemporary ascendancy of positivism assisted in the treatment of social forms as if they were natural scientific categories, and so theories of natural evolution (which were circulating before Darwin published *The origin of species* in 1859) came to be applied to social theory, notably through the work of Herbert Spencer.[38] Darwin's importance lay in the mechanism he proposed for evolution – natural selection – which in some intellectual circles served to attribute differing values to specific ethnic categories or social forms.

In his *Ancient law* of 1861, the English jurist and anthropologist Henry Sumner Maine focused the spotlight on 'tribal societies', defining them as assemblages of kin whose rules were dictated more by kinship than by any state structures. It was only as populations became more sedentary that territoriality began to replace kinship as a principle of social organisation.[39] A decade later and in a similar vein the American anthropologist Lewis H. Morgan published *Systems of consanguinity*

[33] For the Hyrnathioi: *IG* 4.600, 601, 602. For the Skheliadai: *IG* 4.748.   [34] *IG* 4².1.166.
[35] Aristotle, *Politics* 1.2.   [36] Blackwell 1735. See Bernal 1987, 208.
[37] Fustel de Coulanges 1980, 121.   [38] Banton 1977, 90–91.
[39] For a recent assessment of Maine and his work, see Diamond 1991.

and affinity, in which he described kinship as the basic organising principle of clans, defined as lineal and segmented descent groups possessing and working the land in common. In turn, an ensemble of clans formed the tribe, which was for Morgan the necessary evolutionary stage between barbarism and civilisation.[40] Both theories are classic examples of a social evolutionism which still commands a certain degree of adherence today: 'There is a widespread belief to the effect that the tribe constitutes an indispensable stage in the evolution of mankind from primitivity to statehood.'[41] It is within this tradition that one must situate the publication, in 1864, of the first edition of *La cité antique* by Numa Denis Fustel de Coulanges.

Fustel's account of the development of the ancient city was bluntly evolutionist. Making religion the prime determinant of social order, he proposed that the cult of the sacred fire and of the dead ancestors engendered initially the *genos*, which was defined as an extended family rather than an association of families.[42] In evolutionist-laden language, Fustel talks about 'a primitive epoch, when the family was independent of all superior power, and when the city did not yet exist'.[43] In the next stage, groups of *gene* joined in common ritual to form the *phratry*, and several *phratries* in turn formed the *phyle*.[44] It is at this point, immediately prior to the conglomeration of *phylai* within the city, that Fustel's ideas mesh with those being propounded in anthropology. He writes: 'From what remains to us of the tribe we see that, originally, it was constituted to be an independent society, and as if there had been no other social power above it'.[45] Since these tribes each had a religious nature that was specific and unique, they could neither fuse nor admit new families: in other words, mobility across tribal divisions was impossible.[46]

As a consequence, the prehistory of the Dorians was conceived as follows. Originally, the three Dorian *phylai* were separate tribal societies, possibly of diverse origins: it was proposed that the Hylleis originated in Illyria and the Dymanes in the northeast Peloponnese, while the Pamphyloi, whose name appears to mean 'all types', was a residual category of mixed origins.[47] This belief in diverse origins, together with Herodotos' description of the wanderings of the Dorians prior to the migrations at the end of the Heroic Age,[48] dictated that the Dorians were thus initially a migrant, rather than a sedentary, population, and it became commonplace to regard them as practising a pastoral-nomadic type of subsistence. Finally, the three *phylai* banded together in central Greece and pushed southwards, conquering the Peloponnese, the southern Aegean islands and southwest Asia Minor. It was only upon occupying the regions which they were to inhabit in the historical period that the Dorians altered their subsistence patterns. Following the model developed by Maine, they emerged from a tribal, pre-statal type of organisation based on

---

[40] See generally Roussel 1976, 9–10. [41] Crone 1986, 56.
[42] Fustel de Coulanges 1980, 34, 101; see also Gellner 1987, 37. For criticisms of this approach: Roussel 1976, 89; Humphreys 1978, 196–97. [43] Fustel de Coulanges 1980, 104.
[44] Fustel de Coulanges 1980, 110–12. [45] Fustel de Coulanges 1980, 112.
[46] Fustel de Coulanges 1980, 118–19.
[47] Wilamowitz-Moellendorff 1893, 139. See also Roussel 1976, 222; Rubinsohn 1975, 112.
[48] Herodotos 1.56.

11

kinship into a civic, statal social organisation based on territoriality, though retaining the memory of earlier tribal divisions in the names of the *phylai*.[49] In areas where the pre-Dorian population remained, they were incorporated into a fourth *phyle*, but the impermeability of 'tribal' boundaries kept the three Dorian *phylai* 'racially pure'.

There were, naturally, some dissenters to this view. Karl Julius Beloch argued that the sources for the Dorian migration were too unreliable to be granted any credibility at all.[50] Although Beloch could hardly deny that the divisions between the Dorians, Ionians and Aiolians were real enough in the Classical period, he dated their origin to the eighth century BC, positing a desire on the part of the colonies of the Asia Minor coast to carve out distinct identities for themselves: from there, the fashion spread to mainland Greece. Beloch's position was, however, being overtaken by other events – notably the rise of archaeology. Already by 1897, the Greek archaeologist, Christos Tsountas, had attributed the Late Bronze Age destructions of the palaces at Mykenai, Tiryns and Gla to the arrival of Dorian invaders.[51]

The scholarship of the first half of the twentieth century provides ample illustration of the debts that were owed to the intellectual traditions of the previous century. In the first edition of the *Cambridge Ancient History*, Alan Wace observed that 'the inhabitants of classical Mycenae, who might have been supposed *to keep themselves free from alien blood*, wrote in *good, broad* Doric'[52] (my italics). Jardé, while attacking Müller's use of the Peloponnesian War rhetoric for the construction of ethnic consciousness, was happy to talk about Dorian and Ionian 'races'.[53] Werner Jaeger, despite being an *emigré* to the United States, could still attribute the purest ethnic type to Sparta, whose hoplites apparently provided Pindar with the ideal type of the blond warrior;[54] and the great French scholar Georges Dumézil described the Dorians as the most 'nordic' of the Greeks.[55] The ideals derived from romanticism and social evolutionism are poignantly summed up in the otherwise dispassionate study of the Dorians in archaeology, written by Theodore Skeat: 'from the

---

[49] Szanto, however, adopted the opposite viewpoint, arguing that the *phylai* were originally based on land appropriation rather than ethnicity, and that in time a *ius sanguinis* came to be substituted for a *ius soli*: see Roussel 1976, 189.　　[50] Beloch 1890, 559–60.

[51] Tsountas and Manatt 1897, 341. See further chapter 5.　　[52] Wace 1926, 467.　　[53] Jardé 1926, 76.

[54] Jaeger 1933; cited in Schnapp-Gourbeillon 1979, 5. Cf. Myres 1930, xxiv: 'it was apparently common knowledge that the Dorians were blond...' The source of this bizarre belief appears to go back to the poet Alkman. In fr. 37 Bergk, he refers to Megalostrata, the poetess with whom he is obsessed, as 'blond' (*xantha*), while in fr. 13, 54–55 Bergk, he describes the hair of his cousin Hagesikhora as 'golden' (*khrusos*). The assumption is that if Alkman is a Dorian from Sparta, then certainly his cousin and possibly (given the prejudice against 'mixed' unions earlier this century) Megalostrata should also be Dorian. Two points should be made. Firstly, it is not absolutely certain that Alkman was a Spartan – Krates (ap. *Souda*) says that he came from Lydia. Secondly, the term *xanthos* is used of Achilles in *Iliad* 1.197; 23.141; of Odysseus in *Odyssey* 13.399, 431; of Menelaos in *Odyssey* 15.133; of Ariadne in Hesiod, *Theogony* 947; and of Helen in Sappho fr. 13.5 Diehl. This would suggest a heroic or aesthetic rather than ethnic application. Finally, the often cited reference to 'golden haired' Dorians in Pindar, *Nemean Odes* 9.40 is spurious, since Pindar applies it not to Dorians but to the Danaoi.

[55] Dumézil 1939, 157–59; cited in Schnapp-Gourbeillon 1979, 5.

mountainous country of the South-West [of Thessaly] there emerged a small tribe of hillsmen whose strange destiny it was to attain, at the height of their power, the hegemony of the Greeks; their name was the Dorians.'[56]

The course of this particular line of thinking was disrupted by the Second World War. The tragedy of romantic ideology was that its emphasis on the deterministic and immutable character of earth and particularly blood had spawned a succession of racist theories. It is no accident that Joseph Arthur Comte de Gobineau (1816–82), whose arguments for the superiority of the Aryan 'race' guaranteed his later status as a pioneer of Nazi racial philosophy, first became interested in racial theory as a result of his wide reading of German romantic literature.[57] The self-reflection which was required in the wake of the Holocaust left few intellectual disciplines unaffected. Classical scholars had, however, particular cause to reflect soberly on the symbolism that the 'Indogermanic' Dorians had provided for the Nazis, and the way in which the Spartan age-class system had been hijacked as a model for the Hitler Youth.[58] Hitler himself displayed a particular admiration for the Dorians of Sparta, singling out their courageous decision 'to destroy inferior children', and comparing the fate of the 6th Army, cut off in Stalingrad, to that of Leonidas and the 300 Spartans who fell in the Thermopylai pass defending Greece in 480 BC.[59]

The heinous consequences of the ethnic theories of the previous 150 years provoked two reactions within classical scholarship. The first, and by far the more widespread, response has been a greater circumspection: the migrations of the Dorians are generally retained as an *explanans* for the distribution of similar dialects and customs throughout the historical Dorian cities, though the ethnic aspects are played down. In many cases, this simply involved replacing the word 'race' with a more anodyne term, such as 'linguistic group' or 'archaeological culture'.[60] Behind these lexical substitutions, however, much of the nineteenth-century picture remained. The Dorians of the historical period could still, for instance, be described as a 'warrior caste',[61] or – alongside the Akhaians – as one of 'two different strains of people',[62] while their ancestors could be characterised 'as a pastoral people living in crofts and villages in much the same way as their Spartan descendants'.[63]

The second response has been to confront headlong and subvert the dominant Müller paradigm – a strategy heralded in 1956 by Edouard Will's *Doriens et Ioniens,*

---

[56] Skeat 1934, 52.   [57] Banton 1977, 40; 1987, 46–47.
[58] Schnapp-Gourbeillon 1986, 46. See, for example, the anguished comments of the French historian Marrou (1956, 23) writing immediately after the war.   [59] Rawson 1991, 342.
[60] See, for instance, Starr 1962, 72. The word 'race' did, however, still linger in some of the literature: e.g. Andrewes 1956, ch. 5; Jeffery 1976, 44; Boardman 1980, 24. For the concept of an ethnically neutral 'archaeological culture', see Clarke 1978, 365, 369–72.   [61] Tomlinson 1972, 65.
[62] Kelly 1976, 23.
[63] Nixon 1968, xvi; cf. Sakellariou 1990, 231. Nevertheless, a robust and reasoned justification for viewing the Dorians as pastoralists is presented in Cartledge 1979, 94–95 and redefended in Cartledge 1992. The attribution of pastoralism is predicated on the view that the Dorians had originally been a migrant people: e.g. Forrest (1986, 20) talks about 'a long period of chaotic tribal wandering' while Sakellariou (1989, 302) writes, 'The *ethne* from which the groups of refugees came had no state organization. They did, however, have some form of pre-statal structure.'

which set out to question the validity of applying ethnic criteria to the study of Greek history. Will set about his demolition by identifying some key Müllerian themes (for instance, the individualism of Ionians against the discipline of Dorians, or the anti-Dorianism of non-Dorian tyrants such as Kleisthenes of Sikyon) before proceeding to argue against them. He suggests that any common characteristics which appear to be shared by the inhabitants of defined geographical areas are better attributed to sociopolitical or economic, rather than ethnic, factors.[64] Likewise, tyrants are viewed as attacking the dominant classes rather than distinct ethnic groups, with Kleisthenes' actions being interpreted as more anti-Argive than anti-Dorian.[65] Generally, Will rejects the existence of ethnic consciousness within Greece: even its articulation, during the fifth century, in the work of Thoukydides is dismissed as merely a rhetorical device.[66] The ironic aspect of Will's work, however, is that although he dismisses the idea that the Greeks attached any *significance* to ethnic identity, he does appear to believe in the existence of an 'objective' ethnicity in ancient Greece.[67]

Perhaps one of the most interesting aspects of Will's attack on the dominant paradigm is the way in which Müller's beliefs are contextualised. Observing Müller's general interest in the conflict between liberal states such as Athens, and 'closed', conservative states such as Sparta, together with the preferential value placed upon the latter, Will demonstrates that Müller's view of the antagonism between Ionian Athens and Dorian Sparta reflects the conflict between France and Prussia – notably, the Prussian national revolution of 1813 against an alliance with France, which had been defeated in Russia the previous year.[68] Such political stereotypes were even applied to the level of intellectual traditions: thus Fustel de Coulanges contrasted the 'discipline' of the Germans with the 'liberality' of the French.[69]

Another challenge was launched in 1976, this time against social evolutionism in Greek history, by Denis Roussel. Roussel starts from an observation, originally made by Max Weber, that while *phylai* are attested in the *polis*, they are absent from the *ethnos*-state.[70] Yet, if the *phyle* was really the prevailing pre-statal form of social organisation in Greece, one might expect to find traces of it in both *poleis* and *ethne*. In Roussel's opinion, the *phyle* must have emerged at the same time as the *polis*, organically linked to its organisational structure: in other words, there were no Hylleis, Dymanes and Pamphyloi wandering around Greece and the Balkans in the Bronze Age.[71] The 1970s also saw systematic attempts to challenge the historic-

---

[64] Will 1956, 24–25. [65] Will 1956, 38–41. [66] Will 1956, 66–67.

[67] For instance, Will (1956, 53) notes that in fighting aristocrats, tyrants fought against Dorians 'même si eux-mêmes avaient du sang dorien dans les veines'. The romantic terminology in this passage is still very apparent. [68] Will 1956, 11–12. See also Schnapp-Gourbeillon 1979, 2–3.

[69] Fustel de Coulanges 1893; cited in Hartog 1988a, 386.

[70] Roussel 1976, 5. For a definition of the *ethnos* state: Morgan 1991, 131.

[71] The anteriority of the *phylai* to the *polis* has, however, recently been redefended by Van Effenterre (1985, 299–300) and Nagy (1987). Jones (1980, 212) has noted that the three Dorian *phylai* are nearly always recorded epigraphically in the same sequence (Dymanes–Hylleis–Pamphyloi), thus suggesting an original system of seniority which must predate the dispersal of the Dorians.

ity of the Dorian migration, notably in the fields of archaeology and linguistics.[72]

In a sense, those works which seek to deny any validity to ethnicity in Greek antiquity are as much the product of their times as was *Die Dorier*. In this case, the contextual influence derives from the post-war abhorrence towards the direction that ethnic studies had taken. The date of publication of *Doriens et ioniens* is instructive in this respect, since it appeared only two to three years after the Franco-German Steel and Coal Treaty which sought to couple the French and German economies – a not insignificant fact considering that its author was a scholar born and educated in the Franco-German region of Alsace. There was, in the 1950s, not only a rejection of many pre-war values, but also an optimism concerning the future dissolution of ethnic conflict in Europe, exemplified by the 1957 Treaty of Rome which set up the proto-European Community.

What I hope to have shown is that the history of the discourse that has been constructed around the Dorians is multilineal, and that each of its strands needs to be contextualised in the *Weltanschauung* of a particular period or intellectual tradition, be it romanticism, evolutionism, positivism or racism. In many cases, these traditions have combined cumulatively (rather than interacted dialectically) over the past two centuries, so that it is perfectly possible for ancient historians today to promulgate as doctrine certain historical 'facts', the epistemological underpinnings of which may well belong to a current of thought quite alien to that presently in use.

On the other hand, one need not subscribe to a Hegelian vision of history, in which the contextual distortions of earlier studies are berated while one's own work is promoted as somehow more 'objective'. If it is true that all historical knowledge is inevitably embedded in the present, then the current study can hardly be exempt, and it will no doubt be viewed against the background of the ethnic conflicts which re-emerged throughout the world in the 1980s. The job of the historian is not so much to discover the 'objective truth' of a unitary past, but to translate that past so that it makes sense within the cognitive parameters of the present: 'Ogni vera storia è storia contemporanea' ('every true history is a contemporary history').[73] The point is that Müller's *Die Dorier* made perfect sense in terms of the 'worlds of knowledge' in which it was written. Equally, it was entirely proper that Will should have attempted to dismantle the ethnic theories which had informed Nazism – not least, because there was, at that time, little else to replace them.

Today, however, the situation is different. Over the last few decades a vast number of anthropological studies have appeared, prompting new and different approaches to ethnicity which have very little in common with the deterministic and racialist theories of the pre-war period. The aim of the present study is to lift the taboo on Greek ethnicity and to draw upon current anthropological views to effect a realignment of research in which the focus falls not so much on the *ethnic*

---

[72] These challenges are discussed in more detail in chapters 5 and 6.
[73] Croce 1943, 4. For the metaphor of translation, see Overing 1985, 19–20; H. White 1978, 52.

15

group or its 'character', but rather on *ethnic identity* – that is, the operation of socially dynamic relationships which are constructed on the basis of a putative shared ancestral heritage. The endeavour will, I hope, demonstrate that ethnic identity was indeed an important dimension (among others) of social and political action in ancient Greece.

2

The nature and expression of ethnicity: an anthropological view

The rise and fall of instrumentalism

It is fashionable for Western observers, securely ensconced in their own national identities forged in toil and blood several centuries ago, to pour scorn on the rhetorical excesses and misguided scholarship of nationalist intellectuals in nineteenth-century Europe or twentieth-century Africa and Asia. Those whose identities are rarely questioned and who have never known exile or subjugation of land and culture, have little need to trace their 'roots' in order to establish a unique and recognizable identity. Yet theirs is only an implicit and unarticulated form of what elsewhere must be shouted from the roof-tops: 'We belong, we have a unique identity, we know it by our ancestry and history.' It matters nothing that these are so many 'myths' and memories; with them, the English and French are 'nations', without them, just so many populations bounded in political space.[1]

It was once thought that ethnicity was a transient phenomenon.[2] This had much to do with the substitution of an 'instrumentalist' view of ethnic groups for one that was 'primordialist'. Put briefly, the primordialists consider ethnicity (along with religion, race and territory) to be a basic and natural unit of history and humanity. Ethnicity is merely an extension of kinship and the normal vehicle through which common goals might be pursued.[3] As an historical 'given', it is frequently granted a deterministic role: Max Weber, for instance, regarded ethnicity as having played a decisive part in shaping the patterns and directions of economic forces in ancient Israel, China and India, as well as in the Protestant kingdoms of the Reformation period.[4]

The instrumentalist view, on the other hand, considers that ethnic groups exploit the symbol of shared, ancestral association to mask their *real* purpose – the pursuit of political and/or economic interests. According to this stance, ethnicity 'serves purposes other than the cultural goals which its spokesmen proclaim to be its raison d'être'.[5] For historical purposes, the persistence of the ethnic group cannot be assumed, since it is likely to emerge and disappear in tandem with the fluctuating claims to power advanced by competing interest groups. Furthermore, instrumentalists tend to regard the appearance of ethnicity as a fairly recent phenomenon. When Ernest Gellner maintained that the level of stratification and social

---

[1] Smith 1986, 2. [2] Parkin 1979, 31. [3] See Smith 1986, 12. [4] Fishman 1983, 134.
[5] Smith 1986, 9. See also Horowitz 1985, 13.

17

heterogeneity typical of 'agroliterate' societies prior to the Industrial Revolution precluded anything like a 'collective consciousness', he was referring to national identity, but the same argument is sometimes also extended to ethnic identity.[6]

There have been some attempts to reconcile these two opposing points of view. Smith has pointed to ethnicity's 'mutability in persistence and its persistence through change',[7] and Bentley, drawing on Pierre Bourdieu's 'theory of practice', has argued that while the members of an ethnic group may unconsciously inherit an ethnic *habitus* (a system of strategies for ordering experience and informing action), they are equally capable of modifying that *habitus* instrumentally in the pursuit of various goals.[8] Generally, however, it is the instrumentalist view which has been most popular in recent decades.

In fact, the opposition between primordialism and instrumentalism is not simply one of intellectual fashion. It is the primordialist view of ethnicity that is more likely to be held by members of an ethnic group, particularly an ethnic group which perceives itself to be threatened. The reason for this is obvious: if members of an ethnic group do not regard their ethnic heritage as primary, there is unlikely to be much of a basis for cohesion. Conversely, instrumentalism is more frequently the viewpoint of one of two groups: either outsiders, such as anthropologists, or alternatively groups within the state whose identity is not especially threatened. In Rwanda, for instance, the Hutu regard themselves as a cohesive ethnic group on the basis of primordial claims to direct descent from immigrants from Chad and southern Africa; the Tutsi, on the other hand, who have traditionally held the higher status positions, deny any genuine ethnic basis to the conflict by pointing to centuries of intermarriage between the groups.

The political agenda of groups such as the Tutsi is more obvious than in the case of anthropologists. Nonetheless, it cannot be accidental that the anthropological subscription to instrumentalism flourished in the United States during the 1950s and 1960s – a time when there was a wide expectation that economic prosperity and the extension of civil rights would obviate the need for ethnic groups to campaign towards social and economic goals, and that ethnic minorities throughout America would assimilate in the proverbial cultural 'melting-pot'.[9] In other words, the expression of ethnic identity was considered a problem that needed urgent resolution; by adopting an instrumentalist point of view, the 'ethnic problem' could begin to appear less intractable.

Situations in which the instrumentalist view of the anthropologist is set up in opposition to the primordialist view of the ethnic group that s/he is studying conform to the standard anthropological distinction between an 'etic' point of view (that of the outsider) and an 'emic' one (that of the insider). Needless to say, the balance is rarely equal, and the 'rational' and 'detached' view of the outsider has invariably been championed over the 'credulous' and 'self-interested' one of

---

[6] Gellner 1983, 8–14. See Smith 1986, 69; Shennan 1989, 14. [7] Smith 1986, 32.
[8] Bentley 1987. See Bourdieu 1977. [9] Schermerhorn 1974, 3–4.

the insiders. Yet this in itself is symptomatic of the kind of 'Orientalism' attacked by Edward Said and explored so successfully in modern Greece by Michael Herzfeld.[10] There is currently a growing awareness among anthropologists that the distance set up between the etic observer and the emic subject, together with the value judgements exercised by the former about the latter, may simply be assumptions predicated on western cultural arrogance.

The danger of the emic-etic dichotomy in the study of ethnic identity lies in the possibility of establishing a sterile debate between ethnic truth and ethnic fiction. Such a debate contributes little to the understanding of the phenomenon. On the one hand, there is – as we shall see – no doubt that ethnic identity is a cultural construct, perpetually renewed and renegotiated through discourse and social praxis. The ethnic claims that such a group makes on the basis of a 'real' ancestral state of affairs cannot automatically be privileged over the constraints and actualities of the present. On the other hand, there is little to be gained, and much to be lost, by denying that the ethnic group does possess its own realm of reality. The expectation that ethnicity would disappear in the American 'melting pot' was as unrealistic as it was undesirable.[11] Indeed, the American columnist Bob Callahan has argued that Ronald Reagan's re-election to presidential office in 1985 was largely achieved by identifying the failure of the 'melting-pot' ideology, and by appealing to those European ethnic minorities whose existence had ceased to be recognised by the Democratic Party.[12] Similarly, if there is anything to be learnt from the recent ethnic conflicts throughout the world, it is that the refusal to recognise ethnicity is more likely to exacerbate than to eliminate its potency.

Defining the ethnic group

Attempts to find an objective set of criteria which might act as a definition for the ethnic group have ultimately proved futile. The reason for this is that ethnic identity is *socially constructed and subjectively perceived*.[13] This is hardly a revelation to social anthropologists, but it is worth spelling out in some detail, not least because (as chapter 1 demonstrated) its implications remain to be absorbed by many classicists. The fields which are normally invoked to define the ethnic group are genetics, language and religion.

It was maintained in the previous chapter that the Holocaust discredited the racial philosophies that had spawned it, and that, by and large, the term 'race' was replaced by another – most often, 'ethnic group'. However, in many cases it was also quite clear that this new use was purely cosmetic, and that the basic conceptual apparatus of 'race' had remained, despite a change in terminology: "'Ethnic

---

[10] Said 1978; Herzfeld 1982; 1987.
[11] Parsons 1975, 63–64; Greene 1978, 330–31; Tambiah 1989, 335.   [12] Callahan 1989, 232–33.
[13] De Vos and Romanucci-Ross 1995, 350.

19

group" is a collocation often used in covert synonymy for another term, "race"'.[14] Certain sociologists attempted to distinguish 'race' from 'ethnic group' by applying the former to the biological and the latter to the social aspects of group identity.[15] Consequently, biological conceptions of 'race' began to be underplayed and eclipsed by the social dimensions.

In the last few decades, however, attention has again been focused on the biological aspects of groups through the practice of using blood-typing and DNA analysis to 'fingerprint' populations. The irony of having criticised, in chapter 1, the romantic obsession with the 'blood essence' as a diacritical marker of identity lies in the fact that scientists today are using blood-typing to identify discrete populations. So the populations that inhabit the Basque enclave exhibit blood-types with high 'O', very low 'B' and high Rhesus negative frequencies; Celtic populations of Ireland and Scotland, and the populations of Sardinia and the eastern Black Sea area have high 'O' frequencies; western Europeans generally tend to show high 'A' frequencies, while Slavs and other eastern Europeans are typified by high 'B' frequencies.[16]

These biological entities should not be seen, however, as *determining* cultural attributes. In the case of blood-types, the relative frequencies of each group, while being hereditary, are in equal measure a consequence of adaptation to the environment, nutritional norms, child-rearing practices and local epidemics. Experiments carried out in South America and New Guinea have revealed that genetic differences between villages belonging to the same tribe may be almost as great as those between tribes which are culturally or linguistically distinct.[17] From this, the French anthropologist Claude Lévi-Strauss has concluded that culture and genetic make-up are in a symbiotic relationship, though with the determining emphasis placed on culture: 'each culture selects genetic aptitudes, which have a reciprocal influence on the very culture that originally contributed to reinforcing them'.[18] This reversal in the causal connection between 'race' and culture has also been stressed by Clifford Geertz, who regards culture as the prerequisite for biological, psychological and social existence.[19]

At first sight, an emphasis on the sociocultural, rather than genetic, factors which influence ethnicity might seem to contradict experience. After all, is it not genetically derived physical differences that define ethnic groups such as African-Americans and WASPs (White Anglo-Saxon Protestants) in New York City? At this point, Horowitz's distinction between the *criteria* and the *indicia* of ethnicity may be helpful.[20]

The criteria of ethnicity are the definitional set of attributes by which membership in an ethnic group is ultimately determined. They are the result of a series of conscious and socially embedded choices, which attach significance to certain cri-

---

[14] Tonkin, McDonald and Chapman 1989, 16. See also Just 1989, 76.   [15] Banton 1987, xi.
[16] Cole 1965, fig. 4.   [17] Neel 1970.   [18] Lévi-Strauss 1985, 19.   [19] Geertz 1973, 46–49.
[20] Summarised in Horowitz 1975, 119–20. See also Crone 1986, 49.

teria from a universal set while ignoring others (though in practice this will usually concern a putative notion of descent, as will be seen). The indicia, on the other hand, are the operational set of distinguishing attributes which people tend to associate with particular ethnic groups once the criteria have been established. Up until the 1950s, the criterion of membership in an African-American ethnic group was the slightest degree of African ancestry, expressed through the infamous metaphor of 'one drop of Negro blood'; but the operational indicia on which judgements were based were physical characteristics – namely, physiognomy and colour. In Rwanda and Burundi, short stature acts as an operational indicium in identifying the Hutu, though their ethnic identity is ultimately determined not by height but by claimed descent from immigrants from Chad or southern Africa.[21] Similarly, in Western Darfur in the Sudan, the criterion for membership of the Baggara is claimed descent (in this case, from original Arab invaders). The potency of this ethnic criterion is demonstrated by its ability to keep the Baggara culturally distinct from the 'black' Fur, even though it is now virtually impossible to distinguish the two groups on physical grounds.[22] The important point is that ethnic identity is not ultimately defined by such physical indicia. While physical characteristics are for the most part genetically derived, *attitudes* towards such characteristics are historically and culturally situated. This is demonstrated by the fact that ethnic significance does not become attached to *each and every* type of phenotypic variation, but rather to a specific and culturally determined set of variations.[23]

In cases where little genetically derived differentiation exists, physical indicia of ethnicity may be created, either by adopting stylistic differences (coiffure, dress, etc.) or by a form of bodily mutilation (circumcision, tattooing or piercing of the nose, ears, tongue and lips).[24] Indicia of ethnicity need not, however, always be physical. While the indicia of African-American ethnicity are today based on colour, in seventeenth-century America, the differentiating indicia between English settlers and African slaves were based on a religious opposition between Christians and Heathens. Colour only came to replace religion as an important indicium from about ca. 1680, when many slaves had already converted to Christianity.[25]

In rejecting the significance of physical characteristics, many scholars have instead argued that ethnic identity is determined more by language.[26] Certainly, language may act as an important dimension of ethnic identity, especially in situations where an ethnic group possesses few highly distinctive physical indicia – for instance, among the Walloons in Belgium, the French-Canadians in Québec, the Bretons in France or the Welsh in Britain.[27] In Medieval France, the distinction between the partly Romanised Celts of the north and the fully Romanised popula-

---

[21] See Isaacs 1975, 40 n. 7 (citing an article from the *New York Times* for June 17, 1973 which describes how the short Hutu often use a machete to hack off the feet of their taller Tutsi opponents).
[22] Haaland 1969, 59. [23] Wade 1993, 21. [24] Isaacs 1975, 43. [25] Horowitz 1985, 43.
[26] E.g. Renfrew 1987, 2.
[27] Giles 1979, 278; Taylor, Bassili and Aboud 1973, 189; Giles, Bourhis and Taylor 1977, 326.

tions of the south was signalled by a variety of cultural forms: while biennial cropping was practised in the South, triennial cropping was the norm in the North;
while (prior to the Napoleonic Code of 1804) the North established law by prece-
dent, the South had a virtually immutable written law code; and while houses in
the South had flat roofs, those in the North were steeply pitched, despite the fact
that there is apparently no drastic difference in annual rainfall levels. One of the
most significant means of differentiation, however, was indicated by the use of
different linguistic forms for the French affirmative, *oui* – hence, the distinction
between Langue d'oil and Langue d'oc.[28]

On the other hand, language can just as often be irrelevant for an ethnic community. Geary has noted that language is at best a fluid index of ethnicity in
Medieval Europe, since most of the aristocracy was bilingual,[29] and today the identity of Jews in the former Soviet Union is signalled by inherited cultural patterns
and ancestral values rather than language, since most have assimilated to
Russian.[30] Furthermore, linguistic unity is no guarantee against ethnic conflict:
Serbo-Croatian has hitherto been, for all practical purposes, a unified language,
yet that has not prevented violent confrontation between the Orthodox Serbs and
the Catholic Croats.

The non-convergence between ethnic and linguistic boundaries is perhaps
shown most forcefully by Forsythe's study of West German attitudes towards a
Germanic ethnicity (*Deutschstämmigkeit*). On the one hand, some Germans see
Austria and the German-speaking parts of Switzerland as culturally Germanic on
the basis of shared language; on the other hand, fluency in German is sometimes
not enough to be categorised as *Deutsche* rather than *Ausländer*, while others who are
classified as German cannot speak the language.[31] Similarly, Turkey accepts
Bosnian Muslims and Pomaks (Bulgarian-speaking Muslims) as Turks, even though
they speak no Turkish.[32] In short, language cannot be used as an objective definition of ethnic identity.[33] It is an ethnic indicium, rather than an ethnic criterion,
and like other ethnic indicia its significance may be volatile both over time and
through space.

Likewise, religious affiliation is not always a satisfactory basis for defining ethnic
groups. There are cases where religion almost appears to act as a surrogate for
ethnic groups who possess little or no linguistic distinctiveness: for instance,
Christianity in the case of the Egyptian Copts who speak Arabic like the rest of the
Muslim population,[34] or Islam in the case of the Bosnian Muslims who share the
Serbo-Croatian language with Serbs and Croats.[35] Perhaps the observation that
there is little or no linguistic differentiation between the Catholics and Protestants
of Belfast goes some way to explaining the significance attached to religious affilia-

---

[28] Chambers and Trudgill 1980, 122–23.   [29] Geary 1983, 20.
[30] Haarmann 1986, 45. For the lack of isomorphism between ethnicity and language in southeast
Asia: Keyes 1995.   [31] Forsythe 1989, 141–43.   [32] Karpat 1985, 96.
[33] Anderson 1991, 133; Horowitz 1985, 50.   [34] Haarmann 1986, 261.
[35] Horowitz 1975, 116; Gellner 1983, 71–72; Smith 1986, 23; Simić 1991, 19; Gilliland 1995, 209.

tion.[36] On the other hand, religious beliefs need not always be coterminous with ethnic identity. The population exchanges following the Asia Minor Catastrophe of 1923 defined Greeks and Turks according to religious lines. Those who professed Christian Orthodoxy were deemed to be Greek, and those who were Muslim were considered Turkish, despite the fact that in many cases this delineation cut across ethnic and linguistic boundaries: the Turks who had settled in Krete without forswearing their former religion were returned to Anatolia speaking only Greek, while the Karamanli, who were Orthodox Christians but Turkophone and in most cultural respects Turkish, were sent to Greece.[37]

Furthermore, the importance of religion to ethnic solidarity may be transitory. The partition of Pakistan in 1947 on religious (Muslim) grounds failed to prevent the separation in 1972 of Bangladesh on the linguistic claim of self-determination. In 1947, the people of East Pakistan considered their greatest enemy to be the Bengali-speaking Hindus of East Bengal; thirty years later, they were locked in battle with their fellow Muslims of West Pakistan.[38] Alternatively, one religious affiliation may be replaced by another: some African-Americans are now turning away from Christianity (which they perceive as the religion of white racism) and embracing instead Islam.[39] These examples suggest that, like language, religion acts less as a defining criterion of ethnicity and more as an ethnic indicium which may in time give way to other indicia according to local circumstances.

Faced with a situation in which genetic, linguistic and religious boundaries were seldom coterminous, and where no single one of these could stand as an objective set of criteria for defining the ethnic group, scholars fell back on the idea of the ethnic category as a polythetic set of shared cultural forms – that is, a set of cultural attributes where the appearance of any one single attribute is neither necessary nor sufficient on its own to define the set. Initially, this would appear to be a common-sense deduction, related to the social psychological notion that each culture is characterised by a Basic Personality Structure, based on child-rearing practices, family organisation and subsistence techniques, and generating secondary institutions such as art, folklore and religion. In practice, however, the considerable heterogeneity that has emerged in the 'character' of various cultures has thrown doubt on the value of the Basic Personality Structure as a heuristic tool.[40] One of the problems resides in the treatment of cultural traits as a transhistorically static category – a method that Ian Hodder has described as 'dangerous given the propensity of traits or groups of traits to change their meanings in different contexts.'[41]

Another problem arises from the fact that cultural traits, like genetic, linguistic or religious categories, do not map directly onto ethnic groups. David Fischer's examination of the folkways ('the normative structure of values, customs and meanings that exist in any culture')[42] of the Appalachian Backcountry in America

---

[36] Milroy 1981, 44; 1992, 190–91; Trudgill 1986, 122.   [37] Just 1989, 81; Clogg 1992, 101.
[38] Das Gupta 1975, 471; Horowitz 1985, 68–69.   [39] De Vos 1995, 22.   [40] Jahoda 1978, 81–82.
[41] Hodder 1987, 3.   [42] Fischer 1989, 7–8.

reveals a shared common culture, unique in its speech, architecture, family ways and child-rearing practices. This culture exhibits a remarkable homogeneity despite its geographical extension,[43] and its structural content reflects that of the British border regions of northern England, the Scottish Lowlands and Ulster, from where the first Appalachian settlers migrated. Yet this commonality of culture did not eradicate ethnic differences in the Appalachian region: subjects would describe themselves variously as 'Ulster Irish', 'Scots-Irish', 'Irish', 'Scots', 'English', 'Anglo-Irish' or even 'Saxon-Scots'.[44] Conversely, Edmund Leach noted that the Kachin of Highland Burma could not be defined on the basis of shared cultural attributes.[45] The same is true of the Lue of Thailand, who regard themselves as ethnically distinct from their neighbours despite the absence of any perceptible cultural basis for this differentiation.[46]

An example from Mauritius illustrates the difficulty in using shared traits, religion, language or customs as objective definitions for ethnic groups. There are four legally recognised ethnic groups in Mauritius: Hindus, Muslims, Chinese and French/African/Madagascan. At first sight, these groups appear to share no common basis of differentiation: the first two are defined in terms of religion, the Chinese on regional grounds, while the last group represents a residual category. In fact, the majority of members of the French/African/Madagascan group are Catholic, but then so are the majority of the Chinese group, as well as some of the Hindu group.[47] Any quest, then, for an objective definition of an ethnic group is doomed to failure simply because the defining criteria of group membership are socially constructed and renegotiated, primarily through written and spoken discourse. For instance, in finding no commonality of livelihood, language, custom or religion among the Lue of Thailand, Michael Moerman was forced to conclude, 'Someone is Lue by virtue of believing and calling himself Lue'.[48] Furthermore, the fact that ethnicity is subjectively perceived raises the possibility that its meaning may assume varying significations at different times: 'A man might speak a Romance language, dress as a Frank, and claim Burgundian law. How he perceived his ethnic identity, and how he was in turn perceived by others, if in fact anyone thought of his ethnicity at all, is impossible to determine *as an objective category.*'[49]

Once one places an emphasis on the socially and subjectively constructed criteria of group membership, then one is compelled to turn away from an examination of the *content* of an ethnic group, and consider instead its ascriptive boundaries.[50] In other words, we should not begin by identifying a 'core personality' of an ethnic group, tracing the occurrence of this personality, in its varying intensity, centrifugally until we reach the point at which it becomes discontinuous; rather, it is necessary to focus on the conceptual and ascriptive boundary by reference to which category membership is defined. The boundary is set by the criteria

[43] Fischer 1989, 786.   [44] Fischer 1989, 618.   [45] Leach 1954, 281.
[46] Moerman 1965, 1219. Cited in Eriksen 1993, 11.   [47] Eriksen 1993, 34.
[48] Moerman 1965, 1219. Cited in Eriksen 1993, 11.   [49] Geary 1983, 21.
[50] This important shift in research was first proposed by Barth (1969, 14).

of ethnicity which are phrased in the form of a yes or no question – normally, 'can you, or can you not, claim descent from x?' It is the value of the response, affirmative or negative, that dictates group membership or exclusion. In situations where ethnic identity persists over the long term, this is due not to the immutability of ethnic indicia or of an 'ethnic character', but to the maintenance of an ascriptive criterial boundary.

If the ethnic group is a social, rather than a biological category, what distinguishes it from other social groups? Anthony Smith identifies six characteristics: a collective name; a common myth of descent; a shared history; a distinctive shared culture; an association with a specific territory; and a sense of communal solidarity.[51] Not all of these features, however, need be exclusive to the ethnic group. Smith is probably right to suggest that there have never existed ethnic groups which did not use a collective name (ethnonym) encapsulating the 'essence' of the group,[52] though it is easy to think of plenty of collectivities for which a name bestows particular significance (football teams or Oxbridge colleges, for instance). Likewise, it might be possible to attribute a distinctive shared culture, a sense of communal solidarity, and possibly a shared history to economic classes in a stratified society.

While all of these features may be vitally important for ethnic consciousness (as they would be in many other associative groups), I would, nonetheless, suggest that the connection with a specific territory and the common myth of descent are more distinctive characteristics of ethnic groups.[53] The specific territory in question may be the region where the ethnic group currently resides, or there may be a potent memory of an association with an earlier historic territory. Displacement of population may result from boundary changes (the frequent occurrence of this in eastern Europe and the Balkans must bear some responsibility for the salience of ethnic identities in this part of the world) or from voluntary or enforced migration. In these cases, however, the memory of the ancestral homeland is invariably an important component of ethnic consciousness: when the Masai tribe was relocated, its members tried to preserve their identity with their former environment by using the same assemblage of toponyms in their new territory.[54] Alternatively, given the constructive nature of ethnic identity, it is not entirely impossible that an ethnic *Ursprungsland* may in fact be a mythical, utopian territory.

Above all else, though, it must be the myth of shared descent which ranks paramount among the features that distinguish ethnic from other social groups, and, more often than not, it is proof of descent that will act as a defining criterion of ethnicity.[55] This recognition, however, does not vindicate a genetic approach to ethnic identity, because the *myth* of descent is precisely that – a recognition of a *putative* shared ancestry. The genealogical reality of such claims is irrelevant; what matters is that the claim for shared descent is consensually agreed. The putative

[51] Smith 1986, 22–30.   [52] Smith 1986, 23. See also Renfrew 1987, 216.
[53] See Tambiah 1989, 335.   [54] A. White 1978, 375.
[55] Fishman 1977, 17; Keyes 1976, 205–206; Eriksen 1993, 12.

nature of this belief in descent was actually recognised as far back as Max Weber, who defined ethnic groups as 'human groups that entertain a *subjective* belief in their common descent because of similarities of physical type or of customs or both, or because of memories of colonization and migration; this belief must be important for the propagation of group formation; conversely *it does not matter whether or not an objective blood relationship exists*'[56] (my italics).

The genesis and maintenance of ethnic groups

It is precisely the emphasis on a shared myth of descent and the attempt to endow category membership and political claims with an historical legitimation that renders it difficult to trace the genesis of various ethnic groups. The instrumentalist points to sociopolitical or economic imperatives that invest themselves in the garb of ethnicity, though this does not explain exactly *how* an ethnic basis of differentiation comes to be manipulated so successfully in such strategies. Appeals to primordialism, conversely, simply beg the question.

Max Weber's discussion of 'social closure' still has some explanatory value.[57] Social closure indicates 'the process by which social collectivities seek to maximize rewards by restricting access to resources and opportunities to a limited circle of eligibles. This entails the singling out of certain social or physical attributes as the justificatory basis of exclusion'.[58] Frank Parkin defines two types of social closure, the first being a prerequisite for the second. Social closure as exclusion represents 'the attempt by one group to secure for itself a privileged position at the expense of some other group through a process of subordination'. Social closure as usurpation, on the other hand, is a reaction that may, but need not, occur as a result of exclusion, and is the type of social closure employed by the subordinated group in order to 'bite into' the resources and opportunities that have been monopolised by the dominant group.[59]

In contrast to Weber, who suggested that the criteria of exclusion are contingent, and that the choice between a linguistic, religious, ethnic, gender or class basis for differentiation is irrelevant, Parkin argues that exclusionary criteria are never 'plucked out of the air in a purely arbitrary manner'. In the case of ethnic groups, he proposes that exclusion is a result of 'territorial conquest or the forced migration of populations creating a subcategory of second-class citizens within the nation state'.[60] Although this comes close to the nineteenth-century obsession with explaining change by means of exogenous causes such as invasions or migrations, at a very general level there does seem to be some value in such an explanation. Despite the fact that 'migration' has frequently been exploited by prehistorians as a panacea for the problem of explaining culture change in societies about which

---

[56] Weber 1968, 389.   [57] See Weber 1968, 43–46.   [58] Parkin 1979, 44.
[59] Parkin 1979, 45, 74.   [60] Parkin 1979, 95–96.

we otherwise know very little, it cannot be denied that there is a multiplicity of documentation for historically attested migrations. In such situations, and under circumstances whereby the immigrant population quickly assumes a position of domination (English Canadians in Québec or Protestants in Northern Ireland), or alternatively finds itself occupying the lower rungs of the socioeconomic ladder (ethnic minorities in Britain and the United States, and especially *Gastarbeiter* in Germany), then it is not hard to understand why exclusion strategies based on 'descent', however putative, may emerge. On the other hand, the same situation can be caused without any movement of people: the political and social ascendancy of the Walloons in Belgium was not the result of migration, but of a series of territorial demarcations that combined to form the somewhat artificial nation of Belgium.[61]

Furthermore, the idea of social closure by usurpation could have some appeal even to the most dedicated proponents of endogenous change – that is, change resulting from internal, rather than external, factors. Much of the impetus for the separation of a Muslim East Pakistan was due to the fact that the privileged positions of power and domination were held by Hindus. Likewise, the growing militancy among Kurdish groups in Iraq and particularly Turkey has been a consequence of their exclusion from the apparatus of power: in these situations, the increasing salience of Kurdish identity, together with the extreme actions undertaken in pursuit of a policy of usurpation, has further exacerbated their exclusion.[62]

From a demographic point of view, the fact that the resources of any one region are finite militates against the possibility of a vast, single and short-lived influx of newcomers. Yet the arrival of too small a number of settlers or families is not sufficient in itself either to provoke an instance of social closure, or to escape assimilation (particularly intermarriage). In fact, in the initial stages migrant populations tend to reproduce themselves through the process of 'channelised migration', whereby immigrants move to areas on the basis of information provided by friends or relations who have already taken up residence there. Studies in the United States have shown that the vast majority of African-American migrants to Rochester, New York formerly lived in Sanford, Florida or in Williamsburg County, South Carolina, and that high proportions of African-Americans in Norristown, Pennsylvania came from Saluda, South Carolina.[63] This phenomenon is also reflected in the concentrated distributions of Irish in New England, Germans in the Midwest, Scandinavians in the upper Midwest, Poles in Pennsylvania and Italians in Providence, Rhode Island.[64] Outside America, a study of channelised migration in Africa has shown that the vast majority of migrants from the Yemen Arab Republic to Sudan were from a village near Yerim, while those who left Yemen for Chad tended to emanate from another village near Rada.[65]

---

[61] Petersen 1975, 198–200. [62] Nagel 1980. [63] Thompson 1983, 346.
[64] Thompson 1983, 341–42. [65] Thompson 1983, 345.

The process of channelised migration does not last for ever. The migration which carried 80,000 British men, women and children from East Anglia to Massachusetts lasted only eleven years; the migration of southern Englanders, particularly Royalists, to Virginia was completed in a generation; and the transplantation of 23,000 colonists from the north Midlands to the Delaware Valley took forty years.[66] In cases where social closure has resulted from migration, we should probably regard the movement of peoples as lasting from a decade up to half a century. After a certain time, the ethnic community is sufficiently stable that its ascriptive boundaries can be maintained without recourse to immigration.

It is time to focus on these ascriptive boundaries more closely. When one considers the distinction between ascribed (hereditary) and achieved (non-hereditary) statuses, it would seem immediately apparent that ethnic identity is a case of the former. According to Harold Isaacs, 'basic group identity consists of the ready-made set of endowments and identifications which every individual shares with others from the moment of birth by the chance of the family into which he [sic] is born at that given time in that given place'.[67] Yet, ascribed and achieved statuses need not always be mutually exclusive. Sikhism was originally an achieved status, based on recruitment from the ranks of Hindus, though recent years have seen an attempt to prevent conversion and intermarriage between the two groups, with the aim of establishing Sikh identity on a more ascribed basis.[68] Nor does the fact that a myth of shared descent is vitally important to ethnic consciousness necessarily vindicate the notion that ethnicity can only be ascribed through birth. One should rather make the subtle distinction between a situation which views birth as *determining* one's identity, and one in which an individual's identity is justified *by reference to* descent. In fact, ethnic identity can sometimes be a matter of an achieved status which vests itself in the garb of an ascribed one. This happens where an individual manages successfully to persuade his or her peers that s/he fulfils the criteria for ethnic inclusion, *regardless of any objective considerations.*

In most cases, one does assume the ethnic identity of the familial environment into which one is born, but there are plenty of examples which show the feasibility of changing one's ethnic identity, and demonstrate that if an ethnic group is defined by its criterial boundaries, that does not in itself prevent a flow of personnel across such boundaries.[69] This will occur most frequently between ethnic groups which do not practise endogamy.[70] Many subjects in the United States who affirmatively claimed to be Italian were actually found to have Irish and Polish matrilineal ancestors. The employment of a specifically Italian (rather than Italian-Irish or Italian-Polish) identity occurred with marriage, when the Irish or Polish bride began to prepare, cook and eat Italian cuisine; she was henceforth considered by the group – and, more importantly, considered herself – to be Italian.[71] The permeability of ethnic boundaries is also demonstrated in many of the Greek

---

[66] Fischer 1989, 16, 226–27, 421.   [67] Isaacs 1975, 31.   [68] Horowitz 1985, 56.
[69] Barth 1969, 9.   [70] Parsons 1975, 57.   [71] Parsons 1975, 64.

28

villages of Attikí and Viotía (ancient Attika and Boiotia), where Arvanites often form a majority. These Arvanites are descended from Albanians who first entered Greece between the eleventh and fifteenth centuries (though there was a subsequent wave of immigration in the second half of the eighteenth century). Although still regarded as ethnically distinct in the nineteenth century, their participation in the Greek War of Independence and the Civil War has led to increasing assimilation: in a survey conducted in the 1970s, 97 per cent of Arvanite informants, despite regularly speaking in Arvanítika, considered themselves to be Greek.[72] A similar concern with being identified as Greek is exhibited by the bilingual Arvanites of the Eastern Argolid.[73] In sum, the remarkable persistence of ethnic groups is not maintained by permanent exclusion nor by preventing boundary crossing. One might even suggest that it is in the act of crossing boundaries that such demarcations are reaffirmed.

If ethnic groups are not monolithic at the level of the individual, then neither are they static at a collective level, being subject to processes of assimilation and differentiation.[74] On the one hand, ethnic groups may disappear, as in the case of the Franks in France or the Etruscans in Italy. On the other, the phenomenon of ethnogenesis is well attested: for instance, the Sikh identity which emerged out of Hinduism as a religious and military protest against Muslim rule in the Punjab, or the creation of new, overarching categories such as the Malays in Malaysia or the Ibo in Nigeria as a result of the fusion of various subgroup identities.[75] An interesting case is provided by Italian-Americans in the United States. When Italian migrants first left for America, they left not as Italians, but as Neapolitans, Sicilians or Calabrians. Italian-American identity is a fusion of American working-class folkways with the generic South Italian identity that was foisted on the newcomers by those already resident in America.[76]

The fact that ethnic groups have a tendency to persist over long periods of time despite the permeability of their boundaries demonstrates their employment of highly effective adaptation strategies. At this point, however, it is as well to emphasise that this is not a property of a group in itself, viewed as a reified and de-individualised deterministic force. One of the criticisms levelled at the functionalist approach of social scientists such as Parsons or Geertz is that they think in terms of social 'actors', behaving according to a pre-determined script and driven by unseen sociocultural forces, instead of according recognition to active, knowing individuals, who 'possess subjectivity, a sense of self, and biographical uniqueness'.[77] Rather, the maintenance of ethnic groups and ascriptive boundaries operates by means of a dialectic between individual and collectivity.

The dynamics of intergroup behaviour are of a qualitatively different nature from those of interpersonal behaviour, which means that behaviour in groups

---

[72] Trudgill and Tzavaras 1977, 179; Trudgill 1983, 108, 128, 135.   [73] Koster 1977, 43.
[74] See generally Horowitz 1975, 115–18; 1985, 64–70; Haarmann 1986, 41–55; Tambiah 1989, 335–36.
[75] Horowitz 1975, 117; 1985, 66.   [76] Sarna 1978, 371.   [77] Silverman 1990, 124.

cannot be understood by simple extrapolation from dyadic interaction. A group is not merely the composition of its constituent individuals: its principal characteristic is not number, but continuous interaction.[78] Furthermore, it is not attraction to individuals *as individuals* that forms a group, but attraction to individuals *as group members*.[79] In many cases, experiments have shown that the mere perception of belonging to a social category is sufficient for group behaviour, even in the absence of interpersonal relations.[80] According to these terms, intergroup behaviour can be defined as the situation in which individuals belonging to a group interact, collectively or individually, with another group or its members *in terms of their group identifications*.[81]

The knowledge of one's membership in a social group, together with the value and significance that is attached to this membership, constitutes the 'social identity' of a subject.[82] This social identity is the internalisation by the individual of shared group norms and values, and exists alongside a 'personal identity', which is a function of genetically transmitted and familially conditioned variations that distinguish one individual from another. Quite clearly in day-to-day personal interaction it is going to be a question of one's personal identity that is brought to bear. When, however, the identity of a group is threatened, a response on the individual level is mobilised because the identity of the ethnic group has been internalised in the individual, with the consequence that injury to the group is seen as an injury to the self.[83] It would be unwise, however, to insist upon too clear-cut a distinction between social and personal identity: in some cases, individuals who have negated any conscious identification with their ethnic heritage may still internalise its value system and implicitly transfer these values to their children.[84] In this eventuality, what was originally part of a social identity becomes incorporated into one's personal identity.

By considering the individual and collective dimensions of ethnicity, and the distinction between personal and social identity, it is possible to shed more light on the debate about the ascription of ethnic membership. While the criteria of ethnic inclusion are in principle ascriptive and normally exist prior to the birth of the individual, subjects potentially have a choice whether or not to consider their ethnic membership as meaningful. Owing to the duality of personal and social identities in the self-concept of the subject, individuals might choose at different times and under different circumstances to interact with each other as individuals rather than as group-members. In addition, each individual has the potential to choose one or more of a whole repertoire of social identities that make up his or her social *persona*. This is the point that lies behind Orlando Patterson's rather instrumentalist definition of ethnicity as, 'that condition wherein certain members of a society, in a given social context, choose to emphasize as their most meaningful basis of primary, extrafamilial identity certain assumed cultural, national or somatic traits'.[85]

---

[78] Fraser 1978, 177.   [79] Turner 1982, 26.   [80] Turner 1982, 23.   [81] Tajfel 1982, 3.
[82] Tajfel 1982, 2.   [83] Gordon 1975, 92; Horowitz 1985, 147.
[84] Fandetti and Gelfand 1983, 112; Horowitz 1975, 119; Vecoli 1978, 136.   [85] Patterson 1975, 308.

Individuals will, according to Patterson, initially attempt to reconcile their different allegiances (ethnic, class, linguistic, religious, national, etc.), but failing that, they will optimise the one that seems to operate in their best interests; where class interests are in confrontation with other allegiances, it is class that will win.[86]

This may be true at times when one's ethnic identity is not under threat – at times when a group perceives itself as holding a 'positive social identity'.[87] When, however, a group senses that it holds a 'negative social identity', it will attempt to gain a positive identity by one of three strategies. Either it will assimilate culturally and psychologically as a whole with the dominant group; or it will redefine positively characteristics that were previously negatively defined; or it will create new dimensions of comparison to bypass those by which it was formerly disadvantaged.[88]

The feasibility of the first strategy will depend on how rigorously the ethnic boundaries are patrolled. In cases where boundary crossing is relatively easy, an ethnic group may well assimilate with another that appears to enjoy a positive social identity: middle-class Italian-Americans in the United States have tended to converge towards the parental and social values of the dominant society,[89] and many of the Lapp communities in Finnmark in northern Norway have attempted to escape their perceived stigmatised status by 'becoming' Norwegian.[90] Yet, there are a number of Lapps who have also tried to pretend that 'ethnicity does not count', which represents the third strategy mentioned above.[91] In many cases, however, an ethnic group that perceives itself to have a negative social identity will begin to celebrate, rather than apologise for, its values, norms, symbols and cultural forms – the second strategy. Gypsy groups, for example, often achieve this by promoting themselves at the expense of one another. Thus, the Rom argue that the Romnicel and the Ludari are not real 'pure' gypsies, while each of the three groups projects onto the others the stereotypical image of criminality.[92]

The usual consequence of a threat to group identity is a convergence of individual behaviour. This process is sometimes termed Referent Informational Influence, whereby individuals first define themselves as members of a distinct social group, and then learn and apply to themselves the criterial attributes or stereotypic norms of that group. When category membership becomes more salient, their behaviour becomes more normative.[93] In other words, an external threat to the identity of an ethnic group will tend to engender a more uniform and normative behaviour among its members, which will seek to subsume the internal differences that result from personal identity under a more unified social identity. In these circumstances, adherence to an ethnic identity is seldom any longer voluntary in the way that Patterson describes.

---

[86] Patterson 1975, 311–13.   [87] See Giles, Bourhis and Taylor 1977, 320–21; Wetherell 1982, 209.
[88] Giles, Bourhis and Taylor 1977, 320–21.
[89] Fandetti and Gelfand 1983, 125; Vecoli 1978, 136. Nevertheless, many third-generation Italian-Americans (like many other white ethnics in America) are currently searching again for their ethnic roots: De Vos 1995, 30.   [90] Eidheim 1969, 54–55.   [91] Eidheim 1969, 54.
[92] Salo 1979, 84, 93.   [93] See Turner 1982, 31.

31

The occurrence of an increased salience in group membership is often more frequent among those who are socially excluded or politically dominated.[94] Thus within Britain the ethnic identity of the Scots and Welsh is generally more salient than that of the English. Research into the relations of power between groups has suggested that the 'dominant' do not see themselves as being determined by their group membership or social affiliation, but rather as individual human subjects, while the 'dominated' are viewed as objects.[95] That is, those whose position of status and privilege is not threatened tend to operate more according to personal identities than a social identity. Conversely, tests show that those who are dominated define themselves more in terms of group membership and social position than their dominators: 'being dominated produces in the individuals involved a heightened awareness of the social categories which determine their minority status'.[96]

Finally, since the prerequisite for gauging the positive or negative value of a group's social identity is intergroup comparison,[97] then it is fairly obvious that the ethnic identity of a group is only likely to become salient when confronted with at least one other group.[98] Among the U'wa of the eastern Andes, 'it is not until radical differences are met, in terms of language, habitat, food habits and world view, that ethnic and territorial boundaries are drawn'.[99] For this reason ethnicity will rarely be a salient dimension of differentiation in situations where the ethnic group is coterminous with the national group, unless national boundaries are open to question. Irish ethnicity (as opposed to nationality) does not command the same significance within the Republic of Ireland as it does within Northern Ireland.

Summary

By way of summary, it may be useful to enumerate and reiterate the main points of this chapter.

(1) Ethnicity is a social rather than a biological phenomenon. It is defined by socially and discursively constructed criteria rather than by physical indicia.

(2) Genetic, linguistic, religious or common cultural features do not ultimately define the ethnic group. These are symbols that are manipulated according to subjectively constructed ascriptive boundaries.

(3) The ethnic group is distinguished from other social and associative groups by virtue of association with a specific territory and a shared myth of descent. This notion of descent is putative rather than actual, and judged by consensus.

(4) Ethnic groups are frequently formed by the appropriation of resources by one section of the population, at the expense of another, as a result of long-term conquest or migration, or by the reaction against such appropriation.

[94] Schermerhorn 1974, 2; Sarna 1978, 374.   [95] Deschamps 1982, 90.   [96] Deschamps 1982, 91.
[97] Tajfel 1978, 443.   [98] Brass and Van den Berghe 1976, 200; Eriksen 1993, 34.
[99] Osborn 1989, 153–54.

(5) Ethnic groups are not static or monolithic, but dynamic and fluid. Their boundaries are permeable to a degree, and they may be subject to processes of assimilation and differentiation.

(6) Individuals need not always act in terms of their membership of an ethnic group. When, however, ethnic group identity is threatened, its internalisation as the social identity of each of its members entails a convergence of group behaviour and norms, and the temporary suppression of individual variability in the pursuit of a positive social identity. Ethnicity gains varying degrees of salience at different times.

(7) Such behavioural convergence and ethnic salience is more common among (though not exclusive to) dominated and excluded groups.

(8) Ethnic identity can only be constituted by opposition to other ethnic identities.

3

The discursive dimension of ethnic identity

Ethnic groups in ancient Greece

While the term 'ethnicity' apparently made its first appearance only in 1953,[1] the phenomenon which it describes is indisputably more ancient. The genesis of nationalism in the late eighteenth and early nineteenth centuries did not create ethnic consciousness, but demanded that ethnic boundaries should be coterminous with political ones.[2] Thus, although Catalan nationalism may be a product of the modern era, the earlier existence of a distinct Catalan identity is demonstrated by the enrolment of the Catalan *natio* (this time without its political connotations) in the statutes of the University of Bologna in AD 1265.[3] Similarly, Serbian consciousness is not a product of the nationalist movement of the 1980s, but has been preserved in the ritualised songs and epics telling of the conquest of the Old Serbian Kingdom by the Turks.[4]

Although the English words 'ethnic' and 'ethnicity' are derived from the Greek *ethnos* (plural, *ethne*), even the most cursory survey of the ancient sources is sufficient to demonstrate that *ethnos* could embrace a wider variety of meanings than simply 'ethnic group'. While it certainly can describe groups of people, its use does not appear to be strictly circumscribed in any defined sociological sense. On the one hand, it may be applied to the inhabitants of a *polis*, as when Herodotos refers to the Athenian and Attic *ethne*, or the *ethnos* of the Khalkidians.[5] Alternatively, it may refer to a larger population which inhabits several *poleis*. For instance, the Boiotians are described as an *ethnos*,[6] and in describing the peoples of the Peloponnese, Herodotos writes:

> Seven *ethne* live in the Peloponnese. Of these, two – the Arkadians and Kynourians – are autochthonous and are settled in the same territory which they occupied even in the past; one – the Akhaians – did not depart from the Peloponnese but left its own territory and now inhabits a different region. The remaining four of the seven *ethne* – the Dorians, Aitolians, Dryopes and Lemnians – are newcomers. The cities of the Dorians are many and well known; Elis is the only Aitolian city; Hermione and the Asine which is situated opposite Lakonian Kardamyle are Dryopean; and all the Paroreatai are Lemnians.[7]

---

[1] Glazer and Moynihan 1975, 1; Geary 1983, 16.
[2] Gellner 1983; Anderson 1991; Hobsbawm 1992b.   [3] Romeo 1981, 136–37.
[4] Hobsbawm 1992b, 75–76.   [5] Herodotos 1.57.3; 5.77.4; 7.161.3.   [6] Herodotos 5.77.4.
[7] Herodotos 8.73.1–2.

34

Nor is the term restricted to the Greeks. It is used to describe the populations west of the river Halys, over whom the Lydian king Kroisos ruled, or the peoples within the Caucasus region.[8] Here again, the word can refer to groups of varying size: it denotes both the Libyans collectively and each of the groups that are the subdivisions of the Libyans.[9] Similarly, *ethnos* is the word that is applied to the Skythians generally, as well as to Skythian subgroups such as the Alizones, the Tauroi and the Boudinoi.[10]

All of the above examples could loosely be described as population groups. Yet *ethnos* could also be applied more widely. In Homer, it simply designates a class of beings who share a common identification.[11] Thus it is used to describe groups of warriors or young men, the ranks of the dead, flocks of birds and swarms of bees or flies.[12] Its use as a simple collective noun persists through to the fifth century: Aiskhylos refers to the *ethnos* of the Erinyes, or Furies;[13] Sophokles applies the term to bands of wild beasts;[14] and Pindar uses it to designate the male and female sexes.[15] In the fourth century, Plato was to call the Penestai (the serf population of Thessaly) an *ethnos* because they made up a class with a particular function within the relations of production.[16]

Nevertheless, if *ethnos* need not always denote what we would term an 'ethnic group', many of the populations that are referred to as *ethne* are also often described as *gene*. *Genos* is related to the verb *gignesthai*, which means 'to be born', 'to come into being' and so eventually 'to become'. *Genos*, then, can be seen as both the mechanism by which one's identity is ascribed (i.e. birth),[17] as well as the collective group in which membership is thought to be ascribed through birth. The most obvious application of this second definition is to the family unit: so Herodotos employs *genos* to describe the Athenian families of the Gephyraioi or the Alkmeonidai.[18] But *genos* is not reserved exclusively for the family group; it can be applied to a category of any size that recognises its members to be enlisted automatically by birth.[19] Thus Herodotos can describe the population of Attika not only as an *ethnos*, but also as a *genos*, since Athenian citizenship was restricted to those of Athenian birth. Similarly, the Hellenes can be described as both an *ethnos* and a *genos*, since one of the defining criteria of Greekness, along with language, customs and cult, was – for Herodotos at any rate – shared blood.[20]

In one of the standard works of reference for Greek terminology, *ethnos* is defined as a 'nation', and *genos* as a tribal subdivision of an *ethnos*.[21] Quite apart

---

[8] Herodotos 1.6.1; 1.203.1. [9] Herodotos 4.171–72; 4.197; 4.183.

[10] Herodotos 4.5; 4.17; 4.99; 4.108.

[11] Donlan 1985, 295; Tonkin, McDonald and Chapman 1989, 12.

[12] Warriors/young men: *Iliad* 2.91; 3.32; 7.115; 11.724. The dead: *Odyssey* 10.526. Birds: *Iliad* 2.459. Flies: *Iliad* 2.87, 469. [13] Aiskhylos, *Eumenides* 366.

[14] Sophokles, *Philoktetes* 1147; *Antigone* 344. [15] Pindar, *Olympian Odes* 1.66; *Pythian Odes* 4.252.

[16] Plato, *Laws* 6.776d. See Roussel 1976, 162.

[17] Cf. Herodotos 1.6.1; 1.31.2; 3.4.1; 4.147.2; 6.133.1; 7.208.1. [18] Herodotos 5.55; 5.62.2.

[19] See Smith 1986, 21.

[20] Attic *ethnos*: 1.57.3. Attic *genos*: 5.91.1. Hellenic *ethnos*: 1.56.2. Hellenic *genos*: 1.143.2. For the defining criteria of Greekness: 8.144.2. [21] LSJ s.v. γένος, ἔθνος.

35

from the anachronistic application of terminology more appropriate to the modern than the ancient period, the idea that *genos* should be ranked below *ethnos* within the same hierarchical social taxonomy is vitiated by Herodotos' use of the two terms as synonyms. In introducing the Spartans and Athenians into his narrative, Herodotos says that the Spartans belonged to the Dorian *genos* and the Athenians to the Ionian *genos*: while the Dorian *genos* is an *ethnos* that is Hellenic, the Ionian *genos* is an *ethnos* that was originally Pelasgian, but became more Hellenic over time.[22] Thus while *ethnos* can be substituted frequently for *genos*, it is the latter term which has the more specialised meaning, with its focus on the notion (however fictive) of shared descent. Once this is understood, Herodotos' description of the temple of Karian Zeus becomes more intelligible. This was a cult shared by Karians, Mysians and Lydians, though not by other *ethne*, even if they spoke the same language or dialect as the Karians. The reason for this exclusion was that the other homophonous *ethne* did not share in the *ancestry* of the three participating peoples, whose eponymous ancestors, Kar, Lydos and Mysos, were brothers.[23]

An important feature of the *genos*, whether defined as the family unit or a larger collectivity, is the fact that it is subject to the segmentary nature of lineage fission. Thus, while Sparta claimed to belong to the Dorian *genos*, so did the neighbouring *poleis* of Messene and Argos, as well as more remote cities such as Kerkyra or Syracuse. This subscription to the notion of shared descent in the absence of geographical integrity was explained by the belief that the members of the Dorian *genos* had originally cohabited in various parts of northern and central Greece prior to the series of migrations which led to their distribution throughout the Aegean in the historical period.[24] It was because of this former cohabitation that the Dorians, just as the Dryopes, could be described as one of the recently arrived *ethne* in the Peloponnese.[25] The Ionians likewise were supposed to have originally lived together on the northern coast of the Peloponnese, known in the historical period as Akhaia.[26]

In chapter 2, it was argued that an ethnic group should be defined as a social collectivity whose members are united by their subscription to a putative belief in shared descent and to an association with a primordial homeland. It should be clear, then, that a group such as the Dorians, the Ionians or the Dryopes should qualify for the definition, insofar as each claimed to trace both its common descent from eponymous ancestors such as Doros, Ion and Dryops, and its original roots in a territory extraneous to the regions which it inhabited in the historical period. This belief in a common ancestry and an original territory of cohabitation could then engender a sense of ethnic consciousness, or *syngeneia*.

Syngeneia is the regular word for family kinship,[27] though it is important to note that it does not signify an *externally defined* system of cognative relationships between

---

[22] Herodotos 1.56.2. Cf. 1.57.3.   [23] Herodotos 1.171.6.
[24] See Herodotos 1.56.3; 7.99.3; 8.31; 8.43; Thoukydides 1.107.2; 3.92.3.
[25] Herodotos 8.73.2.   [26] Herodotos 1.145–47; 7.94; Strabo 8.1.2; 8.7.1–4; Pausanias 7.1.2–4.
[27] E.g. Herodotos 4.164.4.

siblings and cousins, but rather the kin relationships that a particular individual might recognise at any one time *by reference to shared ancestors in the lineage*.[28] In other words, a *syngenes* is one who is recognised as belonging to the same *genos* as ego, whether or not this is biologically the case. But, just as *genos* can be extended beyond the scope of the family to refer to larger collectivities, so *syngeneia* can refer to the wider kinship that individuals might share with one another by virtue of their belief in shared descent.[29]

Thoukydides' history is replete with appeals to kinship for political or military purposes. Immediately after the Persian Wars (480–479 BC), the recently liberated Ionian cities of Asia Minor are supposed to have asked Athens to assume the leadership over them in place of the Spartans 'according to their *syngeneia*',[30] and in 427 BC, the Sicilian city of Leontinoi appealed to the Athenians for assistance in their war against the Dorians of Syracuse 'on the basis of their ancient alliance and the fact that they were Ionians'.[31] The opportunism of the Athenians' selective recognition of kinship was not lost on Thoukydides, who makes the authorial comment that, in launching the Sicilian expedition of 415 BC, the Athenians wished to be seen to aid their '*syngeneis*' though the real reason behind the campaign was their desire to conquer the island.[32] Similar sentiments are placed in the mouth of the Syracusan statesman Hermokrates, who points out that while the Athenians seemed eager to help the Khalkidian settlers of Leontinoi 'according to [Ionian] *syngeneia*', they had already enslaved the Khalkidian inhabitants of Euboia.[33]

The Ionians were not alone in resorting to appeals based on kinship. For the Korinthian delegation at the allied congress of the Spartans and their allies in 432 BC, the fact that the Dorian inhabitants of Poteideia were being besieged by Ionians from Athens was evidently a sufficient reason for Peloponnesian intervention.[34] Once again, though, Thoukydides exposes the fragility of claims based on supposed kinship. Under siege from the Athenians in 416 BC, the inhabitants of the Dorian island of Melos expressed their confidence that the Spartans would come to their aid 'if for no other reason than for the sake of *syngeneia*'. Such confidence was misplaced: the Melians, abandoned by the Spartans, were forced to surrender to the Athenians in 415 BC, resulting in the execution of all adult males and the total enslavement of women and children.[35]

It has been argued that the appearance in Thoukydides' work of ethnic claims based on kinship is nothing more than a rhetorical device on the part of the author, and that such appeals hardly constitute evidence for a genuine ethnic consciousness either in or before the late fifth century BC.[36] There is, however, a reason for doubting that this is the case. One of the persistent oppositions which pervades

---

[28] Roussel 1976, 29.
[29] For a detailed analysis of the term *syngeneia* in diplomatic treaties between Greek cities, see Curty 1995. [30] Thoukydides 1.95.1. [31] Thoukydides 3.86.3; cf. 6.20.3.
[32] Thoukydides 6.6.1; cf. 7.57.1. [33] Thoukydides 6.76.2. Cf. 4.61.2. [34] Thoukydides 1.124.1.
[35] Thoukydides 5.104; 5.108; 5.116.4. [36] Will 1956, 67; Jardé 1926, 76.

Thoukydides' history is that between the 'specious pretext' and the 'real reason'.[37] The former is frequently articulated through the speeches which Thoukydides introduces into his narrative and which, he claims, represent the sorts of opinions that were current at the time;[38] the latter, instead, is not infrequently presented in the form of authorial comment. The fact, then, that Thoukydides sees through the ethnic pretext of Athenian help to Leontinoi according to *syngeneia* does not detract from the distinct possibility that when the Spartan general Brasidas describes Dorians as courageous and Ionians as weak, or when Hermokrates asserts that Ionians are slavish while Dorians are free, they may be expressing more popularly held opinions.[39] Such appeals are undoubtedly rhetorical, though the success of rhetoric depends upon its being able to draw on, exaggerate or subvert stock themes in current circulation.[40]

Appeals to kinship can always, of course, be a matter of pure invention. In the third century BC, king Areus I of Sparta is supposed to have sent a letter to the High Priest of Jerusalem claiming to have authenticated a document which demonstrated a kin relationship between the Spartans and the Jews.[41] In the case of the rhetorical appeals to kinship in Thoukydides, there can be little doubt that the Peloponnesian War and its prelude provided a particularly salient context for the elaboration of an ethnic opposition between Dorians and Ionians. Indeed, the use of the word *syngeneia* in appeals to ethnic solidarity is not common before the fifth century – Pausanias has the Messenians appealing to the Spartans as '*syngeneis*' at the time of the Second Messenian War in the mid-seventh century, but he is writing some 800 years after the supposed event.[42] Nevertheless, the *notion* of kinship does appear earlier in situations where an ethnic *esprit de corps* is galvanised by reference to shared descent from a common ancestor. In 470 BC, Pindar wrote an ode commemorating the chariot victory of Hieron (tyrant of Syracuse and founder of Aitna) in which the Dorians of Sparta are described as the joint progeny (*ekgonoi*) of Pamphylos, the grandson of Doros, and the Herakleidai, the descendants of Herakles.[43] Two centuries earlier, Tyrtaios had exhorted the Dorians of Sparta by reminding them that they were of the lineage (*genos*) of Herakles.[44]

Aside from occasional appeals to kin relationships, the members of an ethnic group are also often described as sharing certain common social customs.[45] For instance, the sixth-century poet Anakreon mentions a Dorian type of dress,[46] while Euripides refers to a 'Dorian knife'.[47] Thoukydides observes that the Sicilian city of Gela adopted 'Dorian customs' though the Dorian-Ionian foundation of

---

[37] See especially Thoukydides 1.23.5–6.   [38] Thoukydides 1.22.1.

[39] Brasidas: Thoukydides 5.9.1. Hermokrates: Thoukydides 6.77.1. See generally Alty 1982, 6–7.

[40] Alty 1982, 3.

[41] 1 Maccabees 12.19–23; Josephus, *Jewish Antiquities* 12.226. See Bernal 1987, 109–110; Cartledge and Spawforth 1989, 37, 85; Rawson 1991, 96; Malkin 1994, 67.   [42] Pausanias 4.8.2.

[43] Pindar, *Pythian Odes* 1.62–65.   [44] Tyrtaios fr. 11 Edmonds.   [45] E.g. Murray 1993, 9.

[46] Anakreon fr. 54 Page. See also Aiskhylos, *Persai* 182–83; Herodotos 5.88.

[47] Euripides, *Elektra* 836.

Himera did not,[48] and Pindar describes the Spartans as living 'according to the ordinances of Aigimios (a mythical ancestor of the Dorians)'.[49]

Even more significant than common customs were the cults and rituals that were thought to unite the members of an ethnic group. Thoukydides says that the month in which the Karneia (a festival to Apollo Karneios) took place was sacred among the Dorians.[50] Theopompos of Khios explains that the festival was instituted to placate Karnos, a seer of Apollo who prophesied to the Herakleidai on their return to the Peloponnese but was killed on suspicion of espionage.[51] It has, however, been suggested that *karnos* may in fact be a synonym for the word *krios*, which means 'ram', thus referring not only to the preferred sacrificial victim at the festival, but also to the supposed pastoral-nomadic subsistence of the Dorians.[52]

Similarly, while the *cult* of Hyakinthos, originally centred on the Lakonian town of Amyklai, has often been considered as being pre-Dorian (and perhaps even pre-Greek) in character,[53] the *festival* of the Hyakinthia would appear to have had a reasonably wide diffusion among Dorian areas, to judge from the frequent attestation of a month known as Hyakinthios.[54] Certainly, Thoukydides seems to regard the Paian (a hymn frequently associated with the Hyakinthia)[55] as a peculiarly Dorian form of expression: in an incident of 413 BC, during the Sicilian expedition, the Athenians are supposed to have panicked when their Dorian allies, the Argives and the Kerkyraians, joined with the Syracusan enemy in singing the Paian.[56]

There were also certain festivals which were thought to be exclusive to the Ionians. In describing the sanctuaries on and around the Athenian akropolis, Thoukydides says that the custom of honouring Dionysos in the Marsh during the Older Dionysia, held in the month of Anthesterion, was one that was followed even in his own day by 'those Ionians who are originally from Athens'.[57] Herodotos

---

[48] Thoukydides 6.4.3; 6.5.1. [49] Pindar, *Pythian Odes* 1.64. See Van Effenterre 1985, 296–97.

[50] Thoukydides 5.54.2. See also Herodotos 6.106.3; 7.206.1.

[51] Theopompos of Khios *FGrH* 115.357. See also Pausanias 3.13.4.

[52] See generally Burkert 1985, 234–36; Eder 1990; Malkin 1994, 149–57.

[53] The assumption that the cult of Hyakinthos is pre-Hellenic is predicated on the *-nth* suffix which some (though not all) linguists consider to be non-Indo-European in origin. The existence of a double cult to Apollo and Hyakinthos at Amyklai has often been explained historically as the implantation of the Dorian god Apollo alongside the pre-Dorian god Hyakinthos at the time of Dorian Sparta's conquest of Akhaian Amyklai (see e.g. Nilsson 1950, 556–58) though this rests on the erroneous belief that Apollo was an exclusively Dorian deity (see chapter 4). While recognising the difficulties in this explanation, Cartledge (1979, 80–81; 1992, 54) associates the pre-Dorian Hyakinthos cult with the LHIIIB-C phase of the Amyklaion and the Dorian cult of Apollo with the appearance of Lakonian Protogeometric pottery after a break of some 200 years. Other archaeologists (e.g. Demakopoulou 1982; Coulson 1985; Pettersson 1992, 92–109) prefer to see archaeological (and hence, cultic) continuity at the Amyklaion from the Late Bronze Age onwards, and Dietrich (1975) has argued that Hyakinthos was already a Dorian god in the LHIII period. Doubts have, however, been cast on a Late Bronze Age cult to Hyakinthos by Calligas (1992, 39–40, 45–46) and Dickinson (1992, 114).

[54] Dietrich 1975; Cartledge 1979, 81; Burkert 1985, 19; Malkin 1994, 111–13. [55] Burkert 1985, 145.

[56] Thoukydides 7.44.6. [57] Thoukydides 2.15.4. See also Burkert 1985, 237.

defines Ionians as 'those who originate from Athens and celebrate the festival of the Apatouria' – the festival at which new citizens were enrolled into the phratry.[58]

It is here, however, that the weaknesses in a *primarily* cultural-religious definition of Greek ethnic groups are exposed, because Herodotos goes on to say that the Ephesians and Kolophonians do not celebrate the Apatouria: 'these are the only Ionians who do not celebrate the Apatouria, pleading some murder as an excuse'.[59] Yet if the Ephesians and Kolophonians can be considered ethnically Ionian without celebrating the Apatouria, then clearly this festival is not a necessary defining criterion of being Ionian. By the same token, if the Karneia is considered as a vehicle for the expression of an exclusively Dorian identity, it is somewhat strange that Pausanias makes no mention of a sanctuary to Apollo Karneios in the Dorian city of Argos.[60] In fact, Theopompos states that the Argives worshipped Zeus Agetor rather than Apollo Karneios.[61] Even Anakreon's 'Dorian dress' loses some of its significance when we learn that this was the type of garment that was worn by Athenian women before they adopted Ionian attire.[62]

It is these slight though significant discrepancies that appear to vindicate another conclusion reached in chapter 2: namely, that cultural forms may come to reinforce an ethnic identity that has been discursively constructed, but cannot define that ethnicity in the first place. When Pausanias notes that the formerly Athenian region of the Megarid 'changed its customs and its language and became Dorian', he is merely pointing to the most visible *indicia* which distinguished the Dorians of Megara from their Athenian neighbours.[63] Ultimately, however, it was not the adoption of Dorian customs or the Doric dialect which primarily defined the Megarians as Dorians, but rather the fact that they considered themselves to be the descendants of Dorians who had invaded the Megarid when Kodros was king of Athens. Likewise, however 'Dorianised' the inhabitants of Kynouria may have become as the result of long subjection to the Argives, they still remained Ionians.[64] In other words, the primary constitutive elements in the construction of ethnic consciousness were not behavioural but discursive, articulated through myths of ethnic origins which spoke not only of ethnic ancestors but also of primordial territories.

Myths of ethnic origins

Although there is a considerable diversity of approaches to the interpretation of Greek myths in general, myths of ethnic origins present their own peculiar prob-

---

[58] Herodotos 1.147.2. See Burkert 1985, 255; Bruit Zaidman and Schmitt Pantel 1992, 65–66.
[59] Herodotos 1.147.2.
[60] Contrast Pausanias 2.10.2; 2.11.2; 3.21.8; 3.24.8; 3.25.10; 3.26.5–7; 4.31.1; 4.33.4.
[61] Theopompos *FGrH* 115.357.   [62] Herodotos 5.87.3.   [63] Pausanias 1.39.5.
[64] Herodotos 8.73.3. See Faklaris 1990, 31–32.

lems.[65] Typically, as one might expect, they take the form of genealogies, but they are somewhat different from the type of 'family genealogies' which are normally assumed to have been elaborated initially among élite families, partly for the purposes of establishing affiliation and relationships of seniority among one another, and partly to accommodate the political alliances that were forged through intermarriage.[66] Whereas family genealogies allowed individuals to trace their lineage back to three-dimensional characters such as Perseus, Keryx or Eumolpos, ethnic genealogies were the instrument by which whole social collectivities could situate themselves in space and time, reaffirming their identity by appeals to eponymous ancestors such as Doros, Ion or Dryops, who were at the same time the retrojected constructions of such identity.[67]

There is a school of thought, generally termed 'historically positivist', which sees in myths of ethnic origins a hazy and refracted recollection of genuine population movements that occurred at the end of the Late Bronze Age.[68] The series of sometimes contradictory variants in which such myths exist are then understood as pathological aberrations from a 'real' historical memory – a collective amnesia, or even polymnesia, resulting from the passage of time. The task of the historical positivist is to reconcile these contradictory variants within a single, rationalising work of synthesis in order to reveal 'what actually happened'. In fact, there is nothing new in this practice: compilers of 'Universal Histories' such as Ephoros of Kyme, Diodoros of Sicily, or the author of the Pseudo-Apollodoran *Bibliotheka* were confronted with a similar task. As Diodoros comments: 'It has turned out that the old myths have nothing in the way of a simple or consistent story; for this reason, one should not be surprised if some of the antiquarian accounts do not match up exactly with all the poets and historians'.[69]

The problem with the historically positivist approach is that it views myths of ethnic origin as the passive trace-elements of groups whose 'objective' existence is deemed to stand independently of those same myths. If, however, we accept the view that ethnicity is not a primordial given, but is instead repeatedly and actively structured through discursive strategies, then clearly myths of ethnic origins are among the very media through which such strategies operate. They function as cognitive artefacts which both circumscribe and actively structure corporate identity, so that whenever the relationships between groups change, then so do the accompanying genealogies.[70] What enables us to trace this genealogical restructuring is precisely the appearance of mythical variants – that is, the occasional survival of earlier elements which coexist, albeit uncomfortably, alongside later elements. Thus, far from regarding mythical variants as the inevitable consequence of a genuine collective memory in decay, we should rather view them as indicat-

---

[65] For recent approaches to understanding myths in general: Kirk 1970, 42–83, 252–85; Burkert 1979, 1–34; Vernant 1980, 207–40; Detienne 1986, 1–21; Bremmer 1987; Edmunds 1990; Dowden 1992, 22–38.   [66] Finley 1986, 28; Thomas 1989, 157; Dowden 1992, 11.
[67] Nilsson 1951, 65.   [68] E.g. Myres 1930; Hammond 1975; 1976; Wallace and Kase 1978.
[69] Diodoros 4.44.5–6.   [70] Bohannan 1952, 308–312; Vansina 1985, 24.

ing specific stages in the discursive construction of ethnicity. The contradictions, or 'fracture points', which exist between these variants can serve to outline the individual building blocks from which myths of ethnic origins are constituted, reordered and restructured.

The earliest reference to the ethnic groups that are familiar to us in the historical period is found in the *Odyssey*, where Krete is described as inhabited by Akhaians, Eteokretans, Kydonians, Dorians and Pelasgians.[71] The Dorians are described as *trikhaïkes* – a word which some have interpreted as referring to the standard tripartite organisation of the Dorians into three *phylai*.[72] The appearance of the Dorians is somewhat surprising given the fact that the epic narrative is set in the decade after the Trojan War, and thus, according to Thoukydides, some two generations *before* the arrival of the Dorians.[73] In the *Iliad*, for instance, Miletos is not yet home to Greek settlers despite the fact that the archaeological evidence suggests it had been colonised by the eleventh century at the very latest.[74] The apparent anachronism is welcome to those who argue that the Dorians neither invaded nor migrated, but were already part of the Mycenaean world (see chapters 5–6). Nevertheless, Dorians are not envisaged as yet in possession of the Peloponnesian cities of Argos or Sparta, so it is probably best to regard this description of the multilingual situation on Krete as an Iron Age, rather than Late Bronze Age, element in the thickly woven tapestry of oral tradition inherited by the poet of the Homeric epics.[75]

The earliest reference to Greek ethnicity with an explicitly genealogical dimension is what we may term the 'Hellenic genealogy', from the *Catalogue of women*: 'The sons of the war-loving king Hellen were Doros, Xouthos and Aiolos who fights from the chariot'.[76] A recently discovered papyrus fragment from Oxyrhynkhos in Egypt adds two further details: firstly, that 'the spear-famed king Aigimios begat by force in his palace Dymas and Pamphylos'; and secondly that 'by the will of the gods, Xouthos took as his wife Kreousa of beautiful form, the fair-cheeked daughter of godlike Erekhtheus, and she lay with him in love and begat him Akhaios, Ion of the noble steeds and the beautiful Diomede'.[77] It is almost certain that the Oxyrhynkhos fragment also belongs to the *Catalogue of women* and should follow hard on the heels of fragment 9, since Diodoros, who cer-

---

[71] Homer, *Odyssey* 19.177.

[72] See Musti (1985b, 39–40) who compares this passage with the tripartite division of Rhodes under the Heraklid Tlepolemos: Homer, *Iliad* 2.655. Finley (1977, 17) and Roussel (1976, 224) argue instead that *trikhaïkes* has nothing to do with sociopolitical organisation.

[73] Thoukydides 1.12.3.

[74] Homer, *Iliad* 2.868. See Emlyn-Jones 1980, 14; Vanschoonwinkel 1991, 398.

[75] See, however, Van Wees 1992, who argues against the 'patchwork' view of the *Iliad* and prefers to treat it as a coherent work of the early seventh century.

[76] Hesiod fr. 9 Merkelbach/West. For reasons that I intend to elaborate elsewhere, I am unconvinced by arguments for an earlier genealogy in which Hellen's role as *capostipite* was taken instead by Aiolos: see Cassola 1953; Mele 1995, 436.

[77] Hesiod fr. 10(a).6–7, 20–24 Merkelbach/West. A similar genealogy is presented in Pseudo-Apollodoros, *Bibliotheka* 1.7.3.

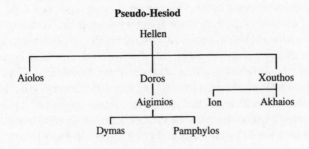

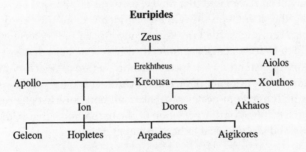

1 The Hellenic genealogy according to Pseudo-Hesiod and Euripides.

tainly made use of this work, has Aigimios as the son of Doros.[78] It is therefore possible to reconstruct, at least partially, the Hellenic genealogy (fig. 1).

Clearly the function of the Hellenic genealogy is to establish the degree of relatedness between the various Greek ethnic groups which are represented by their eponymous ancestors (Hellen, Doros, Aiolos, Ion and Akhaios). Similarly, the appearance of the eponymous Pamphylos and Dymas serves to explain the relationship between the Dorian *phylai* of the Pamphyloi and Dymanes (the non-eponymous Aigimios will be treated later). More than simply providing an answer to the question of ethnic origins, however, the Hellenic genealogy employs the metaphor of kinship to construct a system of *ranked* relationships between the groups that are represented by their eponyms. By depicting Doros and Aiolos, or Akhaios and Ion, as brothers, the Hellenic genealogy projects the idea that Dorians are more related to Aiolians than they are to Akhaians, while Akhaians share a closer affinity with Ionians than they do with Aiolians. At the same time, by having Doros and Aiolos as sons, but Akhaios and Ion as grandsons, of Hellen, the genealogy is implicitly stating that Dorians and Aiolians possess a higher status by being somehow *more* Hellenic.

In antiquity, the *Catalogue of women* was attributed to Hesiod, though in fact it was

---

[78] Diodoros 4.58.6.

43

probably not written down before the sixth century BC – perhaps in Athens.[79] That is not to say that all of the genealogical elements are fictive creations of the sixth century: thus Martin West hypothesises that the tradition concerning the three sons of Hellen may have been in oral circulation since the eighth or even ninth centuries, though the attachment of the daughter of the Argive 'first man', Phoroneus, to the lineage of Doros may not predate the late sixth century.[80] In the final event, the only thing of which we can be fairly certain is that the end of the sixth century is the very latest *terminus ante quem* for the development of the Hellenic genealogy in the form we have it. I shall suggest that it may not in fact predate that *terminus* by many decades.

It has long been recognised that the Persian War of 480–479 BC was a decisive moment in the formation of Greek self-identity: in the words of Simon Hornblower, 'Persia gave the Greeks their identity, or the means for recognizing it.'[81] Even if few *poleis* actually mounted resistance against Xerxes' forces (only thirty-one are named on the 'Serpent Column', set up as a victory monument at Delphi), the looming presence of an external invader was a powerful vehicle in persuading formerly antagonistic cities to make common cause in defence.[82] The invasion acted as a catalyst for the 'invention of the barbarian' – that is, the creation of a derogatory and stereotypical 'other', exemplified best in Aiskhylos' *Persai* of 472 BC.[83]

It is in these terms that we must view the work of Herodotos, born, according to Dionysios of Halikarnassos, a little before the Persian Wars.[84] In an almost certainly fictitious incident just before the battle of Plataia in 479 BC, Herodotos has Athenian envoys chide the Spartans for thinking that they would desert to the Persian side:

> There are many important factors that would prevent us from doing this, even if we wanted to. First and foremost are the statues of the gods and the temples which have been burnt and destroyed; it is necessary for us to avenge this to the best of our ability rather than come to an agreement with him who did it. Secondly, there are the common blood and tongue that we Greeks share, together with the common cult places, the sacrifices and the similar customs; it would not be noble for the Athenians to betray all this.[85]

At first sight, this passage might appear to offer an 'essentialist' definition of Greekness – that is, a definition based on *similarities* between the various Greek communities, be it of kinship, language, cult or customs. When, however, this extract is viewed against the general scheme of Herodotos' *Histories*, a very different interpretation emerges.

---

[79] West 1985, 127–30, 169–71.
[80] West 1985, 59, 144. For Phoroneus' marriage: Hesiod frs. 10(a). 17–19, 10(b) Merkelbach/West.
[81] Hornblower 1991b, 11.
[82] For a less unitary picture of the Greeks after the Persian Wars, however, see Sinn 1994.
[83] See E. Hall 1989, esp. 56–100.　　[84] Dionysios of Halikarnassos, *De Thucydide* 5.
[85] Herodotos 8.144.2.

The greater part of Herodotos' work is taken up with the so-called 'barbarian *logoi*' – ethnographic descriptions of peoples such as the Persians, the Egyptians, the Skythians or the Libyans – though, unlike Aiskhylos, Herodotos respected cultural diversity and refrained from adverse comparison between stereotyped, undifferentiated barbarians and Greeks.[86] Instead, as François Hartog has eloquently and persuasively argued, one of the functions of Herodotos' ethnographic excursuses was to 'hold up the mirror' to his Greek audience, displaying a series of overlapping images of barbarian practices which might thereby act as a mirror reflection of Greek customs.[87] Opposition based on kinship or language was not difficult to establish. While the ancestry of barbarians might be traced back to figures of Greek myth such as Deukalion or Inakhos,[88] it could not be derived from Hellen and so, technically speaking, no barbarians could share in Hellenic blood. Similarly, since the word *barbaros* seems originally to have carried a linguistic connotation,[89] there is good reason to suppose that Greek speakers were aware that barbarians spoke differently, though that is not to imply that they were ever linguistically accomplished enough to decide *exactly* where the linguistic boundaries between Greek and non-Greek always fell – Prodikos was to call Pittakos' Lesbian dialect a 'barbarian register'.[90]

It is the emphasis on 'Greek' religion and customs in Herodotos' definition which is innovative, because from the Greek point of view there were decided differences in the cults and ritual practices of different regions. The only way in which cultural heterogeneity could appear more uniform was by contrasting it with practices that were even more heterogeneous, and this is precisely what Herodotos achieved through the barbarian excursuses. For instance, in describing Persian religious practices, Herodotos says, 'it is not their custom to erect statues, temples and altars, and they think that those who do this are foolish – I suppose, because they do not have the tradition of anthropomorphic gods as the Greeks do'.[91] Herodotos' purpose in this observation is not to deride the Persians: Walter Burkert has even suggested that Herodotos' sympathies lie with the Persian view, which might partially explain why Plutarch regarded the 'father of history' as a *philobarbaros*.[92] It is rather to define *externally* Greek sacrificial practice, with its focus on the trilogy of statue, temple and altar, by opposing it to the alien customs of the Persians. Similarly, in discussing Skythian religion, Herodotos writes, 'it is not their custom to make statues, altars or temples other than to Ares' – by contrast, temple cults to Ares in Greece are few and far between.[93]

The crystallisation of a diametric opposition between Greek and barbarian in

---

[86] Nippel 1990, 14–16. [87] Hartog 1988b. See also Cartledge 1993, 55–56.
[88] E. Hall 1989, 172.
[89] In Homer, *Iliad* 2.867, the Karians are described as *barbarophonoi* ('with barbarian tongue'). See E. Hall 1989, 9–11. [90] Plato, *Protagoras* 341c; E. Hall 1989, 179. See further chapter 6.
[91] Herodotos 1.131.1.
[92] Burkert 1990, 21. For Herodotos as a 'barbarian lover': Plutarch, *Moralia* 857a.
[93] Herodotos 4.59.2. For the scarcity of temple cults to Ares: Burkert 1985, 170.

the fifth century marks a distinct break from the Archaic period. Even though epics such as the *Iliad* celebrated the confrontation between Greeks and Trojans, Homer has the opponents sacrifice to the same gods, and there is little evidence for the Trojans being stereotyped in the derogatory way that Aiskhylos was to practise with regard to the Persians.[94] In essence, the conflict is enacted between the inhabitants of the Greek mainland and those of Anatolia: while Krete and the Dodekanesian islands are already occupied by Greeks, the Kykladic islands and Ionia are not. Furthermore, as Thoukydides had already observed, Homer's Greeks are variously described as Danaoi, Argives and Akhaians, but never Hellenes – a term which is reserved only for the contingent which Akhilleus led from Phthiotis.[95] Richard Buxton has suggested that one of the functions of the *Odyssey* is to explain 'Greekness' by contrast with the behaviour of the diverse peoples which Odysseus visited.[96] It is, however, difficult to discern in the epic any explicit 'Greek' consciousness. The model that is constructed through such oppositions is not so much an ethnic, as it is a socio-cultural paradigm – a way of coming to terms with new conceptions of space and territoriality as populations became more sedentary towards the end of the eighth century. Even the land of the Phaiakians, often taken as a portrait of the early *polis*, is in fact a kind of Utopia, situated between the real and the mythical worlds.[97]

Indeed, the evidence, such as it is, suggests strongly that the Archaic period saw a considerable degree of interaction between Greeks and those who would later be categorised as barbarians. On the one hand, Greeks might serve as mercenaries in eastern armies: the brother of the Lesbian poet Alkaios served the king of Babylon;[98] Psammetikhos I, pharaoh of Egypt between 664 and 610 BC, employed Ionians alongside Karians in his army;[99] and the Greek inscriptions carved ca. 591 BC on the rock-cut statues at Abu Simbel on the Nile testify to Greek mercenaries among Psammetikhos II's expeditionary force to Nubia.[100] On the other hand, members of the Greek élite might forge *xeniai*, or 'guest-friend relations', with non-Greek nobles, perhaps for the purpose of gaining access to resources not readily available closer to home.[101] Herodotos cites the often quoted example of the relationship between Alkmeon, head of the Athenian family of the Alkmeonidai, and king Kroisos of Lydia, and it may be that the Kroisos commemorated by the 'Anavyssos kouros' was given his name by an Alkmeonid father keen to honour his Lydian *xenos*.[102] One of the ways of sealing a guest-friendship was through the exchange of women and this was a practice that continued as late as the fifth century in Athens: the mother of Themistokles was from either Thrace or Karia, while Kimon's mother was a Thracian princess.[103] The accusations of 'medism'

---

[94] Burkert 1990, 5; E. Hall 1989, 21–25; Cartledge 1993, 38.   [95] Thoukydides 1.3.3.
[96] Buxton 1994, 155, 212.   [97] Finley 1977, 100–102; Segal 1962, 17; Vidal-Naquet 1981b, 90–94.
[98] Alkaios fr. 48 Lobel/Page; Cartledge 1993, 38.   [99] Herodotos 2.152.5.
[100] See Boardman 1980, 115–16.   [101] See generally Herman 1987.
[102] Herodotos 6.125. Eliot 1967; Hall 1991.
[103] Themistokles' mother: Plutarch, *Life of Themistokles* 1. Kimon's mother: Plutarch, *Life of Kimon* 4.

(or 'Persianising') that we see behind the ostracisms of the newly democratic city of Athens in the early decades of the fifth century may be as much a condemnation of this élite practice of intermarriage as they were a genuine suspicion of betrayal to the enemy.

Where then does the Hellenic genealogy fit into this picture? Does it not already provide evidence of a Greek identity that embraces, through the genealogical metaphor of Hellen and his sons, the ethnic groups which represented its constituent elements? At first sight perhaps, but it is the omissions from the genealogy that are significant. To the best of our knowledge, the Aitolians were considered Greek, yet their eponymous ancestor, Aitolos, did not derive his descent from Hellen but from Endymion.[104] Similarly, Arkas, the eponymous ancestor of the Arkadians, was the son of Kallisto, who was the daughter of Lykaon and the granddaughter of Pelasgos – a lineage that finds no point of correlation with the Hellenic genealogy.[105] It is clear, then, that the Hellenic genealogy was not an all-inclusive vehicle for defining the groups that occupied what we know as the Greek Aegean.

What has changed between the Archaic and the Classical periods is the *mechanism* of Greek self-definition. It was suggested in chapter 2 that the criteria of ethnicity are set with reference to the ascriptive boundaries rather than to the internal linguistic, physical or cultural content of an ethnic group, and that ethnic identity can rarely achieve a salience in the absence of an 'outgroup' against which an ethnic group can define itself through a process of intergroup comparison. This is precisely what happened after the Persian Wars. By establishing a stereotypical, generalised image of the exotic, slavish and unintelligible barbarian, Greek identity could be defined 'from without', through opposition with this image of alterity. To find the language, culture or rituals of the barbarian desperately alien was immediately to define oneself as Greek. The construction of a sharp symbolic boundary between Greek and barbarian should theoretically no longer leave any doubt as to the Greekness of those on its inside.

If, from the fifth century, Greek self-definition was *oppositional*, prior to the Persian Wars it was *aggregative*. Rather than being defined 'from without', it was constructed cumulatively 'from within'. It was a definition based not on difference from the barbarian but on similarity with peer groups which attempted to attach themselves to one another by invoking common descent from Hellen. Since this cumulative aggregation of identity was enacted in the absence of any clear, determinate boundary between Greek and non-Greek, it is inevitable that the definition of Greekness could hardly be as all-encompassing as that which was later to be established externally and through opposition. In the fifth century BC, Hellanikos of Lesbos attempted to remedy the situation by adding the figure of Xenopatra, daughter of Hellen, to the Hellenic genealogy as a 'general purpose' ancestress of

---

[104] Pausanias 5.1.4; cf. Hesiod fr. 10(a). 58–63 Merkelbach/West. Endymion's father, Aithlios, was the son of Hellen's sister, while his mother, Kalyke, was the daughter of Aiolos. In strict patrilineal terms, however, neither relationship bestows Hellenic descent upon Endymion.
[105] Pausanias 8.4.1.

47

those Greek peoples previously excluded from the genealogy.[106] The solution was not, however, entirely satisfactory – not least because in a patrilineal society appeals to uterine succession must inevitably undermine the legitimacy they seek to validate. In short, while the Hellenic genealogy did not disappear completely during the fifth century, it ceased to be an efficacious means of self identification by comparison with the oppositional definition of Greekness.

In *aetiological* terms, the Hellenic genealogy seeks to explain the ethnic order of the present by means of an evolutionist schema. Greece was originally ethnically homogeneous (Hellen), but gradually became more ethnically diverse (Aiolos, Doros, Akhaios, Ion). Eventually, each of these ethnic groups diversified further as they split into their constituent *phylai* (Pamphyloi, Dymanes, etc.). If, however, we are right to consider the formation of Greek identity in the Archaic period as aggregative, then it should be clear that the *historical development* of the Hellenic genealogy may not follow exactly the unilineal trajectory that it purports to document. That is to say, Pamphylos' and Dymas' filiation from Aigimios and Doros may actually be an historically earlier element in the development of the Hellenic genealogy than Hellen's paternity of Doros.

The character of Hellen himself need not be a late invention: as the son of Deukalion, he is rooted in early Thessalian mythology, and it is in Thessaly that Thoukydides (following Homer) situates the first Hellenes.[107] Furthermore, since the historical Thessaly was inhabited by Aiolians, Aiolos' filiation from Hellen may be an ancient element in the genealogy; the fact that he is the only son to whom an epithet is attached in fragment 9 of the *Catalogue of women* might act as support for the antiquity of this tradition, as may the fact that, unlike Doros, he stands at the head of developed local genealogical traditions (he is, for example, the ancestor of Sisyphos and Bellerophon).[108] On the other hand, Hellen's paternity of the Dorians, Ionians and Akhaians may be a little more recent. As ethnic groups come into increased contact with one another they may wish to find common ground through the metaphor of genealogy, which might anchor in a mythical past the supposed reasons for affinity in the present. In cases of ethnic assimilation or incorporation, the eponyms of the ethnic groups will be conceptualised genealogically as sons and fathers; in cases where two ethnic groups wish to stress an affinity without surrendering their independent identity, their eponymous ancestors need to be brothers, but this necessitates the creation, or adoption, of a common father.

That the Dorians may have felt some affinity with the Aiolians is hardly surprising in light of the fact that both considered their ancestral homeland to be in northern Greece. The first stage in the wider diffusion, from southeast Thessaly, of the term 'Hellene' may thus have been the attachment of the eponymous Doros to the lineage of Aiolos and his father, Hellen. Similarly the perceived affinity

---

[106] Hellanikos *FGrH* 4.125. See Myres 1930, 334.
[107] Thoukydides 1.3.3. See Müller 1830, 12; West 1985, 53; E. Hall 1989, 7.   [108] Myres 1930, 335.

between Ionians and Akhaians was no doubt bolstered by the belief that the ancestral homelands of both were in the Peloponnese.[109] The fact, however, that their shared father is Xouthos, and not Hellen, may suggest that at the time when Ionians and Akhaians felt a sufficient affinity to link their eponymous ancestors within one genealogy, they did not feel that they yet had much in common with Dorians or Aiolians.

This aggregative construction of a Hellenic identity may find its material realisation in the Greek *emporion*, or 'trading settlement' of Naukratis on the Nile Delta. Herodotos writes that this settlement was given to the Greeks by the Egyptian pharaoh Amasis, who reigned 569–525 BC:

> To those who regularly voyaged there, but did not wish to settle permanently, he gave land so that they could erect temples and precincts to the gods. The largest and best known – as well as most frequented – of these is called the Hellenion: the cities which founded it in common were the Ionian *poleis* of Khios, Teos, Phokaia and Klazomenai, the Dorian *poleis* of Rhodes, Knidos, Halikarnassos and Phaselis, and the Aiolian *polis* of Mytilene . . . In addition, the Aiginetans built on their own account a precinct of Zeus, the Samians one to Hera and the Milesians one to Apollo.[110]

Archaeological exploration of the site of Naukratis confirms the presence of material from far afield – from Rhodes, Khios, Samos, north Ionia, Lesbos, Athens, Korinth and Sparta – thus bearing out Herodotos' description of the panhellenic nature of the site.[111] Two buildings in the northern part of the town can almost certainly be identified with the Samian temple to Hera and the Milesian temple to Apollo on the basis of inscribed dedications and architectural fragments. It is also entirely plausible that the corner of a building excavated to the east of the temples by Hogarth in 1899 should be identified with the Hellenion, again on the basis of vase inscriptions which refer to 'the gods of the Greeks'.[112] What is interesting is that while the material from the 'Hellenion' does not appear to predate the reign of Amasis (the mid-sixth century on the conventional chronology),[113] the pottery from the temple of Apollo belongs to the earliest years of the settlement, dated to the last quarter of the seventh century due to the appearance of Transitional and Early Korinthian ware – in other words, some 50 to 75 years earlier than the Herodotean foundation date.[114]

It has to be admitted that our state of knowledge for Naukratis is pitifully meagre. There had already been considerable destruction of the site before Petrie's

---

[109] Mimnermos fr. 9 West; Herodotos 1.145–47; 7.94. See West 1985, 57–58.

[110] Herodotos 2.178.2–3.

[111] Petrie 1886; Gardner 1888; Hogarth 1898–89; 1905; Austin 1970, 22–33; Coulson and Leonard 1982. For a synthesis, see Boardman 1980, 118–29.

[112] See Coulson and Leonard 1982, 366 whose investigations at Naukratis in 1980 and 1981 confirmed that Petrie's original identification of the Hellenion with the so-called 'Great Temenos' was wrong.

[113] For the problems with conventional Egyptian chronology, see James et al (1991).

[114] Boardman 1980, 120–21; Coulson and Leonard 1982, 361.

excavations of 1884 (one third of the site had been dug out by local farmers for use as high-phosphate fertiliser). Furthermore, it is now difficult to rectify the lack of a true stratigraphical sequence due both to the considerable weathering and destruction that has taken place since Petrie's investigations and to the fact that the area of the early excavations is now under water.[115]

Nevertheless, notwithstanding these provisos, it is tempting to see in the archaeological evidence the following developmental stages in aggregative identity. When the Greeks first became involved with Naukratis in the second half of the seventh century, it was as individual citizens who sought sanction for new cult foundations from their mother-cities – hence the Samian and Milesian sanctuaries. However, the fact that the Samian precinct of Hera and the Milesian sanctuary of Apollo were situated *adjacent* to one another may already testify to a notion of affinity between these two cities based on Ionian ethnicity. Finally, towards the middle of the sixth century, the Ionians expressed a new-found affinity with Dorian cities and the Aiolian city of Mytilene in the foundation of the Hellenion, which celebrated the common descent of Doros, Aiolos and Ion from Hellen. The fact that the Akhaians are absent is not too surprising, since such overseas activity as was undertaken by the Akhaians was directed more towards the west than the east. It is also interesting that this aggregative construction of Hellenic identity should see its material realisation outside Greece proper, especially in light of Catherine Morgan's observation that the panhellenic sanctuaries of Olympia and Delphi were an effective arena for competition and emulation between *poleis* precisely because they were outside the territorial orbit of their main participants.[116] The evidence of Naukratis, then, should suggest that we can raise slightly the *terminus ante quem* for the final articulation of the Hellenic genealogy to the mid-sixth century.

If Hellenic identity in the Archaic period was constructed cumulatively from pre-existing Dorian, Ionian or Aiolian identities, we should not assume that the latter constituted the primary and irreducible building blocks in the process. There remains the possibility that even these groups were themselves the product of aggregation or ethnic assimilation. Indeed, this may explain the seemingly puzzling phenomenon of eponymous heroes who appear as leaders rather than ancestors.

Strictly speaking, an eponym should be a common ancestor from whom the members of an ethnic group can profess (albeit without literally believing it) shared descent. For instance, in early Judaic thought the world was populated by Hamitic, Semitic and Japhetic peoples who were descended from Noah's three sons, Ham, Shem and Japheth.[117] Yet, in some of the local variants of Greek ethnic myths, there are occasions when an ethnic group is unable to adduce strict descent from an eponym. Herodotos and Pausanias note that the earlier inhabitants of Akhaia in the northern Peloponnese were originally called Aigialeis, but began to be called

---

[115] Coulson and Leonard 1982, 362–63.   [116] Morgan 1990, 3.   [117] Genesis 9.18–19.

Ionians when Ion arrived from Athens and married the daughter of their king, Selinous.[118] The inhabitants of Argos and Sparta began to call themselves Akhaians only on the arrival in the Peloponnese of the sons of Akhaios, Arkhandros and Arkhiteles.[119] The earliest inhabitants of Lakonia were termed Leleges not because they were descended from Lelex, but because he was their king.[120] It is presumably with the arrival of Ion at Athens that the formerly Pelasgian population of Athens became Ionian (and thus eventually Hellenic).[121] The inference would be that where an eponym is a leader, rather than an ancestor *sensu stricto*, we may have an indication of an act of mythical integration which seeks to attach the identity of one ethnic group to that of another already in possession of a more established ethnic pedigree.

The Athenians: Ionians or autochthons?

According to the author of the Pseudo-Aristotelian *Athenian Constitution*, the early sixth-century Athenian statesman and elegiac poet Solon had referred to Attika as 'the oldest land of Ionia'.[122] The Ionian identity of the Athenians is repeated in Herodotos and Thoukydides,[123] and is normally accepted by modern scholars, partly on the basis of the evident linguistic similarities between the dialects spoken in Attika, Euboia, the Kyklades and Ionia (see chapter 6), and partly due to the fact that the earliest Submycenaean and Protogeometric pottery from the Ionian settlements of Asia Minor appears to display some dependence on Attic styles.[124]

The sources are not, however, so unequivocal. Miletos was supposed to have been founded by Neleus, the son of the Athenian king Kodros (dated by the Parian Marble to 1077 BC),[125] while the foundation of Ephesos was attributed to another son of Kodros named Androklos.[126] Yet Kodros' own Athenian credentials are not beyond dispute, since his father, Melanthos, was a Messenian from Pylos,[127] while another Neleus – this time the son of the god Poseidon – appears in the mythical tradition as the king of Pylos.[128] The possible Messenian connections of the Ionian cities of Asia Minor are not confined to Miletos: a fragment of the seventh-century elegiac poet Mimnermos describes how Kolophon was founded from 'Nelean' Pylos.[129]

Another common tradition held that the Ionians had originally inhabited the

---

[118] Herodotos 7.94; Pausanias 7.1.3.

[119] Pausanias 7.1.3. Strabo 8.7.1, however, has Akhaios himself coming to Sparta and giving his name to the inhabitants there.   [120] Pausanias 3.1.1.

[121] Herodotos 1.57.3. Cf. 1.56.2.   [122] Solon fr. 4 Diehl = Pseudo-Aristotle, *Athenian Constitution* 5.

[123] Herodotos 1.56.2; 1.143.2. Thoukydides 7.57.2.

[124] Coldstream 1968, 264; Desborough 1972, 179–80; Emlyn-Jones 1980, 13; Connor 1993, 196–97. However, Popham (1994) seems to imply that the Euboians also may well have played some part in this colonisation.   [125] Herodotos 9.97; Hellanikos *FGrH* 4.125; Pausanias 7.2.1–2.

[126] Pherekydes *FGrH* 3.155.   [127] Cf. Strabo 14.1.3.

[128] Homer, *Iliad* 11.690–93; Hesiod fr. 33(a) Merkelbach/West. See Nilsson 1972, 153–54; Vanschoonwinkel 1991, 378–80.   [129] Mimnermos of Kolophon fr. 9 West.

northern Peloponnesian region of Akhaia and that they had fled to Athens when their territory was invaded by the Akhaians.[130] Herodotos suggests two reasons why Akhaia may have been considered the metropolis of Ionia. The first is explicitly stated: the fact that membership of the Panionion (the common Ionian sanctuary at Mykale) was restricted to twelve cities was a legacy from when the Ionians had inhabited the region of Akhaia which, in the historical period, supported the twelve regions (*mere*) of Pellene, Aigeira, Aigai, Boura, Helike, Aigion, Rhypes, Patres, Phares, Olenos, Dyme and Tritaies.[131] The second is more implicit: cult at the Panionion was dedicated to Poseidon Helikonios, and the apparent etymological connection with the Akhaian city of Helike may have evoked the belief that the cult had been transferred to Ionia from Akhaia.[132] It would seem that the Peloponnesian origin of the Ionians was already well established by the time it is reported by Herodotos,[133] and this may perhaps explain why Akhaios and Ion are represented as brothers in the Hellenic geneaology.[134]

In addition to Athenian, Messenian and Akhaian origins, Hellanikos of Lesbos traced the foundation of Priene to settlers from Thebes.[135] Indeed, Herodotos caustically observes that the so-called 'Ionian' population of Asia Minor was actually an ethnic mixture of Abantes from Euboia, Minyans from Orkhomenos, Kadmeians, Dryopes, Phokians, Molossians, Pelasgians from Arkadia and Dorians from Epidauros.[136] Even those who had set out from the Prytaneion at Athens and considered themselves to be the purest Ionians had married Karian wives – the implication being that their descendants could hardly be considered 'true blue-blooded' Ionians.

Rather than treating these various foundation myths as reminiscences of genuine population movements, it is perhaps preferable to view them as active attempts on the part of the Greek cities of Asia Minor to anchor their origins in the deeper mythical past of mainland Greece. It has, for example, already been noted that the Helikonian epithet of Poseidon may have evoked a connection with Akhaian Helike: the presence of Boiotian inhabitants (Minyans and Kadmeians) in Herodotos' list of the occupants of Ionia may similarly suggest that a connection was forged with Boiotia on the basis of the apparent etymological relatedness of Poseidon's epithet and the Boiotian mountain Helikon. It may be that as the Ionians began to develop more of a sense of collective identity through the framework of the Panionion, it was considered desirable to reconcile various foundation myths in order to invent a common ancestral homeland.[137] The solution adopted was to trace Ionian origins to Akhaia, but to have them pass through Athens where they could come into contact with Pylian refugees. What is vitally important,

---

[130] Herodotos 1.145; 7.94; Pausanias 7.1.2–4. Strabo (8.1.2; 8.7.1–4) also connects the Ionians with both Akhaia and Athens, though he has the Ionians going *from* Athens *to* Akhaia, supposedly due to overpopulation in Athens.

[131] Herodotos 1.145. For a discussion of the *mere* of Akhaia, see Morgan and Hall 1996, 167–69.

[132] Herodotos 1.148.1. See Vanschoonwinkel 1991, 375.   [133] Vanschoonwinkel 1991, 375.

[134] Parker 1987, 206.   [135] Hellanikos of Lesbos *FGrH* 4.101.   [136] Herodotos 1.146.1–2.

[137] Sakellariou 1990, 137.

however, is the Athenian involvement in this mythical restructuring. Michel Sakellariou has argued that the Attic origin of the Ionians was an Athenian invention which postdated the Ionian Revolt.[138] Yet the Solonian fragment demonstrates that the Athenians considered themselves Ionian by at least 600 BC. The most effective explanation for this is that the Athenians were anxious to attach themselves to the Hellenic genealogy through the figure of Ion. Connor suggests that this was at the initiative of élite families, to whom the cosmopolitan and cultured world of Ionia was particularly appealing.[139] The integration was achieved by having Ion arrive in Athens to assume command of the Athenian army and giving his own name to the Athenians.[140]

If the Athenians were anxious to be thought of as Ionians in the Archaic period, a distinct shift in attitude is easily discernible in the fifth century, when there is a greater emphasis on the theme of the autochthonous Athenians and on the figure of the earth-born Erekhtheus or Erikhthonios – although these were separate figures in Athenian myth, the similarity between their names and attributes suggests that they were 'joint heirs to a single mythological inheritance'.[141] From the time of the *Iliad*, Erekhtheus was treated as a son of the earth, and Herodotos calls him *gegenes* ('earth-born').[142] This in itself is hardly unique. The first king of Lakonia, Lelex, was born from the earth as was Anax, the first king of Miletos, or Pelasgos, the first inhabitant of Arkadia; Phoroneus' birth from the Argive river Inakhos fulfils a similar function.[143] In fact, the primeval figures which typically occupy the upper, cosmogonic reaches of a genealogy normally serve to explain the toponyms in any given landscape. Thus, Lelex's grandson, Eurotas, is supposed to have given his name to the principal river of the Lakonian plain; Eurotas' daughter Sparte, has the most important town in Lakonia named after her; and the name of the Taygetos mountain range, which overshadows Sparta, was explained by reference to Sparte's mother-in-law, Taygete.[144]

There is normally, however, a rupture which intervenes between these 'land genealogies' and the genealogies which explain the sociopolitical existence of that region's population. This rupture is typically marked by the arrival of a 'culture hero' who gives his name to the citizenry (e.g. Danaos at Argos, Miletos at Miletos or Lakedaimon at Sparta).[145] The citizens of Athens, however, were named not after a culture hero, but after the goddess Athena. This was, according to Herodotos, due to Erekhtheus – a figure whose promotion as a civic hero may perhaps first be glimpsed in his selection as one of the eponymous heroes of the ten *phylai* which replaced the original four Ionian *phylai* as part of the political reforms of Kleisthenes in the late sixth century.[146] The creation of ten new *phylai*

---

[138] Sakellariou 1990, 137. [139] Connor 1993, 198–200. [140] Herodotos 8.44.2.
[141] Parker 1987, 201. [142] Homer, *Iliad* 2.547–48; Herodotos 8.55.
[143] Lelex: Pausanias 3.1.1. Anax: Pausanias 7.2.5. Pelasgos: Pausanias 8.1.4; Hesiod fr. 160 Merkelbach/West. Phoroneus: Pausanias 2.15.5. For the structural similarity between birth from the earth and birth from rivers: Dowden 1992, 75. [144] Calame 1987; Malkin 1994, 19–22.
[145] Pausanias 3.1.2 (Lakedaimon); 7.1.7 (Danaos); 7.2.5 (Miletos).
[146] Herodotos 8.44.2. For the reforms of Kleisthenes, see Herodotos 5.66.2.

at the expense of the old Ionian ones may be the earliest indication of an anti-Ionian attitude which was to become more prevalent in the fifth century: Herodotos was to write, 'But now the other Ionians [i.e. the Ionians of Euboia and the Kykladic islands] and the Athenians avoid the name, not wishing to be called Ionian; in fact, I believe that many of them are ashamed of the name'.[147] We can only guess at the reasons for this sense of shame, though it may have been prompted by the fact that the Ionians had offered little in the way of resistance against their annexation by the Persian king Kyros around 545 BC.[148]

Certainly, an anti-Ionian attitude became more prevalent after the Persian Wars.[149] The Athenians are described as autochthonous for the first time in Aiskhylos' *Agamemnon* (first performed in 458 BC).[150] An autochthon is not, as is commonly translated, one who is born from the earth but one who has always occupied the same land.[151] But the reason why the Athenians could regard themselves as having always occupied the same land was because they regarded themselves as descendants of the earth-born Erekhtheus – a notion that is first explicitly articulated in the extant sources in Pindar's second Isthmian Ode, probably to be dated to the 470s BC.[152] If the Athenians were the direct descendants of Erekhtheus and had always occupied the same territory, then they could hardly be Ionians who derived their descent from Ion and traced their origin in the Peloponnese. What made this new subscription to a myth of autochthony desirable was the new position Athens held at the centre of the Delian League. What made it possible, though, was the shift from an aggregative to an oppositional self-definition which rendered obsolete the necessity of continuing to attach one's own ethnic origins to the Hellenic genealogy.

Autochthony offered a number of advantages. Firstly, it served to distinguish the 'ethnically pure' Athenians from those whose descent from ancestors such as Pelops, Kadmos, Aigyptos or Danaos made them 'barbarian' by nature, even if nominally Greek.[153] Secondly, by tracing descent back, through Erekhtheus, to the life-nourishing earth, Athenians subscribed to an ideology of equality in which social existence derived from one and the same territory rather than from differentiated human progenitors.[154] Enrico Montanari draws the parallel between this ideology and the fact that Kleisthenes is supposed to have legislated that Athenians should in future be known by their demotics rather than their patronymics (that is, an identity predicated on territory rather than blood),[155] though, in reality, epigraphical evidence provides no substantial confirmation of this shift in Athenian nomenclature.[156] Thirdly, the Athenians could conceive of themselves as particu-

---

[147] Herodotos 1.143.3. [148] Connor 1993, 199. [149] Rosivach 1987, 297.

[150] Aiskhylos, *Agamemnon* 536. See Montanari 1981, 31.

[151] Cf. Herodotos 7.163.3; Thoukydides 1.2.5; 2.36.1.

[152] Pindar, *Isthmian Odes* 2.19. See Rosivach 1987, 294–97.

[153] Plato, *Menexenos* 245d. See Loraux 1986, 1, 149; Rosivach 1987, 302.

[154] Montanari 1981, 54–55; Loraux 1986, 332; Parker 1987, 195; Rosivach 1987, 303.

[155] Montanari 1981, 54. Cf. Pseudo-Aristotle, *Athenian Constitution* 21.4. [156] Winters 1993.

larly cherished by the gods, since the infant Erekhtheus had been entrusted to the tutelage of Athena and Hephaistos.[157]

This rejection of Ionian ancestry finds a symbolic articulation in the myth of the struggle between Athena and Poseidon for the patronage of Attika, which was depicted on the western pediment of the Parthenon, built between 447 and 432 BC. Not only was Poseidon the patron deity of the Ionians, he was also god of the sea, the god 'who holds the earth' and the god 'who shakes the earth' – functions incompatible with those who treated the earth as their mother. Athena's victory in the contest judged by Kekrops can thus be viewed as the symbolic reflection of the rejection of Ionian ancestry and the adoption of the myth of autochthony.[158]

It was not, however, politically expedient for Athens to reject completely all her Ionian associations. The majority of the allies who paid tribute to Athens for much of the fifth century (ostensibly to buy protection against future Persian aggression) were Ionians, and the motif of Ionian kinship provided a useful means of justification for the exaction of this tribute. In the 440s BC, a series of *horoi*, or 'boundary stones', was set up on the island of Samos to demarcate a sanctuary to Athena, Ion and the four eponymous heroes of the Ionian *phylai*. It has been argued that these testify to a series of cults in the Ionian cities which may have been set up voluntarily at the suggestion of the various members of the Delian League, but whose headquarters was situated in Athens.[159] Another focus of Ionian identity for political purposes was established in 426/5 BC, when the Athenians resurrected, or reorganised, what they claimed was the ancient Ionian festival held on the sacred island of Delos.[160]

There was, then, an urgent need to reconcile the Athenians' own myth of autochthony with the political mileage that was to be gained through promoting a sense of kinship with the Ionian cities of the alliance. One way of achieving this was to regard the Ionians as Athenian *colonists*. Explicit references to the Ionian cities as *apoikiai*, or 'homes from home', appear in the second half of the fifth century,[161] and the cities of Ionia, like other allies, were instructed to send a cow and a panoply to the Great Panathenaia which was held every four years, on the grounds that they were colonists of Athens.[162] This slight 'adjustment' to the relationship between Athens and the Ionians was ingenious. By applying to the Ionian cities the vocabulary of historical colonial foundations, the Ionians could be situated within a unilineal relationship of dependence. The analogy of Kerkyra can serve as an example: while the *apoikia* of Kerkyra could be treated as Korinthian, owing its metropolis respect and certain honours and rights at common festivals,[163] the Korinthians could not be regarded as Kerkyreans. Similarly, the populations of the Ionian cities could be considered to be Athenian colonists, owing their metropolis certain obligations, though this did not make the Athenians themselves Ionians.

55

It is within the context of this reconciliation between Ionian and autochthonous origins that Euripides' *Ion* must be situated. The political intent behind the play, probably dating to the last decade of the fifth century, has long been recognised.[164] Xouthos, who had traditionally been thought of as the father of Ion, is described as a descendant of Aiolos from the Peloponnesian region of Akhaia;[165] in fact, throughout the play he is denigrated as a foreign upstart.[166] But, although the Delphic Oracle has conspired in making Xouthos think that Ion is his son, Ion is in reality the issue of Apollo's rape of Kreousa, the daughter of Erekhtheus, in a cave beneath the Athenian akropolis. Thus Ion is both descended from Apollo and from the noble lineage of Erekhtheus, filtering out any 'foreign blood' in his ancestry.[167] Towards the end of the play, Euripides picks up the theme of the Ionians as colonists sent from Athens. Athena announces that Ion will have four sons – Geleon, Hopletes, Argades and Aigikores (the four eponyms of the Ionian *phylai*) – and that their sons will colonise the Kykladic islands and the mainland on either side of the Hellespont where they will come to be known as Ionians after their ancestor.[168] The vital point is that while the Ionians will take their name from Ion, Ion himself is not an Ionian. Thus autochthony is preserved alongside an emphasis on the *unilineal* genetic relationship between Athenians and Ionians.

Euripides also manages to subvert the Hellenic genealogy which, as we have seen, no longer served a useful purpose (fig. 1). Ion is wrenched from his formerly low status in the second generation of Hellenism and given a divine father – a privilege shared only with Aiolos. Similarly, the formerly close connection between the brothers Akhaios and Ion has been shattered. In fact, Athena tells Kreousa that she will bear two mortal sons by Xouthos: Doros, on whose account the *polis* of Doris will be celebrated throughout the Peloponnese, and Akhaios who will rule over, and give his name to, the peoples of the shore around Rhion.[169] Both in the substitution of Doros for Ion as Xouthos' son, as well as in the attribution of a divine father to Ion but a mortal one to Doros, it is hard not to see a conscious act of propaganda which reflects the antagonistic relationship between Athens and Sparta in the closing stages of the Peloponnesian War.

Dorians and Herakleidai

The fullest information for the arrival of the Dorians and the return of the Herakleidai to the Peloponnese is inevitably to be found in the later, synthetic accounts of Diodoros and Pseudo-Apollodoros.[170] After Herakles' ejection from the Argolid by Eurystheus and his apotheosis on Mount Oita, his sons sought refuge at the court of Keyx, king of Trakhis, but were obliged to leave when Keyx

---

[164] E.g. Müller 1830, 12 n. z.   [165] Euripides, *Ion* 63–64.
[166] Euripides, *Ion* 290, 293, 674–75, 703–04, 808–11, 1058–60.
[167] Parker 1987, 207; Loraux 1993, 184–236.   [168] Euripides, *Ion* 1575–88.
[169] Euripides, *Ion* 1589–94.   [170] For references, see Vanschoonwinkel 1991, 335–66.

was threatened with war by Eurystheus if he continued to offer them shelter.[171] Only the Athenians were prepared to offer hospitality to the Herakleidai, settling them in the town of Trikorythos near Marathon; here a war was waged against Eurystheus, in which he was killed.[172]

Pseudo-Apollodoros goes on to tell how the Herakleidai returned to the Peloponnese, but were beset by plague and advised by the Delphic Oracle to wait for the 'third crop'. Assuming 'crop' to mean 'harvest', Hyllos, the son of Herakles, waited for three years before leading a force against the Peloponnese where he confronted the Peloponnesian army under Atreus at the Korinthian isthmus. It was agreed that Hyllos should engage in single combat against Ekhemos, king of Tegea, on the understanding that were Hyllos to win, the Herakleidai should regain their ancestral land in the Argolid, whereas were he to lose, they would retire for one hundred years – or, according to Diodoros, fifty years. Ekhemos killed Hyllos in the battle and the Herakleidai retreated.[173] The Apollodoran account explains that the Delphic Oracle had meant 'generation', not 'harvest' by its reference to the 'third crop'. Some of the Herakleidai retreated to Trikorythos, while others went to king Aigimios, the king of the Dorians of Hestiaiotis, where they asked for the land which they had been promised.[174] The Heraklid claim to this land went back to an earlier incident. In their war against the Lapiths of Thessaly, the Dorians had implored the aid of Herakles, promising him a third share of the land of Hestiaiotis and the kingship. Having aided the Dorians to victory, Herakles asked Aigimios to safeguard his share of the land for his descendants.[175]

In the third generation after the death of Hyllos, his great-grandson, Temenos, together with the Heraklids Kresphontes and Aristodemos mustered at Naupaktos on the northern shore of the Korinthian Gulf, where Aristodemos was killed by a thunderbolt and succeeded by his sons, Eurysthenes and Prokles.[176] From Naupaktos, the expedition crossed the Gulf and invaded the Peloponnese with the help of Oxylos, an Aitolian, who acted as their guide.[177] After expelling Teisamenos, son of Orestes and the last of the lineage of Atreus, the Herakleidai divided the Peloponnese among them, with Temenos taking Argos, the sons of Aristodemos Sparta, and Kresphontes Messene.[178]

The best way of demonstrating that this tradition is the product of a cumulative aggregation of accounts, rather than a dim reflection of genuine population movements, is to attack it at its weakest point – the account concerning the founda-

---

[171] Diodoros 4.57.2–4; Pseudo-Apollodoros, *Bibliotheka* 2.8.1. Cf. Hekataios *FGrH* 1.30; Pausanias 1.32.6.

[172] Diodoros 4.57.4–6; Pseudo-Apollodoros, *Bibliotheka* 2.8.1. Cf. Herodotos 9.27.2; Thoukydides 1.9.2; Pherekydes *FGrH* 3.84; Euripides, *Herakleidai*; Strabo 8.6.19; Pausanias 1.32.6; 1.44.10.

[173] Pseudo-Apollodoros, *Bibliotheka* 2.8.2; Diodoros 4.58.1–4. Cf. Herodotos 9.26.2–5; Pausanias 1.41.2; 1.44.10; 8.5.1; 8.45.3; 8.53.10. [174] Diodoros 4.58.4–6. Cf. Strabo 9.4.10.

[175] Diodoros 4.37.3–4; Pseudo-Apollodoros, *Bibliotheka* 2.7.7.

[176] Pseudo-Apollodoros, *Bibliotheka* 2.8.2. [177] Pausanias 10.38.10.

[178] Diodoros 7.9.1; Pseudo-Apollodoros, *Bibliotheka* 2.8.4; Pindar, *Pythian Odes* 5.70; Isokrates, *Arkhidamos* 16–21; Plato, *Laws* 3.683c-d; Pausanias 2.18.6–7; 4.3.3–6.

57

tion of Korinth. According to Pausanias, the Dorians attacked Korinth under Aletes, the great-great-grandson of Herakles.[179] The Heraklid origin of the Korinthians is also stated by Thoukydides, who adds that the former population of Korinth was Aiolian.[180] The tradition concerning the Dorian capture of Korinth does not, however, quite accord with the foundation myths of the other Dorian *poleis* in the Peloponnese. In Diodoros' account, Aletes does not initially accompany the Herakleidai on their return to the Peloponnese, but is invited to rule over Korinth once the division has already been made.[181] This might suggest that an originally independent account of the foundation of Korinth has been assimilated to the more general tradition of the Dorian invasion and the return of the Herakleidai – a supposition that receives some further support.

Although Pausanias places Aletes in the same generation as Temenos, Velleius Paterculus places him a generation later;[182] the ancient commentator Didymos similarly places him in the generation *after* the return of the Herakleidai.[183] While Temenos, Kresphontes and the sons of Aristodemos all traced their Heraklid ancestry back through Hyllos, Aletes' descent from Herakles was derived through a quite different lineage.[184] While the Herakleidai sought sanction from Pythian Apollo at Delphi, Aletes took Korinth with the blessing of Zeus, after consultation of the oracle at Dodona.[185] Finally, while the social organisation of the Dorian cities of the Peloponnese was typically based on the three *phylai* of the Hylleis, Dymanes and Pamphyloi, Aletes was credited with the division of the Korinthian citizen body into eight tribes.[186]

The attribution of the Korinthian tribal organisation to Aletes, as well as Pindar's reference to the Korinthians as 'the children of Aletes',[187] testifies that he was recognised as the founding father of Korinth by at least the fifth century.[188] In fact, this tradition may already be attested in the late eighth or early seventh centuries. There was, in antiquity, a well-known proverb proclaiming 'Aletes accepts even a clod' – thus appearing to associate Aletes with the Korinthian soil. Since the phrase scans as the last part of a hexameter verse it is not impossible that it derives from the *Korinthiaka* of Eumelos – the poet who is credited with rewriting Korinthian mythology in the late eighth century.[189] Two other indications also support the idea that the legend of Aletes may have been coined – or, at least, promoted – in the late eighth century. Firstly, this is the date at which a shrine is established on the Solygeia ridge to the southeast of Korinth: according to

---

[179] Pausanias 2.4.3.   [180] Thoukydides 1.24.2; 4.42.2. Cf. 6.3.2.   [181] Diodoros 7.9.2.
[182] Velleius Paterculus 1.3.3.   [183] Didymus *ap.* Pindar, *Olympic Odes* 13.17c. See Salmon 1984, 39.
[184] Robertson 1980, 7; Salmon 1984, 39.
[185] Scholiast to Pindar, *Nemean Odes* 7.155a. See Salmon 1984, 38; Morgan 1994, 137.
[186] *Souda*, s.v. Πάντα ὀκτώ. See Robertson 1980, 5; Morgan 1994, 116. It would appear that these tribes may have been further subdivided into three *trittyes*: see Stroud 1968.
[187] Pindar, *Olympian Odes* 13.14.   [188] Robertson 1980, 5.
[189] See Pausanias 2.1.1. The proverb is attributed to Eumelos by Salmon 1984, 38. Eumelos is thought to have been writing ca. 730 BC, since Pausanias (4.33.2) cites a prosodion that he is supposed to have written for the Messenians prior to the First Messenian War: see Huxley 1969, 62.

58

Thoukydides, Solygeia was the location from which the first Dorian conquerors of Korinth besieged the Aiolians.[190] Secondly, it is the period at which Korinth develops strong links with northwest Greece – thus providing a context for the association of Aletes with the oracle of Zeus at Dodona.[191] Nevertheless, at the risk of resorting to an argument from silence, there is no evidence that Eumelos ever connected Aletes with the Herakleidai.[192] It is, then, far more likely that this association was a later development to the foundation myth. As such, it indicates an attempt, on the part of the Korinthians, to incorporate their own myths of origin within the general pedigree of the Herakleidai and Dorians of the Peloponnese.

The Dorians are invariably mentioned alongside the Herakleidai.[193] The earliest reference is to be found in the seventh-century elegiac poet Tyrtaios, who writes: 'For Zeus, son of Kronos and husband of fair-crowned Hera, has given this city [Sparta] to the Herakleidai, with whom we [Dorians] left windy Erineos and arrived in the broad island of Pelops.'[194] Elsewhere, Tyrtaios addresses the Spartans as the 'lineage of undefeated Herakles'.[195] In the first half of the fifth century, Pindar refers to the sons of Pamphylos and the Herakleidai as Dorians, and hymns the island of Aigina, founded by 'the Dorian army of Hyllos and Aigimios'.[196]

Despite the constant association between Dorians and Herakleidai, they were clearly originally envisaged as two separate groups.[197] It is frequently argued that the motif of the Herakleidai, returning to their ancestral homeland, was a manipulation on the part of the Dorians to justify their conquest of the Peloponnese,[198] though such an explanation is not entirely satisfactory. If the Dorians had wanted to conceal the fact that they had invaded the Peloponnese by invoking a fictitious hereditary right to the land they were to occupy, then it becomes difficult to explain why the tradition of the Dorians' extra-Peloponnesian origin persisted throughout antiquity. Tyrtaios mentions the Herakleidai who occupy Sparta, but he makes no attempt to deny the Dorian origin in 'windy Erineos'.

In fact, if an ethnic group is defined on the twin bases of putative descent and association with a primordial homeland, then the Dorians and the Herakleidai are not ethnically the same. The Herakleidai traced their ancestry back to Herakles, Perseus and Zeus, and their primordial homeland was the Argolid (more specifically, the eastern Argive plain) where, were it not for the wiles of Hera, Herakles should have acceded to the throne.[199] There is no obvious point of connection

---

190 Thoukydides 4.42.2. For the Solygeia shrine (where the earliest pottery is Early Protokorinthian), see Verdelis 1962b. See also Morgan 1994, 136–38. 191 Parke 1967, 129; Morgan 1994, 137.
192 Robertson 1980, 5; Salmon 1984, 38. 193 Thoukydides 1.12.3; Diodoros 7.9.1; Pausanias 2.13.1.
194 Tyrtaios fr. 2 Diehl. 195 Tyrtaios fr. 8 Diehl.
196 Pindar, *Pythian Odes* 1.62–63; *Isthmian Odes* 9.3–4.
197 Wilamowitz-Moellendorff 1959, 68; Musti 1985b, 38; Vanschoonwinkel 1991, 360; Malkin 1994, 38–43.
198 E.g. Müller 1830, 53; Tigerstedt 1965, 28–36; Cartledge 1979, 76; Drews 1988, 220–21; Dowden 1992, 71. 199 Homer, *Iliad* 19.121–24.

between this lineage and that of the Dorians, whose ancestry was traced back to Aigimios, Doros and Deukalion, and whose original homeland was situated in central or northwest Greece, not the Peloponnese.

The lineage of the Herakleidai is, strictly speaking, a 'family genealogy' rather than an 'ethnic genealogy' (see above). To be of the illustrious lineage of Herakles was to guarantee eligibility to the highest office, and it cannot therefore be coincidental that the myth of the Herakleidai served to legitimate the rule not only of the Spartan kings but also of Pheidon, the tyrant of Argos.[200] Nevertheless, if the Herakleidai were not an ethnic group *per se*, the literary sources leave little doubt concerning the ethnic group to which the Heraklid families did belong. Herodotos recounts how the Spartan king Kleomenes was barred from the temple of Athena on the Athenian akropolis on the grounds that it was forbidden for Dorians to enter; his reply to the priestess was that he was not a Dorian, but an Akhaian.[201] Half a century earlier, the Spartans had 'repatriated' the bones of their former Akhaian king, Orestes, in order to achieve victory in their long-standing dispute with Tegea.[202] This accords fully with the tradition that the Akhaians had occupied Argos and Sparta prior to the arrival of the Dorians and that the Danaoi of Argos were local Akhaians who had adopted the name of their leader, Danaos.[203]

Eventually, the Dorians and the Herakleidai were to become so well assimilated that their ethnic specificity could become confused: Plato says that the Dorians were Akhaians who had been driven out of the Peloponnese and had changed their name, while Vitruvius has Doros as the king of the Akhaians.[204] Nevertheless, the difference in proclaimed ancestry and territorial origin between the two groups does point towards their having been originally distinct. Indeed, the artificiality of the assimilation is suggested by the awkward way in which it is achieved: Aigimios adopts Hyllos alongside his own sons, Pamphylos and Dymas, despite the fact that Hyllos was killed at the Korinthian isthmus a hundred years before Pamphylos and Dymas met their ends during the successful return to the Peloponnese.[205] We cannot be totally certain as to the date at which such an assimilation may have taken place. It is sometimes thought that Aigimios' alliance with Herakles may have been told in the now barely extant *Aigimios* (an epic, attributed in antiquity variously to Hesiod or Kerkops),[206] though there is no solid evidence for this.[207] All we can say is that this integration had already taken place by the mid-seventh century, since Tyrtaios groups the properly Dorian *phylai* of the Pamphyloi and the Dymanes alongside the *phyle* of the Hylleis, which should, strictly speaking, be Heraklid.[208]

[200] Spartan kings: Pindar, *Pythian Odes* 10.1–3; Herodotos 7.204; 8.131.2. See Tigerstedt 1965, 29; Cartledge 1979, 343–44; Malkin 1994, 15. Pheidon of Argos: Diodoros 7.17.

[201] Herodotos 5.72.3.   [202] Herodotos 1.67–68. See Hooker 1989, 131; Malkin 1994, 26–32.

[203] Pausanias 7.1.5–7.   [204] Plato, *Laws* 682e–683a; Vitruvius 4.1.3.

[205] Ephoros *FGrH* 70.15; Strabo 9.4.10; Pseudo-Apollodoros, *Bibliotheka* 2.8.3.

[206] Müller 1830, 33–34; Vanschoonwinkel 1991, 366.   [207] Tigerstedt 1965, 29 n. 112.

[208] Tyrtaios fr. 1a Diehl. In this context, an inscription dating to the early second century BC and found on Kos is particularly suggestive. It prescribes that while the Dymanes should offer rites to Apollo (often considered to be a god of particular significance for the Dorians: see chapter 4), the Hylleis should practise rites to Herakles: see Jones 1980, 210.

While many cities in the southern Aegean and Asia Minor traced their foundations back to descendants of Herakles, the explicit idea of a Heraklid 'return' to an ancestral homeland is found only in the Peloponnese.[209] Nevertheless, we should not assume that the appearance of the same myth in different regions of the Peloponnese provides any proof of a genuine migration. Instead the evidence suggests that the motif of the return of the Herakleidai was *diffused* throughout the Peloponnese from one centre, and that this centre was the Argolid.[210] Firstly, there is the question of the ruling families of the Peloponnese. If one of the prime purposes behind the myth of the return of the Herakleidai was to legitimate claims to kingship, then it is interesting to note that only at Argos was the ruling family – the Temenids – named after one of the Heraklid leaders. The Spartan dynasties, which might have been expected to take their name from Prokles and Eurysthenes, were actually known as the Agiads and the Eurypontids, while the ruling family of Messenia took its name from Aipytos rather than Kresphontes.[211]

Secondly, although the Herakleidai based their rights to the Peloponnese on an ancestral inheritance bequeathed by Herakles, it is strictly speaking only the Argolid to which Herakles himself had a legitimate right by birth, and out of which he was cheated. The specious claims to Lakonia are suggested not only by the fact that after fighting to restore Tyndareos to the throne of Sparta, Herakles is promptly rewarded with a gift of the land that he has just recovered for Tyndareos, but also by the fact that after accepting the gift, Herakles then immediately hands it back to Tyndareos 'to guard for his own (i.e. Herakles') descendants'.[212] With regard to Messenia, Herakles had killed king Neleus and all of his sons except for Nestor, to whom he had entrusted the land for his descendants.[213] In the case of both Lakonia and Messenia, then, the territory is Heraklid by right of conquest rather than inheritance – a claim that could be made equally as well by Dorian invaders as by Heraklid exiles.

Thirdly, the Heraklid ancestry of the Spartan kings was traced back to Herakles, but no further.[214] In the Argolid, however, Herakles was situated in a far richer, and presumably more developed, genealogical tradition which traced his descent back through Alkmene, Alektryon and Perseus to Zeus (see chapter 4). The mythological tradition of Herakles and his descendants received something more of a material realisation in the cultic and topographical landscape of the Argolid than of Lakonia or Messenia.[215] A monument was erected to Temenos at Temeneion (the port on the Argolic gulf where Temenos was thought to have originally landed),[216] while Temenos' daughter Hyrnetho, was honoured with a cenotaph at Argos and a monumental tomb just outside Epidauros.[217] Herakles seems to have

---

[209] Malkin 1994, 15.
[210] This idea is rejected by Piérart (1991, 140), but without – it seems to me – any particularly cogent reason.   [211] Tigerstedt 1965, 34; Roussel 1976, 229.
[212] Diodoros 4.33.5; Isokrates, *Arkhidamos* 18. Tigerstedt 1965, 31; Malkin 1994, 23.
[213] Isokrates, *Arkhidamos* 19. Cf. Homer, *Iliad* 11.690–93; Hesiod fr. 33(a) Merkelbach/West. Tigerstedt 1965, 31.   [214] Herodotos 6.52–53. Malkin 1994, 19.   [215] Vanschoonwinkel 1991, 358.
[216] Pausanias 2.38.1.   [217] Pausanias 2.23.3; 2.28.3.

been the recipient of some kind of cult at Tiryns by at least 600 BC,[218] while his great-grandfather, Perseus, was honoured at Mykenai by the third quarter of the sixth century at the very latest.[219] At Sparta, by contrast, 'Herakles . . . is astonishingly obscure in cult'.[220]

The indications are, then, that the tradition concerning the return of the Herakleidai was originally independent from the Dorian ethnic myth of origin, and that it may initially have been developed in the Argolid, from where its obvious utility for claims to kingship caused its diffusion throughout the Peloponnese more generally. Now the Korinthian and Heraklid elements of the tradition have been isolated and deconstructed, it is time to tackle the origins of the Dorians themselves.

According to Herodotos, at the time of Deukalion the Dorians had lived in Phthiotis in southeast Thessaly. During the reign of Doros they migrated to Hestiaiotis, a region between Mount Ossa and Mount Olympos, but after being expelled by the Kadmeians they made their way to the Pindos area of Makedonia. From there they moved to Dryopis and then on to the Peloponnese.[221] This somewhat tortuous and certainly circuitous series of migrations has often been taken to indicate the pastoral-nomadic character of the Dorians.[222] I would suggest, however, that it represents a rationalisation, on the part of Herodotos, of conflicting traditions of Dorian origins. Most authors associate the Dorians with only one homeland, but the exact location of this homeland seems to vary between different regions of central and northern Greece. What Herodotos has done is to reconcile these conflicting areas of origin by proposing a migrationist explanation which will therefore be able to incorporate most, if not all, of these territorial variants.

The earliest, and the most popular, candidate for the Dorian *Ursprungsland* is Erineos – the central Greek region between Mount Oita and Mount Parnassos which was known as Doris in the historical period.[223] Herodotos also notes the Dorian origin in Erineos, though he argues that Doris was formerly called Dryopis.[224] That Erineos presents a serious claim to being the original Dorian homeland may be indicated by the evident (albeit laboured) relatedness between the cognates *Doriees* (Dorians), *Doros* (king Doros) and *Doris* (Doris, the territory around Erineos). Indeed, the fact that the earliest reference to Erineos is to be found in Tyrtaios may suggest that the myth of Dorian origins was first elaborated at Sparta. Thoukydides names Doris as the metropolis of the Spartans in particular,[225] and this relationship was clearly taken seriously by the fifth century, since in 457 BC a Spartan force of 1,500 hoplites came to the aid of the Dorian metropolis when it was invaded by Phokis.[226]

---

[218] Verdelis, Jameson and Papachristodoulou 1975, 183.   [219] *IG* 4.493; Pausanias 2.18.1.
[220] Parker 1989, 146.   [221] Herodotos 1.56.3. Cf. 8.43.
[222] E.g. Nixon 1968, xvi; Cartledge 1979, 94–95; Sakellariou 1990, 231; Malkin 1994, 45.
[223] Tyrtaios fr. 2 Diehl; Konon *FGrH* 26.1.27; Ephoros *FGrH* 70.15; Pseudo-Skymnos 592–96; Strabo 9.4.10; Pausanias 5.1.2.   [224] Herodotos 8.31.
[225] Thoukydides 1.107.2; 3.92.3. Cf. Pindar, *Isthmian Odes* 7.12–15.   [226] Thoukydides 1.107.2.

According to another popular tradition, the Dorians had – together with their king, Aigimios – originally occupied Hestiaiotis.[227] This is a region subject to a certain amount of geographical indeterminacy. In the historical period Hestiaiotis was the area at the northwestern extremity of the island of Euboia, though this is clearly not the Hestiaiotis celebrated in the tradition of Dorian origins. Herodotos placed Hestiaiotis between Mount Ossa and Mount Olympos in northeast Thessaly.[228] Generally, however, Hestiaiotis is imagined to be in the shadow of the Pindos mountain range – that is, in western Thessaly some 100 km to the north of Doris. The apparent incompatibility between an Erinean and a Hestiaiotid origin for the Dorians was not lost on the ancient authors. Andron of Halikarnassos and Strabo attempted to explain away the contradiction by hypothesising that Hestiaiotis had originally been called Doris, and Strabo went a step further by proposing that Pindos denoted not the mountain but a town in Doris.[229]

There are good reasons for suspecting that Aigimios was not originally the ancestor of the Dorians.[230] The fragmentary nature of Tyrtaios' elegies makes it dangerous to attach too much significance to the absence there of Aigimios' name; on the other hand, the appearance there of the *phylai* of the Hylleis, Dymanes and Pamphyloi may presuppose the existence of the eponymous Hyllos, Dymas and Pamphylos. By at least the sixth century these three heroes were the sons of Aigimios,[231] but by analogy with the Ionian situation – where the eponymous heroes of the four Ionian *phylai*, Geleon, Hopletes, Argades and Aigikores, are the sons of Ion – their father should originally have been Doros. The figure of the non-eponymous Aigimios, then, has probably been interpolated between Doros and his sons to act as an adhesive mechanism in the assimilation between two ethnic myths of origin: one, developed in Sparta, in which a Dorian origin was traced to Erineos; the other, developed elsewhere, in which ethnic origins were situated in the region of Hestiaiotis under a king named Aigimios. It is entirely feasible that it was this mythological integration, rather than a Dorian-Heraklid assimilation, that featured in the Pseudo-Hesiodic *Aigimios*.

There are two other territories in the Herodotean account which remain to be accounted for. The inclusion of Phthiotis, in southeast Thessaly, is relatively easy to explain. It is a consequence of the Dorians attaching themselves to the Hellenic genealogy by having Doros as the son of the Thessalian king, Hellen.[232] To reconcile a Thessalian origin with an origin in Erineos or Hestiaiotis, it was only necessary to posit a migration from one to the other.[233]

The other territory is Makedonia. While other sources associated Mount Pindos with Hestiaiotis, Herodotos mentions it in connection with Makedonia, perhaps

---

227 Pindar, *Pythian Odes* 1.66; scholiast to Pindar, *Pythian Odes* 1.121c; Andron *FGrH* 10.16; Diodoros 4.37.3–4; Strabo 9.5.17.   228 Herodotos 1.56.3.
229 Andron of Halikarnassos *FGrH* 10.16; Strabo 9.5.17; 9.4.10.
230 Nilsson 1951, 68; Roussel 1976, 224.   231 Hesiod fr. 10(a).6–7 Merkelbach/West.
232 Vanschoonwinkel 1991, 363.
233 See also Konon *FGrH* 26.1.28; Pseudo-Skymnos 592–95; Strabo 8.7.1.

indicating the northern rather than southern Pindos range. Elsewhere, Herodotos notes that the Spartans, the Korinthians, the Sikyonians, the Epidaurians and the Troizenians are of the 'Dorian and Makedonian *ethnos*'.[234] Although the mention of Makedonia in the Herodotean account of the Dorians' wanderings has often been invoked as support for the idea of an historical invasion from the northern Balkans (see chapter 5), it has every appearance of being a more recent invention. In the *Catalogue of women*, the eponymous founder of Makedonia, Makedon, was the son of Zeus and Deukalion's daughter Thuia.[235] This line of descent *excludes* him from the Hellenic genealogy – and hence, by implication, the Makedonians from the ranks of Hellenism.[236] While Makedon derives descent from the Thessalian 'first man', Deukalion, this is traced through *uterine* succession (the female line) and bypasses Hellen himself. Nor does the fact that Zeus is his father necessarily testify to his credentials as a *bona fide* Hellene: after all, Sarpedon is the son of Zeus, but he is a Lykian not a Hellene. By the second half of the fifth century, the Makedonians did manage to enrol their eponymous ancestor within the Hellenic genealogy, but Makedon's descent was derived not from Doros but from Aiolos[237] – an association that may have been suggested by the fact that both Makedon and Aiolos were given the epithet 'he who fights from a chariot' in the *Catalogue of women*.[238]

The Dorian pedigree of the Makedonians is not attested before the middle of the fifth century and it is tempting to attribute this development to the reign of Alexander I during the first half of that century. Alexander involved himself with the panhellenic world of the Greek *poleis* to a greater degree than any of his predecessors. His qualification to do so was based on his claimed descent not only from a Heraklid ancestor, but from the Temenids of Argos.[239] These credentials were evidently sufficient to persuade the officials whose task it was to prevent *barbaroi* from competing in the Olympic Games, though Herodotos suggests that the integrity of Alexander's genealogy was not sufficient to convince all the Greeks, and this doubt was to be ruthlessly exploited in the fourth century in order to dissuade the Greeks from allying themselves to Philip II.[240] With the promotion of Alexander's Argive Heraklid descent came perhaps the idea that the Makedonians were Dorians after all.[241]

To sum up, the tradition concerning the arrival of the Dorians and the return of the Herakleidai is best regarded as a composite and aggregative system of beliefs which had evolved from disparate origins and for the purposes of defining discrete ethnic groups. At the heart of the tradition it is possible to recognise the existence of two separate myths of ethnic origin – that of the Dorians of Erineos, perhaps

---

[234] Herodotos 8.43.   [235] Hesiod fr. 7 Merkelbach/West.
[236] *Contra* Hammond 1994, 131. See West 1985, 10; E. Hall 1989, 180–81.
[237] Hellanikos *FGrH* 4.74.   [238] Hesiod frs. 7.2; 9.2 Merkelbach/West.
[239] Herodotos 5.22.2; Thoukydides 2.99.3.   [240] E.g. Demosthenes 3.24; 9.31.
[241] Though Badian (1994, 119 n. 13) argues that while the Makedonian kings may have been Greek, the populations over which they ruled were not.

developed first at Sparta, and that of the Herakleidai, engineered in the Argolid. Both were to be diffused throughout the Peloponnese, where they came into contact with the constitutive myths of other ethnic groups who believed themselves to have originated outside the Peloponnese. The end result of a series of mythological assimilations and syncretisms was the tradition of the Dorian invasion which is so familiar to us today. Whether they knew it or not, the assumption by Herodotos and Plato that the Dorians did not receive their name until *after* reaching the Peloponnese may not be so wide of the mark.[242]

Conclusion

In describing the series of disturbances which intervened between the end of the Bronze Age and the beginning of the Iron Age in Greece there is a common tendency (particularly among archaeologists) to dismiss the literary accounts as too confused, mannered or biased to provide any useful evidence for the historicity of the migrations which they describe. In this chapter, I hope to have showed that they possess an immense value, though not chiefly for what light they may shed on any genuine population movements at the beginning of the Early Iron Age. Nevertheless, by isolating the various elements which constitute these myths of ethnic origins, and (where possible) by establishing something approaching a relative chronology for them, we can begin to gain a glimpse of the process by which ethnic groups constructed and reaffirmed their identity through the discursive medium of myth and ethnography.

The sheer complexity of this exercise (not facilitated by the fact that the evidence is so fragmentary) is testimony if not to the original movements of peoples, then at least to the manifest operation of ethnicity and the importance attached to ethnic belonging in Greece during the first half of the first millennium BC. The existence of ethnic consciousness is already in place by the time the earliest texts appear in the eighth and seventh centuries, and it is not unfeasible that ethnic demarcations had become particularly sharp throughout the eighth century as a result of the processes of 'social closure' which forged a new definition of the community of *politai*, or 'citizens'. It is difficult to know precisely what the mechanisms were by which individuals or families might be included in, or excluded from, the embryonic *polis*, but we can be fairly certain that the recitation of ethnic myths, invoking claims and counterclaims to territory and ancestral rights, must have played some part in accession to, or exclusion from, citizen status.

Nor did ethnicity ever really disappear from ancient Greece, even if it was subject to fluctuations in its salience. The ethnic rhetoric of the Peloponnesian War was mainly possible because it expanded on a discourse that pre-existed it. By the second century AD, when the cities of the Aegean were desperate to adduce Greek

[242] Herodotos 1.56.3; Plato, *Laws* 3.682e.

origin in order to be enrolled within the newly founded Hadrianic league of the Panhellenion, ethnic invention is particularly evident. The Phrygian city of Synnada attempted to get the best of both worlds by claiming to be both a Dorian foundation of Sparta and an Ionian colony of Athens, and Hadrian referred to Libyan Kyrene's 'Akhaian, and more precisely, Dorian ancestors'.[243] It is the continued existence, rather than the speciousness, of these ethnic claims which is significant.

[243] Spawforth and Walker 1986.

4

Ethnography and genealogy: an Argolic case-study

The ethnic populations of the Argolid

The Argolid area of the northeastern Peloponnese (fig. 2) is bounded to the north by Korinthia, to the northeast and east by the Saronic Gulf, to the south and southeast by the Argolic Gulf and Kynouria, and to the west by Arkadia. It can be thought of as divided into two distinct regions. The Argive plain itself, which covers an area of approximately 200 square km, is triangular in shape and was formed from black alluvial soil washed down from the surrounding mountains. On the western side of the plain are the settlements of Argos (by far the most important and best documented site of the Argive plain in the post-Mycenaean period) and Lerna (modern Míli). On the eastern side are the settlements of Mykenai (Mikínes), the Argive Heraion, Berbati, Midea (Déndra), Tiryns, Nauplia (Náfplio) and, a little further to the southeast, Asine. The second region is the eastern Argolid, or Aktí Peninsula, divided into two by the Adhéres mountain range which runs like a spine from east to west. On the southern coast of Aktí are the sites of Mases (on the modern Koiládha bay), Halieis (Portohéli) and Hermione (Ermióni), while on the northern coast are the sites of Troizen (Trizína) and Epidauros (Epídhavros) along with the Methana peninsula and the island of Kalaureia (modern Póros).[1]

The reason why the Argolid has been selected to provide a more detailed illustration of the discursive construction of ethnicity is due to the fact that – as figure 3 shows – it is a region whose population is characterised by the literary sources as being multi-ethnic in its composition. It should be stressed that the information presented in this table is drawn from a variety of authors spanning a period of almost a millennium; furthermore, no distinction has been made between references which purport to describe the ethnographic actualities of the historical period and those which recount ethnic myths of origins. For this reason, it would be unwise to take every literary reference at face-value. On the other hand, ethnic charter myths were not (at least originally) simply tales designed for entertainment, but were rather intended to serve as cues in mapping out or renegotiating a sense of belonging. The fact that they were still circulating at the time of

---

[1] For accounts of the geography and history of the Argolid, see Lehmann 1937; Kirsten 1959; Faraklas 1972; Tomlinson 1972; Kelly 1976; Van Andel and Runnels 1987; Foley 1988; Zangger 1991; 1993; 1994; Jameson, Runnels and Van Andel 1995; Hall 1995b.

67

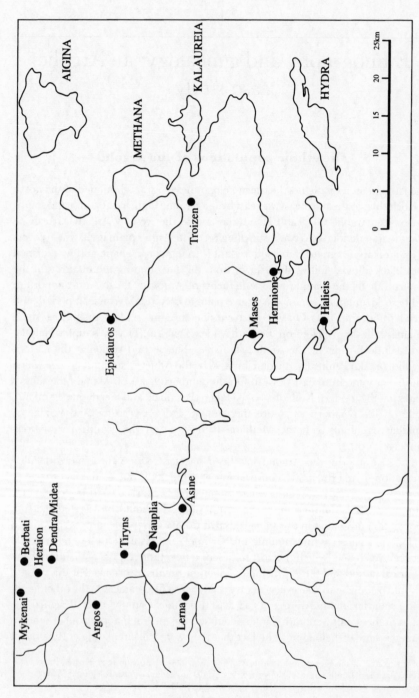

2 Map of the Argolid.

ARGOS	Dorians; Herakleidai (Akhaians); Pelasgians
ASINE	Dryopes
EPIDAUROS	Dorians; Herakleidai (Akhaians); Ionians; Karians
HALIEIS	Dryopes
HERMIONE	Dorians; Dryopes; Ionians; Karians
MIDEA	Herakleidai (Akhaians)
MYKENAI	Herakleidai (Akhaians)
TIRYNS	Herakleidai (Akhaians)
TROIZEN	Dorians; Dryopes; Ionians

3 The distribution of ethnic groups in the Argolid according to literary sources.

the 'Universal Histories' of the fourth century BC (and, it would seem, as late as the time of Pausanias in the second century AD) suggests rather more than a purely antiquarian interest in the past. At the very least, the exercise suggests that the Argolid should provide a fertile field of research in exploring how ancient populations employed discursive strategies in the active construction of identity.

There can be no doubt that by the fifth century Argos was considered to be a typically Dorian city. Its inscriptions were written in the Doric dialect and its population divided among the three standard Dorian *phylai* of the Hylleis, the Dymanes and the Pamphyloi (along with the exclusively Argive Hyrnathioi). Indeed, so strong was this affiliation that in Sophokles' *Oidipous at Kolonos*, Oidipous' son Polyneikes describes Argos as 'Dorian' in spite of the fact that the play is supposed to be set in an era prior to the Dorian conquest of the Peloponnese.[2] Nevertheless, although the arrival of the Dorians was normally considered to have taken place at the end of the Heroic Age (Thoukydides placed it eighty years after the Trojan War),[3] it is not until the sixth century that we find the first explicit reference to the association of Dorians with Argos. In a fragment of the Pseudo-Hesiodic *Catalogue of women*, Argos is mentioned in two consecutive lines immediately prior to the introduction of the Dorian king Aigimios and his two sons, Pamphylos and Dymas.[4] It is now generally accepted that the same extract

[2] Sophokles, *Oidipous at Kolonos* 1301.　　[3] Thoukydides 1.12.3.
[4] Hesiod fr. 10(a).3–4, 6–7 Merkelbach/West.

69

of the *Catalogue* dealt with the marriage of Aigimios' father, Doros, to the daughter of the Argive 'first man', Phoroneus.[5]

Dorians are also recorded by the literary sources in many of the other cities of the Argolid. In an ode to an Aiginetan named Aristokleides who had just won the Pankration event at the Nemean Games, Pindar celebrated the 'Dorian island' of Aigina.[6] Herodotos explains that Aigina was colonised by Dorians from Epidauros, thus implying Dorian populations in both locations, though Strabo somewhat confusingly lists Dorians and Epidaurians separately among the residents of Aigina.[7] Herodotos also implies the presence of Dorians at Troizen when he explains that Halikarnassos was a Dorian city because it was a Troizenian colony.[8] Finally, Pausanias notes that Hermione was settled (apparently peacefully) by Dorians from Argos.[9]

Nevertheless, if Dorians constituted the most populous ethnic group within the Argolid, there is enough literary evidence to suggest that they were not the only residents. As a starting point, we may take the so-called 'servile interregnum'. Herodotos relates how, in ca. 494 BC, the Spartan king Kleomenes launched an attack against Argos at a place named Sepeia in which 6,000 Argives were killed – in other words, virtually the whole adult male population.[10] As a result of this crushing defeat, Herodotos says that Argos was so depleted of manpower that the *douloi* ('slaves') became masters of everything, giving orders and engaging in administration, until the time when the sons of the soldiers who had died came of age.[11]

The sheer magnitude of the catastrophe and the idea of a consequent 'slave revolution' have provided some legitimate grounds for scepticism.[12] Even in antiquity Plutarch expressed his doubts, arguing that what Herodotos meant to say was that the best of the *perioikoi* (literally, 'those who dwell around') were incorporated within the Argive citizenry.[13] Indeed, Aristotle had said that the events of 494 BC compelled the Argives to incorporate within their body 'certain of the *perioikoi*'.[14] Scholars sometimes take this to indicate that residents of 'perioikic' communities such as Mykenai, Tiryns and Midea were granted citizen rights at Argos.[15] On the other hand, Diodoros, following Ephoros, is explicit in his assertion that the Argives freed their *oiketai* (a word normally used for 'house-slaves'), preferring to give these a share of freedom rather than the free residents of perioikic communities a share of citizenship.[16] Similarly, Pausanias mentions that only *oiketai* remained in Argos after the annihilation of the Argive army.[17]

Willetts has attempted to resolve the problem by focusing on terminology. He

---

[5] West 1985, 59. [6] Pindar, *Nemean Odes* 3.3.

[7] Herodotos 8.46.1 (cf. Pausanias 2.29.5); Strabo 8.6.16. [8] Herodotos 7.99.3.

[9] Pausanias 2.34.5.

[10] Herodotos 6.76–80. Cf. Plutarch, *Moralia* 245c-f; Pausanias 2.20.8–10. See Forrest 1960, 221.

[11] Herodotos 6.83.1.

[12] E.g. Forrest 1960, where it is suggested that 'douloi' is a term of abuse used by aristocrats against those advocating political synoikism. [13] Plutarch, *Moralia* 245f. [14] Aristotle, *Politics* 1303a.

[15] Forrest 1960. [16] Diodoros 10.26. [17] Pausanias 2.20.9.

argues that although *perioikoi* can denote the free residents of neighbouring communities, Aristotle regularly uses the word to mean serfs – that is, a class of peasants without political rights who are enslaved to wealthy landowners in the sense of being compelled to pay them tribute.[18] Similarly, a gloss of Hesykhios reveals that the term *oiketai* could act as a synonym for *agroikoi* – again, a word denoting those tied to the land.[19] For Willetts, Herodotos' *douloi* are the same as Aristotle's *perioikoi* and Diodoros' and Pausanias' *oiketai*, and should be equated with the *Gymnetes* – a class of tribute-paying peasants like the Helots of Lakonia, the Penestai of Thessaly or the Klarotai of Krete who, according to Pollux, possessed a status 'between free and slave'.[20]

Certainly, it is difficult to explain the Herodotean account in terms of the extension of citizenship to the free residents of neighbouring communities, since this would have represented a process of synoikism which did not take place in the Argive plain until nearly a generation later, when Argos destroyed Mykenai, Tiryns and Midea.[21] Indeed, the passage from Aristotle's *Politics* is explicitly concerned with *internal* change brought about when one part of the citizen body grows at a disproportionate rate.[22] For this reason, Mauro Moggi regards Herodotos' *douloi* as a class of semi-servile status within Argos itself which was offered freedom (and the right to marry free Argive women) to make up for a chronic shortage of manpower. These rights (particularly any rights over property) would then have been rescinded when the legitimate heirs reached manhood, leading to the expulsion of the *douloi* and their subsequent seizure of Tiryns.[23]

It may be that far too much credence has been given to Herodotos' notice of the Battle of Sepeia, especially since variant accounts of Argive misfortunes exist. Ironically, one of these variants is also recounted by Herodotos and refers to an event that, if it is to be dated at all, should fall shortly *after* the supposed date of the Battle of Sepeia. Herodotos explains how the Aiginetans, threatened by an Athenian attack, appealed to Argos for help. Officially, Argos refused to assist, but unofficially a volunteer force of 1,000, under Eurybates, set out for the island of Aigina where they were promptly massacred by the Athenians.[24] Another variant, not mentioned by Herodotos, has Kleomenes destroy the Argive army at Sepeia, but then meet defeat at Argos itself at the hands of a coalition of house-slaves, elderly men, boys and above all women, organised under the Argive poetess Telesilla.[25]

Nevertheless, it is important to realise that the *function* of all three stories (however fanciful) is to explain the weakness of the Argive élite at the beginning of

---

[18] Willetts 1959, 496. See also Tomlinson 1972, 98–99.   [19] Willetts 1959, 496.
[20] Pollux, *Onomastikon* 3.83. See Willetts 1959, 497; Tomlinson 1972, 98–99; Moggi 1974, 1260–63; *contra* Forrest 1960, 223. The word *gymnetes* seems to mean 'naked', and may refer to the fact that they could not afford a hoplite panoply: Vidal-Naquet 1981a, 192.
[21] Moggi 1974; Hall 1995b.   [22] Moggi 1974, 1260–63.   [23] Herodotos 6.83.1.
[24] Herodotos 6.92.2–3.
[25] Plutarch, *Moralia* 245c-f (citing the Hellenistic historian Sokrates of Argos); Pausanias 2.20.8–10. See Hall 1995b, 588–89.

the fifth century and the (temporary) ascendancy of a new, and formerly inferior, group which we may term, simply for the sake of convenience, the *douloi*. At the very least, the episode should indicate the existence of a conflict between two groups at Argos which was probably still being waged in the middle of the fifth century when Herodotos was gathering his information.

Willetts assumes that the *douloi* belonged to the 'pre-Dorian' population of Argos.[26] No literary source says this, and at first sight the supposition seems to invoke the now rather old-fashioned and monolithic model which has a massive wave of Dorians arrive in the Peloponnese and subjugate an indigenous population without the slightest degree of assimilation. On the other hand, access to power, property and political rights as well as the right to liberty were invariably based in the ancient world on considerations of descent: consider, for example, the Partheniai of Sparta whose imputed illegitimacy (their name means 'maiden-born') seems to have excluded them from full political rights and thus prompted their departure to found the South Italian colony of Taras (Taranto) in 706 BC. Ethnic ascription, which is predicated on notions of descent and belonging, thus represents a particularly efficacious tool within strategies of inclusion in, or exclusion from, the apparatus of power. It is not impossible, then, that Argive citizens justified the inferior status of the *douloi* by assigning them to a pre-Dorian ethnic group, without thereby subscribing to the belief that all *douloi* really were genetically descended from the Bronze Age populations of the Argolid.

According to the literary tradition, two populations inhabited Argos prior to the arrival of the Dorians. The first is the Pelasgians – a name which occurs throughout Greece and which would appear to be used without any particularly precise application to indicate a population that was believed to be aboriginal. The figure of the eponymous Pelasgos occurs frequently in the genealogies of Argive rulers (see figs. 5, 7, 8), and in Aiskhylos' *Suppliants*, he appears as the king of Argos when the daughters of Danaos sought sanctuary there.[27] A fragment of a Sophoklean play names the Argive *Urvater*, Inakhos, as the king of the Tyrrhenian Pelasgians,[28] and Strabo quotes an extract from a lost Euripidean play (probably the *Arkhelaos*) in which the Pelasgians of Argos are described as changing their name to Danaoi upon the arrival at Argos of Danaos.[29]

The second group is the Akhaians. That these were particularly associated with the Argive plain is clear from the numerous references to 'Akhaian Argos' in the *Iliad*. According to Pausanias, the populations of Argos and Sparta began to call themselves Akhaians upon the arrival in both cities of Arkhandros and Arkhiteles, the sons of Akhaios (though in Argos, they were also known as Danaoi).[30] By the fifth century, it was commonly believed that the Akhaians had fled from Argos and Sparta upon the arrival of the Dorians and the Herakleidai, and that their king, Teisamenos (the son of Orestes), had led them to the north Peloponnesian region

---

[26] Willetts 1959, 497, 506. Cf. Kelly 1976, 23.   [27] Aiskhylos, *Suppliants* 850–51.
[28] Sophokles fr. 270 Jebb/Pearson.   [29] Strabo 8.6.9; cf. 5.2.4.   [30] Pausanias 7.1.7.

72

of Akhaia, thus causing the Ionians who were formerly resident there to migrate eastwards.[31] Unless we are willing to accept a highly implausible scenario in which a *whole* population was actually displaced by another, we should treat this belief in the Akhaian migration as a composite myth which serves two very different functions. In the first place, it acts as a foundation myth for the populations of Akhaia itself (and, perhaps more importantly, the inhabitants of the Akhaian colonies in South Italy): what makes the Akhaians of the historical period distinct is not only their descent from Akhaios, but the fact that they once (though no longer) occupied a primordial territory in the Argolid.[32] In the second place, it represents an attempt – presumably on the part of people who felt themselves to be newcomers – to invalidate any claims made by those who sought to derive their descent from the Akhaians of the Heroic Age: there could be no celebration of Akhaian ethnicity if there were no Akhaians left in the Argolid.

If it is true that the tale of the expulsion of the Akhaians was an attempt to silence ethnic claims, then it was a failure. The myth of the Herakleidai, which as we saw in chapter 3 was almost certainly first coined in the Argolid, represented a direct claim to an Akhaian inheritance which had been usurped by those who were to call themselves Dorians. At Argos itself, there seems to have been something of an eventual *rapprochement* between the myths of the Dorians and those of the Herakleidai. Isokrates, for example, says that prior to their return to the Argolid, the Herakleidai went to live with the Dorians in central Greece, and Pausanias, in describing the foundation of the Argive sanctuary of Athena Salpinx by Hegeleos (the grandson of Herakles), describes how Hegeleos 'taught the Dorians with Temenos (the leader of the Argive Herakleidai) how to play the trumpet'.[33]

This *rapprochement* is not, however, so evident at Mykenai and Tiryns. Strabo writes that the Herakleidai expelled the Pelopids from Mykenai and ruled the city until its destruction by the Argives in the fifth century.[34] The historical presence of Herakleidai in Tiryns is not noted, but in Sophokles' *Trakhiniai*, Hyllos (the son of Herakles) announces that while some of his brothers have gone to Thebes, the others have accompanied Alkmene to Tiryns – the location of Herakles' family in Tiryns was, of course, central to the ancestral rights that were to be claimed by the Herakleidai. What is interesting is that Dorians *sensu stricto* are not recorded in the literary tradition at either Mykenai or Tiryns.

Ionians are not specifically associated with any of the cities of the Argive plain, though they are mentioned in connection with the eastern Argolid. At Epidauros, Pausanias records that the last king prior to the arrival of the Dorians was Pitureus, a descendant of Ion, and that he and his people surrendered to the newcomers and left to settle in Athens.[35] Strabo, on the other hand, argues that Ionians only settled

---

[31] Herodotos 1.145; 7.94; 8.73.1; Pausanias 2.18.6–8; 7.1.7–8.
[32] Morgan and Hall 1996, 197.   [33] Isokrates, *Arkhidamos* 17–18; Pausanias 2.21.3.
[34] Strabo 8.6.10. In fact, Strabo says that when the Herakleidai returned to the Argolid they united Argos and Mykenai under their rule. It is clear, however, that he is desperately trying to reconcile *alternative* and *competing* genealogies (see below).   [35] Pausanias 2.26.1–2.

73

in Epidauros upon the return of the Herakleidai,[36] suggesting again a climate of ethnic claims and counterclaims whose context should surely belong to the historical period. Strabo also mentions in the same passage the existence of Ionians at Hermione. At Troizen, there is no direct literary reference to Ionians, though their presence is often assumed due to Pausanias' description of a sanctuary on the offshore island of Sphairia which was dedicated to Athena Apatouria – Herodotos notes that the festival of the Apatouria was a key symbol of Ionian identity.[37]

Other populations supposedly attested in the eastern Argolid include Kretans on the island of Aigina, and Karians at Epidauros and Hermione.[38] Of particular interest, however, are the Dryopes. According to ancient opinion, the Dryopes had originally occupied the central Greek regions of Oita and Trakhis but had been expelled from their homeland by Herakles. For this reason they migrated to Euboia, the Kyklades, Cyprus and the Peloponnese, where Eurystheus (king of Mykenai and arch-enemy of Herakles) is supposed to have allowed them to settle in the eastern Argolic cities of Hermione and Eion, as well as at Asine (geographically connected with the Argive plain rather than the eastern Argolid).[39] Their presence in these cities is further noted by Bakkhylides, Herodotos, Strabo and Pausanias; Kallimakhos adds that they were also resident in Halieis while Nikolaos of Damascus, referring to the intrigues conducted by Deïphontes and Hyrnetho (the son-in-law and daughter respectively of Temenos), mentions Dryopean residents not only at Asine and Hermione, but also at Troizen.[40]

The Dryopes of the Argolid present particular problems for ethnographic analysis because they are, by and large, a 'silent' population. Asine (a site at which only Dryopes are attested) was destroyed by the Argives a little before the end of the eighth century BC;[41] its refugee population was supposedly settled by the Spartans at Koróni (on the eastern coast of the Akritas promontory of Messenia).[42] Yet it is precisely the early date of this destruction which precludes the existence of any epigraphical evidence which might provide *direct* testimony of the significance that was attached at Asine to being Dryopean. In fact, much of the information that is offered about the Asinaian Dryopes by later authors appears to repeat the justifications that the Argives provided for an act of aggression against a people no longer resident.

---

[36] Strabo 8.6.15.   [37] Pausanias 2.33.1; Herodotos 1.147.

[38] Strabo 8.6.15–16. Herodotos (1.171.2) equates the Karians of the islands with Leleges – another group, like the Pelasgians, which was thought to be aboriginal.

[39] Diodoros 4.37.2; cf. Herodotos 8.46.4.

[40] Bakkhylides fr. 4; Herodotos 8.43; 8.73; Strabo 8.6.13; Pausanias 4.34.9; Kallimakhos fr. 705 Pfeiffer; Nikolaos of Damascus *FGrH* 90.30. See Barrett 1954, 427.

[41] Pausanias 2.36.5; 3.7.4; 4.8.3; 4.34.9, who mentions that the Argives spared only the sanctuary of Apollo Pythaeus. For historical and archaeological evaluations: Frödin and Persson 1938, 148; Kelly 1967; Wells 1987–8, 349–52; 1990, 157 (dating the destruction to ca. 720 BC); Foley 1988, 142–43; Morgan and Whitelaw 1991, 82–84; Billot 1989–90, 35, 97; Hall 1995b, 581–83.

[42] The earliest testimony of this New Asine in Messenia is found in Herodotos 8.73.2. However, doubts concerning the authenticity of the tradition are expressed in Beloch 1924, 333 n. 2; cf. Kelly 1967; Billot 1989–90, 38; Hall 1995b, 582.

74

Pausanias does present an account of Asinaian origins told to him by the inhabitants of Koróni, who claimed to be the descendants of the Dryopes expelled from Asine.[43] Nevertheless, even if the Asinaians of Koróni were genuinely descended from the Dryopes of Asine, it is most unlikely that they could have preserved entirely intact the exact account of ethnic origins which had acted as a charter myth at Asine, especially since they had been divorced from the specific context of Argolic claims and counterclaims for over 800 years. Rather, it is more probable that the myths that they recounted to Pausanias served a function that was embedded as much (if not more) within the negotiation of identities in Messenia as it was in their supposed former homeland.

By contrast, those Dryopes who seem to have remained in the eastern Argolic cities of Troizen, Eion, Hermione and Halieis were apparently ashamed of their Dryopean ancestry.[44] In situations where a group perceives itself to have a 'negative social identity' (see chapter 2), we can hardly expect it continuously to rehearse and enunciate the charter myths by which that identity is constituted and perpetuated. On the other hand, the very fact that the Dryopes of the eastern Argolid attempted to escape from what they perceived to be an unfavourable stigma presupposes a certain consensual acceptance that there was, at an earlier period, such a thing as a Dryopean identity in the Argolid.

If we ask what it was that made the Dryopes distinct from other groups, the answer must lie in their myth of collective descent from the eponymous Dryops and their association with a primordial homeland in central Greece. In the fifth century, Herodotos placed this homeland under the shadow of Mount Parnassos,[45] but there are some indications that their *Urheimat* was originally thought of as being situated a little further to the north. According to Pherekydes of Athens (who is almost certainly following an earlier source), the eponymous Dryops was either the son of Sperkheios or the son of Peneios and Polydora, the daughter of Danaos.[46] Since the Sperkheios and the Peneios are both important rivers in eastern Thessaly, it is not unreasonable to suspect that this was the original homeland of the Dryopes. The introduction of Danaos as the father-in-law of Dryops should probably be regarded as the product of a specifically Argolic variant of Dryopean origins.

At Asine, a self-proclaimed Dryopean identity was reinforced by particularly robust cultural indicia, which served to distinguish it from the sites of the Argive plain (see further chapter 5). This may even apply to the *modus vivendi* of her inhabitants, since the very location of Asine, perched on a strategic headland, suggests a mode of subsistence based on sea-activities (including piracy) which would mark a clear departure from the more agriculturally based life-style of the communities that inhabited the Argive plain.[47] Such distinctiveness is also evoked by their name. Dryopes means 'woodpeckers', thus immediately associating them with other

---

[43] Pausanias 4.34.9–10. [44] Pausanias 4.34.11. [45] Herodotos 8.43.
[46] Pherekydes *FGrH* 3.8. [47] See Hall 1995b, 582–83.

75

ethnic groups such as the Pelasgians ('storks'), Meropes ('bee-eaters') and Leleges (also 'storks'), whose migratory nature placed them in direct opposition to the more settled Hellenic groups.[48]

Equally important was the fact that the Dryopes were considered distinctive by outgroups. This was articulated at a mythological level by having the Dryopes come into conflict with the ancestors of other ethnic groups in the pre-migratory period. Thus, according to Herodotos, Bakkhylides and Pausanias, Herakles (the ancestor of the Herakleidai) is supposed to have defeated the Dryopes and to have dedicated them as a 'tithe' to Pythian Apollo at Delphi;[49] Apollo's command was that Herakles should settle the Dryopes at Asine and mark the frontier of their new territory with a twisted olive tree.[50] Marie-Françoise Billot has argued that this myth of Dryopean origins bears all the hallmarks of Argive (rather than Asinaian) invention, particularly in the way that it appears to 'anticipate' and 'justify' the return of the Herakleidai. In her opinion, it must have been developed after the middle of the eighth century, when the Delphic oracle first began to function, and before the early fifth century, when Bakkhylides was writing.[51] In fact, it is more than likely that it first entered into currency at about the time of the Argive destruction of Asine, serving as an aetiological doublet for the Argive action.[52]

Furthermore, the legend of the mythical war between Herakles and the Dryopes was exploited as a means of consolidating not only the fusion between the Herakleidai and the Dorians, but also the integration of Aigimios within the account of Dorian ethnic origins (see chapter 3). The Pseudo-Apollodoran *Bibliotheka* tells how the Dorians were engaged in a war with both the Dryopes and the Lapiths, and that Herakles was asked to lend assistance by the Dorian king, Aigimios. In return, Herakles' son Hyllos was adopted by Aigimios alongside his own sons, Dymas and Pamphylos, and granted an equal share in the inheritance of his dominion.[53]

By tracing their ancestry back through Dryops to either Sperkheios or Peneios, the Dryopes were technically excluded from the Hellenic genealogy (chapter 3), and this may account for why the Dryopes were never regarded as truly 'Hellenic': Strabo was later to regard them as one of the 'barbarian peoples' which settled Greece, along with the Kaukones, Pelasgians and Leleges.[54] Surrounded by neighbours whose self-proclaimed Dorian or Ionian identities served to enrol them within the ranks of Hellenism, the Dryopes of the eastern Argolid must have been acutely aware of the ethnic ascription by which they were disadvantaged, and the fact that they are described as being ashamed of their ethnonym may indicate that they attempted to assimilate (albeit without a spectacular degree of success) with

---

[48] Paraskevaidou 1991.

[49] Herodotos 8.43; Bakkhylides fr. 4 Jebb; Pausanias 4.34.9. The king who leads the Dryopes is named as Phylas in Diodoros (4.37.1) and Pausanias (4.34.9) but as Laogoras in Pseudo-Apollodoros (*Bibliotheka* 2.7.7). [50] Bakkhylides fr. 4.8 Jebb; Pausanias 4.34.9. Cf. 2.28.2.

[51] Billot 1989–90, 43–47. [52] Piérart 1985, 278. [53] Pseudo-Apollodoros, *Bibliotheka* 2.7.7.

[54] Strabo 7.7.1.

the Dorians.[55] Certainly, this might explain the apparent geographical confusion behind Herodotos' assertion that Doris was formerly called Dryopis.[56]

The Asinaians of Koróni, on the other hand, were in a rather different position. Firstly, they were far removed from the ethnic claims and counterclaims specific to the Argolid. Secondly, they appear to have resided in a part of Messenia that was especially given over to populations of a supposedly refugee origin:[57] in this case, their Asinaian origin would be particularly useful in stressing their distinctiveness among neighbours who were similarly immigrants. Thirdly, by the time Pausanias interviewed them, the necessity of proving descent from Hellen had long since ceased to be a defining criterion of Hellenism. The people of Koróni, then, could afford to celebrate – rather than apologise for – their Dryopean identity: in fact, Pausanias notes that they were the only Dryopes to be proud of their ethnonym.[58]

The Asinaians of Koróni made two modifications to the Dryopean myth of origins in order to redefine in a more positive light features which had been viewed somewhat negatively among the Dryopes of the eastern Argolid. On the one hand, they counteracted their exclusion from the Hellenic genealogy by adopting a tactic that had been so successful among the Athenians (see chapter 3) – namely, by asserting that Dryops was in fact the son of Apollo, thus bypassing the Hellenic genealogy altogether.[59] On the other hand, they vigorously denied the Argive accounts of how they had come to be located in the Argolid. While accepting defeat at the hands of Herakles, they refuted the belief that they had been taken prisoner and forcibly installed in the Argolid. Indeed, not only had they been invited to settle in the Argolid, but this invitation had been offered by Eurystheus – the king of Mykenai to whom the mighty Herakles, ancestor of the Herakleidai, had been enslaved.[60]

The genealogies of the Argolid

While eponymous ethnic ancestors could serve to explain origins and the kin-ties that gradually came to be recognised between geographically distant populations in Greece, their universal applicability was expedited by the fact that they were rather shallow personalities to whom few, if any, mythological adventures could be attached. This inevitably made them less 'good to think with' at the more local level of competing claims. For more parochial imperatives, then, the Greeks turned to the royal genealogies which dealt with more three-dimensional characters such as

---

[55] Jameson, Runnels and van Andel (1995, 373) suggest that the population of the southern Argolid was originally Dryopean but later treated as Dorian.   [56] Herodotos 8.31; 8.43.

[57] Methóni, some 25 miles away from Koróni on the other side of the Akritas peninsula, is supposed to have provided home to refugees expelled from Nauplia: Theopompos of Khios *FGrH* 115.383; Strabo 8.6.11; Pausanias 4.24.4; 4.27.8; 4.35.2. See, however, Kelly 1976, 89; Hall 1995b, 583–84.

[58] Pausanias 4.34.11.   [59] Pausanias 4.34.11.   [60] Diodoros 4.37.2; Pausanias 4.34.10.

Herakles, Bellerophon or Oidipous – figures whose mythical association with the local landscape rendered them more effective within strategies of appropriation and legitimation. It is not at all impossible that these royal genealogies were originally elaborated to legitimate the political position of aristocratic families: we have already seen (chapter 3) that the lineage of Herakles and his descendants served to justify the right to rule of the Spartan kings, and the same may be true of the Argive monarchy. Nevertheless, the fact that these genealogies played a central role in both the mythology and ritual of Argolic cities by at least the sixth century (see below) is enough to indicate that they were quickly consumed and employed at a more collective level.[61]

Technically, of course, the personages of the Heroic Age were supposed to have lived prior to the age of migrations, though this seems to have been a cause of concern only to 'rationalist' historians such as Thoukydides or Diodoros. In non- or partially literate populations, a chronological or annalistic consciousness of history is generally limited by the capacity of the human memory and rarely stretches back more than three or so generations from the present. Prior to this, fact and fiction tend to be mixed up in a timeless, 'mythic' consciousness of the past, in which temporal causality – when it does occur – is more often invented *ad hoc* rather than preserved unaltered.[62] As the discussion below will reveal, the protagonists of the Heroic Age could serve as symbolic figureheads not only for those who claimed to be occupants of the Argive plain at the time, but also for those who did not.

The wealth of genealogical myths preserved in a succession of authors from Homer to Nonnos testifies to the fact that the Argives were enchanted no less than the Spartans by tales of heroes, men and civic foundations.[63] Yet even if the recitation of mythical genealogies was intended, from at least the time of Homer, to evoke pleasure in the ear of the listener, its other functions came to be progressively eroded and expunged by the fission which occurred between *muthos* and *logos*, and the transition from oral *myths* circulating in the public domain to a literate *mythology* which was the preserve of an educated élite.[64] While the details of the Pseudo-Apollodoran *Bibliotheka* are not radically different from those to be found in the Pseudo-Hesiodic *Catalogue of women*, the former appears to be fossilised and antiquarian precisely because the myths which it has immutably fixed through the medium of writing have been wrenched from the living context in which they originally circulated and functioned.

The fullest sources for the Argolic genealogies are to be found in Pseudo-Apollodoros and Pausanias, both writing in the Roman Imperial period. Their

---

[61] 'clearly, a city's history is often, in effect, that of its ruling aristocratic family. Presumably that family's preserved traditions would be impressed on the general traditions of that area to become its main traditions': Thomas 1989, 98–99.

[62] Vansina 1985, 23–24; Herzfeld 1982, 63; Sakellariou 1990, 24.

[63] For Spartan attitudes to myth: Plato, *Hippias Meizon* 285d-e.

[64] Veyne 1988, 45–46; Vernant 1980, 186–207; Detienne 1986.

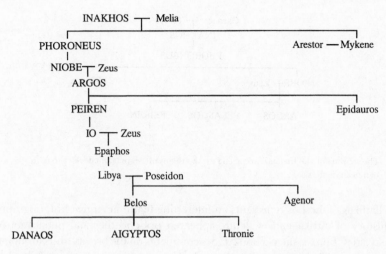

4   The stemma of the Inakhids according to the *Catalogue of women* (capitals refer to more significant figures).

comparative lateness does not necessarily vitiate their validity, since the late appearance of a mythical episode need not automatically entail its late invention.[65] Pausanias' accounts are often favoured because he is assumed to have collected the local variants of myths on his travels,[66] though this is of only limited use in the case of the myths of Mykenai and Tiryns – communities which had been annexed by Argos and already abandoned prior to the Periegete's visits. Yet Pausanias is no mere gleaner of parochial folktales, and he frequently cites references to the earlier writers whose works he has read: for instance, in attempting to determine the genealogies of the Messenians, he mentions that he has read through the Pseudo-Hesiodic *Catalogue of women*, the epic poem *Naupaktia*, and the genealogical writings of Asios of Samos and Kinaithon of Sparta.[67] Indeed in its details, Pausanias' Argive genealogy is very close to the *Catalogue of women*, with the addition of some information derived from Akousilaos of Argos – a writer who, according to Josephus, lived a short time before the Persian Wars (figs. 4, 5, 9).[68]

Pseudo-Apollodoros, too, preserves many of the genealogical elements of the *Catalogue* intact – in fact, the whole structure of the work was modelled on its sixth-century prototype (fig. 10).[69] He also takes account of the Akousilaan variants, though he draws on the mid-fifth-century writer, Pherekydes of Athens, to a greater extent than does Pausanias (fig. 6). The Scholiast to Euripides' *Orestes*, 932 (fig. 8) similarly provides a full account of the early Argive (Inakhid) genealogy, based chiefly on the Pseudo-Hesiodic text but also to a lesser degree on Akousilaos, Pherekydes and Hellanikos (fig. 7).

---

[65] Dowden 1992, 10.   [66] Fossey 1980, 58.   [67] Pausanias 4.2.1.
[68] Josephus, *Contra Apionem* 1.13.   [69] West 1985, 35, 43–44.

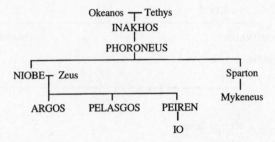

5 The stemma of the Inakhids according to Akousilaos of Argos (capitals refer to more significant figures).

Hellanikos of Lesbos represents an interesting figure in Argive historiography. His history of Attika had evidently appeared prior to the final publication of Thoukydides' Book 1, since Thoukydides comments on the brevity and chronological inaccuracy of his contemporary's work.[70] It is also likely that it was Hellanikos' *Hiereiai* (*Catalogue of the Priestesses of the Argive Heraion*) which was consulted by Thoukydides when he describes the destruction of the Old Temple of Hera at the Heraion which took place when Khrysis was priestess:[71] this should mean that the *Hiereiai* postdates the conflagration of 423 BC. According to Josephus, Akousilaos frequently corrected Hesiod, but Hellanikos was in direct disagreement with Akousilaos,[72] and the limited fragments that we possess tend to support this statement.[73]

The existence of alternative mythical variants is exemplified best by the genealogies of the first rulers of Argos, the Inakhids (figs. 4–10). All accounts seem to agree that Phoroneus (the Argive 'first man', fulfilling the same function as Deukalion in Thessalian myths) was the son of Inakhos, and that Phoroneus' daughter Niobe gave birth to Argos by Zeus; it is only the siblings of Phoroneus, Niobe and Argos that vary between different versions. But the stemma from Argos to the end of the Inakhid dynasty meets with no consensus between any one pair of accounts: the Scholiast to Euripides derives the line from Kriasos, Pseudo-Apollodoros from Ekbasos and Pausanias from Phorbas.[74] Phorbas and/or Triopas appear in Pausanias, the Scholiast, Pherekydes and Hellanikos but not, it would appear, in Pseudo-Apollodoros, Akousilaos or Pseudo-Hesiod. Pelasgos is autochthonous in the Pseudo-Hesiodic *Catalogue*, but can also be the son of Niobe, Triopas, Phoroneus, Argos or Inakhos.[75] Similarly, Argos Panoptes is sometimes viewed as

[70] Thoukydides 1.97.   [71] Thoukydides 4.133. Cf. 2.2.   [72] Josephus, *Contra Apionem* 1.16.
[73] Hellanikos of Lesbos may, in fact, be one of the central figures behind the rapid mythological 'reinvention' in which the Argives engaged immediately after their destruction of Mykenai, Midea and Tiryns in the 460s BC: Hall 1995b, 581, 609–10; cf. Adshead 1986.
[74] Pseudo-Apollodoros, *Bibliotheka* 2.1.2; Pausanias 2.16.1.
[75] Autochthonous: Hesiod fr. 160 Merkelbach/West. Niobe: Akousilaos *FGrH* 2.25. Triopas: Scholiast to Euripides, *Orestes* 932. Phoroneus: Hellanikos *FGrH* 4.36. Argos: Hyginus, *Fabulae* 124. Inakhos: Scholiast to Apollonios Rhodios 1.580.

80

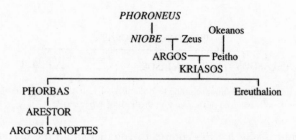

6 The stemma of the Inakhids according to Pherekydes of Athens (capitals refer to more significant figures, italics to restorations on the basis of other texts).

born of the earth, and sometimes as the son of Inakhos, Agenor or Arestor.[76] Finally, Io is sometimes the daughter of a figure who is known variously as Peiras, Peirasos or Peiren,[77] but may also be the daughter of Inakhos or Iasos.[78] In the *Catalogue of women*, the Scholiast and Pseudo-Apollodoros, Io is the ancestress of Danaos, the founder of the succeeding dynasty, though other versions (notably Pausanias) seem to imply a caesura between the Inakhids and the Danaids.

By contrast, the various versions of the Danaid genealogy, including the Proitids and Perseids, are relatively uniform. Such differences as there are rarely alter the basic structure, and typically concern external, matrilineal ancestors: for instance, Alektryon's wife is his niece, Anaxo, in Pseudo-Apollodoros, whereas she is Pelops' daughter Eurydike in Diodoros and Lysidike in Plutarch.[79] In accounting for this uniformity, we may hypothesise that the Danaid genealogy was recited far more frequently than that of the Inakhids, and that it occupied a more central position in the discourse of identity with the result that transformations did not occur lightly. It is also legitimate to wonder how great a role public monumentalisation may have played in the preserved uniformity of the Danaid genealogy. In the mid-fifth century, supposedly after the Battle of Oinoe, the Argives dedicated at Delphi two statue groups of the descendants of Megapenthes, Melampous and Bias who had marched against Thebes.[80] Also in the fifth century, a similar statue group was erected in the *agora* at Argos.[81] A more explicit genealogical succession was dedi-

---

[76] Earth-born: Aiskhylos, *Prometheus* 567, 677; *Suppliants* 305; Akousilaos *FGrH* 2.27. Inakhos: Asklepiades of Tragilos *FGrH* 12.16. Agenor: Pseudo-Apollodoros, *Bibliotheka* 2.1.2. Arestor: Pherekydes *FGrH* 3.67.

[77] Hesiod fr. 124 Merkelbach/West; Akousilaos *FGrH* 2.26. Peiras, Peirasos and Peiren all seem to indicate the same figure: see West 1985, 77. For the political uses of Io's paternity, see Hall 1995b, 609–10.

[78] Inakhos: Aiskhylos, *Prometheus* 589–90; Herodotos 1.1.3; Bakkhylides fr. 18 Jebb. Iasos: Scholiast to Euripides, *Orestes* 932; Pseudo-Apollodoros 2.1.3; Pausanias 2.16.1. The paternity of Io is analysed in greater depth below.

[79] Pseudo-Apollodoros, *Bibliotheka* 2.4.5; Diodoros 4.9.1; Plutarch, *Life of Theseus* 7.1.

[80] Pausanias 10.10.3–4. See also Bourguet 1929, 90; Bommelaer and Laroche 1991, 112–14; Bommelaer 1992. The second group, however, is dated to the third century BC by Amandry (1980, 234).   [81] Pausanias 2.20.5.

INAKHOS
|
PHORONEUS/TRIOPAS

PELASGOS   IASOS   AGENOR

7 The stemma of the Inakhids according to Hellanikos of Lesbos (capitals refer to more significant figures, italics to restorations on the basis of other texts).

cated at Delphi in the fourth century: to commemorate the alliance that the Argives forged with Epameinondas of Thebes to liberate the Messenians, the Argives dedicated a group of ten statues, facing the earlier series across the Sacred Way, which represented the royal line from Danaos, through Hypermestra, Lynkeus, Abas, Akrisios, Danae, Perseus, Alektryon and Alkmene to Herakles.[82] The monumental investiture of the Danaid/Perseid genealogy, especially in the extra-local and panhellenic domain of Delphi, must have acted as an effective dam on the fluid and dynamic properties that oral myths can often exhibit.

It may, at first sight, appear a little surprising that there is almost a complete lack of rapport between the Argolic genealogies and the ethnographic traditions of the Argolid (see above), let alone the Hellenic genealogy (see chapter 3). The only real exception to this is Ion's paternity of Pitureus, the last pre-Dorian king of Epidauros.[83] Aiolos, who is not normally associated with the Argolid, makes a surprising (though only implicit) entrance into the Argive genealogies through his great-grandson, Melampous,[84] while the appearance of Iasos, the father of Io, has tempted some to see an adjective which should originally mean 'Ionian' – either from *Ἰασονες [*Iasones*] > *ΙαϜονες [*Iawones*] > *Ἰαονες [*Iaones*] > Ἰῶνες [*Iones*], or from the attested adjective Ἰάς – Ἰάδος [*Ias – Iados*].[85] It has already been noted, however, that while the literary tradition refers to Ionians in the eastern Argolid, they do not seem to be an ethnographic feature of the Argive plain.

In fact, the reasons why the Argive genealogies and the Hellenic genealogy seem almost incommensurable have already been anticipated. In chapter 3, it was argued that the Hellenic genealogy was the product of an aggregative process of ethnic integration which only took its final form in the middle of the sixth century. While the originally independent myth of the Herakleidai bears the strong imprint of Argolic invention, the strictly 'Dorian' component of the genealogy was almost certainly the result of diffusion from another single centre of origin – probably Sparta. This entails the strong likelihood that the Argolid already had a developed mythical tradition of its origins which eventually had to be accommodated within the developed Hellenic genealogy. The earliest indication of this accommodation may be the hypothesised marriage between Doros and a daughter of Phoroneus in the *Catalogue of women* – a union which bears all the hallmarks of a rather slap-

---

[82] Pausanias 10.10.5. See Bourguet 1929, 41–54; Pouilloux and Roux 1963, 46–51; Salviat 1965; Bommelaer 1984; Bommelaer and Laroche 1991, 114–15.   [83] Pausanias 2.26.1.
[84] See Jost 1992, 173.   [85] Wathelet 1992, 104; Sakellariou 1977, 86.

82

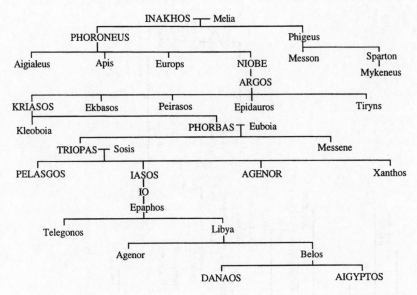

8 The stemma of the Inakhids according to the Scholiast to Euripides, *Orestes* (capitals refer to more significant figures).

dash act of *bricolage*, and which West attributes to a final sixth-century stage in the development of the *Catalogue*.[86] A similarly clumsy attempt at reconciling the two genealogies is found in Pausanias' identification of the Danaids with the Akhaians – achieved through having Akhaios' sons, Arkhandros and Arkhiteles, arrive in Argos and marry two daughters of Danaos.[87]

Decoding the genealogical grammar

It was observed in chapter 3 that, despite criticism from symbolists, functionalists and structuralists alike, a good many approaches to Greek myths are still informed by historical positivism. According to this viewpoint, myths are treated as the refracted memory of 'real' historical events. Thus, Martin Bernal attempts to link the story of Danaos' arrival at Argos from Egypt to a Hyksos invasion of Mainland Greece in the eighteenth century BC, despite the fact that the *Catalogue of women* traces Danaos' ancestry back to the former Inakhid dynasty.[88] Evangelia Protonotariou-Deïlaki argues for an essential continuity in the material culture of Argos from the Early Helladic through to the Hellenistic period, with the exception of a cultural intermission in the Late Helladic: in her opinion, the myths which

[86] Hesiod fr. 10(b) Merkelbach/West. See West 1985, 143.
[87] Pausanias 7.1.7. Cf. Herodotos 2.98.2. See above.
[88] Bernal 1987; 1991. For criticisms of Bernal's approach to myth: Hall 1990, 251; E. Hall 1992.

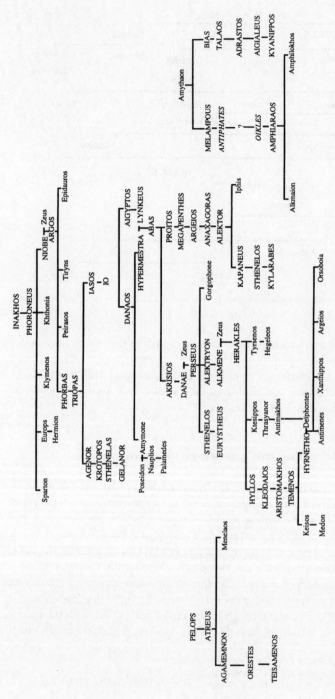

9 The Argive genealogies according to Pausanias (capitals refer to more significant figures, italics to restorations on the basis of other texts).

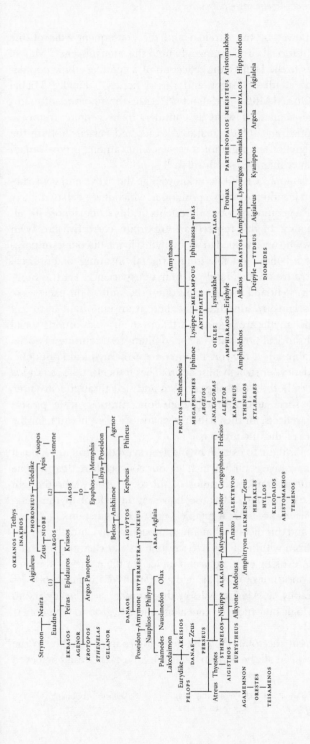

10 The Argive genealogies according to Pseudo-Apollodoros (capitals refer to more significant figures, italics to restorations on the basis of other texts).

tell of the seizure of power by the Atreidai and the consequent exile of the Herakleidai reflect the historical circumstances behind this intermission.[89] Marcel Piérart sees in references to the Danaoi the reflection of a genuine ethnic population which lived to the south of Argos and raised horses.[90] Finally, Michel Sakellariou – like Karl Otfried Müller (see chapter 1) – uses the *distribution* of mythical themes as the trace-element of what he considers to be genuine historical migrations: thus, the appearance of the names Akrisios and Perseus in both the Argolid and Thessaly signifies an origin for these accounts among proto-Danaoi living in Thessaly who later migrated southwards.[91]

The extreme historicist approach fails to acknowledge the active and constructive nature of myth; by relegating myth to a position in which it is a debased, hazy and passive reflection of a genuine history, proponents of this school ignore its relative autonomy and vitality. In this respect, an important corrective has been effected by structuralists, who have wished to see in myth a living discourse, or paralanguage, which, far from being reducible to an original 'meaning' or historical event, acts as a metanarrative on the totality of human experience. Yet two modifications to this view are essential. Firstly, one need not succumb to the excesses of historicist searches for origins by admitting that there is an important historical dimension to myths. Since myths are cognitive artefacts in currency among social groups, the passage of historical time with its concomitant restructuring of social relationships will inevitably affect the form and content of mythical episodes.[92] Secondly, there is a tendency for structuralist approaches to neglect the *sociological contexts* of myths. In short, both historical positivism and structuralism leave little room for knowledgeable social actors through their concentration on the passive character of myth which reflects, for the former, 'real' historical events and, for the latter, the deep structures of the unconscious.

It is perfectly possible for there to exist in myths deep symbolic structures, but it is neither these nor the narrative content which are our concern here. Instead, the present objective is to attempt an identification of the social groups who thought themselves through these genealogies. Because, however, the field of myth is relatively autonomous, it is necessary to treat mythical episodes as phenomena rather than as epiphenomena, and this dictates that any approach should initially be conducted independently 'from within'. That is to say, one should elicit the meaning of the genealogies not by evoking etymological parallels for the names of the protagonists, as Sakellariou does, nor by comparing the locations of mythical episodes with Mycenaean geography, as Martin Nilsson did;[93] rather, it is necessary to understand the internal logic on which the genealogies seek to ground their coherence.

The first step is to treat the totality of the genealogies from Inakhos to the Herakleidai as they appear in all the versions available to us. The result achieved

---

[89] Protonotariou-Deïlaki 1982, 45–47.   [90] Piérart 1992, 125.   [91] Sakellariou 1980, 207.
[92] Bohannan 1952; Burkert 1979, 27.   [93] E.g. Nilsson 1972.

is, of course, somewhat artificial, since in normal social and historical conditions genealogies 'are only rarely expressed as a whole'.[94] It is, however, a vital prerequisite which then allows us to identify the elements of the genealogical syntax, and thus to isolate 'genealogemes' – that is, the basic and irreducible 'building-blocks' of the genealogies, whose generational depth may vary. Faced with both the totality, or system, of the genealogies and the individual genealogemes, one is able to discern how the latter are hierarchically clustered to constitute the former. Yet within the overall system one will also be able to recognise 'fracture points' – that is, nodes which contradict or challenge the internal logic. Sometimes these fracture points will occur *between* variant versions and reflect both authorial and sociopolitical intention, but sometimes they will arise *within* individual accounts which may betray originally diverse social applications.

In the Argive genealogies, one can recognise the following categories of syntactic elements, or common motifs: culture heroes; toponyms; theogeniture; the transition from agnatic to uterine descent; uxorilocality; and conjunctive names. Culture heroes are mythological figures who are to a certain extent treated as patrons of a particular town or region; it is for this reason that more developed tales tend to become attached to them. There are two basic types: primeval and dynastic. The primeval type may be eponymous (Pelasgos and Dryops) or not (Phoroneus and Oros), but his role is that of the 'civiliser' of the earliest humans. So, for instance, Pelasgos initiates humans into the secret of making bread,[95] while Phoroneus is the first to unite humans into communities.[96] Primeval culture heroes typically belong to the upper, 'cosmogonic' reaches of a genealogy,[97] and will normally be either autochthonous like Pelasgos,[98] or the sons of rivers (Phoroneus, for instance, is the son of the Inakhos, while Dryops is the son of either the Sperkheios or the Peneios).[99]

The dynastic type of culture hero is represented by figures such as Danaos at Argos, Perseus at Mykenai, Herakles at Tiryns and Klymenos at Hermione. A distinctive characteristic is the fact that dynastic culture heroes invariably arrive or return from outside the locality to which they come to be attached: Danaos arrives from Egypt, Perseus from Seriphos, Herakles from Thebes and Klymenos from Argos. The phenomenon is not restricted to the Argolid: Kadmos arrives in Thebes from Phoenicia and Theseus arrives at Athens from Troizen. The historicist school, however, is quite wrong in imagining that these mythical arrivals reflect prehistoric migrations or even deep-rooted links between the two localities concerned. It is not the *place of departure* which is as important as the *fact of arrival*, and this is because the Greeks had great difficulties in 'thinking their origins'. In tracing back genealogies from child to parent, there was a danger of an infinite regress to which two solutions were possible – either an autochthonous *Urvater*, or the arrival of a *Stammvater*

---

[94] Vansina 1985, 182.   [95] Scholiast to Euripides, *Orestes* 932.   [96] Pausanias 2.15.5.
[97] Cf. Calame 1987; Malkin 1994, 19–22.   [98] Hesiod fr. 160 Merkelbach/West.
[99] Pherekydes *FGrH* 2.8.

whose ancestry could be ignored since it had no specifically local significance. In most cases the *Stammvater* replaces the lineage descended from the autochthon – the notable exception is Athens (see chapter 3). The arrival of a dynastic culture hero can regularly be viewed as the initiation of a new genealogeme.

Toponymic heroes generally appear in the earlier, cosmogonic phases of genealogies. There are two exceptions: Hermione, daughter of Menelaos and Helen, and Nauplios, grandson of Danaos, son of Poseidon and father of Palamedes. However, the genealogy of Nauplia has been severely truncated, since Nauplios should by rights belong to cosmogony while his son Palamedes should be a contemporary of Agamemnon; it is probably for this reason that Strabo considered the myth to be manufactured.[100] The reason why toponyms are normally consigned to a stage prior to the arrival of the dynastic culture hero is to provide an existing community into which the culture hero may insert himself. Sometimes the toponymic hero founds the city (Epidauros, Tiryns, Mykene(us), Hermion), while at other times he simply gives his name to a pre-existing community: Argos gives his name to the city of Phoroneus, while Troizen's name is given to the cities of Hypereia and Antheia by his brother Pittheus.[101]

The function of the toponymic heroes is clearly to act as linchpins, pegging the genealogies to their consumer cities. They do not, however, appear to be organically or even originally linked with the structure of the genealogy for two reasons. Firstly, there is a far greater variability surrounding their positioning within the genealogy than is the case for non-toponymic heroes: Mykene(us) can be the daughter of Inakhos or the son of Sparton,[102] while Epidauros is in all Argive versions the son of Argos, but in the Epidaurian version the son of Apollo, and in the Elean version the son of Pelops.[103] Secondly, the significance of toponymic heroes seems to be blunted somewhat by their appearance side-by-side with non-toponymic siblings: Phorbas, Ekbasos, Kriasos, Iasos and Peirasos are all named as brothers of Tiryns and Epidauros. Since, however, 'political' history only begins properly with the arrival of the dynastic culture hero, it is a little difficult to maintain that the toponyms express political hierarchies or territorial claims. They may, instead, be a way of comprehending the relative antiquity of a city. In this case, Argos is usually ceded a greater antiquity than Epidauros or Tiryns, although Mykenai can be conceived of as roughly contemporary (Scholiast to Euripides, Pausanias) or even older (Pseudo-Hesiod) than Argos.

At certain points within the genealogies, theogeniture is attested – that is, heroes may have one divine parent instead of two human ones. Such is the case with Argos, son of Niobe and Zeus; Epaphos, son of Io and Zeus; Agenor and Belos, sons of Libya and Poseidon; Nauplios, son of Amymone and Poseidon; Perseus, son of Danae and Zeus; and Herakles, son of Alkmene and Zeus. The conjuncture of single mother and semi-divine child can be taken as signifying a new

---

[100] Strabo 8.6.2. [101] Pausanias 2.30.7–8.
[102] Inakhos: Hesiod fr. 246 Merkelbach/West. Sparton: Akousilaos *FGrH* 2.24; Pausanias 2.16.4; Scholiast to Euripides, *Orestes* 1246. [103] Pausanias 2.26.2.

genealogeme. In the case of Herakles and Perseus, this feature coincides with that of the culture hero.

It was the custom in the majority of Greek cities to trace descent and inheritance through the male ('agnatic') line, and this is generally the rule in the genealogies. At certain points, however, the transmission of hereditary rights passes aberrantly through the female ('uterine') line: for instance, Niobe-Argos; Io-Epaphos; Libya-Agenor and Belos; Hypermestra-Abas; Danae-Perseus; Lysippe-Antiphates; Iphianassa-Talaos; and Deipyle-Diomedes. The coincidence between this transition to uterine descent and theogeniture is fairly high; for this reason, this feature can likewise be said to constitute a new genealogeme. A similar fracture point can be observed when Eurystheus, left heirless, entrusts his kingdom to his matrilineal affines, the Pelopidai. Though this is not strictly a uterine succession, it fulfils a similar function.

As in the case of agnatic descent, the general rule in Greece was one of virilocality – that is, the bride moves to the groom's household upon marriage. The Argive genealogies, however, present some instances of uxorilocality: notably, Lynkeus' marriage to Danaos' daughter Hypermestra; the marriage of Melampous and Bias to Proitos' daughters, Lysippe and Iphianassa respectively; and Tydeus' marriage to Deipyle, daughter of Adrastos. These again signify new genealogemes, but this time the new genealogeme is not attached vertically through descent, but grafted on horizontally through marriage.

Finally, there are several appearances of very shallow figures to whom virtually no tales are attached, and whose name is not infrequently an adjective signalling a warrior virtue. Such is the anonymity of these figures that their names may recur several times within genealogies. For example, Agenor ('manly/heroic') appears both as the son of Libya and Poseidon and as the son of either Phoroneus, Triopas or Ekbasos. Sthenelas/Sthenelos ('strong') makes three appearances: once as the son of Krotopos and father of Gelanor; once as the son of Perseus and father of Eurystheus; and once as the son of Kapaneus and father of Kylarabes (this last Sthenelos is one of the three leaders of the Argive contingent in the *Catalogue of ships*).[104] Similar examples may include Phorbas ('nourishing'), Alkaios ('mighty'), Argeios ('Argive'), Kapaneus ('charioteer') and Triopas ('thrice-sighted').[105] These characters are 'fillers' and are normally encountered sandwiched between better-known personages; they rarely occur at the beginning or end of any genealogeme.

Staking the Heraklid claim

The Pelopid family is one with which a rich store of mythology is associated: Pelops and the chariot race with Oinomaos to win the hand of Hippodameia; Atreus' preparation of a cannibalistic feast for his brother Thyestes; Menelaos' loss of his

[104] Homer, *Iliad* 2.564.
[105] The name Triopas also crops up in Messenia and Thessaly: Calame 1987, 160.

wife, Helen, to Paris; Agamemnon's sacrifice of his daughter Iphigeneia; the expedition against Troy; Klytaimnestra's adulterous relationship with Aigisthos and their murder of Agamemnon; Orestes' vengeance on Klytaimnestra and Aigisthos; and the defeat of Teisamenos by the Dorians and the Herakleidai. It will no doubt, then, seem surprising that the Pelopid family was not originally associated with the Argive plain.

In the Homeric epics, Agamemnon is located at 'well-built Mykenai', though he also holds sway over 'many islands and all of Argos';[106] the *Catalogue of women* describes him as ruling over 'Argos of the broad expanse'.[107] Wathelet has shown how the word 'Argos' may at different times designate the town, the Argive plain, the Peloponnese or the whole of Greece.[108] The reference in Book 2 of the *Iliad* may signify either the Argive plain or the Peloponnese rather than simply Argos itself, but in either case *it cannot exclude the city of Argos*. Yet a scenario in which Argos is under the dominion of Agamemnon immediately clashes with the developed myth in which Argos was ruled by the descendants of Melampous and Bias (see below). It also results in the unconvincing division of territory in the *Catalogue of ships*, whereby the greater part of the Argolid (Argos, Tiryns, Hermione, Asine, Troizen, Eïonai, Epidauros, Aigina and Mases) falls to Diomedes, Sthenelos and Euryalos, while Agamemnon is left with Mykenai.[109] To rehabilitate Agamemnon's status, he is ceded Korinthia and the cities of Korinth, Kleonai and Sikyon – a deft sleight of hand which then requires Bellerophon (a civic hero in Korinth during the historical period) to be consigned to the obscure village of Ephyre.[110] In fact, the Pelopid stemma bears all the hallmarks of having been 'grafted on' to the Argive genealogies.

It has already been observed that fracture points may be signalled by the shift of descent through matrilineal affines. At a narrative level, the tradition stated that upon embarking on his expedition against the Herakleidai, Eurystheus, the Perseid ruler of Mykenai, entrusted his kingdom to his maternal uncle, Atreus. After Eurystheus' death in Attika, Atreus assumed full power and bequeathed the kingdom to his son Agamemnon.[111] The Pelopid stemma, however, did not graft easily onto the Perseid one. The mechanism adopted to allow Perseid domination to pass to the Pelopidai (through Nikippe, the mother of Eurystheus and daughter of Pelops) dictated that Agamemnon and Menelaos should belong to the same generation as Eurystheus and Herakles; indeed, according to the *Iliad*, Hera contrived to have Eurystheus born only a few months before Herakles.[112] Yet Herakles is supposed to have launched his own expedition against Troy *one generation before* the campaign of Agamemnon,[113] and Eurystheus is supposed to have lived *three*

---

[106] Homer, *Iliad* 2.108.   [107] Hesiod fr. 195 Merkelbach/West.   [108] Wathelet 1992.
[109] Homer, *Iliad* 2.559–68, 569–80.
[110] Homer, *Iliad* 6.152. For Bellerophon's associations with Korinth: Nilsson 1972, 51; Musti and Torelli 1986, 211. For Eumelos' epic elevation of Ephyre: Huxley 1969, 61; De Fidio 1992.
[111] Thoukydides 1.9.2; Diodoros 4.58.2.   [112] Homer, *Iliad* 19.114–24.
[113] Pseudo-Apollodoros, *Bibliotheka* 2.6.4.

90

generations prior to the Trojan War.[114] A couple of 'elastoplast' solutions were adopted. *The Catalogue of women*, followed by Aiskhylos, introduced the figure of Pleisthenes as the son of Atreus and father of Agamemnon and Menelaos, thus postposing the latter by one generation.[115] The *Epitome* to Pseudo-Apollodoros' *Bibliotheka* ignored the marital links and had Atreus and Thyestes arrive in a void.[116]

The Pelopid stemma also shows itself to be of a qualitatively different nature to the Perseid genealogy by its repeated motif of uxorilocality. This commences with Pelops himself, who arrives from Asia Minor to Pisa in Elis where he marries Hippodameia. It is repeated when Menelaos moves to Sparta upon marrying Helen, the daughter of the Spartan king Tyndareos; when Aigisthos arrives at Mykenai to pursue his adulterous relationship with Klytaimnestra; and when Orestes' marriage to Hermione, the daughter of Menelaos and Helen, brings him the throne of Sparta.[117]

The numerous fracture points which occur between the Pelopid and Perseid stemmata suggest the development of independent groups of genealogemes. Furthermore, the contradictions generated by attempting to accommodate both within the Homeric account of the mythical geography of the Argolid give us strong reasons for considering the initial construction of the Pelopid genealogy to have taken place in a context outside the Argolid. Wilamowitz-Moellendorff suggested that the Pelopid mythology originated in Asia Minor,[118] and support for such a view has sometimes been sought in the supposed existence of cults to Agamemnon at Klazomenai and Smyrna, the arrival of Pelops in Greece from Anatolia and the apparent existence of Agamemnon's surviving family on Lesbos and at Kyme.[119] However, as we have seen, the dynastic culture hero should normally arrive from outside the territory to which he lays claim, so his point of departure need carry no reference to the diffusion of the myth. Pelops should almost certainly be seen as a hero indigenous to the Peloponnese, where the vast majority of his activities are localised.[120]

That said, if it is necessary to locate the mythical development of Agamemnon anywhere, then the best candidate would be Lakonia. Although Homer generally situates Agamemnon at Mykenai, a passage from the *Odyssey* which describes him as running into a storm off Cape Malea has suggested to several commentators the existence of an alternative early tradition whereby, on his return from Troy, Agamemnon makes not for the Argolid but Lakonia.[121] Such an earlier tradition would certainly explain why it is that, in a vain attempt to appease Akhilleus' wrath,

---

[114] Fossey 1980, 61.

[115] Hesiod fr. 194 Merkelbach West; Aiskhylos, *Agamemnon* 1569, 1602. Cf. Ibykos fr. 282.21–22.

[116] Pseudo-Apollodoros, *Epitome* 2.11. See Fossey 1980, 62.   [117] Pausanias 2.18.5–6.

[118] Cited in Nilsson 1972, 48 and followed by West 1985, 159.

[119] Pausanias 7.5.11; Thoukydides 1.9.2; Cf. Herodotos 7.11.4. See, however, Nilsson 1972, 47–48.

[120] Nilsson 1972, 44; Herrmann 1980, 61.

[121] Homer, *Odyssey* 4.514–18. Heubeck, West and Hainsworth (1988, 224–25) suspect the passage of being an interpolation, but Podlecki (1971, 315) defends the authenticity of the tradition.

Agamemnon is able to offer him seven cities between Lakonia and Messenia,[122] and it may also account for the rather anomalous situation in the *Catalogue of women* where Agamemnon, rather than Menelaos, is named among those seeking the hand of Helen as some sort of 'proxy suitor' for his brother.[123]

The sixth-century poets Stesikhoros and Simonides had apparently located Agamemnon's palace at Sparta, and Pindar has Agamemnon die at Amyklai while his son Orestes is a Lakonian by birth.[124] Pausanias (who follows the Homeric location) refuses to accept the local Lakonian tradition that Agamemnon's tomb was situated at Amyklai,[125] though in fact excavations at Agia Paraskevi near Amyklai have brought to light a shrine whose inscribed dedications identify it as that of Agamemnon and Alexandra (Kassandra). Activity is first attested at the sanctuary in the Late Geometric period and continues through to Hellenistic times, while the earliest dedications to Agamemnon date to the last quarter of the sixth century (thus predating by more than two centuries the earliest inscribed dedications to Agamemnon at the so-called 'Agamemnoneion' near Mykenai).[126]

Agamemnon's rootedness in Sparta would also explain an incident described by Herodotos. Immediately prior to the Persian invasion of Greece, the Spartans sent an embassy to Gelon, the tyrant of Syracuse, seeking assistance. Gelon accepted, but only on the condition that he would assume the supreme command of the Greek defence, to which the Spartan envoy Syagros exclaimed, 'The Pelopid Agamemnon would wail greatly if he learned that the Spartans had been robbed of hegemony by Gelon and the Syracusans.'[127] Finally, the theme of the two brothers Agamemnon and Menelaos launching an expedition to rescue Helen is remarkably similar to the Lakonian myth of the abduction of Helen by Theseus and her rescue by her brothers, the Dioskouroi, first attested in the *Iliou Persis*.[128] Both myths conform to the same structure: the hostess is abducted by the guest and rescued by her brothers (-in-law).[129]

It would appear, then, that Agamemnon and his family are a relatively late addition to Argive mythology.[130] Their introduction probably predates the mid-seventh century when scenes connected with Agamemnon, Klytaimnestra and Orestes appear on a bronze revetment found at a small roadside shrine close to the famous

---

[122] Homer, *Iliad* 9.149–53.   [123] Hesiod fr. 197 Merkelbach/West.

[124] Stesikhoros fr. 39 Page; Scholiast to Euripides, *Orestes* 46; Pindar, *Pythian Odes* 11.24, 47; *Nemean Odes* 11.44. See West 1969, 148–49 and, for a general discussion, Malkin 1994, 31–32.

[125] Pausanias 3.19.6.

[126] Literary references to the cult of Agamemnon (apparently associated with Zeus) and Alexandra: Pausanias 3.19.6; Clement of Alexandria, *Protrepticus* 32; Scholiast to Lykophron 1123, 1369. See Wide 1893, 333–38. A long inscription on a relief-stele of the second or first centuries BC identifies the remains at Agia Paraskevi as the sanctuary of Alexandra: Löschcke 1878. For reports of the excavations at Agia Paraskevi: Christou 1956; 1960; 1961. The earliest inscriptions to Agamemnon and Alexandra are dated to ca. 525 BC by Johnston (in Jeffery 1990, 447). For a general discussion: Hooker 1980, 66–68. I have expressed elsewhere my doubts about the earlier identification of the Khaos shrine at Mykenai as the 'Agamemnoneion': Hall 1995b, 601–03. See also below.   [127] Herodotos 7.159.   [128] *Iliou Persis* fr. 3 Allen.   [129] Dowden 1992, 151.

[130] West 1985, 159; Piérart 1992, 131.

sanctuary of Hera at Prosymna.[131] If Martin West is correct to posit a date after 700 BC,[132] then it is legitimate to wonder whether the development of the Pelopid genealogy in the Argolid was prompted by the circulation of the Homeric epic rather than vice versa. Clearly, it was Mykenai that benefited from the Homeric promotion of Agamemnon, though his importance never quite supplanted that of Perseus: while the latter was the recipient of a hero cult by at least the third quarter of the sixth century, Agamemnon had to wait until the resettlement of Mykenai in the Hellenistic period.[133]

Unencumbered by the presence of the Pelopids, we can now focus on the central constitutive myth of the Argive plain which served to express competing claims and counterclaims – namely, the division of the plain between Akrisios and Proitos. The fullest accounts are found in Pseudo-Apollodoros and Pausanias, but the episode is also treated in Akousilaos and the *Catalogue of women*.[134] According to the common version, the two sons of Abas, Akrisios and Proitos, fell out with each other. Akrisios remained in the town of Argos, while Proitos held 'the Heraion, Midea, Tiryns and the coastal parts of the Argive plain' (Pseudo-Apollodoros adds the detail that Proitos was originally exiled to Lykia, but was forcibly established at Tiryns through the help of his Lykian father-in-law).[135]

Akrisios, who feared an oracle in which he was warned of his murder at the hands of his grandson, confined his daughter Danae within a bronze chamber to prevent her from having any children. Zeus, however, seduced her in the form of a shower of gold and she gave birth to Perseus. Upon learning of the birth of the child, Akrisios had both Danae and Perseus locked in a wooden chest which was set afloat and arrived on the Kykladic island of Seriphos. After a series of episodes (including the beheading of the gorgon Medousa and the rescue of Andromeda) Perseus returned to the mainland to seek reconciliation with his grandfather, Akrisios, but accidentally killed him with the throw of a discus in the course of some funeral games. In atonement, Perseus exchanged his dominion for that of Proitos' son Megapenthes (technically, his mother's first cousin). From this time on, his descendants, who included Eurystheus and Herakles, were thus located in the towns on the eastern side of the plain, and it is on the basis of this lineage that the Herakleidai claimed the right to their ancestral land.

Megapenthes' lineage did not, however, rule the newly gained kingdom of Argos alone. According to Pseudo-Apollodoros, Akousilaos and the *Catalogue of women*, the daughters of Proitos were driven mad (in some versions, they are transferred into cows like Io) and were only cured after Megapenthes ceded two-thirds of his kingdom to the mythical healer Melampous and his brother Bias.[136] Pausanias has a similar version, but it takes place two generations later during the

---

[131] Blegen 1939, 415–17; Kunze 1950, 167; Richter 1949, 21.   [132] West 1985, 159–60.
[133] For the cult of Perseus: *IG* 4.493. See Jameson 1990.
[134] Pseudo-Apollodoros, *Bibliotheka* 2.2; Pausanias 2.16.2–3; 2.18.4; Akousilaos *FGrH* 2.28; Hesiod frs. 129, 135 Merkelbach/West.   [135] Pausanias 2.16.2; Pseudo-Apollodoros, *Bibliotheka* 2.2.1.
[136] Pseudo-Apollodoros, *Bibliotheka* 2.2.2; Akousilaos *FGrH* 2.28; Hesiod frs. 37, 131.

reign of Anaxagoras, and concerns not the daughters of Proitos but the women of Argos generally.[137] This variant can be traced back to Herodotos, and is probably a rationalisation to avoid complicating the simple and direct exchange of kingdoms between Perseus and Megapenthes.[138] It is from Megapenthes, Melampous and Bias that the Argive heroes who marched against Thebes were descended.

There are two features of these genealogies which allow us to identify the fracture points. The motif of territory being divided up among sons is hardly uncommon: one might point to the tripartite division of the Peloponnese which assigned the Argolid, Lakonia and Messenia to the descendants of Herakles, the division of Troizenia between Hyperes and Anthas, or the division of the Argive *khora* between Pelasgos and Iasos in Hellanikos' account.[139] By dividing Abas' kingdom between his two heirs, Akrisios and Proitos, the Argive myth is in any case merely conforming to the Greek norm of equal inheritance rather than a hereditary principle based on primogeniture. Yet some of the ancient commentators knew of versions of the myth in which Akrisios and Proitos were not the only sons of Abas: the Scholiast to Euripides' *Hekabe*, 125 adds the name of Khalkodon. Nor is Abas' positioning within the genealogy totally secure, since he is normally encountered as either an eponym for the Abantes of Euboia, or as a toponymic hero for Abai in Phokis.[140] In fact, Pherekydes of Athens makes Proitos the son not of Abas but of Thersandros,[141] while there is a further version in which Akrisios is not the brother of Proitos but his son.[142] The second feature that should alert our suspicions is the exchange of kingdoms. If the function of the Abas-Akrisios-Proitos triad is to establish a mythologically justified division into two kingdoms, why is it then necessary, in the succeeding generation, to reverse the assigned distributions? Why is Proitos not initially assigned Argos and Akrisios Mykenai, Tiryns and Midea?

The problem is resolved if we view the two stemmata of Akrisios and Proitos not as *complementary* but as *competing* genealogies, in which each protagonist is assigned the whole of the Argive plain to rule rather than just half of it. Reminiscences of such a scenario can occasionally be glimpsed in the tradition. Although the conjunction of Proitos with Argos in the *Catalogue of women* may refer to the geographical region where Proitos lives (i.e. the Argive plain) rather than the precise extent of his dominion,[143] the *Iliad* states that Proitos ruled over the Argives rather than simply the Tirynthians, even though the Proitidai are supposed to have assumed sovereignty over Argos only in the generation succeeding Proitos.[144]

---

[137] Pausanias 2.18.4. Cf. Diodoros 4.68.4; Pseudo-Apollodoros, *Bibliotheka* 1.9.12.

[138] Herodotos 9.34.

[139] Peloponnese: Pindar, *Pythian Odes* 5.70; Isokrates, *Arkhidamos* 16–21; Plato, *Laws* 3.683c-d; Pausanias 4.3.4–5; Pseudo-Apollodoros, *Bibliotheka* 2.8.4. Troizen: Pausanias 2.30.8. Argive *khora*: Hellanikos *FGrH* 4.36.

[140] Abantes: Hesiod frs. 204, 296 Merkelbach/West; Pindar, *Pythian Odes* 8.73; Eustathius' commentary to *Iliad* 2.536. Abai: Pausanias 10.35.1.   [141] Pherekydes *FGrH* 3.170b.

[142] Kastor *FGrH* 250.3; Clement of Alexandria, *Stromateis* 1.103; Tatian, *Oratio ad Graecos* 39.1; Scholiast to Aiskhylos, *Prometheus* 774.   [143] Hesiod fr. 37 Merkelbach/West.

[144] Homer, *Iliad* 6.157–59. Cf. Pindar, *Nemean Odes* 10.77.

Similarly, Eurystheus, who in the developed genealogies ruled over Mykenai, Tiryns and Midea, is described as a worthy lord over the Argives in the epic – as we have seen, it is Eurystheus' panargolic dominion that the Homeric Agamemnon is to inherit.[145] Furthermore, it can hardly be coincidental that the mythical episodes of Perseus and Medousa and of Bellerophon and Khimaira – associated with the lineages of Akrisios and Proitos respectively – look suspiciously like transformations of the same structural prototype: the hero (Perseus, Bellerophon) falls foul of the aged king (Akrisios, Proitos), who fears – totally without justification – that the hero is to usurp his throne through a sexual misdemeanor on the part of the queen (Danae, Stheneboia). The hero is therefore exiled (Seriphos, Lykia), where a foreign king (Polydektes, Iobates) orders him to kill a fantastic monster (Medousa, Khimaira).[146]

The supposition that the Perseid and Proitid genealogies are competing variants would also explain why Perseids and Proitids appear as alternative cult founders: the Nemean Games were believed to have been instituted by *either* the Perseid Herakles *or* the Proitid Adrastos,[147] while Herakles and the Proitid Melampous fulfil a similar function in the foundation myths pertaining to the Dryopes of Asine and the cult there of Apollo Pythaeus.[148] In addition, it may not be accidental that it was the Heraklid descendants of Perseus who helped defend the city of Thebes against the Proitid 'epigonoi'. The solution of consigning each of the competing variants to opposite sides of the plain had clearly suggested itself already by the time of the *Catalogue of women* in the sixth century, but one problem remained. Although Perseus and Herakles were at home in the communities of the eastern plain, Proitos had already become indelibly attached to Tiryns. The course of action adopted was to organise an exchange of kingdoms in the generation *after* Proitos, so that both Proitos and the Perseids could be accommodated east of the river Inakhos.

Having identified the fracture points and contradictions *between* the two competing genealogies, it is now useful to examine each in turn to discern its inner, essential characteristics. The Perseid stemma witnesses two instances of theogeniture (both Perseus and Herakles are sons of Zeus by Danae and Alkmene respectively) and this theogeniture coincides with the fact that the two semi-divine children are fully fledged culture heroes: Perseus at Mykenai, Herakles at Tiryns.

It is because Perseus and Herakles are culture heroes that the vast majority of personages within the Perseid genealogy are firmly localised in the towns on the eastern side of the Argive plain. It is true that most of the adventures of Perseus take place on Seriphos, where in Pausanias' time there existed the major shrine to the hero,[149] but this in no way compromises the rootedness of Perseus at Mykenai.

---

[145] Homer, *Iliad* 19.122–24. [146] See Dowden 1992, 141–43.
[147] See, however, Doffey 1992 who argues that the Heraklean version is syncretic.
[148] Billot 1989–90, 47; Jost 1992, 181.
[149] Pausanias 2.18.1. In any case, Mykenai had already been abandoned by the time of Pausanias' visit there.

After all, many of the exploits of the Athenian hero Theseus took place at Troizen, while Korinth's hero Bellerophon pursued his quests in Anatolia. It is the very fact that fantastic quests have to be situated in the margins of mythological space that actually reinforces the centrality of Mykenai in the Perseus cycle. Indeed, if Evangelia Protonotariou-Deïlaki is right to identify as Perseus a figure carrying a knife and an animal's head which is depicted on a stele dating to the early phases of Grave Circle A at Mykenai, then we may have evidence for an extremely early association between Perseus and Mykenai.[150]

The case of Herakles is slightly more complicated, since he was promoted as a panhellenic hero from the Archaic period onwards. Of the various communities claiming some kind of mythical link with him, it is Thebes which had the strongest claim beside the Argolid, and as early as the Homeric epics Herakles' birth is located at Thebes.[151] Yet despite this, the *Iliad* takes it for granted that the kingdom to which Herakles would have had a claim, had it not been for the wiles of Hera, was the Argolid, and the Pseudo-Hesiodic *Aspis* remedies the situation by having Herakles' stepfather, Amphitryon, flee from Tiryns to Thebes after killing his father-in-law, Alektryon.[152] The evidence connecting Herakles, Alkmene and Alektryon with the eastern half of the Argive plain is so strong that the rootedness of Herakles and his family in this location cannot be seriously challenged.[153]

The Proitid genealogy has no directly attested instances of theogeniture. Instead, it manifests a feature which was absent from the Perseid stemma – namely, uxorilocality. Melampous and Bias acquire their shares in the Argive kingdom by marrying two daughters of Proitos (Lysippe and Iphianassa), and Diomedes accedes to the leadership of the Argive contingent against Troy because his father, Tydeus, took up residence in Argos by marrying Deipyle, the daughter of Adrastos. Nor do the mythical personages in this genealogy seem to be as deeply rooted in the Argive landscape. It is not simply the case that the heroes arrive at Argos from other localities; rather, they seem to enjoy a more panhellenic and less parochial appeal which is signalled by the role they play in the myths of various Greek cities. Melampous and Bias are the best examples of heroes to whom a considerably developed mythological tradition was attached, and who are located in other regions of Greece – Melampous in Thessaly, Messenia, Elis, Arkadia and the Megarid, Bias in Messenia and Megara.[154] Diomedes too is a hero who is encountered in many areas of Greece as well as in the Italian peninsula.[155] Adrastos enjoyed cults at Megara, Sikyon and Attika;[156] Alkmaion received honours at Thebes and Arkadian Psophis;[157] and Amphiaraos had cults near Thebes and at

---

[150] Cited in Jameson 1990, 223.　　[151] Homer, *Iliad* 19.98–99.

[152] Homer, *Iliad* 19.121–24; Hesiod, *Aspis* 78–82.

[153] See Hesiod, *Theogony* 292; Sophokles, *Trakhiniai* 1151–52; Euripides, *Alkestis* 838; Theokritos 13.20; 24.1; Pseudo-Apollodoros, *Bibliotheka* 2.4.6; Pausanias 2.25.9.

[154] Bibis-Papaspyropoulou 1989; Antonetti and Lévêque 1990; Jost 1992.

[155] Farnell 1921, 410; Wathelet 1992, 114.

[156] Herodotos 5.67; Pausanias 1.30.4; Scholiast to Pindar, *Nemean Odes* 9.30. See Farnell 1921, 408.

[157] Pausanias 8.24.7; Scholiast to Pindar, *Pythian Odes* 8.82.

Sparta, apart from in the later and better-known oracular sanctuary at Oropos on the Attic-Boiotian border.[158] The remainder of the stemma is occupied by conjunctive figures, or by the heroes who were defeated at Thebes (the 'Seven') and those who subsequently and successfully assaulted the Boiotian city (the 'Epigonoi').

Indeed, the Theban tenor of the Proitid stemma is very marked. The myth of the madness of the Proitidai is the structural doublet of that of the Bakkhai of Thebes. In the Theban version, the mother and aunts of Pentheus ('mourner') are driven mad because they do not welcome the god Dionysos; in the Argive version, the sisters of Megapenthes ('great mourning') are also subject to divine madness.[159] According to Pseudo-Apollodoros, Akousilaos had attributed the source of this madness to Hera because the daughters of Proitos had scorned the *xoanon* (wooden statue) of the goddess, but the *Catalogue of women* had assigned the cause to their failure to accept the rites of Dionysos.[160] It is interesting to note in this regard the myth which told of the successful resistance mounted against Dionysos and his female retainers by Perseus (the hero of the competing stemma).[161]

There can be no doubt that the legend of the 'Seven against Thebes' was originally developed in Thebes rather than Argos – especially since the name of the defender is Eteokles ('true glory'), while that of the assailant is Polyneikes ('much strife').[162] Nevertheless, from the time of the early epic poem, the *Thebais*, Argos had been indelibly established as the chief adversary of Thebes (the city of Argos is even invoked in the first word of the poem), and there were ways in which Argos derived benefit from the legend. Firstly, the fact that the Peloponnesian army which marched on Thebes had set out from Argos under Argive generals served to establish Argos' centrality and importance within the Peloponnese generally. Secondly, even if the expedition was ultimately a failure, it functioned to justify the second, successful expedition of the Epigonoi – a myth which was almost certainly an Argive creation.

The Perseid and Proitid genealogies find their material realisation in the human landscape of the Argive plain. At Tiryns, Herakles seems to have received a sacred precinct by ca. 600 BC,[163] while officials for the cult of Perseus are attested at Mykenai by the third quarter of the sixth century.[164] As one might expect, traces of the Perseid stemma are not common in the town of Argos itself. The absence of any monuments to Herakles, for example, is particularly striking,[165] while such

---

[158] Herodotos 1.46; 1.49; Pausanias 1.34; 3.12.5; 9.8.3.   [159] West 1985, 147.

[160] Pseudo-Apollodoros, *Bibliotheka* 2.2.2; Akousilaos *FGrH* 2.28; Hesiod fr. 131 Merkelbach/West. West (1985, 78–79) thinks that Hesiod had in fact attributed the origin of the madness to Hera, but in the Argive version of the myth Melampous is central to the healing of the Proitidai, and the close association between Melampous and Dionysos is one that is well attested throughout Greece: Antonetti and Lévêque 1990, 205; Casadio 1994, 51–122.

[161] Pausanias 2.20.4; 2.22.1.   [162] Burkert 1984, 99–106; Dowden 1992, 69; Daumas 1992, 253.

[163] Verdelis, Jameson and Papachristodoulou 1975, 183.

[164] *IG* 4.493; *SEG* 11.300; Jeffery 1990, 174 no. 1. The physical remains of a shrine to Perseus still existed on the road from Mykenai to Argos as late as the second century AD: Pausanias 2.18.1.

[165] Piérart 1992, 129.

Perseid monuments as do exist tend to be situated on the outskirts of the town, beside the road which leads to the location where the accompanying myth was originally located.[166] For instance, the tomb of Likymnios (the son of Alektryon and, according to Strabo, the eponym for the akropolis at Tiryns) was situated on the road leading to Tiryns, while Marcel Piérart believes that the tomb of Medousa and the grave of Perseus' daughter Gorgophone should be located on the road leading through the Eleithuian Gate to Mykenai.[167]

The usurpation of these non-Argive mythological figures and the centripetal crystallisation of the myths of the Argive plain is the epiphenomenon of Argos' synoikism of the plain, and finds its parallel in the Argive practice, during the Roman Imperial period, of awarding to eminent notables 'the honours of Herakles and Perseus' (i.e. the exappropriated culture heroes of the annexed territories of Tiryns and Mykenai).[168] It is impossible to know the exact date of the establishment of the monuments that Pausanias saw, but it is unlikely that Argos monumentalised the myths of Mykenai, Tiryns or Midea before its ascendancy over the plain in the 460s BC: the earliest datable monument which exemplifies this mythical usurpation is the fourth-century 'hemicycle of the kings' at Delphi (see above).

Monuments relating to the Proitid genealogy, on the other hand, are more centrally situated. Statue groups of the Seven and the Epigonoi stood in the *agora* as did the tomb of Talaos, while the house of Adrastos, the sanctuaries of Amphiaraos and Baton and the grave of Eriphyle should be situated somewhere in the centre of the modern town of Argos.[169] The Larissa akropolis was supposedly the repository for a wooden statue of Zeus taken from Troy by Sthenelos, the son of Kapaneus.[170] In the case of the monumentalisation of these myths, some form of chronological control is possible. Anne Pariente's discovery of a mid-sixth century heroon to the Seven against Thebes in the *agora* at Argos proves that the monumentalisation of the Proitid genealogy within a central Argive location predates the political reorganisation of the Argive plain in the fifth century.[171]

It is, then, possible to postulate three stages in the development of the Perseid and Proitid genealogies. Initially, in the Early Iron Age, each was a competing mythology concerned with the domination of the entire Argive plain. By the Archaic period, however, the notion of the shared inheritance had been developed, and the Perseid stemma came to be localised in the eastern half of the plain while the Proitids were firmly situated in Argos. Finally, after the destruction of the eastern communities of the plain in the 460s BC, Argos emphasised her control over the region by usurping her former neighbours' mythology: the absorption of their culture heroes symbolised the new Argive synoikism.[172]

---

166 See generally Piérart 1985; 1990; 1991; 1992.
167 Tomb of Likymnios: Pausanias 2.22.8. Likymnios as the name of the akropolis at Tiryns: Strabo 8.6.11. Tomb of Gorgophone: Pausanias 2.21.5. See Piérart 1990; 1992, 132.
168 *IG* 4.606. See Jameson 1990, 222.   169 Pausanias 2.20.5; 2.21.2; 2.23.2.
170 Pausanias 2.24.3.   171 Pariente 1992.   172 See generally Moggi 1974.

Yet, it was argued earlier that myths are neither completely autonomous nor self-generating: they need a social context. If there existed two competing mythical variants, then there must also have existed two social groups for whom these genealogies were meaningful. The Proitid genealogy is characterised by the persistent theme of arriving newcomers, particularly those having strong associations with central Greece, and is monumentally manifested in the centre of Argos. In other words, we are confronted with an Argive group which appears to use the Proitid dynasty to celebrate its exogenous origins from north of the Korinthian isthmus and its rights of conquest. If this group did not yet begin to call itself 'Dorian' in, say, the eighth century, it would hardly have involved a vast amount of 'remythologising' to effect an eventual attachment to the Dorian pedigree.

The Perseid genealogy, on the other hand, is based on ancestral inheritance through mythical figures who are rooted to their environment, and tends to focus on the communities of the eastern plain (Mykenai, Tiryns and Midea). The obvious conclusion to be drawn is that this genealogy acted as a cognitive artefact for a group, based in the eastern plain, for whom the idea of rootedness was central. This pattern becomes even more suggestive when correlated against the distribution of cults to Hera.

Ethnicity and cult: Hera, Herakles and the Herakleidai

The argument that certain cults may be closely, or even exclusively, linked to ethnic groups is hardly new. Karl Otfried Müller posited an intimate association between Apollo cults and the Dorians (see chapter 1), and Apollo's importance for the Dorians has been emphasised by several scholars since. Adshead, for instance, has argued that 'Apollo Pythaeus was an exclusively Dorian divinity', and Eder has drawn attention to the connection between Apollo Lykeios and Dorian areas, seeking to make the 'Wolf-God' an appropriate apotropaic deity for the pastoral-nomadic Dorians.[173] The case is not, however, quite so straightforward. While it is certainly true that cults to Apollo often assume a particular importance in many Dorian cities, neither Apollo Lykeios nor Apollo Pythios (if, indeed, Pythaeus is an equivalent form of Pythios as is normally assumed) can be exclusively associated with the Dorians, since both are attested in Attika: the former at the Lykeion, which was to give its name to Aristotle's philosophical school, and the latter on the Sacred Way at Dafní.[174] In fact, both the name Apollo (which is almost certainly derived from Northwest Greek *apella*, meaning 'assembly')[175] and the epithet Lykeios (perhaps suggesting age-sets organised in 'packs') indicate that Apollo Lykeios is the god who should preside over the admission of male youths to citizen groups. Clearly, in a Dorian city that god will be associated above all with Dorian

---

[173] Adshead 1986, 35; Eder 1990, 208.
[174] For the Lykeion, see Jameson 1980. For Dafní: Pausanias 1.37.6–7; Sophokles, *Oidipous at Kolonos* 1047–48.   [175] Harrison 1912, 439–41; Burkert 1985, 144–45.

citizens, while in Ionian cities it is admission to Ionian political tribes that he regulates.

A long-needed rejection of the individualistic approach to the Greek pantheon was issued by the 'Paris School', and in particular Jean-Pierre Vernant.[176] Drawing on parallels from Saussurean structural linguistics, Vernant argued that the meaning of an individual deity is not inherently and independently determined, but acquires signification through association and opposition with other elements of the pantheon system. Vernant's stance is a necessary revision to the individualistic model, and yet is limited by its implicit assumption that one can talk of a panhellenic 'thought' or 'subconscious'. For example, on the ritual level at which Greek religion ultimately operated,[177] there is little evidence that the Homeric vision of the society of gods, headed by the patriarchal Zeus, found much of an early material realisation in the cultic geography of the various Greek *poleis*. The earliest Zeus cults do not occupy the focal point of a city (a position held rather by Apollo or Athena) but are situated in more remote areas such as Olympia or Dodona.[178]

Furthermore, with the current trend towards a more contextualised regionalism in Greek archaeology, it is reasonable to ask if religious beliefs might not differ from area to area.[179] Certainly, the importance of the Dioskouroi in the Peloponnese in general, but at Sparta in particular, is not uniformly consistent throughout the rest of Greece.[180] Similarly, despite Euripides' attempts at reconciliation,[181] the Iphigeneia whom epic myth remembered as the innocent daughter of Agamemnon bears very little resemblance to the Iphigeneia who was worshipped at Brauron as the alter-ego of Artemis: while dedications would be made to Artemis after successful childbirth, the clothes of those women who died in labour were dedicated to Iphigeneia, whose very name means 'violent birth'. Without, then, reverting to Müller's 'idol of the tribe', we might allow for the possibility that the pantheon was articulated differentially according to area, and that this was as valid a mechanism for the maintenance of group identity as was the employment of linguistic and material symbols. It is not, after all, modern but ancient writers who associate certain gods and festivals with the Dorians.[182]

Modern reconstructions of ancient cultic landscapes tend to be heavily dependent upon the testimony of Pausanias,[183] though by the time of the second century AD Greek cities were crowded with various temples, shrines and altars, whose original significance and articulation within a dynamic cultic system had been blunted by their fossilised preservation as repositories for a Greek cultural identity that had already vanished.[184] It is here, however, that archaeology can assist. The sanctuaries that are the first to be registered in the archaeological record would also

---

[176] See, for example, Vernant 1980, 92–109.　[177] Cartledge 1985, 98.
[178] Polignac 1995, 81; Morgan 1990, 28; 1993, 31. See also Nilsson 1972, 246–47.
[179] Morgan 1993, 19.　[180] Malkin 1994, 25.　[181] Euripides, *Iphigeneia in Tauris* 1462–69.
[182] E.g. Thoukydides 5.54.2; Pausanias 3.13.4; 4.8.2. See chapter 3.
[183] For the application of Pausanias' descriptions to the topography of Argos, see Piérart 1982; 1983; Aupert 1987.　[184] See Habicht 1985; Elsner 1992; Arafat 1995.

appear to be, by and large, the most important to judge from the quality and quantity of offerings dedicated. In addition, the archaeological evidence suggests that these early sanctuaries often continued in use throughout most of antiquity. Given this, it is not unreasonable to assume that the divinities worshipped at such sanctuaries commanded a particular importance for the local communities.

If this line of argument is accepted, then it is interesting that the cultic landscapes of the Argive plain and the eastern Argolid appear to be constructed differently. Figures 11–12 show the distribution of sanctuaries in Argos and the Argolid respectively, as well as the dates at which the first votives are attested. What is notable is that in the eastern Argolid, cults to Apollo and Poseidon assume an early importance: the former at Epidauros, Halieis and possibly Troizen;[185] the latter on the island of Kalaureia and at Hermione. Indeed, Poseidon's importance in the eastern Argolid may also be reflected in the genealogical traditions of Troizen where he invariably fathers the important local heroes – a function normally exercised by Zeus at Argos, Mykenai and Tiryns.[186] We have already seen in chapter 1 that Müller regarded Poseidon as commanding a particular importance for the Ionians,[187] particularly due to his patronage of the Panionion at Cape Mykale.[188] It is worth noting, then, that the ethnographic record (fig. 3) displays a strong Ionian component in the eastern Argolid, especially at Hermione and Troizen – a city which is normally thought to have controlled the sanctuary on Kalaureia.[189]

Müller also believed that Demeter was a popular deity in Dryopean settlements.[190] Again, then, it is interesting to note that Demeter cults make a relatively early appearance in sites associated with Dryopes by the literary tradition (fig. 3). A seventh-century deposit east of the akropolis at Halieis has been associated with Demeter on the basis of the finds, which include terracotta lamps and figurines of a goddess carrying pigs (the preferred sacrificial victim in Demeter cults). Similarly, the discovery of some 1,200 miniature lamps among an Archaic votive deposit just outside the city walls at Troizen matches up well with Pausanias' description of the suburban sanctuary of Demeter Thesmophoros.[191] Finally, a series of inscribed bronze cows, dated to the fifth century, appears to belong to the sanctuary of Demeter Khthonia, located at the Church of the Archangel in Hermione. Demeter's importance at Hermione is further corroborated by her appearance on the local coinage and by the fact that she was the subject of a poem by the sixth-century poet Lasos of Hermione.[192]

---

[185] For references, see the keys to figures 11–12. The Apollo identification of the *agora* sanctuary at Troizen is not entirely secure. Welter (1941, 18) attributed it to Artemis Soteira, whose name can be read on an inscription in the nearby church of Agios Georgios. On the other hand, this goddess's name also appears in an inscription built into the Episkopí church, which lies 1 km further to the west. The reasons for assigning the sanctuary to Apollo Thearios are due, firstly, to the appearance of his name in another inscription (*IG* 4.748) in Agios Georgios and, secondly, to the fact that Pausanias (2.31.6) believed this sanctuary to be the oldest at Troizen.

[186] Cf. Pausanias 2.33.1. [187] Müller 1830, 266. [188] Herodotos 1.148.

[189] Faraklas 1972, 23; Schumacher 1993, 76. [190] Müller 1830, 414. [191] Pausanias 2.32.8.

[192] Lasos fr. 702 Page. See Jameson, Runnels and Van Andel 1995, 592–93.

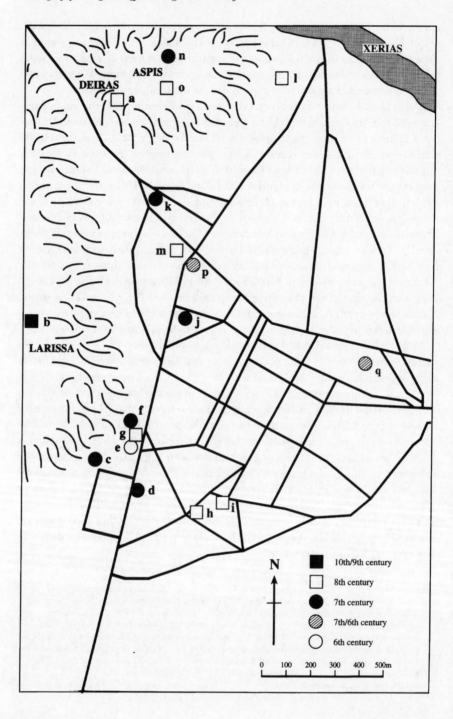

XERIAS

ASPIS

DEIRAS

LARISSA

N

10th/9th century
8th century
7th century
7th/6th century
6th century

0   100   200   300   400   500m

11 Distribution of sanctuary deposits at Argos.

	Location	Deity	References
a	Deiras ridge	Apollo Pythaeus	Vollgraff 1956; Roux 1957; Bergquist 1967, 18–19; Foley 1988, 140; Billot 1989–90, 52–57; Hägg 1992, 12.
b	Larissa	Athena Polias	Vollgraff 1928; 1934, 138; Béquinon 1930, 480; Roes 1953; Courbin 1955, 314; 1966, *passim*; Boardman 1963, 122; Foley 1988, 140–41; Billot 1989–90, 56; Hägg 1992, 11.
c	Odeion	Aphrodite	Daux 1968; 1969; Foley 1988, 141.
d	Bonoris Plot	Hera Antheia?	Kritzas 1973–74, 230–42; Touchais 1980, 599; Foley 1988, 141; Hall 1995b, 605.
e	Odos Gounari		Courbin 1956, 366; Daux 1957, 674–77; Courbin 1980; Foley 1988, 141; Marchetti 1993.
f	Sondage 73		Daux 1959, 761; Foley 1988, 142.
g	Pilios Plot		Deïlaki 1973, 108–09; Hägg 1992, 12.
h	Koros Plot		Consolaki and Hackens 1980.
i	Maniates/ Tsoukrianis Plots		Kritzas 1973–74, 212, 228; Foley 1988, 142.
j	Yeorgas Plot		Kritzas 1972, 198; Foley 1988, 142.
k	Siamblis Plot		Deïlaki 1973–74, 208.
l	Mikhalopoulos Plot		Protonotariou-Deïlaki 1980, 191.
m	Church of Timios Prodromos		Protonotariou-Deïlaki 1982, 39.
n	Aspis, north slope		Touchais 1980, 698.
o	Aspis, south slope	Hera Akraia?	Vollgraff 1907, 155–61; 1956, fig. 23; Musti and Torelli 1986, 290; Foley 1988, 142; Hall 1995b, 604–05.
p	Athanasopoulos Plot		Kritzas 1973, 130–32.
q	Peppas Plot		Kritzas 1972, 203.

Demeter's importance in the eastern Argolid is not, however, matched in the Argive plain itself. Indeed, Herodotos states that when the Peloponnese was overrun by the Dorians, the festival of the Thesmophoria (which was celebrated in honour of Demeter) was no longer practised except by those Peloponnesians, such as the Arkadians, who did not abandon their homes.[193] Evangelia Protonotariou-Deïlaki has suggested that a rustic shrine in the village of Kourtaki, 8 km east of Argos, should be attributed to Demeter Mysia, though this rests on no epigraphical evidence.[194]

In the Argive plain, it is instead Hera who appears to preside over many of the functions (e.g. mysteries, fertility and marriage) which are the preserve of Demeter in the eastern Argolid, and this may explain why it is that artefacts such as terracotta pomegranates, loomweights and *koulouria* (representations of cakes) are dedicated to Demeter in the eastern Argolid and to Hera in the Argive plain.[195] Certainly, Pausanias' description of Polykleitos' famous statue of Hera at the Heraion reveals that Hera and Demeter both shared the iconographical elements of the polos, the wreath and the pomegranate.[196] Interestingly, while Demeter cults are comparatively rare in the Argive plain, Hera cults are conversely underrepresented in the eastern Argolid – even as late as the second century AD, Pausanias reports only two cults to Hera in the whole of the eastern Argolid.[197]

Hera cults are most conspicuous on the eastern side of the Argive plain. Myth recounted how the Kanathos spring near Nauplia was where Hera went annually to renew her virginity,[198] and she had received sanctuaries at Tiryns, the Heraion and a small terrace shrine near the Heraion by the eighth century at the very latest.[199] It is not unlikely that Hera was the recipient of eighth-century cult on the citadel at Mykenai and at the nearby 'Agamemnoneion',[200] while a sanctuary near Agios Adriános, dating to the late eighth or early seventh century, was probably also dedicated to her.

By contrast, Hera's importance within the local pantheon of Argos itself is less evident. Indeed, it was only after Argos assumed control over the Heraion in the 460s BC that the goddess began to appear on the local coinage – for instance, a coin struck in 421 BC to commemorate the alliance between Argos and Elis.[201] Prior to that, the coins of Argos bore the representation of Apollo Lykeios whose sanctuary, situated in the *agora* of Argos, was by the Classical period regarded as

---

[193] Herodotos 2.171.3.
[194] Protonotariou-Deïlaki 1970, 156; 1982, 40. See also Charitonidou 1967, 178–79; Papachristodoulou 1968, 131–32.
[195] Pomegranates, loomweights and *koulouria* are found both at the Heraion and at the sanctuary of Demeter Thesmophoros at Troizen.   [196] Pausanias 2.17.4.
[197] Pausanias 2.29.1 (Epidauros); 2.36.2 (Halieis).   [198] Pausanias 2.38.2.
[199] For bibliography, see key to figure 12.
[200] For the Hera identification of the Citadel sanctuary (at which cult may actually predate the eighth century): Wright 1982, 194 n. 44; Foley 1988, 144; Antonaccio 1994, 88; Hall 1995b, 599–600. For the 'Agamemnoneion' as a Hera shrine: Marinatos 1953, 87–88; Polignac 1995, 142 n. 37; Morgan and Whitelaw 1991, 89 n. 50; Antonaccio 1993, 67 n. 36; 1994, 91; Whitley 1994, 220; Hall 1995b, 601–03.   [201] Jeffery 1990, 151; Hall 1995b, 606.

the oldest and most important at Argos.[202] Unfortunately, the sanctuary has not yet been located, so to date the earliest archaeologically attested cult at Argos is that of Athena Polias on the Larissa akropolis, where the earliest votives date back to the middle of the eighth century, if not earlier. There are only two sanctuaries at Argos that may plausibly be assigned to Hera: one was planted towards the end of the eighth century on the southern slopes of the Aspis hill in the northwest sector of the city,[203] while the other was established approximately a century later on the western side of the *agora*.[204] Neither sanctuary, however, matches the importance or antiquity of the Athena cult on the Larissa.

The fact that the principal sanctuaries to Hera appear on the eastern side of the Argive plain may not be entirely accidental, especially since this is the area which was the heartland of the plain during the Late Bronze Age. That Hera was worshipped in the Bronze Age is confirmed by the attestation of her name in Linear B, but she may not always have been the scheming and jealous consort of Zeus that Homer describes.[205] Linear B tablets from Pylos and Thebes mention a goddess named Diwija, which is the feminine form for Zeus and should identify her as Zeus' original wife.[206] Similarly, on etymological grounds, Hera's original husband should be not Zeus, but Hero.[207] The supposition that Zeus' and Hera's union is a post-Mycenaean act of mythical integration would certainly go some way in explaining why the two were never to sit very comfortably together.[208]

In the Argive plain during the historical period, Hera presided over so many functions (e.g. flora, fauna, warfare, adolescent transitions, marriage and even virginity),[209] that it is hard not to see her as the original Bronze Age 'divine mistress'. This memory appears to be preserved in the Homeric epics, where Hera is intimately associated with the Akhaians and names Mykenai as one of her favourite cities.[210] It cannot, then, be entirely coincidental that the most important sanctuaries of Hera should be found in precisely the area of the Argive plain where the ethnographic tradition placed the Akhaian Herakleidai and the genealogical tradition situated the Perseidai – in other words, the legendary descendants and ancestors respectively of Herakles, whose very name means 'Glory of Hera'.[211] In short, cult and myth served to articulate ancestral claims to the Argive plain which

---

[202] For the coins: Gardner 1887 s.v. Argos; Dengate 1988, 202; Eder 1990, 208. For the importance of the sanctuary of Apollo Lykeios: Aiskhylos, *Agamemnon* 1257; Thoukydides 5.47.11; Pausanias 2.19.3; Scholiast to Euripides, *Elektra* 6. See further: Roux 1953; Courtils 1981; Hall 1995b, 606.

[203] Hall 1995b, 604–05.   [204] Hall 1995b, 605.   [205] See generally O'Brien 1993.

[206] The Pylos tablet is Py Tn316. The evidence from Thebes has recently come to light in excavations undertaken by Dr V. Aravantinos.   [207] Pötscher 1961; 1987, 1–2.

[208] Burkert 1985, 132; Pötscher 1987, 1.   [209] Polignac 1995, 42–43; Pötscher 1987, 139.

[210] Homer, *Iliad* 4.52.

[211] In the later traditions, Hera was notoriously hostile towards Herakles, but Walter Pötscher (1987, 28–29) has argued that Herakles' earlier function was to pursue dangerous quests not only for his own renown but also for the glory of Hera. Eventually, the nature of these ordeals began to appear so perilous that the relationship between Herakles and Hera came to be misunderstood and represented as hostile in nature. See also Jameson 1990, 220; Hall forthcoming.

helped to forge ethnic distinctions between the populations of Mykenai, Tiryns and Midea on the one side and the self-styled *parvenus* of Argos on the other.

Conclusion

From the evidence of genealogy (supplemented by archaeology), a very clear pattern emerges which serves to distinguish the western from the eastern side of the Argive plain. It is essentially structured around the oppositions between continuity and discontinuity, rootedness and mobility. While the Perseid ancestors of the Herakleidai were central to the identity of Mykenai and Tiryns, Argos structured its own ideology around the Proitid descendants of Melampous and Bias and the heroes who marched against Thebes – figures who were not as deeply rooted in the Argive landscape and whose only firm connection with Argos was the fact that the *Thebais* had them set out from there on their fateful expedition against Thebes. Furthermore, while the communities of the eastern side of the plain accorded particular honour to the ancient goddess Hera, Argos itself preferred to promote the cults of Athena and Apollo (who is, tellingly, the traditional god of newcomers).

It was argued above that the Perseid and Proitid stemmata were originally competing variants which each sought to place the entire Argive plain under the dominion of one or the other. There are, however, indications that the ancestral claims that were pursued in support of a Heraklid identity had not always been restricted to the eastern side of the plain – indeed, the ethnographic tradition records the presence of Herakleidai at Argos (see fig. 3). In the eighth century, for instance, the northwestern (Aspis/Deiras) sector of the city joined with the communities of the eastern plain in pursuing a range of 'ancestralising' strategies (see further chapter 5) and towards the end of that century a sanctuary was established to Hera on the slopes of the Aspis hill.[212]

Nevertheless, the archaeological links between northwest Argos and the communities of the eastern plain and the former's appeals to the ancestral past appear to subside in the early seventh century, and it may be that those for whom the Herakleidai and a sense of rootedness were so central managed to reconcile themselves with those whose identity was predicated on their exogenous origins. This would then match up with the already proposed *rapprochement* that was later articulated through the myths which told of the peaceful arrival at Argos of both Dorians and Herakleidai. Certainly, towards the end of the seventh century the alliance appears to have been sealed by the establishment of a sanctuary to Hera in the area of the Argive *agora*. It is pure speculation to wonder whether that enigmatic figure Pheidon may have had a hand in this, though Diodoros was to record

[212] For the material connections between the Aspis/Deiras area and the eastern Argive Plain: Hall 1995a, 13–15.

that he traced his ancestry back to the Heraklid, Temenos.[213] In any case, from this time up until the middle of the fifth century BC, it was the communities of the eastern plain which continued to proclaim an exclusively Heraklid identity.

If those who adopted discursive and behavioural strategies to appeal to the ancestral past can be associated with the Herakleidai, can we treat as Dorians those with whom they were to assimilate (at Argos, at any rate), and who appear to have been less concerned with rootedness than with celebrating their exogenous origins and the territorial rights that conquest yields? It is possible: we have, after all, already seen the assimilation of the myth of the Herakleidai with that of the Dorians at Sparta by the middle of the seventh century BC.[214] On the other hand, it is not totally impossible that it was not until the sixth century that those Argives whose identity was predicated on extraneous origins sought to attach themselves to the general myth of the Dorians – an act of mythical integration achieved in one of the final stages of composition of the *Catalogue of women* by having Doros marry the daughter of Phoroneus.[215]

---

[213] Diodoros 7.17. It is, however, impossible to determine when exactly Pheidon is supposed to have lived: Hall 1995b, 586.

[214] Tyrtaios fr. 2 Diehl. See chapter 3.

[215] Hesiod fr. 10(b). See West 1985, 143.

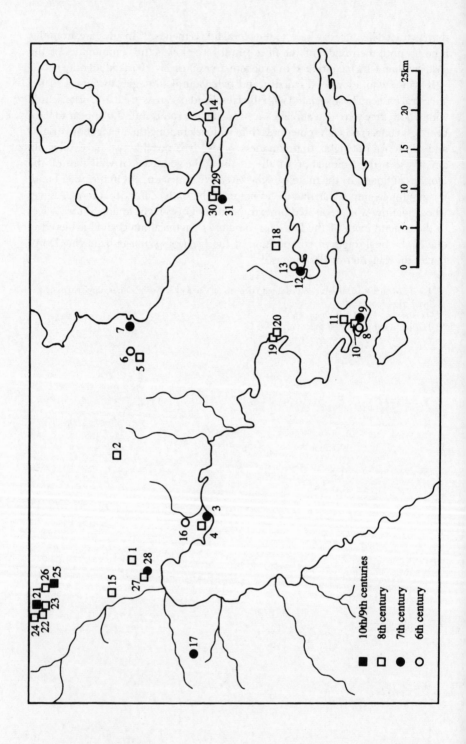

12 Distribution of sanctuary deposits in the Argolid.

	Location	Deity	References
	Profitis Ilias (Agios Adrianos)	Hera?	Protonotariou-Deilaki 1963, 65–66; Alexandri 1964; Foley 1988, 150; Hall 1995b, 597.
1	Mount Arakhnaion	Zeus & Hera?	Rupp 1976; Foley 1988, 150; Hägg 1992, 19.
2	Akropolis, Asine		Frödin and Persson 1938, 26 fig. 8c, 32 n. 1.
3	Barbouna Hill, Asine	Apollo Pythaeus?	Frödin and Persson 1938, 148–51; Vollgraff 1956, 31; Barrett 1954; Wells 1987–88; 1990; Foley 1988, 142–43; Billot 1989–90; Hägg 1992, 18; Hall 1995b, 581–82.
4	Mount Kynortion, Epidauros	Apollo Maleatas	Papadimitriou 1949; Lambrinoudakis 1975; 1978–79; Tomlinson 1983, 92–94; Foley 1988, 147–48; Hägg 1992, 19.
5	Arkhéa Epidhavros	Asklepios	Kavvadias 1900; Burford 1969; Tomlinson 1983.
6	Paléa Epidhavros	Artemis?	Arkhontidou-Argiri 1975, 60; 1977, 46.
7	Akropolis, Portohéli-Halieis	Athena?	Jameson 1969, 320–21; 1974, 74; Foley 1988, 149.
8	East of akropolis, Portohéli-Halieis	Demeter?	Jameson 1969, 340; Foley 1988, 149; Jameson, Runnels and Van Andel 1995, 424.
9	Flamboura, Portohéli-Halieis		Jameson, Runnels and Van Andel 1995, 423.
10	Harbour, Portohéli-Halieis	Apollo	Jameson 1972; 1973–74; Dengate 1988, 199, 231–34; Foley 1988, 149; Mazarakis-Ainian 1988, 117–18; Billot 1989–90; Bergquist 1990; Cooper 1990, 65–77.
11	Bisti promontory, Hermione	Poseidon?	Philadelpheus 1909, 177–79; McAllister 1969; Jameson, Runnels and Van Andel 1995, 488–89, 589–90.
12	Pron Hill, Hermione	Demeter?	Jameson, Runnels and Van Andel 1995, 489.
13	Kalaureia	Poseidon	Wide and Kjellberg 1895; Welter 1941; Kelly 1966; Bergquist 1967, 35; Coldstream 1968, 405; Foley 1988, 148; Billot 1989–90, 62–65; Hall 1995b, 584–85.
14	Saravakos Plot, Kourtáki	Demeter Mysia?	Charitonidou 1967, 178–79; Papachristodoulou 1968, 131–32; Protonotariou-Deilaki 1970, 155–56; 1982, 40; Foley 1988, 150; Hägg 1992, 13.
15	Lefkakia	Apollo?	Vollgraff 1956, 33.
16	Magoula	Artemis?	Vollgraff 1907, 180; Foley 1988, 150.
17	Magoula sta Ilia		Jameson, Runnels and Van Andel 1995, 519.
18	Koiládha Bay, Mases		Jameson, Runnels and Van Andel 1995, 469.
19	Kastráki, Mases		Jameson, Runnels and Van Andel 1995, 440–41.
20	Citadel, Mykenai	Hera?	Kuruniotis 1901; Wace 1939, 210; 1949, 24, 84–86; Foley 1988, 143; Hall 1995b, 598–600.
21	House of the Oil Merchant, Mykenai		Verdelis 1962a, 85–87; Drerup 1969, 28; Fagerström 1988, 30; Foley 1988, 144; Hägg 1992, 16.
22	'Agamemnoneion', Mykenai	Hera?	Cook 1953; Marinatos 1953, 87–88; Foley 1988, 144; Morgan and Whitelaw 1991, 89; Hägg 1992, 17; Antonaccio 1995, 147–52; Hall 1995b, 601–03.

12 (cont.)

24	Asprókhoma	Enyalios	Mylonas 1965, 95–96; 1966, 111–14; Foley 1988, 145.
25	The Heraion	Hera	Waldstein 1902; 1905; Blegen 1937a; 1939; Amandry 1952; 1980; Caskey and Amandry 1952; Courbin 1959; 1983; Bergquist 1967, 19–20; Plommer 1977; 1984; Snodgrass 1980, 53; Wright 1982; Strøm 1988; 1992; 1995; Foley 1988, 135–39; Antonaccio 1992; Hägg 1992, 14–15; Pfaff 1992; Hall 1995b.
26	Prosymna shrine	Hera	Blegen 1939, 410–12; Antonaccio 1992, 100–01; Hägg 1992, 15; Hall 1995b, 601.
27	Citadel, Tiryns	Hera?	Schliemann 1886, 229; Frickenhaus, Müller and Oelmann 1912; Müller 1930, 134–39; Drerup 1969, 17–18; Jantzen 1975, 99, 159–61; Verdelis, Jameson and Papachristodoulou 1975; Kilian 1981, 159–60; Wright 1982, 201; Rupp 1983; Fagerström 1988, 29; Foley 1988, 145–46; Jameson 1990; Hägg 1992, 17; Hall 1995b, 598.
28	East gateway, Tiryns	Athena?	Jantzen 1975, 105; Foley 1988, 147; Hall 1995b, 598.
29	Agora, Troizen	Apollo Thearios?	Legrand 1893, 93; 1905, 281–82; Welter 1941, 18.
30	Episkopí, Troizen	Hippolytos?	Welter 1941, 34; Billot 1989–90, 71.
31	West of Troizen	Demeter Thesmophoros?	Legrand 1905, 302–03; Welter 1941, 21–25.

5

Ethnicity and archaeology

Excavating the ethnic group

It was argued in chapter 1 that, in the course of the nineteenth century, the study of ethnicity in Greek antiquity came to be dominated by the twin movements of romanticism and positivism. It was, therefore, only natural that the nascent discipline of archaeology, with its seemingly objective materiality, should be harnessed to the pseudo-scientific quest for the *Volksgeist*. At first sight, the archaeological record appears to provide a number of dimensions in which to search for the ethnic group. An examination of ceramics might indicate the decorative styles favoured by certain ethnic groups as well as the types of vessels its members used for the storage, preparation, cooking and consumption of their food. Floral and faunal analysis could identify dietary preferences. A study of metalwork could reveal the sort of adornment favoured (and perhaps, by extension, the mode of dress worn) as well as the tools, implements and weapons employed in times of peace and war. Finally, an architectural survey might bring to light the preferred type of house-form.

Above all other classes of information, it is the evidence of burial which has traditionally ranked paramount in archaeological approaches to social phenomena. There are two principal reasons for this. Firstly, the conscious action of placing a corpse or a cinerary urn in a trench results in a 'closed' (or self-contained) deposit. This means that the grave goods, and particularly the ceramic objects, are likely to remain relatively intact: it is no coincidence that the vast majority of Greek pots displayed on museum shelves originate from burials rather than other contexts. It also means that for periods such as the Greek Dark Ages, when domiciles were constructed of perishable and insubstantial materials and sanctuaries had generally not yet begun to receive much in the way of architectural investment, the subterranean preservation of graves makes them virtually the only source of information. Furthermore, the grave and its contents should ideally represent a single historical moment, uncontaminated by what may be termed 'post-depositional' disturbances, though in practice graves could be reused in antiquity or cut through by later building activity, leading to the presence of 'intrusive' material from other periods. Alternatively, certain graves that are known to contain valuable grave offerings (notably, Mycenaean or Etruscan tombs) may be subject to systematic looting over the centuries.

Secondly, archaeologists are able to draw on a long tradition of research into death and burial carried out by social anthropologists. Among early anthropologists, and particularly pioneers of the British 'classical' anthropological school such as E. B. Tylor or J. G. Frazer, funerary ritual offered access to both the eschatological beliefs of a certain society as well as the psychological answers that its members might adopt in order to explain natural phenomena. Funerals were the direct expression of a society's beliefs in the after-life and other-world.[1] An important modification to this approach came about with the rise of modern sociology. Refuting the deterministic emphasis placed on religion by his teacher Fustel de Coulanges, Emile Durkheim affirmed the primacy of the social order as the fundamental underpinning of religious ideas.[2] As a consequence, the focus of attention shifted somewhat away from the psychological functions of burial ceremony to illuminate the ways in which social structure may be articulated and projected through funerary ritual.[3]

There is, however, one further characteristic of mortuary evidence which has sometimes been thought to offer distinct advantages in the study of ethnicity – namely, the physical anthropological evidence of the skeletal remains themselves. The eighteenth century saw the emergence of the pseudo-science of craniometry, which operates on the principle that cranial measurements can assign skeletal remains to 'racial groups'. In 1775, comparative illustrations of Caucasian and Ethiopian skulls appeared in Blumenbach's *De generis humani varietate nativa*, and in 1799, the Manchester surgeon Charles White compared the anatomical measurements of more than 50 'Negro' skulls to the figures for whites, and concluded that 'Negroes' bore a stronger resemblance to apes than did Europeans.[4] More influential was a footnote written by the Philadelphia doctor Samuel George Morton and appended to his *Crania Americana* of 1839. After comparing the internal cranial capacity of Caucasian, Mongolian, Malay, American and Ethiopian skulls, Morton argued that whites had the biggest brains and blacks the smallest. Despite the fact that several errors in calculation were made, his conclusions were greatly to influence the work of racial theorists such as Carl Gustav Carus or the Comte de Gobineau.[5]

Quite apart from its pernicious pedigree, there are a number of methodological problems inherent in craniometry. One illustration of this is Robert Charles' analysis of the skeletons excavated at Argos by the Ecole Française between 1952 and 1958. On the basis of cranial types, Charles divided the ancient Argive population into Cromagnoid, Grimaldoid, Atlantic-Nordic and 'Mixed Origin' groups. These were then further subdivided: the Cromagnoid group included the Ancient Mediterranean, Alpine-Mediterranean and Alpine sub-groups; the Atlantic-Nordic group included the Cordé, Danubian and Dinaroid sub-groups; and the

---

[1] Huntington and Metcalf 1979, 6; Binford 1972, 209.
[2] Durkheim 1915; see Gellner 1987, 37–38.
[3] See generally Huntington and Metcalf 1979; Morris 1987, 29–43; 1992, 1–30.
[4] Banton 1987, 14–15, 21.   [5] Banton 1987, 34–35, 47.

'Mixed Origin' group included Alpine-Grimaldoid, Neo-Mediterranean and Hybrid types. Charles concluded that the Grimaldoid and Cordé types are found only in the Middle Helladic and Late Helladic cemeteries, and that the arrival of Dorian newcomers to Argos can be traced by an increase in the proportion of Atlantic-Nordic types during the Early Iron Age.[6] However, as Thomas Kelly has pointed out, the figures that Charles gives are hardly significant: Atlantic-Nordic types account for 5.9 per cent in Late Helladic, 7.7 per cent in Protogeometric and still only 14.2 per cent in the Geometric period.[7]

Today, many archaeologists criticise craniometry for its statistical imprecision and inaccuracy,[8] and considerable doubt has been expressed as to whether any cranial categories other than the major divisions of Europoid, Negroid, Australoid and Mongoloid can be studied with certainty.[9] We can, however, go further. Any approach which attempts to deduce ethnic identity from physiognomic factors is immediately flawed for the reasons that were set out in chapter 2 – namely, that while physical characteristics may occasionally operate as indicia of ethnicity, they cannot be treated as defining criteria. Furthermore, in the case of craniometry it is becoming increasingly apparent that cranial morphogenesis may be as much, if not more, the result of environmental, rather than genetic, factors. Kenneth Beals's study of cranial data for various populations throughout the world suggests that as one proceeds from hot to cold climates, the cephalic index increases (i.e. heads become rounder). This might indicate that the process of cranial adaptation is a slow, long-term, background adjustment of the species.[10] Alternatively, cranial morphogenesis may be influenced by rainfall. Neil Brodie has noted that the cranial index of British skulls steadily increased throughout the Medieval period before declining again during the seventeenth century. These oscillations in the cranial indices were not accompanied by any documented major population influxes, though they do seem to move in tandem with the increasingly dry climate experienced in Britain between the thirteenth and seventeenth centuries.[11] Perhaps most striking of all is Kobyliansky's examination of the cephalic indices for 718 Israeli Jewish males of east European, central European, middle eastern and north African origin, which demonstrates that the cephalic index decreases significantly even within one generation after migration to Israel.[12]

The rejection of craniometry need not invalidate the potential contribution of physical anthropology to ethnic studies. The evidence of pathology, for instance, may be especially illuminating, particularly when it can be attributed to dietary behaviour:[13] the symbolic value of distinctive cuisine is, after all, evident enough in the Little Italys and Chinatowns of many modern western cities as is the way culinary peculiarities like roast beef, *cuisses de grenouilles* or *Sauerkraut* may be used to stereotype outgroups. There are currently new research projects to study the archaeological applications of bone marrow and DNA analysis within diet and

---

[6] Charles 1963, 72–73.   [7] Kelly 1976, 16.   [8] E.g. Renfrew 1987, 4.
[9] Dolukhanov 1989, 269; Morris 1992, 91.   [10] Beals 1972, 90.   [11] Brodie 1994, 71–74.
[12] Kobyliansky 1983.   [13] McGuire 1982, 163.

kinship studies (notably at the University of Sheffield and the University of Athens), but it is fair to say that such work is still in its infancy. For this reason, the archaeological examination of ethnicity must remain content with the material symbols that past populations used, rather than with the physical characteristics of those populations. The problem lies, however, in establishing precisely what the relationship is between the expression of ethnic identity and the archaeological record. This is best illustrated by examining the arguments and counter-arguments that have been made concerning the historicity of the so-called 'Dorian invasion'.

Archaeology and the 'Dorian invasion'

The pioneering excavations undertaken by Heinrich Schliemann, Wilhelm Dörpfeld and Christos Tsountas which brought to light the palatial culture of the Mycenaean world simultaneously raised a problem which needed urgent resolution – namely the reasons for the collapse of this system towards the end of the LHIIIB period.[14] As more Mycenaean sites were excavated, a recurrent pattern of violent disruption appeared to emerge, with claims being made for complete or partial destruction at Mykenai and Tiryns in the Argolid, Zygouries in Korinthia, the Menelaion in Lakonia, Krisa in Phokis, Iolkos in Thessaly and possibly Gla in Boiotia.[15] Since late nineteenth-century archaeology was essentially philological in nature,[16] it was to the literary texts that archaeologists turned and found their answer in the shape of the Dorians. Not only did the literary sources display a surprising unanimity in their belief that the Dorians, accompanied by the Herakleidai, had entered and taken possession of the Peloponnese in the generations after the Trojan War, but the invasion hypothesis appeared entirely satisfactory to scholars who at that time tended to attribute cultural discontinuity to exogenous factors. One of the earliest accounts explicitly to link the Dorians with the end of the Mycenaean palaces was the grand work of synthesis, written by Tsountas and Manatt in 1897.[17]

Once the connection had been established between the Dorians and the end of the Mycenaean world, it was relatively easy to find further supporting evidence in the archaeological record. The strengthening of the fortification walls at Mykenai and the measures taken to safeguard water-supplies at Athens, Mykenai and Tiryns during LHIIIB were taken to indicate some anticipation of hostility, while the erection of what was interpreted as a fortification wall across the Korinthian Isthmus in the same period seemed to suggest that the attack was expected from the north.[18] The consequences of the attack, on the other hand, were thought to be reflected

---

[14] For an account of the early excavations of Mycenaean palaces, see McDonald and Thomas 1990.
[15] Ålin 1962, 58–59, 122–23, 130–31, 142–44; Stubbings 1975, 352–53.
[16] Bianchi Bandinelli 1985.   [17] Tsountas and Manatt 1897, 341.
[18] Ålin 1962, 10–11; Stubbings 1975, 352–53; Broneer 1966; Vanschoonwinkel 1991, 56–66, 108–09.

in the disappearance of the stylistically homogeneous LHIIIB pottery and its replacement by the more regionally variable LHIIIC styles.[19]

The Dorian invasion was also held responsible for the evident demographic shifts that accompanied the collapse of the palaces. In Lakonia, recent estimates suggest that only sixteen of some fifty LHIIIB sites continued to be occupied into LHIIIC, while only five of twenty-two LHIIIB sites in Messenia remained in use in the subsequent phase.[20] In the case of Lakonia, Paul Cartledge has argued that the archaeological 'gap' apparent in the Amyklaion sequence between LHIIIC artefacts and the first appearance of Protogeometric pottery ca. 950 BC, together with the fact that the latter appears to demonstrate little if any typological or stylistic filiation from the former, should argue for the arrival of a new population in the middle of the tenth century. Arguing that Lakonian Protogeometric appears stylistically to belong to a common West Greek pottery tradition, Cartledge has suggested that the most economic hypothesis is to assume that this new population is the Dorians of the literary tradition.[21]

On the other hand, a number of new sites, sometimes interpreted as 'refugee settlements', are attested for LHIIIC in areas such as the Ionian islands, Krete, Cyprus, Perati in east Attika, Koukounaries on the island of Paros and Palaiokastro in Arkadia.[22] One of the most interesting of the currently attested sites is Teikhos Dymaion in Akhaia, particularly given the ancient belief that Akhaia had been invaded (and named) by Akhaians who had left the Argolid and Lakonia upon the arrival in those regions of the Dorians.[23]

In the early decades of this century, it was commonly believed that an ethnic group should possess distinctive and exclusive behavioural and cultural patterns. The task that awaited archaeologists, then, was to identify the appearance of new material cultural artefacts that might reflect the arrival of Dorian newcomers at the end of the Bronze Age. At first sight, the most obvious innovation appeared to be the metallurgical shift from bronze to iron which (somewhat erroneously) gives the Iron Age its name, and some scholars argued that by tracing the spread of iron-working from the northern Balkans to Greece it was possible to map the Dorians in their migration southwards.[24]

The transition from the Bronze Age to the Iron Age also witnesses the appearance of new types of pottery. 'Barbarian Ware' (also known as 'Handmade Burnished Ware') is the name given to a type of burnished, handmade pottery which is fired at a low temperature and whose only decoration consists normally of a horizontal band beneath the lip with incisions or thumbprints. It is rarely

---

[19] Desborough 1964, 9–10; 1975, 659.
[20] Demakopoulou 1982, 97–120; Vanschoonwinkel 1991, 172–73. The surviving sites in Lakonia are chiefly situated in the southern Eurotas valley and thus suggest a Lakonia 'without focus': Dickinson 1992, 114.
[21] Cartledge 1979, 87–88, 96; 1994; Coulson 1985, 29. Followed by Parker 1995.
[22] Desborough 1975, 659, 663; Vanschoonwinkel 1991, 103, 119, 172, 175, 178, 302–305.
[23] Herodotos 7.94; Strabo 8.7.1; Pausanias 7.1.5. For Akhaia as a refugee area: Papadopoulos 1979, 183–84.   [24] E.g. Foltiny 1961, 295.

attested in tombs and this, together with the restricted range of shapes (principally cooking-pots, pithoi and amphorai), suggests that it was used for domestic purposes, particularly cooking. It first appears towards the end of the Bronze Age at sites such as Tiryns, Mykenai and Asine in the Argolid, Korakou in Korinthia, the Menelaion in Lakonia, Aigeira in Akhaia and Kommos and Khania on Krete, and is often understood as the pottery brought by an immigrant population of simple technology. Though analogies with the Subappenine and Protovillanovan wares of Italy and the coarse ware of Troy VIIb have all been proposed, the view that it is derived from either the Urnfield Culture of the middle Danube or northwest Greece has been taken as signifying the presence of an intrusive northern (though not necessarily Dorian) population during the LHIIIC period.[25] A similar attribution is sometimes made in the case of 'Incised Ware' – a handmade pottery, found throughout central and southern Greece in the Early Iron Age.[26]

The Dorians have also, however, been credited with the introduction of 'Protogeometric' pottery, popular throughout Greece (and particularly central Greece) in the tenth century BC. Its lineal decoration and preference for tauter shapes seemed to present a clear contrast with LHIIIC vessels, and Theodore Skeat argued that it was possible to trace its origin and diffusion through a stylistic analysis, particularly of the characteristic concentric circle motif. Skeat argued for an early appearance of this motif in Thessaly and Makedonia, from where it was diffused southwards, and attributed its passage to the series of migrations which brought the Dorians to the Peloponnese.[27]

Another important feature perceived to be new at the beginning of the Iron Age was the practice of cremation. Archaeologists used to draw a clear distinction between inhumation and cremation as alternative methods of mortuary disposal. Some even attempted to equate mortuary practice with subsistence strategies: inhumation was associated with the sedentary, agricultural populations of the Mediterranean, whose attachment to the land is preserved even in death by burying the defunct on ancestral soil; cremation, on the other hand, was associated with pastoral-nomadic Nordic populations, for whom the soul might roam free in death as in life.[28] Thus, the introduction of cremation into Greece was taken by many scholars as indicating the arrival of a new Nordic and nomadic population, and if some retained a degree of circumspection, attributing it to 'northern ele-

---

[25] From central Europe: Rutter 1975; 1990; Deger-Jalkotzy 1977. From northwest Greece: Kilian 1978. Mountjoy (1988, 30) also attributes the handmade pottery found in the Kerameikos to an intrusive element, though while not necessarily ruling out a northwest Greek derivation she prefers to situate its origins closer to Attika.

[26] The association is noted in Vanschoonwinkel 1991, 241–42. Karl Reber (1991), who does not accept this derivation, distinguishes three types of Early Iron Age handmade ware: (i) Dark Ware, which appears throughout central Greece from Submycenaean times, particularly in graves; (ii) Argive-Korinthian Ware, attested in both settlements and graves from the Submycenaean period through to the seventh century BC; and (iii) Attic Incised Ware, found mainly in Attic graves (especially those of women and children) between the Submycenaean and Middle Geometric periods. [27] Skeat 1934, 28–29. [28] See Audin 1960, 312.

ments' rather than to Dorians specifically,[29] others credited it to the Dorian descendants of the cremation-practising Urnfield populations who occupied Illyria and Bosnia in the Late Bronze Age.[30]

Regardless of any supposed opposition between cremation and inhumation, there is, even within the practice of inhumation, a variety of choices to be made concerning the exact disposal facility employed, and again the introduction of a new grave type was often associated with the arrival of a new population group. It has been argued, for instance, that the appearance of shaft graves at Mykenai ca. 1600 BC marks the arrival of a new 'Akhaian' population, especially since the graves contain new types of grave goods for which the closest parallels are furnished by south Russia.[31] In terms of the Dorian question, a similar stress was laid on the cist grave – a rectangular pit, lined with stone slabs and closed by either a stone or a wooden cover. The cist grave was originally designed for the interment of a single burial and, as Desborough observed, this represented a complete break from the Mycenaean preference for multiple burial within chamber tombs, which 'had been so universal and persistent that it seems inconceivable that the elimination of this should not entail some radical change in the population'.[32] That the origin of this new population should be the supposed Dorian *Urheimat* of northwest Greece seemed to be confirmed by the early appearance of cist graves at Kalbaki in Epeiros, Kozani, Vergina and Khaukhitsa in Makedonia, and Retziouni, Palaiokastro, Iolkos, Theotokou and Halos in Thessaly.[33]

Attention also focused on the more personal objects that the Dorians supposedly brought with them. Among the most common metal artefacts of the Early Iron Age are dress pins and fibulae (brooches) whose original function was to act as shoulder-fasteners for female and, in a few cases, male dress. They may be iron, though are more commonly bronze, and are found predominantly in graves and sanctuaries. According to Herodotos, they were only used to fasten the Dorian dress (*peplos*), since the Ionian *khiton*, or tunic, did not require them.[34] Furthermore, the dress that Herodotos (and other authors) termed 'Dorian' was a heavy woollen garment, suggesting to some an origin in cooler northern climes. For this reason, the infiltration of a new northern population was associated with the appearance in quantity of the so-called 'violin-bow' fibula – originally dated to the transition between LHIIIB and LHIIIC.[35]

The same date was also originally given for the appearance of a new type of slashing-sword known variously as the Naue II sword, or *Griffzungenschwert*, after its characteristically tongue-shaped hilt.[36] The distribution of the slashing-sword

[29] E.g. Wiesner 1938, 125–56; Bouzec 1969, 126.
[30] Audin 1960, 320. The appearance of cremation burials in central Krete in the mid-tenth century is explicitly attributed to the arrival of Dorians by Parker (1995, 148). Nicolas Coldstream (1984, 314, 317) also notes the shift to cremation, though he dates the arrival of the Dorians to the eleventh century when there is an abrupt break in tomb usage and the appearance of a new non-Minoan Submycenaean ceramic style.   [31] Muhly 1979.   [32] Desborough 1964, 37.
[33] Desborough 1964, 37–40. See also Bouzec 1985, 205.   [34] Herodotos 5.87.
[35] See Desborough 1964, 56.   [36] Desborough 1964, 56.

117

throughout northwest Greece, the northeast Peloponnese, the islands of the southern Aegean and Cyprus, together with its absence from Thessaly, central Greece and Makedonia, were cited as evidence for its derivation from northwest Greece and the Adriatic.[37] Similarly, the distribution of a type of spearhead known as the Höckmann Type K only in Epeiros during LHIIIB, but throughout northwest Greece, Akhaia, the southern Aegean, central Greece, Thessaly and the Peloponnese during LHIIIC, was employed to propose a centre of diffusion for this particular artefact in Epeiros.[38]

The picture of the Dorians generated by this particular configuration of the archaeological evidence was not so dissimilar to the romantic vision of the Dorians that was outlined in chapter 1. The destruction of the Bronze Age palaces, together with the appearance of a new type of sword and spearhead, marked them out as fierce warriors, while their possible involvement in the advent of ironworking and Protogeometric pottery established them as the true ancestors of Hellenism. It is also interesting to note that the original point of diffusion for these supposedly intrusive artefacts was as geographically imprecise as the locations offered for the Dorian homeland by the literary tradition (see chapter 3), wavering between Epeiros, Makedonia and Thessaly.

While most archaeologists prior to the war tended to accept the historicity of the Dorian invasion, it would be misleading to suggest that all of the above associations between the Dorians and supposedly intrusive elements of material culture were granted equal validity.[39] Nevertheless, it was only after the war that a systematic attack was launched against the arguments adduced in support of the Dorian invasion. To a large degree, this counter-assault was conditioned by the growing realisation that culture change need not be explained through resort to exogenous factors (in fact, the reaction against invasion hypotheses spawned new internalist and 'processual' explanations that were just as religiously observed). In part, however, the *volte face* was also a direct consequence of the post-war reaction against the romantic obsession with *Völkerwanderung* (see chapter 1).

In terms of the settlement evidence, decades of further excavation and greater refinement in the classification and chronology of Mycenaean pottery have served to complicate rather than clarify the traditional picture. It is now patently clear that various Mycenaean sites suffered a series of destructions throughout the Late Helladic period rather than a single, simultaneous destruction at the end of LHIIIB2. Furthermore, the major destructions which affected Mykenai and Tiryns at the end of LHIIIB2 have recently been attributed not to the hostile action of invaders but to the effects of a violent earthquake.[40] Indeed, the only certain

---

[37] Hiller 1985, 138–39.
[38] Höckmann 1980; Hiller 1985, 139. In fact, Hammond (1975, 687) regards Epeiros as the cradle of the Dorians.
[39] Interesting in this respect is Myres 1930, 400–63. Desborough (1964) is also rightly critical of many of the elements often adduced as evidence for the Dorian invasion.
[40] Kilian 1980; 1985; Iakovidis 1986.

evidence for hostile action is constituted by the appearance of arrow heads associated with the last of no fewer than six destructions which affected the citadel of Tiryns in LHIIIC – the other destructions being attributed to either seismic activity or inundations.[41] Alternatively, it has been argued that the collapse of the Mycenaean palaces is better attributed to a natural disaster such as climatic change leading to drought,[42] or to economic collapse resulting from either excessive specialisation in agriculture or a debilitating increase in central expenditure,[43] than to any widescale destruction delivered by marauding Dorians.

In Lakonia, the supposed 'gap' between LHIIIC and Protogeometric is now beginning to be plugged. At the upper end, it would appear that LHIIIC in Lakonia may linger on until the middle of the eleventh century,[44] while at the lower end, the appearance of a Lakonian Protogeometric sherd at Asine in a context which is supposed to be securely dated to the eleventh century ought to suggest that the Protogeometric style develops in Lakonia at much the same time as in Attika or the Argolid, rather than some 100–150 years later as previously supposed.[45] If true, the consequence would be that there is in Lakonia little (if any) break in cultural continuity. In Akhaia, the belief in new settlements populated by refugees from the Argolid and Lakonia has encountered the twin objections that there is not the slightest trace of Argive influence on Akhaian ceramics and that there is no evidence for depopulation of the Argive plain during LHIIIC. Instead, Klaus Kilian preferred to see LHIIIC as a period of synoikism rather than depopulation within the Argive plain, hypothesising that the twenty-five hectares around Tiryns may have supported a population as large as 10,000.[46]

Equally strong objections have been voiced in the case of customs and cultural forms deemed diagnostic of the Dorian arrival. In describing the transition from bronze to iron, Anthony Snodgrass has detected three stages: a first phase, when the high value of iron dictates that it is used for ornamental rather than functional objects; a second phase, when iron does begin to be used for the functional parts of cutting and piercing implements, though the use of bronze still dominates; and a third phase when iron begins to be used widely (though without supplanting bronze) for jewellery, weapons and tools.[47] The very fact that the intensive adoption of ironmaking technology is such a gradual and drawn-out process makes it difficult to attach too much significance to the dates of individual iron finds in various parts of the Mediterranean and central Europe. However, if it is necessary to look for an exogenous origin for the advent of ironworking in Greece, Cyprus or the near east provide a more plausible candidate than the north Balkans.[48]

[41] Kilian 1985, 77. [42] Carpenter 1966. [43] Betancourt 1976; Small 1990.
[44] Demakopoulou 1982, 90.
[45] The Asine sherd: Wells 1983, 42, 124, though Cartledge (1992, 53) is sceptical. Dates for the beginning of the Lakonian Protogeometric sequence vary. Cartledge (1979, 92) set it at ca. 950 BC. Coulson (1985, 65) thinks that this may be a little too low, while Snodgrass (1971, 131) preferred a later date of ca. 900 BC. [46] Kilian 1980; 1981–82. See also Papadimitriou 1988.
[47] Snodgrass 1980b, 336–37; 1982b.
[48] Snodgrass 1965; 1967, 36; Pleiner 1969. See Vanschoonwinkel 1991, 273–74.

The Dorian claim to the introduction of Barbarian Ware into Greece was only ever one among many, but the fact that some pieces have come to light in LHIIIB2 levels at Mykenai and Tiryns – i.e. before the major destructions – and that this type of pottery may actually have influenced some Mycenaean LHIIIB2 forms rather undermines the view that it was introduced by external invaders during the Early Iron Age.[49] Observing that Barbarian Ware is almost always of local manufacture, Walberg invoked endogenous causes and attributed its appearance to a change in the conditions of pottery production after the palatial destructions, whereby large-scale workshops were replaced by smaller, local workshops with a more limited domestic production.[50]

In the case of Protogeometric pottery, Desborough pointed to what he saw as the technological revolution involved in the simultaneous invention of a faster wheel, resulting in tauter shapes, and a new combined multiple-brush and compass which allowed the execution of concentric circles and semicircles. In his opinion, this could only mean that the Protogeometric style had been developed in one, single centre rather than evolving independently in various regions of Greece out of local Mycenaean styles. Since it was in Attika that the Protogeometric style reached its zenith of perfection, Desborough attributed its invention to Attic workshops.[51] Yet in the literary tradition, if there was one region of Greece which escaped the Dorian invasion, it was Attika.

Among the earliest cremations in Greece are those of the LHIIIC cemetery at Perati in eastern Attika, while during the Submycenaean phase the rite is particularly favoured in the Pompeion cemetery in the Athenian Kerameikos, the Arsenal cemetery on the offshore island of Salamis and the cemeteries of Lefkandi on Euboia. Again, all are traditionally 'Ionian' areas that are said to have escaped the Dorian onslaught.[52] In fact, with the exception of a LHIIIC/Submycenaean cremation platform at Khaniá, near Mykenai,[53] and an instance at Nikhoria in Messenia,[54] the predominantly Dorian Peloponnese studiously avoided the rite of cremation. Furthermore, the hypothesis that there is an ethnic significance to the choice between cremation and inhumation runs the risk of being weakened by instances where both rites are practised alongside one another in the same cemetery, as is the case in the cemetery at Perati and the Protogeometric cemetery at Fortetsa, near Knossos on Krete.[55] In some cases (for instance, the Athenian Kerameikos or the cemeteries at Eretria on Euboia), cremation is the mode of disposal favoured for adults, while children are inhumed.[56] The most telling example,

---

[49] Small 1990, 8. See Vanschoonwinkel 1991, 234, 239.
[50] Walberg 1976. Small (1990) attributes its appearance to economic stress, caused by an increase in expenditure by the central authorities and the consequent disappearance of the élite. Nevertheless, petrographic analysis of Barbarian Ware from the Menelaion has revealed the occurrence of 'grog tempering' – a technique which, if found to be present in samples from other sites, could possibly be invoked as the inheritance of an originally common technological tradition: see Whitbread 1992.   [51] Desborough 1952, 119–26.
[52] Kraiker and Kübler 1939, 170–71; Vanschoonwinkel 1991, 119, 191–92.   [53] Hägg 1987, 211.
[54] Vanschoonwinkel 1991, 192.   [55] Perati: Paidoussis and Sbarounis 1975. Fortetsa: Brock 1957.
[56] Mazarakis-Ainian 1987, 16.

however, is that of Lefkandi where it would appear that, in some cases at least, the funerary ritual combined *both* cremation *and* inhumation.[57]

Again, the cist grave finds favour in non-Dorian areas such as the Pompeion and Arsenal cemeteries.[58] In this case, however, its appearance in the Early Iron Age does not represent any cultural innovation. Desborough knew that the cist grave was a popular mode of burial during the Middle Helladic period, though he believed that the period of time between the end of Middle Helladic and Submycenaean was too long for there to be any connection.[59] Jean Deshayes, on the other hand, attributed its reappearance to the cultural reawakening of a population that had been subjected by the Mycenaeans during the Late Helladic period.[60] In fact, the cist grave never really disappeared from Greece. Examples from LHI are attested in the Argolid,[61] while cists make a widespread appearance during LHIIIB throughout the Argolid, Messenia, Elis, Akhaia, Arkadia, Lakonia, Attika, Boiotia, Phokis and Thessaly.[62]

Even the evidence of the violin-bow fibula and the slashing-sword fails to stand up to closer scrutiny. Firstly, while the testimony of Herodotos associates pins and fibulae with the 'Dorian dress', this does not allow us to assume that the wearing of the *peplos* was exclusive to a Dorian group – in fact, Herodotos goes on to say that prior to the ancient war between Athens and Aigina, *all* women wore the 'Dorian dress'.[63] Secondly, the use of pins and fibulae – along with the Naue II sword – is already attested in the Mycenaean world, prior to the supposed date of the Dorian arrival.[64]

The list of archaeological objections to the traditional view of the Dorian invasion is impressive. Reflecting on the paradox of 'an invasion without invaders',[65] James Hooker wrote, 'We may therefore boldly postulate that there never was a "Dorian invasion", in the sense that speakers of Doric forcibly entered some of those areas of Greece previously occupied by Mycenaeans.'[66] For the 'Dorosceptics', either there never was a Dorian invasion, or (if one wants to concede some value to the literary tradition) the Dorians were already so heavily 'Mycenaeanised' that the cultural forms they employed are archaeologically indistinguishable from those of the Mycenaeans.[67]

Has the 'Dorian invasion', then, finally been laid to rest? Many archaeologists evidently think so,[68] though many ancient historians are insistent that the literary tradition cannot be jettisoned so easily.[69] In fact, reports of the death of Dorian archaeology have been greatly exaggerated, as the continuing controversy over Protogeometric pottery and cist graves will demonstrate.

---

[57] Popham, Sackett and Themelis 1980, 210–14.   [58] Snodgrass 1971, 314.
[59] Desborough 1964, 37.   [60] Deshayes 1966, 250.
[61] Alden 1981, 78; Barakari-Gleni 1984, 172–75.
[62] For a full list with bibliography: Vanschoonwinkel 1991, 184–85.   [63] Herodotos 5.88.
[64] Kilian 1987–88, 155; Snodgrass 1971, 307–309; Van Soesbergen 1981, 39.
[65] Snodgrass 1971, 312.   [66] Hooker 1979, 359.   [67] Snodgrass 1971, 312.
[68] E.g. Morris 1990, 64: 'The deconstruction of the Dorians recommends a similar elimination of the Indo-Europeans from the arena of Aegean archaeology'.
[69] Musti 1990, 66–74; 1991, 31; Brillante 1984.

Desborough's arguments for the single Attic origin of Protogeometric pottery were predicated on the simultaneous adoption of a faster wheel and the multiple-brush compass. However, both of these innovations have been questioned by Harrison Eiteljorg.[70] The presumption of a faster wheel was based on the fact that Protogeometric shapes appear tauter and more cylindrical by comparison with their more 'saggy' Submycenaean predecessors, but Eiteljorg has argued that the characteristically dumpy shapes of Submycenaean pottery cannot be due to technological incompetence since the pot would have had to pass through a more cylindrical shape, akin to Protogeometric forms, during the throwing process. In the case of the multiple-brush compass, Eiteljorg demonstrates how the use of a multiple brush on curved surfaces would result in strokes of different thicknesses. This, together with the fact that on many Protogeometric pots some individual 'stray' arcs of concentric semicircles appear to continue further than others, should suggest that the compass was used with a single, rather than multiple, brush – a technique which was already familiar within pottery decoration.

If the development of Protogeometric pottery is not to be linked with technological advances, then there is no particular need to assume that it had to evolve only in Athens. Indeed Margrit Jacob-Felsch has pointed to the existence of compass-drawn concentric circles on neck-handled amphorai in Submycenaean levels in the sanctuary of Artemis Elaphebolos at Kalapódhi (north of Livadhiá). She argues that the concentric circle motif should have developed first in Thessaly and Doris and that it was carried to other areas by migrating Dorians – a hypothesis that in many respects echoes that of Skeat in the 1930s.[71]

The archaeological objections to associating the cist grave with the Dorians have already been noted. In her archaeological study of the Argolid in the eighth and seventh centuries, Anne Foley does not seek to posit a general and universal correlation between cist burial and Dorian groups throughout Greece, but she does suggest that in Argos and the Argolid cist burial was the mode of disposal favoured by the Dorians.

Foley provides three basic arguments in support of her suggestion. The first is an apparent spatial differentiation in the choice of grave-types, with cist graves being found in the centre of Argos, while pithos and pit burials are located on the periphery of the city. The second is the fact that cist graves account for the majority of burials during the eighth century, and the third is that cist graves are richer than pithos burials:

> It is thus tempting to equate the popularity of the main grave types in Argos with
> different social groups living there at the time. The Dorians, who were the high
> class in Argos, would most probably have favoured cist graves, the cists being in
> general wealthier burials, while the subordinate class would most likely have used

---

[70] Eiteljorg 1980.
[71] Jacob-Felsch 1980. A Thessalian origin for Protogeometric pottery was also proposed by Verdelis (1958).

the pithos and pit burials, which on the whole are not so rich. In Argos those using cists, perhaps mainly the Dorians, were in the majority while those using pits and pithoi were a relatively small group in comparison.[72]

It is worth subjecting these claims to more critical analysis.

Foley is certainly not alone in seeing cist burial as a higher-status mode of mortuary disposal: Robin Hägg has argued that aristocratic families preferred cist graves while poorer people tended to bury their dead in pithoi.[73] Nevertheless, it is important to remember that the Geometric graves that archaeologists have retrieved in Argos are merely a *sample* of the total number of mortuary disposals made between 900 and 700 BC. Unfortunately, we cannot be sure that this sample is entirely representative, or that we possess the complete *social range* of disposal. Morris has argued, in the case of Attika, that up to the middle of the eighth century and for most of the Archaic period the retrieved graves represent only the disposal remains of an élite group or class which excluded its social inferiors from such formal burial.[74] Informal disposal, which might include exposure (or, as in the case of Rome, collective pits outside settlement areas or even city moats),[75] will often be archaeologically invisible. On the other hand (by way of a theoretical *caveat* rather than a concrete proposal), we might have a situation where the exhumed graves of Argos represent the lower end of the social spectrum: the graves of Argos are not, after all, fabulously wealthy when compared with some other areas of Greece.[76] Edmund Leach noted that in India it is only unsocialised infants and moral criminals who are likely to be buried; respectable corpses would be cremated and their ashes scattered to the winds.[77]

Even if the sample we possess is reasonably representative, it is not always an easy task to determine the socioeconomic status of the deceased from the mortuary evidence. The number and quality of interred grave goods might be thought to act as an accurate indicator of the status of the deceased, but some caution should be exercised. Gordon Childe noted that after the Early Bronze Age in Europe, the number and richness of grave goods decreased, although the cultures to which they belonged were undoubtedly richer than before.[78] This difficulty in differentiating rich or poor burials on the basis of grave goods was taken up by Peter Ucko, who notes that the valuable goods displayed at the funerals of high-ranking and wealthy priests among the Yoruba of Nigeria seldom find their way into the grave.[79] Similarly, Parker Pearson's study of the city cemetery in Cambridge revealed little or no correlation between the expense of a funeral and the rateable value of the deceased's property: in fact, the more lavish brick-lined graves and vaults were used by Gypsies and showmen – groups which also held the most expensive funerals in Cambridge.[80] In short, ethnographic comparisons

---

[72] Foley 1988, 40.   [73] Hägg 1990, though no ethnic distinction is implied.   [74] Morris 1987.
[75] Hopkins 1983, 208–09.   [76] Foley 1988, 37.   [77] Leach 1977, 162.
[78] Childe 1944, 85–88. Cited in Ucko 1969, 266.   [79] Ucko 1969, 266–67.
[80] Parker Pearson 1982, 102–04.

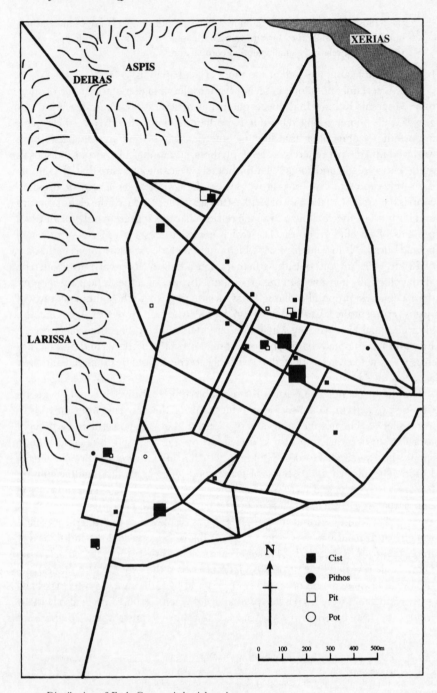

13 Distribution of Early Geometric burials at Argos.

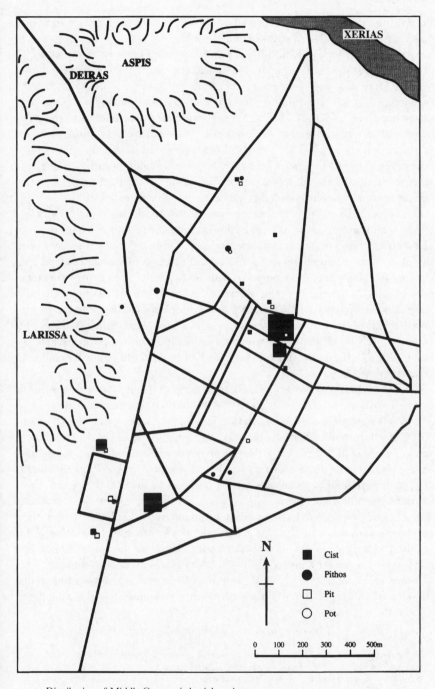

14 Distribution of Middle Geometric burials at Argos.

suggest that 'there is no *general* correlation between grandeur in graves and grave goods and wealth and high status among the living'.[81]

Proposals that seek to establish a direct relationship between the wealth of a grave and the status of its occupant fail to take account of the fluidity of attitudes that a society may hold concerning the dead, the expression of status and the exchange of goods. For instance, the types of artefacts that were deposited in Greek burials up until the end of the ninth century BC (particularly personal ornaments such as pins and fibulae) came to be offered at sanctuaries during the course of the eighth century.[82] The eventual disappearance of such items from graves reflects not a decline in general prosperity but new attitudes towards divinities, the emergent state and the sumptuary display of wealth, whereby the value of prestige artefacts may be safeguarded by taking them out of circulation.[83]

It is certainly true that, in general, the cists of the Argolid are slightly better furnished with grave goods than pithoi. Almost three out of four cist burials of the Geometric period contain at least one artefact, as opposed to slightly over one in three pithos burials. Similarly, a mean average of three ceramic and two metal artefacts are found in cist graves, compared with an average of one ceramic artefact in pithos burials.[84] Nevertheless, this differential is hardly significant enough to posit any extreme social divisions between those who employed cist burial and those who adopted pithos burial, and disguises the fact that while a good many cist graves contained no gifts at all, certain pithoi could be richly furnished – for instance, an infant pithos burial in the Theodoropoulos Plot in northern Argos had fourteen ceramic gifts.[85]

With regard to the grave facility itself, Foley suggests that pithoi 'were convenient and perhaps less costly than cists and no doubt were a quicker method of burial'.[86] This is not, however, so self-evident as it might initially appear. In terms of expenditure of effort, both required a pit to be dug first, and if the horizontal dimensions of the cist pit were greater than those required for a pithos, a considerably deeper pit had to be dug for the larger pithoi. It is difficult to know whether funerary pithoi were bought specifically for the purposes of disposal or whether existing domestic pithoi were pressed into service. On the other hand, the number of human hours required to make a pithos would almost certainly dictate that their purchase was more costly than the acquisition of a few roughly hewn stone slabs. In any case, the type of cist lined with orthostat slabs is not the most common: the majority are of poorer construction from sundry pieces of stone and rock.[87]

Nor is Foley's claim for a central clustering of cist graves and a peripheral distribution of pithos burials particularly convincing.[88] Figures 13–15 show the distri-

---

[81] Leach 1977, 162.   [82] Snodgrass 1980a, 52–54; Coldstream 1977, 333; Polignac 1995, 14–15.
[83] Morris 1986a.
[84] These figures are based on a sample of 269 Geometric graves from Argos. See Hall 1993, ch. 4 and Appendix A.   [85] Protonotariou-Deïlaki 1980, 63 (grave 48).
[86] Foley 1988, 38. For a criticism of simplistic relationships between tomb types and social class in Mycenaean Greece, see Voutsaki 1995.
[87] For a typology of cist graves: Hägg 1974, 109; Courbin 1974, 109.   [88] Foley 1988, 39–40.

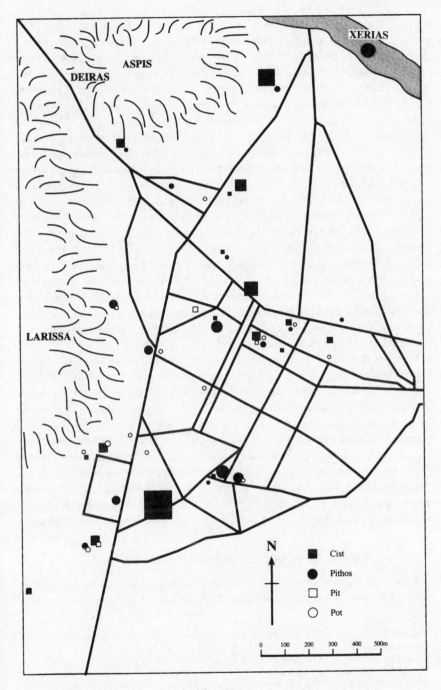

15   Distribution of Late Geometric burials at Argos.

bution of Early, Middle and Late Geometric burials at Argos. What the maps show is that pithoi appear alongside cists in the central part of the town, while cists are attested alongside pithoi both to the north and to the south. In fact, Foley's core-periphery model for the spatial distribution of burials is predicated on the existence of a focalised and unified settlement pattern, though there is good evidence to suggest that this did not emerge prior to ca. 700 BC, when formerly discrete settlement clusters expanded to meet one another.[89]

Not only do cists, pithoi, pit graves and pot burials all occur in varying proportions throughout Argos, they also coexist within the same cemeteries. For instance, in the Theodoropoulos Plot at Argos there is a variety of cist, pithos and pit graves with a uniform orientation.[90] A similar phenomenon recurs at neighbouring Tiryns, where an Early Geometric pithos in the Southwest Nekropolis is quite consciously oriented on the contemporary and earlier cists that surround it.[91] This is a very strange situation if each grave type bears a diacritical reference to a specific ethnic group. Indeed, if Foley's thesis linking cist burials to Dorians and pithos and pit burials to non-Dorians were correct, then we would have to accept a situation in which members of different ethnic groups were buried alongside one another. Ethnographically this seldom happens,[92] and in the case of the Argolid it is most improbable *unless* ethnicity was really not a salient dimension of local identity, in which case the likelihood of a direct correlation between a particular grave type and an ethnic group breaks down anyway.

A further objection is that cists account for over two-thirds of burials at Asine – a site where no pithoi have yet been found that postdate the Middle Helladic period.[93] This figure represents the highest proportion of cists for any site in the Argive plain,[94] yet if there is any *polis* in the Argolid for which a non-Dorian identity is stressed by the literary tradition, it is Asine (see chapter 4). Finally, Foley's argument is hard pressed to explain why the cist grave suddenly disappears throughout the whole Argolid around 700 BC, giving way to pithos and pot burial. If grave types were so intimately related to ethnic groups, is it likely that the Dorians suddenly adopted a mode of disposal that was previously associated with another, lower-status ethnic group? On balance, it is difficult to maintain that cist burial in the Argolid represents an exclusively Dorian mode of mortuary disposal.

Ethnic groups and archaeological cultures

The apparent *impasse* between the proponents and opponents of an archaeologically visible Dorian invasion arises from the fact that both camps subscribe to the

[89] Aupert 1982, 24; Hall 1996. *Contra* Hägg 1982, 300; Siriopoulos 1989, 324. For a parallel development at Korinth: Williams 1982.   [90] Deïlaki 1973, 98–99.
[91] Frickenhaus, Müller and Oelmann 1912, 130; Hägg 1974, 138 (grave 19).
[92] Brown 1981, 37; Parker Pearson 1982, 104.   [93] Hägg 1974, 160.
[94] Cists account for 53 per cent of Geometric burials at Argos, 43 per cent at Mykenai, 39 per cent at Nauplia and 26 per cent at Tiryns.

same fallacy – namely, that an ethnic group must necessarily be identifiable in the archaeological record. According to this view, the presence of new artefacts will indicate an ethnic influx, while the absence of any new elements will argue against it. Yet, history suggests otherwise. Both the Celtic invasion of Asia Minor and the Slavic migration into Greece are historically attested movements which have left little or no archaeological trace.[95] Similarly, for all their military and political dominance, it is difficult to identify archaeologically the Vandals in Europe, the Mongols in China or the Tutsi in Rwanda and Burundi.[96]

This fallacy stems from the 'culture-historical' approach of Gordon Childe, which was itself influenced by the 'settlement archaeology' method of Gustav Kossinna.[97] Both approaches begin by identifying 'archaeological cultures' (complexes of regularly associated traits) before equating the areas where these archaeological cultures are found with the areas occupied by specific populations. The assumption was that an archaeological culture should be the 'material expression of what today would be called a people'.[98] Thus, Kossinna used the dispersal of a type of pottery known as 'Corded Ware', along with other associated artefacts, to trace the original homeland of the Indo-Europeans to north Germany.[99]

Childe was eventually careful to distinguish between a 'race' and what he termed a 'people' – a supposedly more anodyne term for the groups he defined in the archaeological record.[100] On the other hand, Kossinna's claims for an Indo-European *Ursprungsland* in northern Germany were exploited by the Nazi party to bolster their claims for the cultural supremacy of the Germanic *Volk*,[101] and this is undoubtedly one of the reasons why the culture-historical approach has been widely discredited since the last war. By the 1950s it was recognised that an archaeological culture may have little, if any, social reality,[102] and this was developed further by David Clarke, who saw no *a priori* reason why archaeological patterns should equate with ethnic ones.[103] While promoting the reality of an archaeological culture *as* an archaeological culture, he stressed that it could not be treated as identical to an historical, political, linguistic or racial entity.[104]

The reasons for rejecting the culture-historical approach, however, extend beyond the merely ideological. A number of anthropological studies among contemporary societies have concluded that it is doubtful whether material culture need be ethnically diagnostic.[105] Among the Pokom of the Guatemala valley, ceramic differences between communities are more often related to the availability of ceramic resources than to any ethnic affiliation.[106] Equally, a study in Sierra Leone revealed that the form and style of ceramics there varied geographically and temporally rather than ethnically. Despite the existence of three distinct ethnic groups (the Limba, the Yalunka and the Kuranko), variations in the overall

---

[95] Winter 1977; Hodder 1978, 5; Musti 1985b, 47. [96] Martens 1989, 63; Van den Berghe 1976, 24.
[97] Veit 1989, 37–39; Trigger 1980, 44. [98] Childe 1929, v-vi; Renfrew 1984, 33; 1987, 215.
[99] Kossinna 1902; Renfrew 1987, 15. [100] Renfrew 1987, 215. [101] Renfrew 1987, 4.
[102] Willey and Phillips 1958, 49; Renfrew 1984, 34. [103] Clarke 1978, 365.
[104] Clarke 1978, 369–72. [105] Collett 1987, 106. [106] Arnold 1978, 58.

material cultural assemblage were due to factors other than ethnicity, such as climate, topography or history.[107]

It might be thought that the ritual opportunities which a funeral offers should provide a particularly efficacious *locus* for the expression of a range of social roles and identities.[108] In fact, the sort of problems which we have already encountered in attempting to associate burial practices such as cremation or the cist grave with the Dorians are not confined to the field of classical archaeology. For the anthropologist Edmund Leach, the whole practice of mortuary archaeology was something of a wasted exercise, since what archaeologists rather grandiosely call 'mortuary practice' is, in reality, simply the material residue of burials rather than the totality of rituals associated with the funeral. The exaggerated importance which is thus placed on burial distorts the fact that it is just one of a whole range of possibilities included in mortuary rites.[109] Even those anthropological archaeologists, such as Lewis Binford, who have proposed direct links between mortuary variability and social complexity remain unconvinced that it is possible to establish any correlation between mortuary rites and ethnic affiliation,[110] and the ancient historian Moses Finley pointed out that the Jewish community of Sicily provides a good example of an archaeologically invisible group, since it spoke Greek and adopted gentile burial practices.[111] The difficulties are highlighted even today by funerary practices in America, which preserve a high degree of uniformity despite regional, social and ethnic divisions.[112]

Further scepticism concerning the detection of ethnicity in burial practice is expressed in O'Shea's study of Plains Indian cemetery sites in Nebraska and South Dakota.[113] Each site was the reserved burial location for one of three ethnic groups: the Pawnee and the Arikara of the Northern Caddoan language group, and the Omaha who speak Dhegihan Sioux. Archaeological analysis detected elements of social ranking but not of kin-based social divisions, unless these were expressed in archaeologically invisible ways such as pre-mortuary rituals, the use of degradable materials, or coiffure.[114] On average, Pawnee sites were only marginally more similar to each other than to sites of other ethnic groups; the two Arikara sites were more similar to sites in other groups than to each other; and when artefacts found in association with sub-adults were tabulated, the levels of within-group similarity turned out to be lower than similarity between groups.[115] O'Shea asks whether it is 'reasonable to suppose that the placing of a particular artefact in the grave or the direction in which the body is oriented will communicate an individual's cultural association to the next tribe up the river?'[116]

The reasons for this archaeological *aporia* have already been anticipated in chapter 2. The failure of the culture-historical approach was to regard artefactual assemblages as *defining criteria* of ethnic identity. Instead, as we have seen, the crite-

---

[107] DeCorse 1989, 137. [108] Morris 1987, 42–43. [109] Leach 1977, 162.
[110] Binford 1972, 208–43. See also Brown 1981, 28. [111] Finley 1968, 168–69.
[112] Huntington and Metcalf 1979, 187. [113] O'Shea 1981; 1984. [114] O'Shea 1981, 49.
[115] O'Shea 1984, 289, 296. [116] O'Shea 1984, 287.

ria for ethnic inclusion are subjectively and discursively constructed. If one's ethnic identity cannot be determined in the first place by physiognomy, language or religion, then it is illusory to imagine that inanimate objects will prove to be a better candidate. The difficulty with archaeological research is that it does not have direct access to the self-conscious identifications by which the ethnic group is constituted.[117]

The archaeology of social praxis

The rejection of the culture-historical approach does not necessarily mean that archaeology has no role to play in the study of ethnic identity. In fact, one can find ethnographic parallels which do attest the expression of ethnicity through mortuary practices. In 1977, Michael Parker Pearson studied the differential treatment accorded to ethnic groups in the city cemetery of Cambridge. Certain reserved areas of the cemetery were set aside for Catholics, Jews and Muslims, and during the course of the twentieth century it is only ethnic minorities, and particularly Gypsies, who can be said actively to 'compete between themselves in death ritual'.[118] Parker Pearson attributes this to the fact that ethnic groups are positioned within vertically stratified relationships of power and domination: 'Social advertisement in death ritual may be expressly overt where changing relations of domination result in status re-ordering and consolidation of new social positions.'[119]

The reason why the Plains Indian and the Cambridge cases are so different is due to one of the principles set out in chapter 2 – namely, that ethnic identity is more likely to be salient in multi-ethnic situations. In the case of the Plains Indians, the three ethnic groups were positioned horizontally on a basis of relative autonomy and equality, and each cemetery was the burial ground for members of only one ethnic group. Therefore, such symbolic competition as existed was concerned with positions of power and influence *within* – rather than *between* – each ethnic group. The Cambridge case, on the other hand, exemplified the more common situation of 'ranked ethnicity':[120] that is, a scenario where different ethnic groups are vertically situated within the same ranked society and therefore confronted with one another on a generally unequal basis. In such circumstances, a group may well use material symbols to define itself, particularly when it either perceives itself to be threatened or is seeking to advance itself.

For earlier archaeological theorists, an archaeological culture was assumed to be the *passive* reflection of a group's behavioural patterns.[121] The types and distributions of artefacts were considered to be the direct result of their being used and discarded in accordance with rules which have arisen from human adaptation to

---

[117] Shennan 1989, 14.　　[118] Parker Pearson 1982, 104, 109.　　[119] Parker Pearson 1982, 112.
[120] Horowitz 1985, 22–24.　　[121] E.g. Piggot 1957, 2–3, 126; Daniel 1967, 17.

131

local environments, which are transmitted and learned through familial and societal institutions and which are unconsciously replicated every day. While these 'learned modes of behaviour'[122] *may* sometimes arise from ethnic enculturation, they are (as the comparative examples demonstrate) equally likely to be the consequence of technological or environmental factors. In some cases, such modes of behaviour may begin by having an ethnic significance, but come to be so deeply engrained that they continue even in the absence of any ethnic consciousness. In any case, at our historical remove, it will seldom be clear whether such behaviour can justifiably be termed 'ethnic' or not.

Conversely, the *active* 'social advertisement' of the ethnic groups in the Cambridge cemetery suggests that ethnic groups can engage in a form of social action which is more fully self-conscious and purposive than action which is simply denoted 'behaviour', and which we might term 'praxis'. As Shennan puts it, 'the creation of ethnic identities should have repercussions in terms of the self-conscious use of specific cultural features as diacritical markers, a process which might well be reflected in the archaeological record'.[123] In other words, certain cultural forms and artefacts may sometimes actively serve as *indicia* of ethnic identity, fulfilling a function similar to that of physiognomy, language or religion.

This proposition is not very dissimilar from recent views on archaeological 'style' – a term which describes the information-bearing element of material culture. Traditionally, the importance of style in archaeological analysis was to identify dates and populations, tracing discontinuities arising from invasions, migrations and diffusion.[124] It then came to stand as an index of social interaction: the similarity of stylistic attributes between social units was assumed to reflect the degree of interaction between them as well as social norms such as endogamy or exogamy, matrilocal or patrilocal patterns of residence.[125] In both cases it was viewed as a passive trace element – the unconscious, unintended residue of behaviour.

Current thinking tends to view style as being also used actively to convey messages about social or ethnic affiliations.[126] When viewed in this active role, style is termed 'iconological'.[127] It is considered to function as a mode of social integration and difference, targeted at individuals beyond the immediate scope of the household or residence group. At the same time, the range of this messaging is bounded, since its meaning would have little effect among socially distant populations.[128] It is for this reason that 'certain objects dispose of a genuine ethnospecific force only in the immediate vicinity of their own ethnocultural entity'.[129]

There is by no means, however, absolute consensus on this issue, and the passive nature of style has been eloquently championed by James Sackett's theory of isochrestism – a Greek neologism for 'equal use'.[130] According to Sackett, there exists a spectrum of equivalent alternatives or equally viable options for attaining any

---

[122] Clarke 1978, 18. [123] Shennan 1989, 16. [124] Shanks and Tilley 1987b, 138.
[125] Shanks and Tilley 1987b, 140–41. [126] Shennan 1989, 16; Shanks and Tilley 1987a, 85.
[127] Conkey 1990, 13. [128] Wobst 1977. [129] Bálint 1989, 189. [130] Sackett 1977.

given end in the manufacture and use of material culture. Style is then the choice of a few or just one among the range of possible isochrestic options, and is dictated by the technological traditions in which its users have been enculturated.[131] Isochrestic behaviour (i.e. that which conforms to and perpetuates the isochrestic options imposed by technological traditions) is therefore no different from conforming to the sorts of gestures, linguistic idioms, ways of disciplining children and magical practices that are appropriate to the culture in which such traditions are fostered.[132] According to Sackett, the unique conjunction of isochrestic options should be capable of 'fingerprinting' specific and discrete social groups.

Traditionally, the style of an artefact has been separated from its function. Thus, the function of a Greek pot – defined in terms of whether it was intended for transportation (hydriai or large amphorai), storage (pithoi and some kraters), distribution (oinokhoai) or consumption (cups, skyphoi and plates) – tends to be treated separately from any painted decoration on its surface. For Sackett, however, style inheres in function, because there are isochrestic choices to be made between different clays, tempers and degrees of firing or thickness as much as between different decorative elements. Style then becomes 'the specific ethnically bounded isochrestic choice assumed by functional form'.[133] The argument is in general a good deal more sophisticated than earlier treatments of style. It is still, however, predicated on the belief that an ethnic group is necessarily defined by its learned behavioural codes. The method may certainly be able to identify a range of social groups which find a cohesive identity through shared technological traditions, but there is no reason why such groups should be exclusively ethnic.

In chapter 2, it was necessary to elucidate the relationship between the individual and the collectivity. The same is true for a discussion of stylistic messaging, since it is individual potters, sculptors and metalsmiths (rather than faceless, anonymous groups) who manufacture artefacts. The importance of the dialectic between individual and society lies behind Ian Hodder's definition of style as 'the referral of an individual event to a general way of doing'.[134] Just as an individual's self-concept comprises a personal and social component (see chapter 2), so there is an individual and collective dimension to style, which William Macdonald terms 'panache' and 'protocol' respectively. Panache refers to the social processes and related behaviours aimed at an emphasis on the individual as a unique element. Protocol, on the other hand, refers to the similar processes aimed at the promotion of group identity and may, or may not, conflict with the individual level.[135]

This distinction between panache and protocol is similar to Polly Wiessner's distinction between 'assertive' and 'emblemic' style.[136] Assertive style is the consequence of a conscious or unconscious expression of personal identity, while emblemic style has a distinct referent, and seeks to transmit a clear message to target populations about a conscious social identity.[137] Emblemic style, then, will

---

[131] Sackett 1990, 33.   [132] Sackett 1990, 35.   [133] Sackett 1990, 34.   [134] Hodder 1990, 45.
[135] Macdonald 1990, 53.   [136] Wiessner 1983.   [137] Shennan 1989, 18–19.

be a consequence of group identity being 'switched on' by situations such as fear, intergroup competition, aggression, the need for co-operation to attain certain goals, or imposed political control that requires group action.[138]

As an example of the varying emphasis placed on social and personal identities respectively, Wiessner cites the use of style in the dress of the Eipo in eastern Irian Jaya. When participants competed in intravillage dances, their personal identity was more salient and they consequently displayed considerable variation in the sorts of dress that they wore. When, conversely, they competed in intervillage dances, they exhibited a much greater homogeneity of dress because the contest was concerned with group – rather than individual – expression.[139] The example is an instructive illustration both of the fluctuating salience in individual and social identities and of how, at certain times, artefacts can be employed actively to act as indicia of such social identities. To illustrate this active employment of material cultural forms for ethnic purposes further, we can take three ethnographic examples. One is concerned with settlement patterns, one with architecture and one with costume.

Traditionally, one of the most striking characteristics about Italian-Americans was their concentration in certain discrete areas within cities: in the early 1970s, over 90 per cent lived in urban areas such as Boston's North End, New York's South Brooklyn or South Side Philadelphia. This can hardly be attributed to a pattern of urban behaviour practised back home in Italy and replicated unconsciously in America, since the vast majority of Italian émigrés set out from rural areas such as the Mezzogiorno or Sicily. The establishment of these 'Little Italys' was rather a strategy to establish stable residence patterns, free from assimilation and focused on the centrality of *trattorie* and *drogherie*, which served to promote a key Italian virtue – namely, family solidarity.[140] The important thing is that this particular residential pattern resulted from conscious action rather than unconscious behaviour. Furthermore, it seems reasonable to expect that a 'Little Italy' would leave distinctive traces in the archaeological record.

In nineteenth-century America, German-Americans 'lacked a common religion, common regional or class origins, a common political ideology, a common immigrant predicament, in short, most of the generally accepted bases for the crystallization of ethnic sentiment'.[141] This did not, however, prevent them from celebrating and consolidating their ethnic identity, particularly through the frequent staging of festivals and pageants. By the 1880s, German-Americans who had achieved a certain level of status within some American cities began to erect public and private buildings in the German baroque style. Again, since there had been no pre-existing tradition of such a style of architecture in America up to that date, the phenomenon can hardly be regarded as a deeply-engrained 'way of doing'. Rather, the action was a conscious one, in line with the contemporary baroque revival in the *Vaterland*.[142]

---

[138] Wiessner 1990, 109.   [139] Wiessner 1989, 59–60.   [140] Vecoli 1978, 123–25.
[141] Conzen 1989, 48.   [142] Conzen 1989, 64.

The two American examples involved attempts to signal an identity that was distinct. The final example, on the other hand, concerns the active use of dress in order to assimilate ethnically with another group. The Muslims of Mauritius are, by and large, the descendants of merchants and indentured labourers from British India. In the 1970s, however, when it became increasingly apparent that Arab countries represented a considerable force on the world stage, they consciously attempted (ultimately unsuccessfully) to redefine themselves as Arabs by having the women adopt veils and the men long white robes.[143]

Thus cultural features such as costume, architecture or settlement patterns can be used in an active sense to signal a particular ethnicity. The last example is, however, particularly instructive. The Muslims of Mauritius committed the same mistake as adherents to the culture-historical approach, since they believed that material symbols could act as defining criteria of ethnic identity – they thought that to dress like an Arab was to *become* an Arab. Instead, the most that artefacts can achieve is to act as indicia which serve to reinforce the boundaries already established by ethnic criteria.

Nevertheless, it was argued in chapter 2 that indicia such as physiognomy, language or religion are labile, one often giving way to another over time, and the same is true of material cultural items. There are two reasons why any particular artefact need not always carry an ethnic connotation. The first is that ethnic identity is itself subject to varying degrees of salience over time. The second is that while material morphologies may remain stable, their social functions and attributed meanings can be volatile.[144] Indeed, it is precisely the ambiguity and multi-referentiality of symbols such as artefacts which makes them efficacious, because they can be consumed and employed in common by the members of an ethnic group while simultaneously meaning something different to each individual.[145]

To summarise thus far, we may legitimately conclude that the long-term *overall character* of an archaeological assemblage is as likely to be the consequence of factors such as technology, climate or access to resources, as it is of ethnicity. What an ethnic group does is actively and consciously to select *certain artefacts from within the overall material cultural repertoire* which then act as emblemic indicia of ethnic boundaries. In the words of Catherine Morgan, 'ethnic behaviour affects only those categories of artefact selected to carry social or political meaning under particular circumstances, rather than the totality of a society's material culture'.[146] This selectivity in the choice of material cultural items can be demonstrated by the case of Cyprus.

According to later Greek tradition, Paphos on the island of Cyprus was colonised by Agapenor, king of the Arkadian city of Tegea,[147] and supporters of this tradition often appeal to the fact that Mycenaean-type chamber tombs with dromoi begin to appear on the island in the eleventh century BC.[148] That the adop-

---

[143] Eriksen 1993, 72.   [144] Davis 1990, 21.   [145] Cohen 1985, 20–21, 55.
[146] Morgan 1991, 134.   [147] Strabo 14.6.3; Pseudo-Apollodoros, *Epitome* 6.15; Pausanias 8.5.2–3.
[148] Coldstream 1985, 47.

tion of chamber tombs is not simply a trend that has been borrowed from the Mycenaean mainland is suggested by a bronze *obelos* (spit) in Tomb 49 at the site of Palaipaphos-Skales (ancient Paphos), which bears the inscription *o-pe-le-ta-u* ('Οφελταυ). The inscription is normally assigned to the eleventh century, and while the script used is the Cypriot syllabary (derived from an indigenous Cyprominoan syllabic script employed in the Late Bronze Age) the language is Greek. In fact, the *-u* ending of the genitive identifies the dialect as closely associated with Arkadian.[149] Whether or not the chamber tombs and the inscription really testify to the arrival of a new population, it does seem fairly clear that they represent the active attempts on the part of a certain group on Cyprus to establish links with the Greek mainland. What is interesting, however, is that the scope of such signalling is not extended to the ceramic medium: the pottery deposited in the chamber tombs is decorated in the indigenous Proto-White Painted style of Cyprus.[150]

The problem that remains is how to distinguish active praxis from passive behaviour in the archaeological record. Much of the current work which stresses the active nature of material culture is derived from the field of ethnoarchaeology – a sort of 'back-to-front' archaeology that examines *contemporary* social behaviour in order 'to develop ethnographic analogies which concern the principles which relate material patterning to adaptive and cultural contexts'.[151] This is, however, a luxury that is unattainable for those who work at an historical remove. Instead, there is no choice but to proceed initially from a passive viewpoint, in which it is the artefact, rather than the social actor, that is encountered directly.

The chief aim of active signalling would appear to be the deliberate emphasis on cultural distinctiveness in circumstances where such distinctiveness is not otherwise immediately apparent, or on cultural conformity in situations where such conformity is not necessarily universally accepted. It therefore seems logical to expect that active signalling represents something of a *deviation* from the type of behaviour that one might normally expect. Thus, to identify instances of active praxis, it is necessary to examine the *context* of an archaeological phenomenon, since it is only by forming a picture of how a particular community typically uses various elements of material culture that one can discern apparent deviations from the norm. Furthermore, it is far more likely that artefacts or cultural forms selected for the active marking of boundaries will possess a *short-term* rather than a long-term diacritical value, and that the choice of medium for such expression will change over time. This dictates that the search for active signalling must be conducted in more than one channel of archaeological evidence.

In chapter 4, it was noted that in the ethnographic record the Dryopes of Asine constitute one of the most distinctive identities within the Argolid. It is not, then, altogether surprising that the strategies by which the population of Asine sought

---

[149] Coldstream 1985, 50; Jeffery 1990, 425; Sacconi 1991, 46–47. [150] Coldstream 1985, 48.
[151] Hodder 1982, 40.

to distinguish itself should extend also to material culture. The settlement plan of Asine appears to be unparalleled in the Argive plain,[152] and in the eighth century its pottery is influenced by Attic styles to a degree not witnessed at other Argolic sites.[153] Furthermore, there are at Asine several circular stone platforms (interpreted as the foci of ancestor cult) which find their closest parallels in Attika and on the Kykladic island of Andros.[154]

Indeed, it is in the area of mortuary practices that the divergent behaviour of Asine is most evident. The attested instances of cremation on the Barbouna hill and east of the akropolis mark a strong contrast to the overwhelming preference for inhumation elsewhere in the Argive plain.[155] While other sites in the plain (and especially Argos and Tiryns) exhibited a growing preference for pithos burial throughout the eighth century, Asine is exceptional for its retention of cist burial to the exclusion of pithos and pot burial. While skeletons were buried in a 'contracted' position at Argos and Tiryns, burials at Asine were outstretched and supine, resulting in longer and narrower cists.[156] Finally, while westerly orientations for graves were generally preferred at Argos and Tiryns, Asine seems to favour east or northeasterly orientations – a tendency which is not determined by any topographical factors though does represent a continuation of the practice during the Protogeometric period.[157] There is, then, good reason to recognise in the material culture of Asine a clear existence of active praxis, intended to signal an identity self-consciously distinct from other neighbouring sites.

Another example of active signalling through material culture is provided by the Akhaian colonies of South Italy – Sybaris, Kroton, Kaulonia and Metapontion. In archaeological terms these settlements have a good deal in common with one another, but they also display a distinctive and original blend of diverse stylistic influences – particularly in the fusion of Doric and Ionic architectural elements – which serves to distinguish them from their Dorian and Ionian neighbours in South Italy.[158] It is, however, particularly interesting that while the Akhaian colonies display a distinctive material cultural identity within South Italy, this owes virtually nothing to the material culture of their professed motherland, Akhaia.[159] There could be no clearer warning against equating archaeological cultures with ethnic groups.

The active marking of boundaries is a necessary criterion to be fulfilled in the

---

[152] Morgan and Whitelaw 1991, 82.   [153] Hägg 1965; Bohen 1980.

[154] The circles, whose diameters varied between 1m and 1.5m, contained sherds and animal bones. Absence of extensive burning seems to suggest that they are not so much hearths as platforms for ritual dining: see Hägg 1983; Fossey 1989. It is possible that there are two further parallels in Grave Circle B at Mykenai: Papadimitriou 1953, 207–09.

[155] Frödin and Persson 1938, 192–94; Hägg 1965, 128–29; 1974, 52; Courbin 1974, 115; Fossey 1989. The only certain instance of cremation elsewhere in the Argive plain is a Late Geometric funerary pyre in a circular pit in the Pronoia area of Nauplia: Charitonidis 1953, 194.

[156] Hägg 1990. Supine burial is also attested at Lerna: Courbin 1974, 123.

[157] Hall 1993, 103. For Protogeometric orientations, see Hägg 1980, 123.

[158] Mertens 1976; 1990.   [159] See Morgan and Hall 1996, 213.

archaeological search for ethnic identity. It is not, however, a sufficient criterion on its own, since it need only signify the existence of a self-conscious group identity: there is no automatic ethnic dimension involved. In 'the Thatcher years', for example, the self-conscious adoption by 'yuppies' of braces and filofaxes did not turn them into an ethnic group. Similarly, in the 1970s the active employment of safety-pins marked punks out, without bestowing upon them any putative ethnic heritage. In chapter 2, it was argued that ethnic groups differ from other social groups in their subscription to an ancestral territory and, particularly, to a shared myth of descent. Ideally, then, there should also be some kind of 'ancestralising' strategy behind the active employment of certain artefacts or cultural forms.

Again, the Argive plain may provide some examples of ancestralising strategies. In chapter 4, it was noted that the communities on the eastern side of the Argive plain (and – at least for a short period – the northwestern sector of Argos) found a common focus of identity in the myth of the Herakleidai. This myth expressed ancestral rights to the Argive plain and was reinforced by the practice of cult to Hera, the original Bronze Age mistress of the plain. It can hardly be coincidental, then, that it is precisely the same areas which witness, in the course of the eighth century, material appeals to the Bronze Age past.

One way in which these ancestral appeals might be articulated was by establishing Geometric and Early Archaic sanctuaries in areas of Late Helladic activity. This is the case with the citadel sanctuaries at Tiryns and Mykenai, the Heraion, the smaller Prosymna shrine, the sanctuary on the southern slopes of the Aspis hill at Argos and the cultic deposits in the Siamblis and Mikhalopoulos plots in northern Argos and in the House of the Oil Merchant at Mykenai.[160] At Tiryns, a square altar, dated to the Late Geometric period, incorporated a round Late Helladic predecessor (fig. 16),[161] while at Mykenai the decision to orient the Geometric sanctuary on the same east–west axis as the Mycenaean palace may not have been simply by chance.[162] Similarly, the construction of the 'cyclopean' terrace wall at the Heraion (fig. 17) in a style which imitates the Late Helladic masonry at Mykenai and Tiryns can hardly be regarded as anything other than a conscious appeal to the Bronze Age past.[163]

Another locus for ancestral legitimising strategies is provided by the Bronze Age chamber tombs and tholoi of the Argive plain. Towards the end of the eighth

---

[160] For the bibliography of these sites, see the key to figures 11–12. By contrast, the eighth-century deposits in the Koros, Maniates and Tsoukrianis plots in southern Argos are not associated with Late Helladic remains. There are Late Helladic traces beneath the sanctuary of Aphrodite by the Odeion of Argos, though the archaeological evidence suggests that cult was not established here until the very end of the seventh century. [161] Müller 1930, 134–39; Rupp 1983.

[162] Hall 1995b, 604. By contrast, the terrace which supported the seventh-century sanctuary was oriented north–south.

[163] The terrace wall was dated to the Mycenaean period by Plommer (1977, 76; 1984, 183–84), though is normally assigned to the eighth century: Blegen 1939, 427–28; Wright 1982, 186–92; Foley 1988, 135–36. There have, however, been some suggestions that it need not predate the construction of the first stone temple in the seventh century: Drerup 1969, 57–89; Antonaccio 1992, 95–98.

16 The Geometric altar on the citadel at Tiryns.

century votive offerings begin to appear in chamber tombs in the Prosymna cemetery in the immediate vicinity of the Heraion, in some of the tholoi and chamber tombs at Mykenai and in several chamber tombs in the Deiras cemetery at Argos.[164] Although once interpreted as 'hero cults', they are probably better treated as instances of tomb cult intended to forge a link with distant (and almost undoubtedly fictive) ancestors for the purposes of legitimating territorial and sociopolitical claims.[165]

Alternatively, a link could be forged with 'the ancestors' through the practice of reusing Bronze Age tombs for Iron Age inhumations – something which is attested in the ninth century at Dendra, and in the eighth and seventh centuries on the Deiras ridge at Argos, and at Berbati, Prosymna and Mykenai.[166] In the northern sector of Argos several Geometric and Early Archaic graves were consciously cut into Bronze Age tumuli.[167] This pattern appears all the more significant when it is contrasted with the practice in southern Argos of reusing Iron Age tombs for burial (fig. 18).

[164] Prosymna: Blegen 1937b; Antonaccio 1995, 56–64. Mykenai: Wace 1921–23, 292, 295, 312–13, 320, 329, 366, 387; 1932, 23, 32–33; Wace, Hood and Cook 1953, 80; Desborough 1954, 263; Antonaccio 1995, 32–45. Argos: Vollgraff 1904, 366–67; Deshayes 1966, 215–19; Antonaccio 1995, 17–22.

[165] For a general discussion of 'hero cult' and 'tomb cult': Coldstream 1976; Snodgrass 1982a; 1988; Morris 1986b; 1988; Whitley 1988; 1994; 1995; Antonaccio 1993; 1994; 1995; Hall forthcoming.

[166] Dendra: Persson 1931, 42, 67; Antonaccio 1995, 27–28. Argos: Hägg 1974, 35–36; Antonaccio 1995, 19. Berbati: Säflund 1965, 35–37, 81–90; Antonaccio 1995, 26–27. Prosymna: Antonaccio 1992, 99 n. 41; 1995, 58–60. Mykenai: Wace 1932, 115–17; Antonaccio 1995, 44–46.

[167] Protonotariou-Deïlaki 1980; 1982, 41.

17   The terrace wall at the Heraion.

While the custom of reusing Bronze Age tombs for burial represents an appeal to an ancestral, remote and even mythical past, the tendency towards mortuary disposal in Iron Age graves appears rather to invoke kinship ties in the present and very recent past, perhaps with the aim of strengthening family and kinship ties.[168]

Nevertheless, a note of caution needs to be sounded. The attestation of ancestral legitimising strategies within the archaeological record of the Argive plain only becomes truly significant when set against the context of the discursive construction of Heraklid identity that was traced in chapter 4. We cannot, however, assume that any one of these phenomena *per se* need indicate the operation of ethnic boundary marking. For instance, in Attika (which was supposedly ethnically homogeneous) it is difficult to maintain that the later deposition of votive offerings in the tholos tomb at Menídhi represents an ethnic strategy – indeed, James Whitley has suggested that the Menídhi tomb cult arose as a reaction on the part of an established community against the 'recolonisation' of the Attic countryside.[169] Similarly, it is not easy to determine whether the 'cyclopean' terrace wall which was built to support an Archaic Doric temple at Mases in the eastern Argolid (fig. 19) represents an ethnic appeal to the ancestral past or simply emulates the more famous (and – almost certainly – slightly earlier) terrace wall at the Heraion.[170]

[168] See Snodgrass 1971, 194–96; Hägg 1980, 122.
[169] Whitley 1988, 178. For the Menídhi tholos: Lolling 1880.
[170] Jameson, Runnels and Van Andel 1995, 469.

140

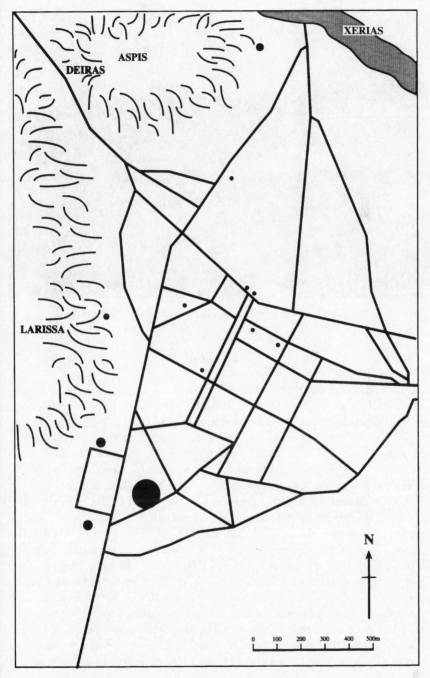

XERIAS

ASPIS

DEIRAS

LARISSA

N

0   100   200   300   400   500m

18   Distribution of Argive burials in reused Iron Age graves during the Late Geometric period.

19 The terrace wall of an Archaic sanctuary at Mases.

Conclusion

It seems fairly clear that there needs to be a radical reconsideration of archaeology's role within the study of ethnicity. It has been argued that since artefacts *never* served as defining criteria of ethnic identity in the past, it would be fallacious for archaeologists to treat them as such now. It is, therefore, hopeless to believe that archaeological evidence can *identify* ethnic groups in the past. Artefacts can, however, be taken and consciously employed as emblemic indicia of ethnic boundaries in much the same way as language or religion. The task, then, that should be reserved for archaeology, and for which it is well equipped, is to illuminate the ways in which ethnic groups actively employed material culture in marking boundaries that had already been discursively constructed.

Such a realignment is, in fact, similar to the so-called 'postprocessual' emphasis on the active nature of material culture.[171] There are, however, some provisos. Firstly, material culture is not *always* used actively: this depends on fluctuations in the salience of ethnic identity. Secondly, when it is used actively, this need not continue indefinitely. Thirdly, material culture is just one medium among others which may come to be selected for such active signalling. The obvious conclusion to be drawn – unpalatable perhaps to some – is that the entire enterprise has little chances of success in situations where the *only* evidence to hand is archaeological.

[171] For 'postprocessual' archaeology, see Hodder 1991.

142

6

Ethnicity and linguistics

One of our most important sources for an ethnolinguistic understanding of the Greek language is the epigraphical evidence furnished by formal inscriptions and dedications carved on bronze or stone tablets, as well as graffiti and dipinti casually scribbled on personal items. Relatively free from the artificial literary idioms that characterise the literary corpus from as early as the time of the Homeric epics, inscriptions (unlike the literary manuscripts which have been subjected to centuries of textual transmission) bear the unmediated mark of their scribes.

Two sorts of information are present in inscriptions. The first is linguistic: slight differences in speech and dialect can be discerned through phonological, morphological and sometimes even lexical variations. The second is strictly speaking stylistic rather than linguistic and involves variations in the *manner* of writing.[1] The existence of localised chirographic traditions and conventions means that the provenance of inscriptions can often be ascertained from the shapes of letter forms. It is, however, the existence of a repertoire of *alternative* letter forms which presents each community with the need to choose between them. As with elements of material culture, this choice is seldom random and may well indicate a conscious selection intended to stress local identities. It is to these non-linguistic variations that we turn first.

Scripts and alphabets

The ancient Greeks attributed the invention of writing to mythical figures such as Hermes, Prometheus, Palamedes and Kadmos, though the earliest alphabetic inscriptions do not generally predate the eighth century BC – ironically, some of the earliest were found in Italy.[2] In the four or so centuries which intervene between

[1] Bile and Brixhe 1983, 122.
[2] See generally Jeffery 1990, 2–3. At present, the credit for the earliest Greek inscription is often claimed by Osteria dell' Osa, where four or five letters of the Greek alphabet were found scratched on the surface of a small, globular flask that is unlikely to be later than the first half of the eighth century (and may even be a little earlier): see Bietti Sestieri 1992, 184. It is important to note, however, that these letters do not seem to constitute anything particularly intelligible and may not even be Greek: Holloway 1994, 112. A kotyle, found at Pithekoussai on the island of Ischia in the Bay of Naples, has provided one of the earliest verse inscriptions in the form of three retrograde hexameters, probably to be dated to the last quarter of the eighth century: see Buchner and Russo 1955; Johnston 1983; Ridgway 1992, 55–57.

143

the collapse of the Mycenaean palaces ca. 1200 BC (when the syllabic Linear B script ceased to be used) and the attestation of an alphabetic script in the eighth century, it is widely assumed that the art of writing was lost in mainland Greece.

Considerable controversy exists over exactly when and where the Greeks adopted the alphabet to represent their language. Most philologists assume that the Greek alphabet is a modified form of the North Semitic, or Phoenician, alphabet whose transmission cannot therefore predate the resumption of communication between Greeks and Phoenicians – an event often dated to the second half of the eighth century BC.[3] However, recent decades of archaeological exploration (particularly the excavations at Lefkandi) suggest that this contact may never have been entirely lost during the Dark Ages,[4] while Joseph Naveh has argued that irregularities in the direction of the script and the shape of certain letter forms – especially *alpha* and *sigma* – suggest borrowing not from the North Semitic alphabet, but from an earlier Canaanite alphabet ca. 1050 BC.[5] Nonetheless, until alphabetic inscriptions predating the eighth century are found in mainland Greece, the consensus of opinion still tends to opt for a late date for the transmission of the alphabet, albeit with a slight upward modification.[6]

It is generally agreed that the alphabet was transmitted in one place only, since all the variant local scripts demonstrate the same divergences from the North Semitic model,[7] though the place of transmission is disputed. Margherita Guarducci favours Krete for three reasons: firstly, the Kretan alphabet shows some of the closest similarities with the Phoenician script; secondly, there are well-established links between Krete and Phoenicia;[8] and thirdly, Krete had distinct advantages in being able to disseminate the alphabet to the rest of the Greek world.[9] Lilian Jeffery, on the other hand, thought that since the script of Rhodes (which is the most important island closest to Krete) is very different from that of Krete, both islands must have derived their alphabet from a third source. She opted for Al Mina, the commercial settlement on the river Orontes in Syria,[10] though some doubts have recently been expressed as to whether there was any significant Greek presence at this site from such an early date.[11] Alternatively, Alan Johnston has suggested that Cyprus also hosted a considerable degree of interaction between Greek and Phoenicians and is thus a strong candidate for the place of transmission of the alphabet.[12]

---

[3] Jeffery 1990, 3.   [4] See especially Shaw 1989.   [5] Naveh 1973.

[6] Johnston, in Jeffery 1990, 425; Guarducci 1987, 20.   [7] Jeffery 1990, 6; Guarducci 1987, 17.

[8] Sznycer 1979; Shaw 1989.   [9] Guarducci 1987, 18. See also Sacconi 1991, 51.

[10] Jeffery 1990, 11–12.

[11] Boardman (1980, 39–46) argues for a Euboian presence at Al Mina by 800 BC at the latest. However, Kearsley (1989) believes that the pendent semicircle skyphoi at Al Mina cannot predate ca. 750 BC, which appears a little too late for the transmission of an alphabet that was by this date, if not slightly earlier, already in use in the west. Snodgrass (1994, 4–5) similarly suspects that an early Greek presence at Al Mina may be somewhat phantomatic, though Popham (1994, 26) rejects Kearsley's chronology and redefends the early presence of Euboians at Al Mina.

[12] Johnston 1983. The claims for Pithekoussai as the place of transmission have been dismissed by Johnston in Jeffery 1990, 426.

20 The evolution of the letter forms for *alpha, epsilon, theta* and *xi*.

The mere attestation of alphabetic literacy in any given region of Greece is not in itself sufficient to inform us as to the extent of literacy among the population of that region or the uses for which writing may have been employed. To determine this, it is necessary to situate the earliest incriptions within their regional epigraphical context. To this end Simon Stoddart and James Whitley have identified two diametrically opposed models for the social context of literacy in Archaic Greece. In the first, typified by Attika, the number of personal inscriptions, including onomastic graffiti, personal dedications and inscribed tombstones, greatly outweighs the number of (generally later) official inscriptions such as law codes and decrees. From this, they argue that literacy was relatively widespread in Attika. In the second model, however, which is represented by Krete, the earliest inscriptions are of a more official nature and include a number of law codes; conversely, personal inscriptions are less in evidence. They conclude that the uses of literacy were more restricted on Krete, and that the recording of laws was not a democratic activity designed to communicate directly with the populace, but rather a symbolic action engineered not only to stress the immutability of the laws, but also to endow them with a certain 'mystique'.[13] Most other regions of mainland Greece – notably, Euboia, Korinth, the Argolid, Lakonia and possibly Boiotia – appear to follow the Attic model. By contrast, the pattern of literacy in Elis seems closer to the Kretan model, though possibly for different reasons – the early inscriptions of Elis tend to concern themselves with the administration of the sanctuary of Zeus at Olympia.

The important feature to observe about the Greek alphabetic scripts is that the representation of certain letters varies over time and through space. It is principally for this reason that texts can be assigned to specific places and periods in much the same way as material cultural artefacts. The general stylistic evolution over time of certain letter forms is illustrated in figure 20. For instance, the slanting cross-bar of *alpha* gradually assumes the horizontal; *epsilon* loses its tail, and its cross-strokes cease to slant; the diagonal cross of *theta* is eventually replaced with a single point; and the vertical bar of *xi* becomes shorter, until it disappears alto-

[13] Stoddart and Whitley 1988.

21 Regional variations between some of the more diagnostic letter forms ca. 600 BC.

gether.[14] Figure 21, on the other hand, illustrates some regional variants of the more diagnostic letter forms in the years around 600 BC. Thus, the lunate *gamma* of Korinth is very different to the more familiar form found in Argos, Sparta and Boiotia, while the Attic *gamma* is more similar to the Spartan *lambda*. Similarly the symbol used to represent *iota* at Korinth bears a strong similarity to that used to represent *sigma* in Boiotia (the reason why the sign for *sigma* does not appear in Korinth, Argos or Krete is because at this period, these areas were using *san* to represent the sibilant).

[14] For a more detailed analysis, see Guarducci 1987, 31–32.

146

Within these general principles, however, a certain degree of caution needs to be exercised. Firstly, individual chirographic variations will blur the patterns somewhat, and there is no necessary reason why state-sponsored inscriptions need show an evolution of letter forms that exactly parallels or keeps pace with personal graffiti. Secondly, it is not impossible that two letter forms may be simultaneously used in the same region: Harold Mattingly has shown that, contrary to the view which sees a three-bar *sigma* giving way to a four-bar *sigma* in the Attic alphabet ca. 445 BC, the use of the two types of *sigma* in fact overlapped during the period 440–418 BC.[15] Thirdly, too rigorous a definition of regional letter forms is monolithic, and fails to take into account the mobility of craftspeople or the availability of skilled labour, not to mention possible social or ethnic divisions within communities. For instance, it was originally believed, on the basis of letter forms attested in a sacral law dating to the first half of the sixth century, that the alphabet of Tiryns could be grouped with the alphabets of Kleonai and Phleious – cities which lie between Korinthia and the Argolid.[16] However, with the discovery in 1962 of a longer sacral law from the Tirynthian citadel it became clear that the local script of Tiryns was closer to that of Argos than those of Kleonai and Phleious.[17] For this reason, the excavators assigned the provenance of the former sacral law to Kleonai rather than Tiryns, though a more economic hypothesis would be to assume that the Tirynthians employed a stone-cutter who had been enculturated in the chirographic traditions of Kleonai.[18]

While analysis of letter forms can serve to identify regional groups of scripts, these regional groups themselves are not always uniform or homogeneous. A good example of this is provided once again by the Argive plain, where the settlements of Argos, Mykenai and Tiryns exhibit slight, though distinctive differences in chirographic conventions despite their evident geographical proximity to one another. Figure 22 tabulates the letter forms attested at the principal settlements of the Argolid in the sixth century.[19] The reason why the sixth century has been chosen is due to the quantity of epigraphical evidence in the Late Archaic period by comparison with the seventh century or the fifth century (in the course of which Mykenai and Tiryns were destroyed and abandoned), though it is important to

---

[15] Mattingly 1982; 1992.

[16] Jeffery 1990, 145. For the sacral law: Peek 1941, 198–200; Jeffery 1990, 150 no. 8; *SEG* 11.369.

[17] Verdelis, Jameson and Papachristodoulou 1975; Koerner 1985; Foley 1988, 124; Hall 1995b, 587.

[18] Verdelis, Jameson and Papachristodoulou (1975, 187) deem the provenance of the former sacral law to be unreliable, though the reported find-spot, based on the testimony of a former *phylax* at the Nafplio Museum, should not perhaps be so readily dismissed. Evidence for the presence of Kleonaians in the Argive Plain may be provided by the appearance of the 'false *epsilon-eta*' of Kleonai on a graffito, scratched on a two-handled globular cup dating to the mid-seventh century and found at the Prosymna terrace shrine: see Blegen 1939, 425; Jeffery 1990, 150 no. 11; *SEG* 11.306.

[19] The data is based on a sample of 40 inscriptions taken from Jeffery 1990, 168–69, 174, 150, 181, 444–45, with the addition of Waldstein 1905, 172, 185–86, 262, 332, 337; Kunze 1950, nos 76, IIIa, XXIVw, XXIXb, XXIX*bis*a, XXXd, XXXIIb; Verdelis, Jameson and Papachristodoulou 1975; Pariente 1992; Piérart and Thalmann 1987, 595; *IG* 4.1203; *SEG* 11. 308; 14.315.

22 Letter forms in sixth-century Argolic inscriptions.

note that the sixth century also witnesses a relatively rapid pace of change in the evolution of letter forms so that not all the variants recorded in figure 22 need be contemporary with one another.

Although the same letter forms are frequently found at Argos, Mykenai and Tiryns, variations arise from the fact that these settlements tend to cling tenaciously to single variants for some letters while employing a number of variants for others. For example, Tiryns uses *alpha* forms with both slanting and horizontal cross-bars, but Argos prefers the slanting variant and Mykenai the horizontal variant. Similarly, Mykenai displays three variants of the *nu* form, while Argos retains only one. That this is not simply a matter of the chronological spread of the sample is demonstrated by the more recent of the two sacral laws at Tiryns in which a number of variants for the same letter – notably *alpha, theta, lambda* and *khi* – appear in the same document.

These variations are brought out more strikingly in figure 23, which charts the highest correlations between local scripts on the basis of the information in figure 22. The coefficients have been calculated by counting the number of positive matches in letter forms between each pair of local scripts, and then expressing that figure as a percentage of the total number of cases in which *both* scripts provide evidence for a letter form. The arrows indicate only the highest correlation score for each script: double-arrows denote pairs of sites whose highest correlation is mutual. What is noticeable is that although there are evident similarities between the scripts of Argos, Mykenai, Tiryns and the Heraion (which, as a neutral meeting-place for the communities of the plain, is likely to show features in common with them), the levels of correlation are not as high in absolute terms as one might perhaps have expected. Given the fact that Argos, Mykenai and Tiryns used various items of material culture to differentiate themselves from one another (especially during the Geometric period),[20] it is entirely feasible that the variability noted in these chirographic traditions is also due to active manipulation rather than arising simply from localised behavioural patterns. On the other hand, such active praxis could easily be intended to signal the *civic* identity of these emergent *poleis* rather than acting as part of any broader ethnic strategy.

From a more regional perspective, however, figure 23 appears to show that the Argive plain and the eastern Argolid formed separate and distinct enclaves. Indeed, the correlation rate between Argos and Troizen is only 37.3 per cent, while that between Tiryns and Epidauros is as low as 22.2 per cent. The distinction between the two regions arises in part from the differential treatment accorded certain letter forms – notably *gamma* and *lambda* – but the most significant variations are firstly, that the east Argolic scripts prefer the 'red' alphabet while the

---

[20] See generally Morgan and Whitelaw 1991 (ceramic style); Hall 1995a, 13–14 (burial practices and votive behaviour); 1996 (settlement patterns). In the case of cult, the division between the eastern and western sides of the Argive Plain is perpetuated throughout the Archaic period: see further chapter 4 and Hall 1995b, 596–608.

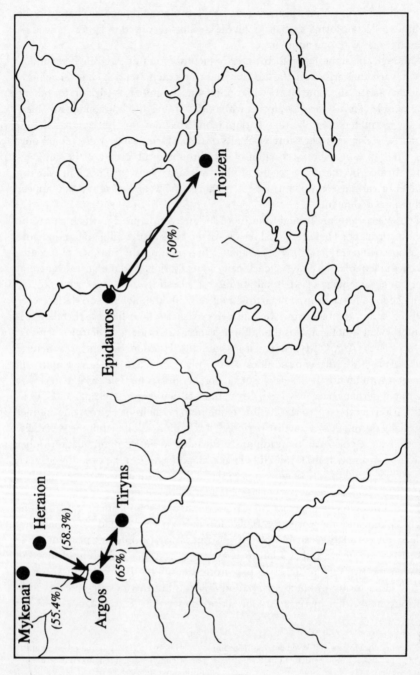

23 Highest correlations between Argolic scripts in the sixth century.

	Blue	Red	Green
xi	‡	✕	Κ Μ
phi	Φ	Φ	Γ Η
khi	✕	Ψ	Κ Η
psi	Ψ	Φ Ϛ	Γ Μ

24 The differential treatment accorded to *xi*, *phi*, *khi* and *psi* by the 'blue', 'red' and 'green' alphabets.

Argive plain favours the 'blue' alphabet,[21] and secondly, that while *sigma* is used to render the sibilant in the eastern Argolid, the Argive plain generally tends to employ *san*.

The 'blue', 'red' and 'green' alphabets derive their name from the colours that Kirchoff used on a map intended to illustrate the differences between the scripts of eastern, western and southern Greece.[22] The distinctions are based on the treatment of the signs for *xi*, *phi*, *khi* and *psi* (fig. 24). So the eastern ('blue') group, which included eastern Greece together with Korinth, Megara and the Argive plain, represented *xi*, *phi*, *khi* and *psi* with the signs that are familiar to us from the later adoption of the Ionic alphabet. The western ('red') group, which included much of the mainland as well as the western colonies, used 'blue' *khi* for *xi*, 'blue' *psi* for *khi*, and a combination of *phi* and *sigma* to represent *psi*. The southern ('green') groups, found in Krete, Melos and Thera, initially lacked signs for *xi*, *phi*, *khi* and *psi*. *Xi* was denoted by a combination of *kappa* and *san*, and *psi* by a combination of *pi* and *san*, while Melos and Thera (though not Krete, where the 'psilotic' dialect lacked aspiration) attached an aspirate to *pi* and *kappa* to render *phi* and *khi*.

Although Argos was certainly using the letter *sigma* for the sibilant in the early fifth century,[23] the seventh- and sixth-century inscriptions of both Argos and Tiryns regularly employ *san* – a usage in stark contrast with the eastern Argolid where Archaic inscriptions show that *sigma* was the preferred form. In fact, the historical development of *san* and *sigma* suggests that the decision to use one or the other is more properly a matter of phonology rather than simply orthography. The

[21] Jeffery 1990, 153, 175. See also Fernández Alvarez 1981, 43.   [22] Kirchoff 1877.
[23] It appears on a stele recording the dedication of Aiskhyllos to the Dioskouroi and dated to 500–480 BC: *IG* 4.561; *SEG* 11.328; Jeffery 1990, 169 no. 17.

151

Phoenicians had four signs to represent sibilants: *zayın, sāmek, ṣadē* and *šīn*. While the Greeks collectively adopted *zayın* to signify the Greek *zeta*, two different Phoenician characters were borrowed to express the sibilant: the *ṣadē* sign, which in Greek scripts was called *san*, and the *šīn* sign, which the Greeks called *sigma*.[24] Nevertheless, in borrowing the signs to fit their phonemes, the Greeks confused the *names* of the signs – *san* is derived etymologically from *zayın* while *zeta* is a corruption of *ṣadē*. This suggested to Jeffery that *san* and *sigma* were originally pronounced differently, with *san* being the voiced and *sigma* the unvoiced sibilant.[25]

There are marked cultural differences between the Argive plain and the eastern Argolid,[26] but what is more important for our purposes is the fact that the ethnographic traditions of the Argolid distinguish between the ethnic compositions of the two areas, assigning Dorians and Akhaians to the plain and Ionians and Dryopes to the eastern Argolid (see chapter 4, esp. fig. 3). Is it possible, then, that the differences that emerge between the two regions with regard to the choice between the 'red' and 'blue' alphabets on the one hand and between *san* and *sigma* on the other possess an ethnic significance?

It is certainly true that the Ionic islands of Khios and Samos shared the 'blue' alphabet with the Ionian cities of Asia Minor, and that the Akhaian colonies of South Italy adopted the same 'red' script as their mother-cities in the north Peloponnese. On the other hand, Attika used the 'blue' *khi*, while neighbouring Ionian Euboia used the 'red' *khi*, and the island of Rhodes adopted 'red' forms, while her Dorian neighbour Knidos preferred 'blue' forms.[27] In the eastern Argolid, while 'red' *xi* and *khi* are attested at Hermione,[28] the settlement of Halieis provides evidence for both 'red' *khi* and 'blue' *xi*.[29] Furthermore, if the communities of the eastern Argolid were really concerned with using an alphabetic script to signal an ethnic identity that was distinct from the Dorian settlements of the Argive plain it is somewhat surprising that they should opt for the 'red' alphabet that was in use at Dorian Sparta.

Turning to the *san-sigma* opposition, an observation of Herodotos initially seems promising. Commenting on Persian nomenclature, he writes: 'There is this one other noticeable feature about them; the Persians themselves are unaware of it but it has not escaped our attention. All their names, which express physical characteristics or magnificence, end in the same letter, which the Dorians call *san* and the Ionians *sigma*.'[30] Quite apart from the fact that Herodotos has mistaken Greek transliterations of Persian nomenclature for the Persian declension of proper names, the passage appears to provide clear testimony for an ethnic distinction between the use of *san* and *sigma*. Unfortunately, the observation does not stand up

---

[24] Guarducci 1987, 22.   [25] Jeffery 1990, 26–27.
[26] See generally Foley 1988; Hall 1995a, 11–13. For the differential articulation of the pantheon, see chapter 4.   [27] Jeffery 1990, x.   [28] One exception is however admitted: Jeffery 1990, 178.
[29] The 'red' *khi* appears on a bronze plaque, found on the akropolis at Halieis and dated to the sixth century. The evidence for 'blue' *xi* appears on an inscribed Korinthian skyphos, dated ca. 630–580 BC: Jameson 1974, 70–71.   [30] Herodotos 1.139.

to closer inspection. Dorian Megara used *sigma*, as did the Dorian Hexapolis, the Dorian cities of Sicily and South Italy and even Sparta itself, arguably the most Dorian of any Greek city. In the Argive plain, Mykenai was certainly using *sigma* to express the sibilant from the third quarter of the sixth century, though there is no evidence to suggest the presence there of Ionians.[31]

To conclude this section, it seems unlikely that there is a direct or unmediated relationship between the script that a community employed and the ethnic identity which it professed. This conclusion does not preclude the possibility that communities might at certain times select certain letter forms from a broader repertoire of graphic symbols in order to reinforce a range of identities (including ethnicity), but it does mean that one cannot simply 'read off' ethnic identity from patterns in chirographic practices. A similar observation holds with regard to the choice between dialectal variants.

Greek dialect history: a synopsis

It was noted in chapter 1 that many classical scholars have sought to reduce the ethnic groups of the literary tradition to the status of linguistic groups. Thus, Chester Starr argues that 'the terms "Dorian", "Ionian" etc., are simply linguistic in character'.[32] It is my intention in the remainder of this chapter to demonstrate that collectivities such as the Dorians, Ionians or Aiolians are not – indeed cannot be – *simply* linguistic groups, though language may certainly be an important tool (among others) in strategies of ethnic proclamation.

The field of Greek philology, and especially dialectology, represents a distinct and often seemingly arcane enclave within the discipline as a whole, rendered all the more bewildering by the fact that universal consensus rarely exists. It may, therefore, be helpful first of all to outline briefly some of the principal points of view that have been held on the subject.

The language that we term Ancient Greek was in reality a collection of regionally specific (or epichoric) dialects which can be traced by identifying isoglosses. In modern linguistics, an isogloss is a line drawn across a map that marks the *limits* of the geographical extent of a certain linguistic phenomenon. An isogloss applies to a single linguistic feature and can be graded at several levels: lexical, phonological, morphological or syntactic. A lexical isogloss distinguishes between vocabulary variants: for instance, in northeast England and parts of Scotland the traditional

---

[31] The earliest attestation of *sigma* at Mykenai is on a fragment of a law, recovered from the citadel and dated by Jeffery to ca. 550–525 BC: Mylonas 1964, 71; Jeffery 1990, 174 no 1A. Michael Jameson (1990, 215) has, however, drawn attention to what appears to be a *san* in an unpublished inscription which may have originally served as the base for an inscribed shaft which was later incorporated within the Hellenistic Perseia Fountain House (*IG* 4.492; *SEG* 11.300). The base may be a little earlier than the shaft, which Jameson assigns to the early fifth century though Jeffery (1990, 174 no. 1) had dated it to ca. 525 BC.   [32] Starr 1962, 72.

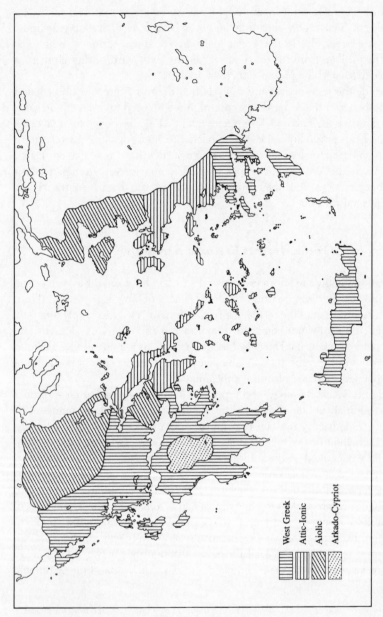

West Greek

Attic-Ionic

Aiolic

Arkado-Cypriot

25 Dialect map of Greece.

dialect word for 'child' is 'bairn' – a legacy of the Danelaw (cf. modern Norwegian *barn*).[33] A phonological isogloss distinguishes between consonantal and vocalic values: e.g. Low German (standard modern Dutch) *dorp* ('village') as opposed to High German (standard modern German) *dorf* – a consonantal shift that seems to coincide with the northward expansion of the Frankish Empire.[34] A morphological isogloss distinguishes between variant word-forms: for example, prior to the seventeenth century the standard English form for the third-person singular ending was *-eth* (as in 'he weareth'), while the *-s* ending ('he wears') was properly a northern dialect form.[35] Finally, a syntactic isogloss distinguishes between variant sentence constructions: e.g. the postposed definite article in Albanian (as in *mik-u*, 'friend the') as opposed to the normal position before the noun in modern Greek (o φίλος [*o filos*, 'the friend']).[36]

The identification of a dialect area only becomes truly significant with the concurrence of several isoglosses (termed a 'bundle'), preferably graded at various levels. Often, morphological distinctions will rank above phonological or lexical ones, and it is morphological isoglosses which tend to distinguish a dialect from an accent (normally defined in terms of only phonological and phonetic variation).[37] Lexical isoglosses in particular may not prove very enlightening because of the phenomenon of lexical borrowing, where a word or expression is transferred from one culture to another, usually as an accompaniment to the item signified:[38] for instance, no structural linguistic relationship can be posited between English and Turkish on the basis of the Turkish loan-word 'coffee'.

Despite the undeniable fact that almost every Greek-speaking community in antiquity possessed its own individual dialect, the identification of isoglosses permits us to classify these local dialects within four major dialect-groups: West Greek, Attic-Ionic, Aiolic and Arkado-Cypriot (fig. 25). The West Greek dialect group denotes the dialects spoken in: (i) the northwest Greek regions of Epeiros, Akarnania, Phthiotid Akhaia, Malis, Ainia, Oitia, Doris, Aitolia, West Lokris and Phokis; (ii) the southern Greek regions of the Megarid, Korinthia, the Argolid, Lakonia, Messenia, Elis and Akhaia; (iii) the islands of Melos, Thera, Krete, Rhodes and Kos; and (iv) the southwestern coastline of Asia Minor. Although it was once thought that the West Greek dialect group could be divided into Northwest Greek, spoken north of the Korinthian Gulf, and Doric, spoken in the Peloponnese and the Aegean islands, Antonín Bartoněk has argued that Northwest Greek cannot be opposed to all the other West Greek dialects, and that it is preferable to regard West Greek as being subdivided into seven groups: (i) the Northwest dialects; (ii) the Saronic dialects (Megarian, Korinthian, East Argolic); (iii) the West Argolic dialect; (iv) the East Aegean dialects (Rhodes, Kos); (v) the Kretan dialects; (vi) the Lakonian, Messenian and Akhaian dialects; and (vii) the dialect of Elis.[39]

---

[33] Trudgill 1990, 112–13.   [34] Bynon 1977, 174–82; Romaine 1994, 135–37.   [35] Trudgill 1990, 95.
[36] Bynon 1977, 246.   [37] Chambers and Trudgill 1980, 5; Romaine 1994, 18.
[38] Haarmann 1986, 159–60; Hall 1990, 250.
[39] Bartoněk 1972, 220–21. See also Méndez Dosuna 1985.

The Attic-Ionic group includes the Attic dialect spoken in Athens and its environs as well as the Ionic dialects spoken in the neighbouring offshore island of Euboia, the Kykladic islands (with the exception of Melos and Thera) and the central coastline of Asia Minor. To the Aiolic group belong the dialect of the island of Lesbos, the dialects spoken along the northern stretch of the Asia Minor coast (particularly in the area of the Troad) and the dialects spoken in the central mainland areas of Thessaly and Boiotia. Finally, the Arkado-Cypriot group designates the dialects of the central Peloponnesian region of Arkadia and of the island of Cyprus.

Traditionally, this particular distribution of the Greek dialect groups has been explained as resulting from the migrations that are described in the literary tradition and which are generally dated to the end of the second millennium BC. Meillet, for example, maintained that the Doric dialects contain many phonetic innovations which argue strongly for their late arrival to the areas in which they are attested in the historical period (though see below).[40] The distribution of the Doric dialects in southern Greece and the southern Aegean was thus compared with the legends which told how the Dorians and Herakleidai occupied the Peloponnese, before colonising the cities of Krete, the Dodekanese and southwest Asia Minor, while the marked similarities between the Doric dialects and the Northwest Greek dialects spoken north of the Korinthian Gulf could be invoked to trace the route of the Dorian invasion.[41]

Variations appear, however, between local 'epichoric' dialects *within* the Doric dialect group. These are normally explained by the unique and regionally specific admixtures between the 'adstrate' Doric dialect of the invaders and the 'substrate' linguistic idioms of the remaining indigenous population.[42] For instance, the fact that throughout Krete the definite articles are οἱ, αἱ [*oi, ai*], rather than the standard Doric forms τοί, ταί [*toi, tai*], is often explained as one of a series of substrate influences exercised by an Akhaian population on the Doric dialect,[43] as is the existence of the demonstrative pronoun ὄνυ [*onu*] for ὅδε [*hode*] at Axos, Eleutherna and Arkades, since this particular pronoun is normally only found elsewhere in Arkado-Cypriot (the dialects thought by many philologists to be closest to the 'Old Akhaian' spoken in the Bronze Age).[44] The 'Akhaian substrate' hypothesis can be illustrated in more detail by a brief consideration of the linguistic characteristics of West Argolic (the dialect of the Argive plain).

Given the cultural, cultic and epigraphic differences that have already been traced between the Argive plain and the eastern Argolid, it will come as no surprise that the two regions are also differentiated on the basis of dialect.[45] For instance,

---

[40] Meillet 1965, 80.   [41] Chadwick 1975, 813.   [42] Ruijgh 1986, 453.
[43] Bartoněk 1972, 92; Risch 1985, 18; Duhoux 1988; Brixhe 1991b, 60–76.   [44] Brixhe 1991b, 60–75.
[45] Originally Argolic was treated as an essentially homogeneous dialect, albeit with some minor variations, within the Doric dialect group: Buck 1955; Meillet 1965; Coleman 1963. Some dialectal variations were noted between the Argive plain and the eastern Argolid by Thumb (1932, 112), though the first systematic attempt to classify these differences appears in Bartoněk 1972.

while West Argolic employs *qoppa* (ϙ) before *-o-* and *-u-*, East Argolic uses *kappa* (κ).[46] While West Argolic aspirates the 'intervocalic secondary' *-s-* (as in the name of Φραhιαριδας [*Phrahiaridas*] on a bronze plaque from the citadel at Mykenai),[47] East Argolic preserves it (e.g. ἐποιεσε [*epoiese*, 'he made'] on the base of a statue dedicated by the people of Hermione at Delphi).[48] And while West Argolic keeps the two dative plural endings *-οις/-οισι* [*-ois/-oisi*], East Argolic keeps just the first.[49] By far the most significant distinction between the two areas, however, resides in the response adopted to the so-called 'compensatory lengthenings'.

The first, second and third compensatory lengthenings describe three separate linguistic events which confronted many Greek dialects between the end of the Bronze Age and the seventh century B C. In all three, the simplification of consonantal clusters resulted in the 'compensatory' lengthening of the preceding vowel.[50] However, the precise 'grade' of the new 'secondary' long vowel created by the compensatory lengthenings varied between the two Argolic regions. East Argolic – like Megarian, Korinthian and the Northwest Greek dialects – created two new 'close' long vowels to represent 'secondary' $\bar{e}/\bar{o}$ phonemes (phonetically signified by $\dot{e}/\dot{o}$). Conversely, West Argolic – like Rhodian, Koan, Theran, Kyrenean, Kretan, Lakonian, Heraklean, Messenian, Elean and Akhaian – assimilated the 'secondary' $\bar{e}/\bar{o}$ phonemes created by the compensatory lengthenings with the 'primary' (existing) $\bar{e}/\bar{o}$ phonemes.[51] The distinction is not evident in the inscriptions of the Archaic and Early Classical periods due to orthographic constraints, though emerges clearly after the adoption of the Ionic alphabet ca. 400 B C. Thus, the word for 'I am' was spelled ἠμι (< $\bar{e}mi$ < *$esmi$) in the Argive plain but εἰμι (< $\dot{e}mi$ < *$esmi$) in the eastern Argolid; similarly, the word 'council' was spelled βωλα (< $b\bar{o}la$ < *$bolsa$) in the Argive plain but βουλα (< $b\dot{o}la$ < *$bolsa$) in the eastern Argolid. In short, the long vocalic system of the Argive plain was different from that of the eastern Argolid: the former had 5 *timbres* and 3 grades, the latter 7 *timbres* and 4 grades (fig. 26). Furthermore, while West Argolic effected the third compensatory lengthening but ignored the second, East Argolic embraced the second, but ignored the third.[52]

46 Fernández Alvarez 1981, 93–94.
47 *IG* 4.492; *SEG* 11.299; Jeffery 1990, 174 no. 2. The intervocalic secondary *-s-* arises through palatalisation, reduction of consonantal groups or analogy. It is eventually lost altogether in West Argolic. See generally Fernández Alvarez 1981, 151–55.
48 Courby 1922, 234; Colin 1930, 221; Jeffery 1990, 182 no. 7.   49 Fernández Alvarez 1981, 186–88.
50 See further Bartoněk 1972, 99–100; Fernández Alvarez 1981, 49–54.
51 Ahrens (1843) terms the first group *Doris mitior* ('Mild Doric') and the second group *Doris severior* ('Severe Doric'). However, Bartoněk (1972, 117) assigns West Argolic, Rhodian and Koan to a mediatory category, *Doris media*, since they fail to distinguish between primary and secondary long vowels as a result of the compensatory lengthenings, but create new 'close' long vowels with the isovocalic contractions of the seventh century B C. It is normally believed that the creation of the 'close' long vowels by the dialects of *Doris mitior* represents an innovation that distinguishes this group from the more conservative *Doris severior*. See, however, Ruijgh (1986; 1989) who argues that *all* Doric dialects originally created 'close' long vowels, but that the dialects of *Doris severior* and *Doris media* later merged these with the 'open' vowels.
52 Bartoněk 1972, 101, 215; Fernández Alvarez 1981, 51, 54, 66.

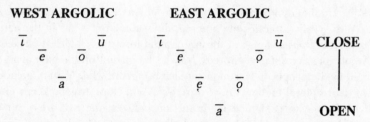

26 The long vocalic systems of the West and East Argolic dialects by the time of the third compensatory lengthening.

The reason for the assimilation of secondary $\bar{e}/\bar{o}$ to primary $\bar{e}/\bar{o}$ in West Argolic is sometimes attributed to the influence of an 'Old Akhaian' substratum, since the phenomenon is also attested in Arkadian and in those dialects such as Lakonian, Messenian and Central Kretan in which 'Old Akhaian' elements have frequently been recognised.[53] 'Old Akhaian' substrate influences have also been invoked to account for the attestation of the preposition πεδά [*peda*] in West Argolic, Arkadian, Kretan and Theran,[54] and the assibilation of -*ti*- to -*si*- (as represented in Ποσειδάν [*Poseidan*, 'Poseidon'] rather than the standard West Greek Ποτειδάν/Ποτιδάν [*Poteidan/Potidan*]) in Argolic, Kretan, Melian, Rhodian and Akhaian.[55] To proponents of the 'Old Akhaian' substrate hypothesis, the fact that the literary tradition records the existence of Akhaians in the Argive plain, but not in the eastern Argolid (see chapter 4, esp. fig. 3), would go a great way in accounting for the differences in dialect between the two areas.

The notion of a Dorian invasion has been central in traditional philological theory not only to the interpretation of West Greek dialect geography but also in explaining the distribution of the other major dialect groups. The decipherment, in 1952, of 'Linear B' (a largely syllabic script used for inventory purposes and inscribed on clay tablets and storage vessels in the larger Mycenaean palatial centres) revealed not only that the Mycenaean language was Greek, but that it bore several affinities with the Arkado-Cypriot dialect group. It is therefore often supposed that the Arkadians of the historical period were the descendants of 'Akhaian' Mycenaeans whose occupation of the relatively inaccessible and mountainous zone of Arkadia left them largely unaffected by the arrival of the Dorians; the Cypriots, on the other hand, are frequently regarded as the descendants of Mycenaeans who colonised the island in the thirteenth century BC.[56] Similarly, the distribution of the Ionic dialects is thought to reflect the passage of refugees, first of all to Attika, and then eastwards to the Kykladic islands and Asia Minor. In this case, however, it is seldom made explicit whether the Ionians are meant to be

---

[53] Bartoněk 1972, 90–92, 107–108, 196. See Risch 1985, 18.   [54] Bartoněk 1972, 107–108, 196.
[55] Lejeune 1972, 64 n. 8.
[56] See, however, Parker (1995) who dates the Arkadian arrival in Cyprus to the tenth century BC.

fleeing the Dorians, or whether they have been driven out from the Peloponnese by displaced Akhaians, as ancient authors affirmed.[57]

This traditional view of the dialect history of Greece assumes that the West Greek, Aiolic, Arkado-Cypriot and Attic-Ionic dialect groups, while tracing their descent back to a common Greek language (or 'proto-Greek'), were already distinguished from one another before the end of the second millennium.[58] Yet even among those who subscribe to what may be described as the 'mainstream' view, there is a considerable diversity of opinion as to when such dialectal divergence may have taken place.

It is widely believed, on the basis of what appear to be non-Greek elements in the Greek language, and particularly in proper nouns, that the earlier inhabitants of Greece were not Greek speakers.[59] Thus the *-nth-* element in toponyms such as Κόρινθος [Korinth] or Τίρυνθος [Tiryns], or the *-ss-* element in Ἁλικαρνασσός [Halikarnassos] are usually deemed to be the substrate influences that an earlier, subjugated linguistic community has exercised on the language of the newcomers. The natural inference is, therefore, that Greek speakers originated from outside the area which they were later to inhabit, and a popular theory earlier this century held that the Greek language was, for the most part, already divided into the major dialect groups prior to the arrival of Greek-speakers, who infiltrated Greece in three migratory waves.[60] The first to come were the 'proto-Ionians' towards the beginning of the second millennium BC. They were followed by 'proto-Akhaians' who, once in Greece, divided into a northern 'proto-Aiolic' branch and a southern 'proto-Arkado-Cypriot' branch (these would have been Homer's 'Akhaians', and their date of entry into Greece should coincide with the emergence of a recognisably Mycenaean culture ca. 1600 BC). Finally at about ca. 1200 BC the Dorians entered Greece.

Kretschmer's reconstruction is generally no longer accepted.[61] Instead the majority of philologists now believe that Greek-speakers entered Greece in one single migratory wave, and that the dialect groups began to diverge from one another within Greece – a proposition that had already been put forward by Karl Julius Beloch.[62] For most scholars, the appearance of the Linear B tablets acts as a *terminus ante quem* for the arrival of the Greek language. The task is then to determine exactly when Greek speakers entered Greece by examining the archaeological record in order to identify any cultural break which might indicate the arrival of a new people – an exercise which is itself, as we have seen, fraught with problems (chapter 5).

Previously, it was thought that the beginning of Middle Helladic (ca. 1900 BC) marked the appearance of radically new cultural forms such as apsidal houses, burial tumuli with cist graves and the use of a wheel-made pottery resembling

---

[57] Herodotos 1.145; Strabo 8.1.2; Pausanias 7.1–5. See Hammond 1976, 151.
[58] Palmer 1980, 74–77; Hainsworth 1982.   [59] Palmer 1980, 9.   [60] Kretschmer 1909.
[61] Bartoněk 1991, 242.   [62] Beloch 1924, 71.

metallic vessels and known as Minyan Ware.[63] Today, it is fairly apparent that all of these features appear slightly earlier, and the commonly accepted date for the arrival of the Greeks is currently the beginning of the Early Helladic III period, ca. 2100 BC.[64] There are, however, dissenters. Robert Drews inclines towards a date ca. 1600 BC, maintaining that the lack of highly differentiated dialects at the end of the Bronze Age argues for a shorter, rather than longer, period of occupation in Greece.[65] Colin Renfrew, adopting a more macroscopic approach which treats the whole area of Europe and Asia in terms of the 'Indo-European question', fails to find any significant cultural break in the archaeological period after the Neolithic period, which leads him to believe that Greek speakers entered the Balkans in the course of the sixth millennium BC.[66] At the other extreme, Sinclair Hood remains unconvinced that the language of the Linear B tablets really is Greek and prefers to date the arrival of the Greeks to ca. 1200 BC.[67]

Unsurprisingly, the mainstream view that the four major dialect groups were distinguished before the end of the second millennium has been subject to several objections in recent decades. Building on a theory first developed by Porzig, Ernst Risch has argued that the Greek dialects can be classified according to a very basic opposition between whether or not they are subject to assibilation (where a -*ti*-sound shifts to a -*si*- sound).[68] Neither the West Greek dialects nor the Aiolic dialects (with the exception of Lesbian) are subject to assibilation, while Arkado-Cypriot, Attic-Ionic and Mycenaean (i.e. Linear B) do share in this particular linguistic innovation: thus, the first group would write δίδωτι [*didōti*, 's/he gives'], while the second group would write δίδωσι [*didōsi*]. From this, Risch deduced that in Mycenaean Greece there were only two dialects: assibilating South Greek (proto-Arkado-Cypriot-Attic-Ionic), which included the language represented by the Linear B script, and non-assibilating North Greek (proto-West Greek-Aiolic).[69]

According to this view, the emergence of four dialect groups is therefore a *post-Mycenaean* event, and comes about through dialect contact. Since Attic-Ionic and West Greek generally accord with one another in the cases where Attic-Ionic diverges from Arkado-Cypriot, it is Risch's opinion that the more conservative Arkado-Cypriot maintains a purer form of the original South Greek dialect, while Attic-Ionic, under the influence of the North Greek dialect, separates itself as a more innovative dialect.[70] Similarly the West Greek dialects maintain more original North Greek forms than the more innovative Aiolic dialects, which have come into contact with the South Greek dialect. The Attic-Ionic dialects distinguish themselves particularly by the post-Mycenaean innovation of shifting an - $\bar{a}$ - phoneme to an - $\bar{e}$ - phoneme (e.g. W. Greek δᾶμος [*dāmos*, 'people'] compared with Attic-Ionic δῆμος [*dēmos*]). The Aiolic dialects are distinctive because they

---

[63] Haley and Blegen 1928.
[64] Finley 1981, 13; Sakellariou 1980, 257–58; Bartoněk 1991, 242. The idea of simultaneous destructions and the arrival of Greek speakers at the end of EHII is, however, doubted in Forsen 1992. [65] Drews 1988. [66] Renfrew 1987. [67] Hood 1967, 126.
[68] Porzig 1954; Risch 1985; 1991. [69] Risch 1985, 27. [70] Risch 1985, 27–28.

have collapsed original labiovelars and labials (Boiotian πέτταρες [*pettares*, 'four'] compared with Attic τέτταρες [*tettares*] < I.E. *$k^w etuóres$).[71]

Risch's views have found some favour,[72] though criticism has been levelled against him for his failure to distinguish linguistic innovation from linguistic archaism. While willing to concede some significance to the fact that both Attic-Ionic and Arkado-Cypriot share in the innovation of assibilation, philologists are generally reluctant to attach the same importance to shared archaisms on the assumption that the imperatives of communication generally favour retention or continuity of linguistic idioms. Therefore, the fact that Aiolic and West Greek do not participate in assibilation presents no argument for their relatedness.[73]

An equally radical challenge to the traditional view of Greek dialect history has been mounted by John Chadwick, who argues that far from invading at the end of the second millennium, Dorian speakers were already present in the Mycenaean world.[74] In 1966, Risch proposed that two dialects could be identified in the Linear B tablets – a 'normal' dialect and a 'special' dialect.[75] Chadwick attributes the first to the Mycenaean élite, and the second to a subjugated proto-Dorian element of low social class and status. He then goes on to suggest that a small incursion of non-Greeks from the area of the Pindos mountains caused the collapse of the Mycenaean palaces, thus enabling the downtrodden Dorians to assume the authority that had been exercised by their former masters. The historical Doric dialect results from the fusion of proto-Doric with this northwestern dialect. Chadwick's challenge is thus the linguistic parallel to the systematic attack on the historicity of the Dorian migration launched by archaeologists (chapter 5).

Quite apart from questions about its historical credibility, Chadwick's hypothesis has met with a great deal of opposition from linguists.[76] Certainly, until we can be sure that we possess a truly representative sample of the Linear B script from the various sites of the Aegean, and until there is a greater consensus over the value to be attributed to certain of the graphic symbols,[77] one may legitimately wonder whether the evidence is yet susceptible to the fine level of sociolinguistic analysis that Chadwick proposes. Furthermore, the hypothesis rests on the very questionable assumption that the written Linear B script reflects closely the contemporary spoken idioms of the Mycenaean population (see below).

On the other hand, the hypothesis has also won its supporters,[78] and the Spanish philologists Antonio López Eire and María Pilar Fernández Alvarez have argued that there is no linguistic necessity for either a Dorian migration or substrate influence on Doric dialects: in fact, in the case of the Argolic dialects, one might have expected a scenario which involved Doric speakers swamping a pre-existing substratum to have produced a greater number of linguistic innovations than are actu-

---

[71] For the reconstruction, see Hamp 1991, 908–909. [72] E.g. Drews 1988, 39.
[73] Bartoněk 1973, 308–309; Palmer 1980, 71. [74] Chadwick 1976; 1985.
[75] Risch 1966, 150–57.
[76] E.g. Moralejo Alvarez 1977; Méndez Dosuna 1985; Consani 1989, 165; Brixhe 1991a, 252.
[77] See the comments of Ruipérez (1972, 136). [78] E.g. Thomas 1978.

ally attested.[79] Both scholars point to the fact that the Doric and Northwest Greek dialects possess no common innovatory trait which is not also found in at least one other non-Doric dialect, and that therefore the Doric dialects have evolved in strict contact both with one another and with non-Doric dialects.[80] Thus, the West Argolic fusion of primary and secondary $\bar{e}/\bar{o}$ is an innovation shared with Lakonian and Arkadian which need carry no substrate significance, while the East Argolic differentiation of primary and secondary $\bar{e}/\bar{o}$ is shared with Megarian, Korinthian and Attic.[81] They conclude that the Doric dialects are not descended from a proto-Doric ancestor, but have emerged directly from proto-Greek, taking on a certain similarity through lateral contact.

Problematising linguistic diversity

The diverse, and sometimes contradictory, reconstructions of the dialect history of Greece can perhaps be understood better when they are situated against the background of a long-running philological debate concerning the relative merits of two (not necessarily mutually exclusive) models of linguistic change: *Stammbaumtheorie* and *Wellentheorie*.

In its most traditional formulation, the orthodox view of Greek dialect history conforms to the *Stammbaum*, or 'family-tree', model proposed by Schleicher to account for the correspondences between Indo-European languages.[82] This essentially 'geneticist' model operates on the principle that structural similarities between different languages allow them to be grouped together in *Sprachfamilien*, or 'speech families'. Separate, but related, languages arise through divergence from a common ancestor, and the greater the similarity displayed by a pair of languages, the more recent such separation is deemed to have taken place. Thus, the marked structural correspondences between the 'Romance' languages (French, Spanish, Italian) argue for a more recent divergence than the split between the structurally related, though less close, Germanic, Slavic, Celtic and Greek languages. Since, however, these last languages do possess some phonological, morphological and syntactic correspondences, they must in turn be derived from a common parent language – in this case, proto-Indo-European. The important thing to observe about *Stammbaumtheorie* is that linguistic diversification is normally attributed to the physical displacement of part of the speech group – due to either expansion, migration or colonisation – leading to loss of contact.[83]

It is the *Stammbaum* model which appears in most introductions to the Greek dialects. The close structural correspondences between, say, Argolic, Lakonian,

---

[79] Fernández Alvarez 1981, 39.
[80] López Eire 1978, 293, 296; Fernández Alvarez 1981, 11, 39. Though see Bile et al 1988, 77.
[81] Fernández Alvarez 1981, 63–64.
[82] Schleicher 1863. For the term 'correspondence' rather than 'similarity', see Hamp 1992.
[83] Bynon 1977, 65, 272.

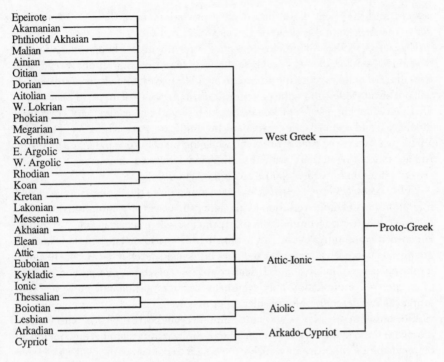

27 *Stammbaum* model for the Greek dialects.

Korinthian and Kretan dictate that they should all be descended from a common proto-Doric ancestor, while the structural homogeneity of Attic, Euboian, Parian and Milesian argues for a common descent from proto-Attic-Ionic. While the major dialect groups (Attic-Ionic, Arkado-Cypriot, West Greek, Aiolic) show fewer structural correspondences between themselves than do the dialects within each of them, they are nevertheless enough related to suggest descent from a common ancestor, proto-Greek (fig. 27).

In historical terms, the *Stammbaum* view of the Greek dialects thus translates as follows. Proto-Greek is the language spoken by the Greeks prior to their arrival in Greece. Once established in mainland Greece, geographical separation led to the divergence from proto-Greek of four dialects: proto-Attic-Ionic, spoken in Attica and the Peloponnese; proto-Arkado-Cypriot, spoken in the Peloponnese; proto-West-Greek, spoken in northwest Greece; and proto-Aiolic spoken in Thessaly. Finally, the end of the second millennium saw a further series of migrations: the speakers of proto-Attic-Ionic were forced out of the Peloponnese and drifted across the Kykladic islands and into Asia Minor; the speakers of proto-Arkado-Cypriot who had not colonised Cyprus were pushed back into Arkadia; the speakers of proto-West-Greek overran the Peloponnese and the southern Aegean

163

islands; and the speakers of proto-Aiolic pushed southwards into Boiotia and across the Aegean to the island of Lesbos.

Wellentheorie is the name given to a model for linguistic change that was first developed by Schmidt.[84] According to this view, linguistic innovations spread from one area to another (generally adjacent) area like waves, though successive waves will not always follow the same pattern of diffusion.[85] Speech areas, or *Sprachbünde*, are thus defined by a series of isoglosses which result from a whole series of lateral influences and contacts: for instance, in southeast Asia, Chinese, Thai and Vietnamese share the feature of 'tone', while the Indo-European languages of the Indian subcontinent share with the unrelated Dravidian languages a series of retroflex consonants which contrast with the dental series.[86]

Unlike *Stammbaumtheorie*, *Wellentheorie* does not require the explanatory device of migrations. Instead, the diffusion of the linguistic waves is accomplished by what is termed 'linguistic accommodation'. In principle, when speakers from two different speech communities come into contact with one another, communication is greatly facilitated if each speaker modifies his or her speech in favour of the other for the purposes of intelligibility. If such contact is repeated frequently enough over time, such accommodation may eventually become permanent. However, geographical and demographic considerations may weigh heavily: geography is relevant because members of a speech community will normally come into contact most with those living closest to them; demography is important because members of small communities are more likely to come into contact with speakers of large communities than *vice versa*.[87]

The most obvious (and generally least significant) example of linguistic change as a result of lateral contact is provided by loan words. Thus the Welsh word *mur* ('wall') is borrowed from Latin *murus*, while the German word *Wein* ('wine') is from Latin *vinum*.[88] There are, however, plenty of examples from the field of historical linguistics that exemplify *Wellentheorie* at the morphological level. The Balkan languages share a number of linguistic features which appear to have been laterally diffused, rather than inherited from any shared ancestral language. Those features that are shared by all the languages are termed 'primary Balkanisms': for instance, the fusion of original genitive and dative cases; an analytic comparison of adjectives (e.g. Greek πίο καλός [*pio kalós*, 'more good/ better']); the adoption of an analytic future which employs an auxiliary verb meaning 'to wish' or 'to want' (e.g. Greek θα γράφω [*tha gráfo*, 'I shall write'] – cf. Bulgarian *šte rabotja*); or the use of a postposed possessive pronoun (e.g. Greek η μητέρα μου [*i mitéra mou*, 'my mother']).[89] In addition, there are a number of

[84] Schmidt 1872.

[85] A clear example of the gradual and 'step-like' diffusion of linguistic innovations is provided by the 'Rhenish Fan' – a series of parallel isoglosses bisecting the Rhine valley which demarcate the multiple linguistic boundaries between High and Low German: Bynon 1977, 174–82; Romaine 1994, 135–37.   [86] Bynon 1977, 245.

[87] Trudgill 1986, 2, 39; Saville-Troike 1989, 86; Giles, Bourhis and Taylor 1977, 309.

[88] Haarmann 1986, 159–60; Bynon 1977, 218.

[89] Hock 1988, 286–87; Chambers and Trudgill 1980, 185.

'secondary Balkanisms', or features that are shared by some, though not all, of the languages: Greek, Bulgarian, Romanian and Serbo-Croat retain the use of the vocative case, though Albanian does not, while Romanian, Bulgarian and Albanian (but not Greek) use a postposed definite article.[90] In most cases, Greek appears to be the prime donor of these innovations, suggesting perhaps that the Balkan *Sprachbund* is the linguistic expression of the unity imposed on the area by the Byzantine Empire.[91]

One of the most enthusiastic proponents of *Wellentheorie* as a plausible model for Greek dialectology was Wyatt, who attributed the emergence of the historical Greek dialects to a series of linguistic innovations, radiating from south Greece as a result of linguistic accommodation between social classes.[92] The model has also, however, clearly influenced the work of linguists such as López Eire and Fernández Alvarez (see above).[93] Certainly, it is an undeniable fact that many of the Greek historical dialects bear the strong imprint of diffusional influence. The proximity of the island of Lesbos to the Ionic-speaking communities of Asia Minor has resulted in a certain amount of Ionic influence on the Aiolic dialect of the Lesbians: thus, unlike Boiotian and Thessalian, Lesbian assibilates;[94] and while Boiotian and Thessalian use the preposition ἐν [*en*, 'into/to/towards'], Lesbian employs the Ionic form εἰς [*eis*].[95] Similarly, the Doric dialect of Aigosthena in the Megarid bears the mark of neighbourly influence from Aiolic-speaking Boiotia.[96] The Boiotian dialect itself shares traits with its Northwest Greek and Attic neighbours,[97] while the Aiolic dialects generally share a large number of linguistic features with the West Greek dialects.[98] The possibility of lateral influence was even recognised in antiquity: the 'Old Oligarch' states that the Athenian dialect has been influenced by a variety of Greek and barbarian dialects.[99]

Wellentheorie is regarded as a complementary, rather than alternative, model to *Stammbaumtheorie*. For example, most linguists, while recognising the evident diffusional influence of Latin and Norman French on English would be reluctant to discount the 'inherited' features of proto-Germanic. Indeed, in order to determine whether isoglosses identified in a *Sprachbund* represent retentions, shared innovations or borrowings, it is often necessary to relate them to the *Sprachfamilie* of the languages concerned.[100]

However, one of the major problems with both *Stammbaumtheorie* and *Wellentheorie* (or, at least, Wyatt's formulation of it) is that too often both are informed by the simultaneous operation of a twin fallacy: (i) that linguistic development is, by nature, *evolutionist*, proceeding from homogeneity to heterogeneity; and (ii) that there is automatically a *social reality* to linguistic traits. This second fallacy is the legacy of the so-called Neo-Grammarian movement of the late nineteenth

[90] Hock 1988, 288–89. [91] Bynon 1977, 246. [92] Wyatt 1970.
[93] López Eire 1978; Fernández Alvarez 1981. See also Diebold 1987, 28; Consani 1989, 159; Brixhe 1991a, 270–71. [94] Bartoněk 1991, 248. [95] Bartoněk 1979, 124. [96] Bartoněk 1972, 88.
[97] Bartoněk 1972, 192; 1979, 121; Risch 1985, 22.
[98] Bartoněk 1972, 192; 1979, 126–27; Risch 1985, 23.
[99] Pseudo-Xenophon, *Athenian Constitution* 2.8. [100] Bynon 1977, 194.

165

century.[101] Although the Neo-Grammarians were undoubtedly correct to emphasise that language has no existence independent of humans – a reaction against the view of earlier linguists (especially Schleicher) who viewed language as an independent 'natural' organism – their belief in universal and mechanical laws governing sound change denied the meaningful and conscious mediation of human actors, resulting in the now discredited notion that social groups and linguistic groups are isomorphic (see chapter 2).[102] In fact, the clustering of dialects within dialect groups is 'a scholars' heuristic fiction':[103] it is, in other words, a convenient taxonomic system for describing a pattern of linguistic relationships in terms of proximity and distance. Once, however, one endows it with a social reality, a series of historically implausible scenarios results.

Like the proponents of the *Stammbaum* model of Greek dialectal development, Wyatt assumes an initial phase in which Greek was a dialectally homogeneous language,[104] and some scholars have wanted to believe that the linguistic uniformity of the Linear B tablets argues for a dialectal homogeneity in Late Helladic Greece.[105] Certainly the geographical distribution of the Linear B tablets (Pylos on the western coast of the Peloponnese, Thebes in Boiotia, Mykenai, Tiryns and Midea in the Argolid, and Knossos on Krete) is surprising when compared with the lack of dialectal differentiation found between the tablets. Yet Linear B is neither a demotic language, nor a language of literature. It is, instead, a language of accountancy with a limited vocabulary, and its formulaic character suggests an archaising and conservative linguistic form which almost certainly screens a much greater variety within the contemporary spoken idioms.[106] The fact that the knowledge of the Linear B script was lost forever after the palatial destructions at the end of the second millennium seems to indicate that only a very few scribes possessed such literary competence, while the strict uniformity of linguistic forms and spelling criteria, as well as of calligraphy, suggests strongly that the scribes of Pylos were trained alongside the scribes of Knossos.[107]

It is important not to underestimate the cognitive revolution involved in using a graphic system to represent speech patterns. All the ideograms and about 90 per cent of the syllabograms of Linear B were taken from the earlier (and still undeciphered) Linear A script, which was in use mainly on Krete and on some of the Kykladic islands, although one instance has been recorded at Agios Stephanos in Lakonia.[108] There is, however, as yet no evidence that Linear A represented a Greek language: indeed, all the indications seem rather to incline towards it being non-Indo-European. In other words, the ability to render vocal sounds by graphic signs – something which we take for granted today – was hardly a habit to which

---

[101] For the 'Neo-Grammarian manifesto', see Osthoff and Brugmann 1878 (English translation: Lehmann 1967, 197–209). See also Morpurgo Davies 1986.

[102] For a criticism of the mechanical and uniformitarian principles of the Neo-Grammarians: Romaine 1994. [103] Collinge 1973, 295. [104] Wyatt 1970, 624.

[105] E.g. Bartoněk 1991, 249.

[106] Palmer 1980, 174; Brixhe 1991a, 253–59; Morpurgo Davies 1985, 84.

[107] Crossland 1985, 338–39; Morpurgo-Davies 1985, 84. [108] Sacconi 1991, 45.

the Greeks of the Mycenaean period had had time to grow accustomed. It is not, in fact, unlikely that individual scribes initially learnt to reproduce the same graphic signifier to represent a signified (e.g. 'chariot' or 'bronze') which was then mechanically repeated on subsequent occasions, rather than that they sat down and thought about which syllabogram they should employ to render their own idiolects or dialects. In short, it would be extremely rash to attempt to use Linear B as the direct reflection of a linguistic situation in Late Bronze Age Greece.

In fact, as has been argued in the case of the proto-Indo-Europeans,[109] it is difficult to imagine a single, undifferentiated language ever having been spoken over a continous area such as an *Urheimat*. Rather than subscribing to an evolutionist view in which language development pursues a unilineal trajectory towards greater differentiation, it is preferable to regard linguistic forms as constantly subject to processes of both convergence and divergence. An example of dialectal convergence is provided by the southeastern counties of Britain today, where originally diverse dialects such as those of Suffolk or Hampshire are gradually giving way to a more homogeneous southeastern dialect.[110] The limitations of a strictly evolutionist approach can be illustrated further by a consideration of the Italian language.

The dialects that are still spoken in the Italian peninsula can be clustered within dialect groups: (i) the Galloitalic-Venetian dialects spoken in Piemonte, Lombardia, Liguria, Emilia Romagna and Veneto; (ii) the Central-Southern dialects spoken in Marche, Umbria, Lazio, Abruzzo, Campania, northern Calabria, northern Puglia and northern Basilicata, and related to the Sicel-Calabrian-Salentine group spoken in Sicily, southern Calabria and southern Puglia; (iii) the Tuscan-Romanesque dialects spoken in Toscana and northwest Lazio; (iv) the Sardinian dialect; and (v) the Rhaeto-Romance dialects spoken in Friuli and Trentino. According to the *Stammbaum* model, their common descent from proto-Italic can be justified by the close structural correspondences between all the Italian dialects.

Yet there never was a period when an undifferentiated proto-Italic was spoken throughout the Italian peninsula. The origins of the modern Italian dialects are already inscribed within the linguistic diversity of Iron Age Italy, where Latin-speakers existed alongside Ligurians, Etruscans, Gauls, Piceni, Iapygi, Greeks, Sicels and Phoenicians. Furthermore, despite Drews' surprising claim that while dialects of the same language can influence one another, dialects belonging to different languages cannot,[111] the specific identity of many of the Italian dialects is, to a greater or lesser extent, due to linguistic influence from outside the Italic *Sprachfamilie*. So, for instance, the Sicilian dialect shows clear signs of linguistic borrowing from Norman French: e.g. *puma* ('apple'), *racina* ('grape') and *ciareddu* ('lamb') are connected to French *pomme*, *raisin* and *charelle*, rather than Italian *mela*,

---

[109] Drews 1988, xiii. [110] Trudgill 1990, 33 map 9, 63 map 18, 75–76.
[111] Drews 1988, 219–20.

uva and *agnello*. At the more significant level of syntactic influence, the appearance of the particle *mi* in Calabrian *voggju mi dormu* ('I want to sleep') reveals the influence of modern Greek syntax (θέλω να πλαγιάσω [*thelo na playiaso*]), in contrast to the standard infinitive construction of modern Italian (*voglio dormire*).

Interestingly enough, the Italian experience runs counter to the expectations generated by an evolutionist view of language development. If one asks at what date a relatively undifferentiated Italic language was spoken throughout the Italian peninsula, the answer would be, theoretically, not much before the nineteenth century, when the Florentine dialect (whose employment by Dante and Petrarch had ensured its status as a 'high' literary dialect) came increasingly to serve as a *lingua franca* in post-unification Italy; even then, the first prime minister of the Italian state, Count Camillo di Cavour, felt more comfortable in French or the Piedmontese dialect than in Italian. In practical terms, however, it is probably fair to say that Italian did not become widely spoken throughout Italy until after the Second World War, when its diffusion was facilitated by greater educational regulation and the mass media; even today it often continues to coexist with (rather than replace) the regional dialects.

The Italian example is not an isolated one, and is matched in Spain, where the national Spanish language is based on the Castilian dialect and in France, where the national language is derived from the dialect spoken in Île-de-France. At the time of the French Revolution in 1789, only half of the adult male population spoke French (as opposed to dialect) and only twelve to thirteen per cent of those spoke it correctly.[112] Similarly, both the Irish language and Nynorsk (the language of Norwegian literature) are essentially modern creations, derived from pre-existing dialects.[113] Closer to home, one would be hard pressed to imagine a period in which an undifferentiated language was spoken throughout England, let alone Britain.

The situation may not have been so radically different in ancient Greece. While some references to the 'Greek tongue' appear in writings of the fifth century BC,[114] this appears to have existed at an abstract level only,[115] and may have more to do with the ethnic divisions which were demarcated in the wake of the Persian Wars rather than strictly linguistic criteria (see chapter 3). In fact, in Greece – as in early modern Italy – it is only relatively late that one can truly speak of a standardised language, developed from one particular dialect. While the Florentine dialect provided the model for Italian, in Greece it was the Attic dialect that formed the basis of the new *koine*, or 'common language' which began to replace local scripts and dialects (at least in formal inscriptions) from the fourth century BC onwards. Even then, it is important to note that the *koine* was characterised by the ancient grammarians as simply another dialect of Greek, alongside Attic, Ionic, Aiolic and Doric.[116]

---

[112] Hobsbawm 1992b, 60.
[113] Hobsbawm 1992b, 106–08; Eriksen 1993, 102–03; Romaine 1994, 95.
[114] E.g. Herodotos 4.78.1; 8.135.3; Thoukydides 2.68.5.   [115] Morpurgo Davies 1987, 17.
[116] Clement of Alexandria, *Stromateis* 1.142.4; Quintilian 11.2.50. See Morpurgo Davies 1987, 14.

168

If the structural similarities between the Italian dialects provide no argument for their descent from a common, undifferentiated proto-Italic language spoken throughout the whole of the Italian peninsula, then cannot the same principle be applied to the Greek dialects? Indeed, Vittore Pisani doubts the heuristic utility of a concept such as 'proto-Greek', arguing that many of the Greek dialects share traits with other Indo-European, but non-Greek, linguistic traditions. This means that the Greek dialects, far from *diverging* from a common proto-Greek ancestor on Greek soil, have in fact *converged* from originally disparate sources – in other words, the *Stammbaum* of the traditional model, with its apex of convergence at the top of the diagram, has actually been upturned.[117]

Pisani's point of view is in part, no doubt, informed by the now somewhat outmoded belief that groups such as the Dorians comprised a strong Illyrian element (see chapter 1), and one could be forgiven for thinking that we have returned, via a lengthy deviation, to Kretschmer's three-wave hypothesis. Nonetheless, it does have the benefit of demonstrating the existence of alternatives to the standard, evolutionist approach towards dialectal differentiation. The point is that there are no compelling grounds to believe – and in fact good reasons for rejecting – the supposition that a single, undifferentiated speech was ever originally spoken in Greece. If true, then the standard evolutionist model, which derives the local dialects from dialect groups, and the dialect groups from proto-Greek, is clearly no longer tenable. That does not mean that the historical Greek dialects had already crystallised in the Late Bronze Age. One could argue that it is the very existence of dialectal diversity in Late Bronze Age Greece which provides the necessary impetus for a complex series of linguistic divergences and convergences, from which the dialects of the first millennium result.

It has not been my intention in this section to replace the *Stammbaumtheorie* or *Wellentheorie* models with an alternative one, but rather to problematise some of the assumptions which sometimes lie behind many of the conventional views of Greek dialect history. Preferring to regard the historical Greek dialects as the consequence of linguistic divergence and convergence excludes neither the possibility of population movements nor lateral influence between static groups. Yet it is clear that the undeniable existence of dialect contact and linguistic accommodation means that the *Stammbaum* model in its most simplistic form cannot stand without major modifications. Such lateral influence entails that linguistic forms need not be the exclusive property of single speech communities in a way that the *Stammbaum* model suggests, and that therefore it is methodologically unsound to identify specific social or ethnic groups from linguistic patterns alone.

The classic example here is provided by Halikarnassos (modern Bodrùm) on the coast of Asia Minor. Herodotos is at pains to stress that Halikarnassos is a Dorian city, founded by the Dorians of Troizen in the eastern Argolid.[118] Yet the earliest inscriptions found from the city, dating to the second quarter of the fifth century,

---

[117] Pisani 1955. See also Consani 1989, 159–60.   [118] Herodotos 1.144; 2.178; 7.99.

are written not only in the East Ionic script (a habit that was shared by Halikarnassos' neighbours) but even in the Ionic dialect.[119] The contradiction cannot be explained away by positing ignorance on Herodotos' part, since he was a native of Halikarnassos; nor is it easy to see that he could pretend, for his own purposes, that Halikarnassos was Dorian if his audience knew better. Nor do we need to be as dramatic as Lilian Jeffery, who postulated a complete change of population towards the end of the sixth century. Instead, we should be prepared to admit the possibility that Halikarnassos adopted over time the dialect of her Ionian neighbours without this having the slightest effect on her continued proclamation of a Dorian ethnicity.

There is, however, one further consequence which arises from the discussion so far. If one rejects the idea of a unilineal evolution from an undifferentiated proto-Greek language to the dialects of the historical period, then there is perhaps no necessary reason to retain the intermediate dialect-group stage (Aiolic, West Greek, etc.) of that trajectory, unless one accepts the highly implausible scenario in which diverse Late Bronze Age dialects all converged *simultaneously* to form four simplified dialects – Attic-Ionic, Arkado-Cypriot, West Greek and Aiolic. It would then follow that dialect groups such as Attic-Ionic or Arkado-Cypriot are, like proto-Greek itself, purely abstract terms used by modern scholars to define structural correspondences between dialects that are certainly 'real', but which may have resulted from a far more complicated series of linguistic processes than mere descent from a common proto-dialect.[120] If, however, the existence of the proto-dialects is illusory, then the questions which pose themselves are: (i) did ethnic groups in Greek antiquity really attach an ethnic significance to their speech patterns, and (ii) if so, was this on the basis of linguistic or non-linguistic factors? To attempt to answer these issues, it is necessary to turn from the study of linguistics to that of 'metalinguistics' – the attitudes a speech community holds towards language and linguistic facts.[121]

The Greek attitude to dialect

In attempting to determine to what degree the Greeks were aware of dialectal diversity and what attitudes they held towards such diversity, two factors are of vital importance. The first is the extent to which the various Greek dialects were mutually intelligible, and the second is the degree of proficiency that the Greeks possessed in classifying dialects.

There are some references to dialectal diversity and attitudinal responses in the literary sources, but – surprisingly perhaps – such evidence is far from copious. We are then compelled to fall back on the internal linguistic evidence of the dialects

---

[119] Jeffery 1990, 353; Craik 1980, 57.   [120] Morpurgo Davies 1987, 18.
[121] Morpurgo Davies 1985, 84.

themselves, as displayed through the medium of epigraphy. This in itself, however, is a far from unproblematic exercise. Firstly, the epigraphical evidence is unevenly scattered in geographical terms: we know, for instance, far more about the dialect of Athens and Attika than we do of Akarnania. Secondly, the ability to identify isoglosses can only operate effectively with a larger sample of material. This, however, means that we are often compelled to treat synchronically a number of inscriptions from varying periods, with the consequent risk that we may identify a number of linguistic features which belong to differing stages of a dialect's history and which never actually co-existed.[122] Additionally, the fact that the number of Hellenistic and Roman inscriptions far outweighs the number of Archaic and Classical ones raises the problem as to how far the *koine* has already penetrated the local dialect.[123] Thirdly, there is always the strong possibility – as noted with regard to Linear B – that the written text conceals a considerably greater differentiation in the spoken idioms.[124] Herodotos, for instance, notes that there are four dialect groups among the Ionic speakers of Asia Minor: a 'Karian' group, which includes Miletos, Myous and Priene; a 'Lydian' group embracing Ephesos, Kolophon, Lebedos, Teos, Klazomenai and Phokaia; a group which includes Khios and Erythrai; and the dialect of Samos.[125] The only group of these four which can be traced epigraphically, however, is the Khios-Erythrai group, in which Aiolic features are noticeable.[126] All of these difficulties need to be borne in mind for much of what follows.

It might be supposed that two dialects of the same language should experience greater mutual intelligibility than would be the case between two dialects of different languages. In fact, experience demonstrates that this is not always the case. Many north Italians are more capable of following standard Spanish than they are of comprehending the Sicilian dialect.[127] Similarly, while the separate languages of Norwegian, Swedish and Danish are largely mutually intelligible, there are certain dialects of German which are all but alien to the speakers of other German dialects.[128] Nor is intelligibility always mutual: Danes claim to understand Norwegians better than Norwegians understand Danes, while Norwegians and Danes collectively profess to comprehend Swedish better than Swedes understand Norwegian or Danish.[129]

The problematic relationship between 'language' and dialect is illustrated well by the phenomenon of 'dialect continua'. A dialect continuum is a cumulative linguistic chain, stretching over several national borders, in which nearest neighbours experience little difficulty in understanding one another. So in a contiguous chain, dialects *a* and *b*, *b* and *c*, and *c* and *d* understand one another, though this mutual intelligibility is not necessarily experienced by dialects *a* and *c*, *a* and *d*, or *b* and *d*. The important feature, however, is that the dialect continuum may actually cut across the linguistic boundary between Language A and Language B. Several

[122] Bartoněk 1972, 34.   [123] Brixhe 1991a, 262.
[124] Morpurgo Davies 1987, 10; Duhoux 1983, 14. See also Osthoff and Brugmann 1878.
[125] Herodotos 1.142.3–4.   [126] Duhoux 1983, 14.   [127] Morpurgo Davies 1987, 8–9.
[128] Chambers and Trudgill 1980, 4.   [129] Romaine 1994, 13–14.

dialect continua have been identified in Europe: for instance, the West Romance Dialect Continuum, which stretches from Portugal, through Spain, France, southern Belgium and western Switzerland to Italy, or the West Germanic Dialect Continuum, which stretches from the Netherlands, through Flemish Belgium, Germany, Switzerland and Austria to northeastern Italy.[130]

What allows for this at first sight surprising phenomenon is the fact, noted above, that a 'national language' is seldom a higher order linguistic category which embraces and subsumes its constituent dialects. It is, rather, an invention which rarely precedes the nineteenth century and which owes its existence to reasons 'that are as much political, geographical, historical, sociological and cultural as linguistic'.[131] From a linguistic point of view, there is little or no difference between a standardised national language and a dialect in terms of their hierarchical ranking within the historical structure of a language. What does distinguish a national language from a dialect is the fact that it is spoken by a greater number of people over a wider area.

There was no standardised 'national' Greek language before the fourth century BC,[132] and even then it is doubtful that the *koine* really qualifies for this title. The possible existence of dialect continua without the straitjacket of a standardised national language raises a number of interesting issues, which cannot be treated here, as to how clear cut the division between Greek and non-Greek speakers may have been on the fringes of the Greek world (a division which becomes even more blurred if the possibility of bilingualism is taken into account). For our current purposes, however, the preceding discussion serves to demonstrate that the apparent relatedness of the Greek dialects provides no *a priori* reason for assuming their mutual intelligibility.

Despite this, there is a common belief that there is not enough structural diversity between Greek dialects to suggest that they acted as an effective barrier to communication.[133] Those who suscribe to this view tend to quote a passage from Plato, in which Sokrates asks to be excused for his unfamiliarity with legal language, 'just as if I were really a *xenos* (i.e. a non-Athenian Greek), you would certainly forgive me if I spoke in the speech and manner in which I had been brought up'.[134] The implication appears to be that Greek visitors to Athens tended not only to speak in their own dialects, but to be largely understood. Similarly, when the Boiotian and Megarian in Aristophanes' *Akharnians*, or the Spartans in Aristophanes' *Lysistrata*, deliver what is normally assumed to be a reasonably faithful rendition of their local dialects (given due allowance for comic effect and the need to be understood by an Athenian audience), the inference appears to be that the Athenians are able to comprehend the dialects of Boiotia, Megara and Sparta.

None of this literary evidence is particularly convincing. To argue that the paucity of references to communicational difficulties is evidence for interdialectal

---

[130] Chambers and Trudgill 1980, 6; Romaine 1994, 12.
[131] Chambers and Trudgill 1980, 5. See also Hobsbawm 1992a, 3.   [132] Morpurgo Davies 1987, 9.
[133] E.g. Hainsworth 1982, 865.   [134] Plato, *Apology* 17d.

intelligibility is an argument from silence: there is, after all, no hint of any impediment to verbal communication between the Greeks and the Trojans in the *Iliad*. The Plato quotation may argue for a certain intelligibility between the speakers of two different dialects, but the need to be *forgiven* for speaking in dialect is testimony rather to Athenian tolerance than to the comparative ease with which *xenoi* were understood. In the case of the dialect-speakers in Aristophanes, the matter is complicated by two factors: firstly, we simply do not know what the exact relationship is between what we now read in the manuscripts and what the Athenian audience actually heard on stage in the fifth century; secondly, it is difficult to know what Aristophanes wanted to signify phonologically since he was constrained by the orthographic conventions of the Attic dialect.[135] What cannot, however, be denied is that Aristophanes' dialects are characterised by both inconsistency and occasionally inaccuracy.[136] More negatively, Thoukydides claims that the Eurytanes of Aitolia speak 'a most unintelligible' dialect, and in Plato's *Protagoras*, Prodikos describes Pittakos' Lesbian dialect as 'a barbarian register'.[137]

In fact, the likelihood is that when a *xenos* stood up to address the Athenian courts, he would have made a conscious effort to modify his speech patterns towards those of his audience, thus adopting a register somewhat different to the one he would use back home with friends and family. If this is true, and if the passage of Plato really does suggest that – even after linguistic accommodation – the comprehension of other dialects was not completely without difficulties, then the logical inference to be drawn is that the Greek dialects were not quite as linguistically similar at the level of comprehension as has sometimes been assumed. Such a conclusion can hardly be refuted by the argument that the Greek dialects are structurally similar and hence mutually intelligible, since this is an argument predicated on analysis of written texts which, as we have seen, may screen a far greater oral diversity. In other words, the language of the formal inscriptions (which, by virtue of their length, furnish more of our evidence for dialectal isoglosses than casual graffiti and dipinti) almost certainly represents a register that is both more uniform and more conservative than the variety of more vernacular idioms in use in the same dialect area.

Rather than arguing either for or against mutual intelligibility, it is surely more reasonable to suppose that there were varying degrees of intelligibility between any one pair of dialects throughout Greece. The degree of intelligibility need not, however, be directly proportional to the *structural* similarity between two dialects – it may, instead, be a function of contact. That is to say, one is more likely to understand those dialects with which one comes into contact more regularly, especially in cases where speakers of two dialects are strongly motivated to comprehend one another, perhaps for the purposes of economic exchange. Thus, neighbouring speech communities are more likely to understand one another than geograph-

---

[135] Colvin 1995, 45. Harvey (1994, 44) suggests that the apparent authenticity behind, say, the Lakonian dialect in *Lysistrata* is the work not of Aristophanes himself but of a learned editor.
[136] Verbaarschot 1988; Colvin 1995.   [137] Thoukydides 3.94.5; Plato, *Protagoras* 341c.

ically distant ones. Furthermore, a city like Athens, which continually played host to artists, craftsmen, traders, intellectuals and deputations from abroad, constitutes a more fertile arena for the possibility of mutual comprehension than a mountain village in Arkadia. We may also deduce, by extension, that the more mobile élite was more proficient at understanding other dialects than the landbound peasantry.

The discussion so far suggests that, even in cases where little difficulty was experienced in comprehending another dialect, there was at least an awareness of dialectal difference.[138] This is exemplified by a passage from Aiskhylos' *Khoephoroi*, where Orestes and Pylades, attempting to disguise themselves, 'both utter the speech of Parnassos, imitating the Phokian dialect'.[139] It does not matter that Orestes actually continues to speak in the conventional Attic dialect of tragic theatre; what is important is the fact that Aiskhylos recognises that the people who live in Phokis, under the shadow of Mount Parnassos, speak the Phokian dialect. Is, however, Aiskhylos capable of understanding the *linguistic characteristics* that define the Phokian dialect? That is to say, would he manage to pick out the Phokian dialect in a 'blind test'? Or is it rather the case that he knows that the people who live in Phokis speak in a different way to those who live in Athens and Sparta, and that they must therefore speak the Phokian dialect? More appositely for the current study, if an Athenian met a Megarian, would the Athenian recognise *on purely linguistic considerations* that the Doric speech of the Megarian was related to the Doric dialects of Lakonia, Messenia, Krete or Thera?

It was only comparatively late that Greek grammarians began to interest themselves in dialectology. Even then, the linguistic divisions that are posited by generations of scholars from Herakleides of Krete in the third century BC, through Strabo in the first century BC to Gregory of Korinth in the twelfth century AD are not quite those that are recognised by most philologists today. The ancient grammarians recognised four groups (Attic, Ionic, Doric and Aiolic) and it is the absence of Arkadian together with the separation of Attic from Ionic that gives us good reason to suspect that these divisions are predicated on *literary* dialects rather than strictly linguistic features.[140] Since the Archaic period, certain literary dialects had been intimately associated with specific genres: for example, lyric poetry was traditionally written in a form of Doric, melic poetry in a form of Aiolic, tragic poetry in Attic, and prose in Ionic. These literary dialects were, however, too stylised to offer any meaningful linguistic analysis of Greek dialectology. Furthermore, the dialect in which an author wrote often bore little resemblance to that which he or she spoke: Pindar wrote not in his native Aiolic dialect of Boiotian, but in a stylised form of Doric, while Hellanikos of Lesbos wrote in the Ionic dialect rather than the Aiolic dialect of Lesbos.

To understand the poor understanding of dialect classification in antiquity, it is necessary to return to the principle by which dialects are recognised as distinctive –

---

[138] Morpurgo-Davies 1987, 15.   [139] Aiskhylos, *Khoephoroi* 560–64.
[140] Buck 1955, 14–15; Hainsworth 1967, 73–74; Bartoněk 1972, 6; Cassio 1984, 118.

namely, the isolation of isoglosses. As has been mentioned earlier, a dialect or a dialect group can be identified by any number of isoglosses. Not all isoglosses, however, are deemed to have the same importance. For instance, if one decided to draw an isogloss distinguishing between dialects which preserve intervocalic $-rr-$, and those which innovate to $-rs-$, then most of the conventional dialect groups would be sliced in half: the innovation is present in Arkadian, but not Cypriot; in Attic and west Ionic, but not in central Ionic or east Ionic; in Rhodian, but not in Kretan or Koan.[141] Similarly, the preposition πεδά [*peda*] acts as a substitute for μετά [*meta*, 'with'] in Argolic but not Lakonian, in Boiotian but not Thessalian, and in Arkadian but not Cypriot,[142] while the isogloss $*r > ra/ar$, instead of $*r > ro/or$ groups the Attic-Ionic dialects with the Doric dialects (e.g. Attic στρατηγός, Doric στραταγός [*stratēgos, stratāgos*, 'general'], as opposed to Lesbian στρόταγος [*strotagos*]).[143]

Nor is it always methodologically valid to operate on the assumption that the greater number of linguistic features a pair of dialects shares, the more related they are. Robert Coleman attempted to determine the relatedness of the various Greek dialects by tabulating correlation coefficients between pairs of dialects, based on shared features.[144] Although a certain degree of caution needs to be exercised with regard to the results, especially since the shared traits that are identified need not all be contemporary with one another, it emerges that there can be a surprisingly high level of linguistic diversity within any one dialect group. For example, the Aiolic dialect of Boiotia appears to demonstrate more similarity with Doric Lakonian (61 per cent) than it does with the other Aiolic dialects of Thessalian (58 per cent) or Lesbian (35 per cent), while the Doric dialect of Messenia is as similar to Boiotian as it is to the Doric dialect of Rhodes (70 per cent).

Such linguistic diversity can even exist within an epichoric dialect. In Arkadian, original labiovelars are represented by -σ- [-*s*-] at Mantinea, -but by -(τ)ζ- [-*(t)z*-] at neighbouring Tegea, while infinitives end in -εν [-*en*] at Tegea but in -ην [-*ēn*] at Lykosoura.[145] In Western Argolic, Mykenai simplified medial and terminal -*ns*-clusters to a simple -*s*- after the 'second compensatory lengthening' of the ninth century BC, while Argos and Tiryns retained the clusters intact: thus the former wrote τος [*tos*] and the latter τονς [*tons*] for the accusative masculine plural of the definite article.[146] Finally, in Kretan, evidence for dialectal diversity is demonstrated by the fact that Dreros writes κόσμος [*kosmos*, 'legislature'] with an initial *kappa* while Gortyn writes ϙόρμος [*kormos*] with an initial *qoppa*.[147]

In order to determine the more significant isoglosses that distinguish dialects, it

---

[141] Collinge 1973, 295. See also Bartoněk 1972, 193.   [142] Bartoněk 1972, 194.

[143] Risch 1991, 237.   [144] Coleman 1963.   [145] Palmer 1980, 65.

[146] Hall 1995a, 14 with *IG* 4.493 and Verdelis, Jameson and Papachristodoulou 1975. At Argos, the clusters are still being retained in the third century BC.

[147] Van Effenterre 1991, 81. Monique Bile (1988; cf. Brixhe and Bile 1991) argues for a more homogeneous Kretan dialect, attributing variants to idiolectal synonyms rather than true dialectal alternatives. Conversely, Van Effenterre (1991) believes that the apparent dialectal unity of Kretan is simply due to the fact that literacy was restricted to a small group of scribes (or *poinikastai*) for which Krete was famous in antiquity.

is necessary to resort to some *ranking* procedure. For our purposes, it is helpful to distinguish between *primary* features, which are shared by a greater number of local dialects and serve to assign them to one of the four dialect groups, and *secondary* features which distinguish the various local dialects within each dialect group. Thus, one of the primary features of the West Greek dialects (though not yet attested in all dialects) is the so-called 'Doric future': so, W. Greek κλεψέω [*klepseō*] as opposed to Attic κλέψω [*klepsō*, 'I shall steal']. One of the primary features of Attic-Ionic is the already mentioned shift from -ᾱ- to -η-. Arkado-Cypriot is primarily distinguished by, among other features, the use of the pronoun ὄνυ [*onu*] for ὅδε [*hode*, 'this man'], while a primary feature of the Aiolic dialects is the use of the feminine form of the numeral ἴα [*ia*] for μία [*mia*, 'one']. Among secondary features, just a few examples will suffice: within the Arkado-Cypriot group, the conditional particle is εἰ [*ei*, 'if'] in Arkadian, but ἤ [*ē*] in Cypriot; within Attic-Ionic, Attic displays θάλαττα [*thalatta*, 'sea'] for Ionic θάλασσα [*thalassa*]; and the Kretan dialect distinguishes itself from other Doric dialects by using the forms οἱ, αἱ [*oi, ai*] for the masculine and feminine plural forms of the definite article, normally rendered in Doric by τοί, ταί [*toi, tai*].

It is important to point out that the very ability to rank isoglosses is occasioned by the distanced overview that modern scholars are privileged enough to hold over the extant epigraphical corpus. Despite undeniable gaps in our knowledge, the current classification of the Greek dialects is the result of confronting, and identifying patterns in, a vast body of material drawn from all over the Greek-speaking world over a period of many centuries. In other words, the complex patterning of isoglosses which identifies dialects and clusters them within dialect groups emerges only with 'the whole picture' – or something approaching it.[148]

The Greeks of antiquity, however, were part of that picture. Condemned to a singular position in time and space, it was impossible for them to gain anything approaching an overview, not least because there was no standardised language against which to compare the local dialects.[149] They would certainly have been able to recognise lexical isoglosses, but the dialect groups are defined more on the basis of 'combinations of phonological and morphological distinctions which could hardly be apprehended and classified without the benefit of a formal grammar'.[150] It is highly improbable, then, that the Greeks were able to rank isoglosses – a hypothesis that finds a certain amount of support in a passage from the Hellenistic poet Theokritos. In a rare instance in extant literature in which direct reference is made to a phonological idiom, a stranger accuses two Syracusans in Alexandria of 'uttering everything with a broad tone':[151] an ancient commentary to the passage explains that this refers to the Doric tendency to use long -ā- vowels. Yet, the long -ā- grade is not an exclusive Doric feature: it is, in fact, shared by *all* the dialects except those belonging to the Attic-Ionic group.[152]

[148] A general linguistic principle already recognised by Gilliéron (1919, 118).
[149] Morpurgo Davies 1987, 9.   [150] Hainsworth 1967, 64–65.   [151] Theokritos, *Idylls* 15.87–93.
[152] Risch 1985, 20.

To sum up, it seems barely credible that the Greeks were capable of using linguistic criteria to assign local dialects to dialect groups. Firstly, they lacked the ability to rank isoglosses, and hence to identify the more significant isoglosses which attach certain dialects to the same dialect group. Secondly, they could not operate on the basis of greater or lesser mutual intelligibility, because this may be a function of social, geographical and demographic factors as much as linguistic ones. This is the reason for rejecting Starr's view that terms like 'Dorian' or 'Ionian' are simply linguistic in character, but it is also due to these considerations that the Hesiodic reference to Doros, Aiolos and Xouthos as the sons of Hellen (chapter 3) must refer primarily to ethnic, and not to linguistic divisions (not least, because there never existed a dialect group known as Xouthian).[153] To return to the question posed earlier, if an Athenian recognised that the speech of a Megarian was related to that of a Lakonian or a Kretan, it would not be on *purely linguistic* grounds, but rather because he knew that the Megarians, Lakonians and Kretans all claimed a common Dorian ethnic identity.[154] Sure enough, when Strabo affirms that the Peloponnesian dialects are a mixture of Doric and Aiolic, it quickly emerges that this observation is predicated not on linguistic grounds, but on the fact that Strabo believes Aiolians to have occupied the Peloponnese prior to the arrival of the Dorians.[155]

The role of language in ethnicity

The arguments so far are sufficient to demonstrate that ethnic groups were not in the first place defined by the dialects that they spoke, and that we cannot therefore use linguistic features to trace them. Language and dialect – like forms of material culture (chapter 5) – cannot be regarded as criteria of ethnicity. That does not, however, prevent them from occasionally acting as indicia of ethnicity: in other words, the relationship between language and ethnicity is unidirectional. This is the point that Harald Haarmann is keen to emphasise when he places the emphasis not on the interrelationship *between* language *and* ethnicity, but on the role of language *in* ethnicity. For Haarmann, language can be used actively to mark ethnic boundaries, but it cannot be treated as a stable feature in ethnic identity because it is merely one parameter, among many others, which may manifest different variations in different settings.[156] Nevertheless, as in the field of archaeological inquiry, the difficulty arises over how to determine when linguistic forms are being used *actively* to mark ethnic boundaries, and when they are simply the passive consequence of non-ethnic factors.

It was noted earlier that there is no hint of linguistic diversity in the *Iliad*. The same is true of the *Odyssey*, with one notable exception. In Book 19, Odysseus describes the multilinguistic situation on Krete, where Akhaians, Eteokretans,

---

[153] Cassio 1984, 115.   [154] See Hainsworth 1967, 66; Morpurgo-Davies 1987, 13.
[155] Strabo 8.1.2.   [156] Haarmann 1986, 260–62. See also Romaine 1994.

Kydonians, Dorians and Pelasgians co-exist in ninety cities, and where 'one language is mixed with another'.[157] Among these different speech communities, it is the Eteokretans that provide particular interest, partly because their name identifies them as the 'true' Kretans – a significant consideration in light of the discursive construction of ethnicity (chapter 3) – and partly because a number of documents written in the non-Greek language of Eteokretan have come to light, especially from the eastern Kretan cities of Dreros and Praisos.

The inscriptions provide clear proof that the Eteokretan language was already in use in the Early Archaic period. One of the earliest texts is a religious law, found at Dreros, and dating to ca. 650 BC. However, at about 600 BC, a Greek text (assumed to be a translation of the law) was appended to the Eteokretan text, and it has been inferred that by this period the Eteokretan language was already in decline at Dreros, though – on the principles outlined earlier – that certainly does not mean that there no longer existed at Dreros a group which called itself Eteokretan. At Praisos the earliest Eteokretan inscriptions date to the sixth century BC, and while the first coins that Praisos mints (450–400 BC) carry legends in Greek, the Eteokretan language is still attested for official inscriptions as late as the second century BC.[158]

Throughout the world and throughout history, multilingualism is the norm rather than the exception,[159] and it is difficult to believe that those who spoke the Eteokretan language did not also possess at least a basic proficiency in Greek. The coexistence of coins with Greek legends and formal documents in Eteokretan may point in that direction, as may Homer's assertion that the various languages of Krete *were mixed together*. It has, however, already been seen that the sheer bulk of public and legal inscriptions compared with private dedications or onomastic graffiti suggests that the majority of the Kretan population, however multilingual, was also largely illiterate.[160] Nor is the phenomenon limited to the Archaic period. Among the 300 or so inscriptions at Gortyn, dating from the third to first centuries BC, only thirty can be identified as of a definitely private nature.[161] The implication is, then, that literacy was extremely restricted on Krete, and Simon Stoddart and James Whitley have estimated that perhaps no more than 300 people could read and write during the Archaic period.[162]

The hypothesis of a bilingual and largely illiterate Eteokretan population has important consequences. Firstly, it means that the appearance of inscriptions in Eteokretan during the sixth century at Praisos (and a century earlier at Dreros) is likely to be a 'real' event, rather than simply an 'archaeological' event. That is to say, the earliest texts may actually be among the first documents to have been inscribed in the Eteokretan language rather than the first to survive the unpredictability of depositional and post-depositional factors. Secondly, it means that the

---

[157] Homer, *Odyssey* 19.172–77. See Morpurgo Davies 1985, 86.   [158] Brixhe 1991b, 54–58.
[159] Romaine 1994, 33.   [160] Stoddart and Whitley 1988.   [161] Brixhe 1991b, 55.
[162] Stoddart and Whitley 1988, 766 (though, of course, reading and writing skills need not be isomorphic).

178

decision, in the Archaic period, to use a graphic system to render the Eteokretan language was hardly the consequence of a long tradition of writing in Eteokretan; it was not, in other words, the unconscious replication of a deeply engrained literate behaviour. Thirdly, it means that the decision to inscribe official documents and laws in Eteokretan can hardly have been dictated by communicational factors for the benefit of a population that was unable to read them. The conclusion is inescapable: the decision to inscribe in the Eteokretan rather than Greek language represents a conscious and active choice of the Archaic period. The only purpose it can usefully have served is to act as a reinforcing indicium of an Eteokretan identity.

The undeniable distinctiveness of Eteokretan makes it a particularly good illustration of how language was used within ethnic strategies. The example does, however, have a wider application in that it warns against the passive and mechanistic view of language change that tends to be inherent in both *Stammbaumtheorie* and *Wellentheorie*. Ultimately, there is no automatic necessity for substrate dialects to influence adstrate dialects, nor for neighbouring dialects to assimilate partially with one another. Both models fail to take account of the social dimension of language contact or of the attitudinal factors which may determine the desirability of linguistic convergence or divergence.[163]

Philologists classify linguistic features according to whether they represent innovations, choices between two or more alternatives, or archaisms. It has already been observed that it is normally only innovations which are regarded as significant. No doubt this is a reasonable policy if one is interested in gauging the purely linguistic relatedness between dialects. In ethnolinguistic terms, however, we should perhaps hesitate before totally relegating the categories of choices and especially archaisms (not least because it was demonstrated in chapter 5 that the retention of what are regarded as ancestral cultural forms is a particularly efficacious ethnic strategy). It is certainly true that the retention of an archaism may sometimes represent an economy of effort that possesses little conscious salience. On the other hand, in situations where an archaism is retained when neighbouring communities are busy innovating, it is hard to regard this as anything other than conscious effort. Indeed, to resist the prevailing trend takes considerably more energy than to be carried along with it. Solon describes how he repatriated Athenians 'who no longer spoke the Attic tongue, due to their widespread journeying'.[164] Had the expatriates retained their native speech the fact would have been a good deal more significant.

I would suggest, then, that innovations, choices and archaisms may all represent legitimate attempts to effect conscious linguistic convergence or divergence, though we can be more certain that they represent active signalling when they occur in communities which can be shown to employ other, non-linguistic symbols in a boundary-marking function. From this point of view, the assimilation of

---

[163] Romaine 1994, 223. [164] Solon fr. 36.10.

primary and secondary $\bar{e}/\bar{o}$ in West Argolic need not be due simply to the mechanistic influence of an Akhaian substrate or passive idleness; it may instead represent an active and deliberative refusal to effect linguistic change with the intention of creating yet another dimension of distinctiveness between the communities of the Argive plain and those of the eastern Argolid.

If archaisms are accepted as significant to ethnolinguistic inquiry, then new light may be shed on the Doric dialects of Lakonian and Messenian – characterised by Bartoněk as the 'fossil survival of the ancient Doric dialectal basis' due to their resistance to the linguistic innovations attested in the rest of the Peloponnese.[165] Lakonian is the slightly more innovative of the two, though many of these innovations are effected in isolation from neighbouring dialects, thus blunting their significance.[166] The orthodox view of Lakonian linguistic conservatism attributes it to Lakonia's self-imposed isolation from the other regions of Greece from the middle of the sixth century onwards. On the other hand, if a more active view of language is adopted, then the Lakonian retention of archaisms could be regarded as a more conscious and deliberate process, specifically designed to maintain a distinct Lakonian identity and to identify the Spartans as the true Dorians of the Peloponnese.

Messenian tends to be characterised as an even more conservative dialect, full of archaisms and with one of the lowest innovation coefficients among all the West Greek dialects.[167] Again, this is normally explained by the fact that Messenian was isolated from many of the other Doric dialects and impeded from linguistic development – this time by almost four centuries of Lakonian domination. Yet, the vast bulk of the linguistic data for the Messenian dialect dates to *after* the foundation of Messene in 369 BC – an event that was achieved through the participation of Thebans, Argives and Arkadians, as well as by the repatriation of Messenians of the *diaspora* (which stretched as far afield as Sicily and Libya).[168] One would normally, then, have expected the Messenian dialect to be rather diverse and heterogeneous. The fact that it is instead so conservative may in fact represent a deliberate and conscious policy on the part of a community that was anxious to equip itself with the history, traditions and general ancestral identity which had been denied to it for so long.

Conclusion

In analysing the role of language within Greek ethnicities, it is essential to challenge two notions which have tended to dominate much thinking in ancient history. The first is that linguistic groups can be equated with ethnic groups. It has already been noted in chapter 2 that language need not be a stable dimension within ethnic

---

[165] Bartoněk 1972, 186.   [166] Bartoněk 1972, 201.   [167] Bartoněk 1972, 91, 159, 185.
[168] Pausanias 4.26.2; 4.27.11.

identification and that consequently it should be regarded as an ethnic indicium rather than an ethnic criterion. A closer examination of the situation in Greece has only served to corroborate this observation. The inhabitants of Dorian Halikarnassos wrote in (and probably also spoke) an Ionic dialect, while the Akhaian communities of South Italy traced their ethnic solidarity back – via the northern Peloponnesian region of Akhaia – to the 'pre-Dorian' inhabitants of Lakonia and the Argolid despite the fact that their West Greek dialects are closely related to the Doric dialects.[169] Furthermore, the lateral operation of linguistic accommodation between dialects belonging to different dialect groups and the considerable heterogeneity within these dialect groups means that the Greeks themselves were incapable of identifying ethnic groups through linguistic cues alone.

The second is the tendency to adopt too materialist a view of language as a determinant of social praxis – a notion not too dissimilar from the now discredited 'Whorfian' hypothesis of linguistic relativity whereby language is treated as a mould which shapes thought.[170] It cannot be denied that language may be subject to substrate influence or to lateral borrowings, but in both cases the role of human agency tends to be neglected. Rather than simply documenting these factors in linguistic development, it is necessary to ask why dialect speakers would wish to modify or maintain their speech patterns. Rather than considering ethnic groups to be held hostage by language, it is surely preferable to envisage them as being confronted by a range of linguistic possibilities (archaisms, choices and innovations), the selection of which – as in the case of items of material culture – may represent a conscious and deliberative decision intended to stress (or deny) ethnic distinctiveness.

[169] Morgan and Hall 1996, 197, 214.
[170] See generally Cole and Scribner 1974, esp. 40–41.

7

Conclusion

I have insisted throughout on the constructive nature of ethnicity. Like all ethnic groups, collectivities such as the Dorians, the Ionians, the Akhaians, the Pelasgians or the Dryopes should not be viewed as 'essential' categories. There is no evidence to suggest that any one of these groups can be traced by a direct and exclusive association with a certain type of pottery, a particular class of dress ornament, a distinctive form of burial ritual or a specific dialect. Nor is there any reason to suppose that they will ever be identified by running DNA tests on their skeletal remains. Ethnic identity is not a 'natural' fact of life; it is something that needs to be actively proclaimed, reclaimed and disclaimed through discursive channels. For this reason, it is the literary evidence which must constitute the first and final frame of analysis in the study of ancient ethnicity. In saying this, I am certainly not advocating a general principle of granting to literary evidence a primacy in *all* approaches to antiquity; it is simply that the very nature of ethnic identity demands this.

It is, of course, easy to see why the practitioners of a more objectivist view to the past should have turned their back on the literary references to ancient ethnicity. Accounts which purport to be ethnographic records of historical populations are interspersed with tales which belong more to the realm of fantasy. What historical validity are we entitled to give, for instance, to the migrations of the Dorians, Ionians and Akhaians, or the return of the Herakleidai or Herakles' removal of the Dryopes? In addition, what are we to make of the fact that different accounts of these tales are so contradictory? Does this not indicate that literary evidence is ultimately untrustworthy and that the ethnic consciousness which it appears to articulate is both fragile and illusory?

In fact, it indicates the opposite. What makes ethnic identity distinct from other social identities is precisely its historical (or quasi-historical) dimension. The consciousness that it engenders is explained and legitimated by reference to the past: the answer to 'who am I?' invariably involves 'how did I get here?' For the ancient Greeks (at least in the period we have been considering) there was no clear division between the historical past and the mythical past: Danaos, Perseus and Herakles were personages as real as Homer, Pheidon or Kleomenes. It is the very appearance in the literary record of these myths of ethnic origin which testifies to the continuing proclamation of the ethnic identity which it is their principal function to construct. Furthermore, the fact that such myths exist in a number of sometimes conflicting variants is not so much the consequence of a decaying memory of a 'real' dim and distant prehistoric past as it is an indication of the dynamic and complex interplay between ethnic claims and counterclaims which occurred intermittently throughout the course of the historical period.

Although ethnic identity is constructed primarily through discourse, it can certainly be bolstered by cultural forms. We have seen, for example, how the Dryopes of Asine used pottery style, mortuary practices, settlement pattern and the practice of a highly original ancestor cult to distance themselves culturally from the communities of the Argive plain. The Akhaians of South Italy adopted an eclectic blend of architectural style to signal their own distinctiveness among their Ionian and Dorian neighbours, and many of the communities of Cyprus expressed their affiliation with the Greek mainland through the medium of funerary architecture.

None of these instances are isolated cultural manifestations. The legends of the Dryopes and their 'dedication' by Herakles were probably already in currency by the end of the eighth century and if they were an Argive invention, coined in order to justify the sack of Asine ca. 720 BC (i.e. a *post hoc* 'externalist' definition of the Asinaian Dryopes), their efficacy would have been severely compromised had there not been a consensual acceptance that the Dryopes had been somehow 'different'. The expression of an Akhaian cultural identity in South Italy has to be seen within the context of the foundation myths which were being elaborated in the course of the sixth century (if not earlier). The Akhaian cities appealed to the pre-Dorian patrimony of the Peloponnese by attributing their foundation to Akhaian heroes returning from Troy, thus establishing claims to a glorious heroic past from which their Dorian neighbours (notably Taras) were inevitably excluded.[1] On Cyprus, the Arkadian inscription which is attested on an *obelos* in an eleventh-century chamber-tomb at Palaipaphos-Skales may provide an astonishingly early context for the foundation myths which derived the origins of Paphos from the Arkadian city of Tegea.

Ritual behaviour – and especially the primacy attributed to certain deities within the pantheon – could also serve as an indicium of ancient ethnicity. This is most obviously the case at Athens, where a pre-eminent significance was bestowed upon the goddess who had supposedly given her name to the city. Yet the depiction, on the west pediment of the Parthenon, of Athena's victory over Poseidon may symbolise the substitution of the Athenian myth of autochthony for the earlier subscription to an Ionian ancestry. During the Late Bronze Age, Poseidon was clearly one of the more important deities at Messenian Pylos[2] – a site which, as we have seen, was sometimes claimed as the metropolis of the Ionian cities of Kolophon, Miletos and Ephesos. In the Archaic period, it was Poseidon who presided over the meetings of the Ionian Dodekapolis, and according to popular tradition it was

---

[1] See Morgan and Hall 1996, 213.
[2] Burkert 1985, 44. Cf. Nestor's sacrifice to Poseidon in Homer, *Odyssey* 3.4–66.

Poseidon's sanctuary at Helike which had served as the focus of Ionian identity during their occupation of Akhaia.[3]

While the 'Akhaian/Heraklid' communities of the eastern Argive plain accorded a particularly salient veneration to Hera – the goddess who almost certainly acted as the 'Divine Mistress' of the Argive plain during the Late Bronze Age – the cult of Hera is far less evident at Argos, where the earliest cult to be registered in the archaeological record would appear to be that of Athena. In the absence of further archaeological exploration it would be premature to guess the date at which the cult of Apollo Lykeios (the principal deity of Classical Argos) was established. This is an important gap in our knowledge, because although Apollo enjoyed no exclusive link with Dorian groups, he does figure prominently within the cults of many Dorian cities. Nevertheless, despite these provisos, it may not be entirely contingent that a small, square building in the Gounaris plot which has been plausibly connected with the sanctuary of Apollo Lykeios dates to the middle of the sixth century BC – the date at which the integration of the Argive genealogies within the general Dorian pedigree is first attested in the *Catalogue of women*.[4]

Finally, linguistic idioms could be harnessed as a symbol of ethnic identity. This is most obviously the case with the Eteokretans who, in the course of the seventh and sixth centuries, took the active decision to give a material, epigraphic form to their language despite the fact that few could have derived any communicational benefit from this action. It has, however, been suggested tentatively that both the Lakonians and the Messenians consciously preserved a more archaic form of the Doric dialect (unless they periodically subjected their own dialects to a purifying *katharevousa*) which served to articulate their competing claims to be the true guardians of the Dorian heritage.

I cannot perhaps end without at least attempting an answer to a question I have studiously ignored up to now. It is the irksome issue of whether the Dorian invasion 'ever actually happened'. That the beginning of the Iron Age in Greece witnessed a considerable degree of population mobility is beyond doubt. The fact that we do not know the ancient names of such key sites as Lathouresa in Attika, Lefkandi on Euboia, Nikhoria in Messenia, Zagora on Andros, Emborio on Khios or Koukounaries on Paros is due precisely to the fact that they were intermittently occupied and abandoned prior to the historical period.[5] If, however, by the 'Dorian migration' we mean a single, massive influx of immigrants from central Greece, then the answer must be no. If we mean that every member of the population of Dorian cities in the Classical period was genetically descended from an original inhabitant of central Greece, then again – no. And if we mean that 'real blood ties'

---

[3] Herodotos 1.148.1; Pausanias 7.24.5.

[4] The building in the Gounaris plot is certainly in the general area where the sanctuary of Apollo Lykeios should be situated. More positively, the retrieval of two tortoise-shell lyres from the enclosure matches well with Pausanias' description (2.19.7) of a statue which depicted Apollo making a lyre out of a tortoise-shell and which stood within the sanctuary of Apollo Lykeios. See Daux 1957, 674; Courbin 1980; Marchetti 1993; Hall 1995b, 606.

[5] Snodgrass 1980, 19; 1987, 172–73.

existed between the populations of cities as distant as Argos, Melos and Halikarnassos, then – almost certainly not. It is not the evidence of archaeology or linguistics that provides us with these answers: the presence or absence of artefacts is not, as we have seen, a sufficient index of the arrival or non-arrival of a new population, and the acceptance of linguistic assimilation does not in itself preclude the possibility of migration. It is rather the recognition that the Dorian myth of origins is a gradual and cumulative aggregation of originally independent accounts which told of different ancestors and different homelands. The final form in which we have it dates back no further than the mid-sixth century – that is some five or six centuries after the supposed date of the migration.

That is not to say, however, that there was no reality to 'being Dorian' in the sixth or fifth centuries. Ethnicity is not unique in purporting to represent itself as the inescapable destiny of a past that it has to a large degree created. Yet to privilege a supposedly objective and externalist account of the past over the 'social reality' of the present is to subscribe to a history devoid of humanism, and ultimately meaning. To understand the ethnic group we must learn how the ethnic group understands itself, and this is rarely achieved by establishing a dichotomy between ethnic fact and ethnic fiction. That is a lesson that could still usefully be learnt far beyond the frontiers of ancient Greece.

Chronological table

All dates are approximate.

Bronze Age

Early Helladic I	EHI	2800–2400 BC
Early Helladic II	EHII	2400–2200 BC
Early Helladic III	EHIII	2200–1900 BC
Middle Helladic I	MHI	1900–1800 BC
Middle Helladic II	MHII	1800–1700 BC
Middle Helladic III	MHIII	1700–1550 BC
Late Helladic I[1]	LHI	1550–1500 BC
Late Helladic II	LHII	1500–1425 BC
Late Helladic IIIA	LHIIIA	1425–1300 BC
Late Helladic IIIB	LHIIIB	1300–1230 BC
Late Helladic IIIC	LHIIIC	1230–1050 BC

Early Iron Age / 'Dark Ages'

Submycenaean	SM	1050–1000 BC
Protogeometric	PG	1000–900 BC
Early Geometric I[2]	EGI	900–875 BC
Early Geometric II	EGII	875–850 BC
Middle Geometric I	MGI	850–800 BC
Middle Geometric II	MGII	800–760 BC
Late Geometric I	LGI	760–735 BC
Late Geometric II	LGII	735–700 BC

[1] The Late Helladic period is also known as the Mycenaean period.
[2] The dates for the Geometric period presented here are based on the pottery sequence of Attika. Pottery sequences of other areas follow slightly different rhythms.

186

Historical period

Archaic	A	700–480 BC
Classical	CL	480–323 BC
Hellenistic	HL	323–146 BC
Roman	R	146 BC–AD 395

Chronological table of authors cited in the text

700 BC	Eumelos of Korinth; Homer; Hesiod
650	Tyrtaios Mimnermos of Kolophon
600	Alkaios of Mytilene; Solon Stesikhoros
550	Pseudo-Hesiod? Asios of Samos? Kinaithon of Sparta? Ibykos Anakreon of Teos Lasos of Hermione; Simonides of Keos
500	Akousilaos of Argos; Aiskhylos; Pindar Bakkhylides of Keos
450	Hellanikos of Lesbos; Pherekydes of Athens Herodotos Thoukydides; Sophokles; Euripides; Hippokrates
400	Xenophon; Plato Isokrates
350	Aristotle; Demosthenes Theopompos of Khios; Ephoros of Kyme; Asklepiades of Tragilos
300	Andron of Halikarnassos Lykophron; Theokritos; Kallimakhos
250	Apollonios of Rhodes; Herakleides of Krete Parian Marble
200	Demetrios of Argos?
150	Apollodoros of Athens; Moskhos
100	Pseudo-Skymnos Lucretius
50	Diodoros of Sicily; Vitruvius; Strabo; Didymos Dionysios of Halikarnassos; Konon; Nikolaos of Damascus Kastor of Rhodes Velleius Paterculus

50 AD	Quintilian
	Plutarch; Josephus
100	Pseudo-Apollodoros?
150	Pausanias; Hyginus
	Clement of Alexandria; Tatian; Pollux
200	
	Nonnos
400	
	Hesykhios

Bibliography

Adams, J. P. (1983) 'The *larnakes* from Tomb II at Vergina', *AN* 12: 1–7.

Adshead, K. (1986) *Politics of the Archaic Peloponnese: the transition from Archaic to Classical politics*. Aldershot and Brookfield VT.

Ahrens, H. (1843) *De graecae linguae dialectis* II. Göttingen.

Alden, M. (1981) *Bronze Age population fluctuations in the Argolid from the evidence of Mycenaean tombs*. Göteborg.

Alexandri, O. (1964) 'Une broche dédalique laconienne', *BCH* 88: 525–30.

Ålin, P. (1962) *Das Ende der mykenischen Fundstätten auf dem griechischen Festland*. Lund.

Alty, J. (1982) 'Dorians and Ionians', *JHS* 102: 1–14.

Amandry, P. (1952) 'Observations sur les monuments de l'Héraion d'Argos', *Hesperia* 21: 222–74.

  (1980) 'Sur les concours argiens', *Études Argiennes* (*BCH* Supplement 6), 211–53. Paris.

Anderson, B. (1991 [1983]) *Imagined communities: reflections on the origins and spread of nationalism* (2nd edition). London.

Andrewes, A. (1956) *The Greek tyrants*. London.

Antonaccio, C. M. (1992) 'Terraces, tombs and the early Argive Heraion', *Hesperia* 61: 85–105.

  (1993) 'The archaeology of ancestors', in C. Dougherty and L. Kurke (eds.), *Cultural poetics in Archaic Greece: cult, performance, politics*, 46–70. Cambridge.

  (1994) 'Placing the past: the Bronze Age in the cultic topography of early Greece', in S. E. Alcock and R. Osborne (eds.), *Placing the gods: sanctuaries and sacred space in ancient Greece*, 79–104. Oxford.

  (1995) *An archaeology of ancestors: tomb cult and hero cult in early Greece*. Lanham MD.

Antonetti, C. and Lévêque, P. (1990) 'Au carrefour de la Mégaride. Devins et oracles', *Kernos* 3: 197–209.

Arafat, K. W. (1995) 'Pausanias and the temple of Hera at Olympia', *BSA* 90: 461–73.

Arkhontidou-Argiri, A. (1975) 'Παλαιά 'Επίδαυρος', *Deltion* 30B: 59–60.

  (1977) 'Παλαιά 'Επίδαυρος', *Deltion* 32B: 46–49.

Arnold, D. (1978) 'Ceramic variability, environment and culture history among the Pokom in the valley of Guatemala', in I. Hodder (ed.), *The spatial organization of culture*, 39–59. London.

Audin, A. (1960) 'Inhumation et incinération', *Latomus* 19: 312–22, 518–32.

Aupert, P. (1982) 'Argos aux VIIIᵉ-VIIᵉ siècles: bourgade ou métropole?', *A.S.Atene* 60: 21–32.

  (1987) 'Pausanias et l'Asclépieion d'Argos', *BCH* 111: 511–17.

Austin, M. M. (1970) *Greece and Egypt in the Archaic age* (*PCPS* Supplement 2). Cambridge.

Badian, E. (1994) 'Herodotos on Alexander I of Macedon: a study in some subtle silences', in S. Hornblower (ed.), *Greek historiography*, 107–30. Oxford.

Bálint, C. (1989) 'Some ethnospecific features in central and eastern European archaeology during the early Middle Ages: the case of Avars and Hungarians', in S. Shennan (ed.), *Archaeological approaches to cultural identity*, 185–94. London.

Banton, M. (1977) *The idea of race*. London.

(1987) *Racial theories*. Cambridge.

Barakari-Gleni, K. (1984) Ἀνασκαφή τάφων στο Ἄργος', *Deltion* 39A: 171–204.

Barrett, W. (1954) 'Bacchylides, Asine and Apollo Pythaieus', *Hermes* 82: 421–44.

Barron, J. P. (1964) 'Religious propaganda of the Delian League', *JHS* 84: 35–48.

Barth, F. (1969) 'Introduction', in F. Barth (ed.), *Ethnic groups and boundaries: the social organization of culture difference*, 9–38. London.

Bartoněk, A. (1972) *Classification of the West Greek dialects at the time about 350 BC*. Prague.

(1973) 'The place of the Dorians in the Late Helladic World', in R.A. Crossland and A. Birchall (eds.), *Bronze Age migrations in the Aegean: archaeological and linguistic problems in Greek prehistory*, 305–11. London.

(1979) 'Greek dialects between 1000 and 300 BC', *SMEA* 20: 113–30.

(1991) 'L'evoluzione dei dialetti greci nella dimensione geografica delle età oscure', in D. Musti et al. (eds.), *La transizione dal miceneo all'alto arcaismo: dal palazzo alla città*, 241–50. Rome.

Beals, K. L. (1972) 'Head form and climatic stress', *AJPA* 37: 85–92.

Bell, D. (1975) 'Ethnicity and social change', in N. Glazer and D. Moynihan (eds.), *Ethnicity: theory and experience*, 141–74. Cambridge MA.

Beloch, K. J. (1890) 'Die dorische Wanderung', *Rh.M* 45: 555–98.

(1924 [1893]) *Griechische Geschichte* I.1 (2nd edition). Berlin and Leipzig.

Bentley, G. (1987) 'Ethnicity and practice', *CSSH* 29: 24–55.

Béquinon, Y. (1930) 'Chronique des fouilles et découvertes archéologiques dans l'orient hellénique, 1930', *BCH* 54: 452–528.

Bergquist, B. (1967) *The Archaic Greek temenos: a study of structure and function*. Lund.

(1990) 'Primary or secondary temple function? The case of Halieis', *Op.Ath* 18: 23–37.

Bernal, M. (1987) *Black Athena: the Afroasiatic roots of classical civilization* I: *the fabrication of ancient Greece, 1785–1985*. London.

Betancourt, P. (1976) 'The end of the Greek Bronze Age', *Ant* 50: 40–47.

Bianchi Bandinelli, R. (1985 [1976]) *Introduzione all' archeologia* (5th edition). Rome and Bari.

Bibis-Papaspyropoulou, A. (1989) 'Μελάμπους, ο μέγας θεραπεύτης του Ἄργους', *Peloponnesiaka* Supplement 14: 49–56.

Bietti Sestieri, A. M. (1992) *The Iron-Age community of Osteria dell' Osa: a study of sociopolitical development in central Tyrrhenian Italy*. Cambridge.

Bile, M. (1988) *Le dialecte crétois ancien*. Paris.

Bile, M. and Brixhe, C. (1983) 'Review of M. P. Fernández Alvarez, *El Argolico occidental y oriental*', *Kratylos* 28: 121–28.

Bile, M. et al. (1988) 'Bulletin de dialectologie grecque', *REG* 101: 74–112.

Billot, M-F. (1989–90) 'Apollon Pythéen et l'Argolide archaïque: histoire et mythes', *Archaiognosia* 6: 35–100.

Binford, L. (1972) *An archaeological perspective*. New York.

Blackwell, T. (1735) *Enquiry into the life and writings of Homer*. London.

Blegen C. W. (1937a) *Prosymna: the Helladic settlement preceding the Argive Heraeum*. Cambridge.

(1937b) 'Post-Mycenaean deposits in chamber tombs', *Arch.Eph*, 377–90.

(1939) 'Prosymna: remains of post-Mycenaean date', *AJA* 43: 410–44.

Boardman, J. (1963) *Island gems: a study of Greek seals in the Geometric and early Archaic periods.* London.

(1980 [1964]) *The Greeks overseas: their early colonies and trade* (2nd edition). London.

Bohannan, L. (1952) 'A genealogical charter', *Africa* 22: 301–15.

Bohen, B. (1980) 'A Geometric horse pyxis from Asine', *Op.Ath* 13: 85–89.

Bommelaer, J-F. (1984) 'Delphes, 3: hémicycle des rois d'Argos', *BCH* 108: 857–58.

(1992) 'Monuments argiens de Delphes et d'Argos', in M. Piérart (ed.), *Polydipsion Argos: Argos de la fin des palais mycéniens à la constitution de l'état classique* (*BCH* Supplement 22), 265–303. Paris.

Bommelaer, J-F. and Laroche, D. (1991) *Guide de Delphes: le site.* Paris.

Borza, E. N. (1981) 'The Macedonian royal tombs at Vergina: some cautionary notes', *AN* 10: 73–87.

Bourdieu, P. (1977) *Outline of a theory of practice.* Cambridge. (Originally published as *Esquisse d'une théorie de la pratique, précédé de trois études d'ethnologie kabyle.* Paris, 1972.)

Bourguet, E. (1929) *Fouilles de Delphes III: épigraphie, inscriptions de l'entrée du sanctuaire au trésor des Athéniens.* Paris.

Bouzec, J. (1969) *Homerisches Griechenland im Lichte der archäologischen Quellen.* Prague.

(1985) *The Aegean, Anatolia and Europe: cultural interrrelations in the second millennium.* Göteborg.

Brass, P. and Van den Berghe, P. (1976) 'Ethnicity and nationalism in world perspective', *Eth* 3: 197–201.

Bremmer, J. (ed.) (1987) *Interpretations of Greek mythology.* London.

Brillante, C. (1984) 'L'invasione dorica oggi', *QUCC* 16: 173–85.

Brixhe, C. (1991a) 'Du mycénien aux dialectes du Ier millénaire. Quelques aspects de la problématique', in D. Musti et al. (eds.), *La transizione dal miceneo all'alto arcaismo: dal palazzo alla città,* 251–72. Rome.

(1991b) 'La langue comme reflet de l'histoire, ou les éléments non doriens du dialecte crétois', in C. Brixhe (ed.), *Sur la Crète antique: histoire, écritures, langues,* 43–77. Nancy.

Brixhe, C. and Bile, M. (1991) 'Le dialecte crétois: unité ou diversité?', in C. Brixhe (ed.), *Sur la Crète antique: histoire, écritures, langues,* 85–136. Nancy.

Brock, J. K. (1957) *Fortetsa: early Greek tombs near Knossos.* Cambridge.

Brodie, N. J. (1994) *The Neolithic-Bronze Age transition in Britain: a critical review of some archaeological and craniological concepts* (*BAR* New Series 238).

Broneer, O. (1966) 'The cyclopaean wall on the isthmus of Corinth and its bearing on Late Bronze Age chronology', *Hesperia* 35: 346–62.

Brown, J. (1981) 'The search for rank in prehistoric burials', in R. Chapman, I. Kinnes and K. Randsborg (eds.), *The archaeology of death,* 25–37. Cambridge.

Brown, K. S. (1994) 'Seeing stars: character and identity in the landscapes of modern Macedonia', *Ant* 68: 784–96.

Bruit Zaidman, L. and Schmitt Pantel, P. (1992) *Religion in the ancient Greek city.* Cambridge. (Originally published as *La religion grecque.* Paris, 1989.)

Buchner, G. and Russo, C.F. (1955) 'La coppa di Nestore e un' iscrizione metrica da Pithecusa dell' VIII secolo av. Chr.', *RANL* 10: 215–34.

Buck, C. D. (1955 [1928]) *The Greek dialects* (2nd edition). Chicago.

Burford, A. (1969) *The Greek temple builders of Epidauros.* Liverpool.

Burkert, W. (1979) *Structure and history in Greek mythology and ritual*. Berkeley.

(1984) *Die orientalisierende Epoche in der griechischen Religion und Literatur*. Heidelberg.

(1985) *Greek religion, Archaic and Classical*. Oxford. (First published as *Griechische Religion der archaischen und klassischen Epoche*. Stuttgart, 1977.)

(1990) 'Herodot als Historiker fremder Religionen', in W. Burkert et al. (eds.), *Hérodote et les peuples non grecs (EAC* 35), 1–32. Geneva.

Buxton, R. (1994) *Imaginary Greece: the contexts of mythology*. Cambridge.

Bynon, T. (1977) *Historical linguistics*. Cambridge.

Calame, C. (1987) 'Spartan genealogies: the mythical representation of a spatial organization', in J. Bremmer (ed.), *Interpretations of Greek mythology*, 153–86. London.

Callahan, B. (1989) 'Is ethnicity obsolete? The European immigrant response', in W. Sollors (ed.), *The invention of ethnicity*, 231–34. New York and Oxford.

Calligas, P. G. (1992) 'From the Amyklaion', in J. Sanders (ed.), *ΦΙΛΟΛΑΚΩΝ: Lakonian studies in honour of Hector Catling*, 31–48. London.

Carpenter, R. (1966) *Discontinuity in Greek civilization*. Cambridge.

Cartledge, P. A. (1979) *Sparta and Lakonia: a regional history 1300–362 BC*. London.

(1985) 'The Greek religious festivals', in P. Easterling and J. Muir (eds.), *Greek religion and society*, 98–127. Cambridge.

(1992) 'Early Lacedaimon: the making of a conquest state', in J. Sanders (ed.), *ΦΙΛΟΛΑΚΩΝ Lakonian studies in honour of Hector Catling*, 49–55. London.

(1993) *The Greeks: a portrait of self and other*. Oxford.

Cartledge, P. A. and Spawforth, A. (1989) *Hellenistic and Roman Sparta: a tale of two cities*. London.

Casadio, G. (1994) *Storia del culto di Dioniso in Argolide*. Rome.

Caskey, J. and Amandry, P. (1952) 'Investigations at the Heraion of Argos, 1949', *Hesperia* 21: 165–221.

Cassio, A. (1984) 'Il 'carattere' dei dialetti greci e l'opposizione Ioni-Dori: testimonianze antiche e teorie di età romantica', *AION (L)* 6: 113–36.

Cassola, F. (1953) 'Le genealogie mitiche e la coscienza nazionale greca', *RAALBA* 28: 279–304.

Chadwick, J. (1975) 'The prehistory of the Greek language', *CAH* (3rd edition) II.2, 805–19.

(1976) 'Who were the Dorians?', *PP* 31: 103–17.

(1985) 'I Dori e la creazione dei dialetti greci', in D. Musti (ed.), *Le origini dei Greci: Dori e mondo egeo*, 3–12. Rome.

Chambers, J. and Trudgill, P. (1980) *Dialectology*. Cambridge.

Charitonidou, A. (1967) 'Ἀργολίς. Κουρτάκι', *Deltion* 22B: 178–79.

Charitonidis, S. (1953) 'Ἀνασκαφαὶ ἐν Ναυπλίᾳ', *Praktika*, 191–204.

Charles, R. (1963) *Étude anthropologique des nécropoles d'Argos: contribution à l'étude des populations de la Grèce antique*. Paris.

Childe, V. G. (1929) *The Danube in prehistory*. Oxford.

(1944) *Progress and archaeology*. London.

Christou, C. (1956) 'Ἀνασκαφὴ εν Ἀμύκλαις', *Praktika*, 211–12.

(1960) 'Ἀνασκαφὴ Ἀμυκλῶν', *Praktika*, 228–31.

(1961) 'Ἀνασκαφὴ Ἀμυκλῶν', *Praktika*, 177–78.

Clarke, D. (1978 [1968]) *Analytical archaeology* (2nd edition). London.

Clogg, R. (1992) *A concise history of Greece*. Cambridge.

Cohen, A. P. (1985) *The symbolic construction of community*. London.

Coldstream, J. N. (1968) *Greek Geometric Pottery.* London.

(1976) 'Hero-cults in the age of Homer', *JHS* 96: 8–17.

(1977) *Geometric Greece*. London.

(1984) 'Dorian Knossos and Aristotle's villages', in *Aux origines de l' Hellénisme: la Crète et la Grèce. Hommages à Henri van Effenterre*, 309–22. Paris.

(1985) 'Archaeology in Cyprus 1960–1985: the Geometric and Archaic periods', in V. Karageorghis (ed.), *Archaeology in Cyprus, 1960–1985*, 47–59. Nicosia.

Cole, M. and Scribner, S. (1974) *Culture and thought: a psychological introduction*. New York.

Cole, S. (1965) *Races of man*. London.

Coleman, R. (1963) 'The dialect geography of ancient Greece', *TPS* 61: 58–126.

Colin, G. (1930) *Fouilles de Delphes* III: *épigraphie, inscriptions de la terrasse du temple et de la région nord du sanctuaire*. Paris.

Collett, D. (1987) 'A contribution to the study of migrations in the archaeological record: the Ngoni and Kololo migrations as a case study', in I. Hodder (ed.), *Archaeology as long-term history*, 105–16. Cambridge.

Collinge, N. E. (1973) 'The dialectology and prehistoric development of Greek', in R. A. Crossland and A. Birchall (eds.), *Bronze Age migrations in the Aegean: archaeological and linguistic problems in Greek prehistory*, 293–304. London.

Collingwood, R.G. (1946) *The idea of history*. Oxford.

Colvin, S. (1995) 'Aristophanes: dialect and textual criticism', *Mnem* 48: 34–47.

Conkey, M. (1990) 'Experimenting with style in archaeology: some historical and theoretical issues', in M. Conkey and C. Hastorf (eds.), *The uses of style in archaeology*, 5–17. Cambridge.

Connor, W. R. (1993) 'The Ionian era of Athenian civic identity', *PAPS* 137: 194–206.

Consani, C. (1989) 'Storia e preistoria dei dialetti greci antichi: a proposito di una recente publicazione', *QUCC* 33: 157–68.

Consolaki, H. and Hackens, T. (1980) 'Un atelier monétaire dans un temple argien?', *Études Argiennes* (*BCH* Supplement 6), 279–94. Paris.

Conzen, K. N. (1989) 'Ethnicity as festive culture: nineteenth-century German America on parade', in W. Sollors (ed.), *The invention of ethnicity*, 44–76. Oxford.

Cook, J. M. (1953) 'Mycenae 1939–1952: the Agamemnoneion', *BSA* 48: 30–68.

Cooper, N. (1990) 'Archaic architectural terracottas from Halieis and Bassai', *Hesperia* 59: 65–93.

Coulson, W. D. E. (1985) 'The Dark Age pottery of Sparta', *BSA* 80: 29–84.

Coulson, W. D. E. and Leonard, A. (1982) 'Investigations at Naukratis and environs, 1980 and 1981', *AJA* 86: 361–80.

Courbin, P. (1955) 'Argos: quartier sud', *BCH* 79: 312–14.

(1956) 'Argos III, quartier sud', *BCH* 80: 366–76.

(1959) 'Dans la Grèce archaïque. Valeur comparée du fer et de l'argent lors de l'introduction du monnayage', *Ann.ESC*, 209–33.

(1966) *La céramique géométrique d'Argolide*. Paris.

(1974) *Tombes géométriques d'Argos*. Paris.

(1980) 'Les lyres d'Argos', *Études Argiennes* (*BCH* Supplement 6), 93–114. Paris.

(1983) 'Obéloi d' Argolide et d' ailleurs', in R. Hägg (ed.), *The Greek renaissance of the eighth century: tradition and innovation*, 149–56. Stockholm.

Courby, M. (1927) *Fouilles de Delphes* II: *topographie et architecture, la terrasse du temple*. Paris.

Courtils, J. des (1981) 'Note de topographie argienne', *BCH* 105: 607–10.

Craik, E. (1980) *The Dorian Aegean*. London.

Croce, B. (1943 [1917]) *Teoria e storia della storiografia* (5th edition). Bari.

Crone, P. (1986) 'The tribe and the state', in J. Hall (ed.), *States in history*, 48–77. Oxford.

Crossland, R. A. (1985) 'La tradizione greca sulla migrazione dorica', in D. Musti (ed.), *Le origini dei Greci: Dori e mondo egeo*, 335–40. Rome.

Curtius, E. (1857) *Griechische Geschichte* I. Berlin.

Curty, O. (1995) *Les parentés légendaires entre cités grecques. Catalogue raisonné des inscriptions contenant le terme συγγένεια et analyse critique*. Geneva.

Danforth, L. M. (1995) *The Macedonian conflict: ethnic nationalism in a transnational world*. Princeton.

Daniel, G. (1967) *The origins and growth of archaeology*. Harmondsworth.

Das Gupta, J. (1975) 'Ethnicity, language demands, and national development in India', in N. Glazer and D. Moynihan (eds.), *Ethnicity: theory and experience*, 466–88. Cambridge MA.

Daumas, M. (1992) 'Argos et les sept', in M. Piérart (ed.), *Polydipsion Argos: Argos de la fin des palais mycéniens à la constitution de l'état classique* (*BCH* Supplement 22), 253–63. Paris.

Daux, G. (1957) 'Chronique des fouilles et découvertes archéologiques en Grèce en 1956', *BCH* 81: 496–713.

(1959) 'Chronique des fouilles et découvertes archéologiques en Grèce en 1958', *BCH* 83: 567–793.

(1968) 'Argos: secteur δ', *BCH* 92: 1021–39.

(1969) 'Argos: secteur δ', *BCH* 93: 986–1013.

Davis, W. (1990) 'Style and history in art history', in M. Conkey and C. Hastorf (eds.), *The uses of style in archaeology*, 18–31. Cambridge.

DeCorse, C. (1989) 'Material aspects of Limba, Yalunka and Kuranko ethnicity: archaeological research in northeastern Sierra Leone', in S. Shennan (ed.), *Archaeological approaches to cultural identity*, 125–40. London.

De Fidio, P. (1992) 'Un modello di 'mythistorie': Asopia ed Efirea nei 'Korinthiaka' di Eumelo', in F. Prontera (ed.), *Geografia storica della Grecia antica*, 233–63. Bari.

Deger-Jalkotzy, S. (1977) *Fremde Zuwanderer im spätmykenischer Griechenlands. Zu einer Gruppe handgemachter Keramik aus den mykenischen IIIC Siedlungschichten von Aigeira*. Vienna.

Deïlaki, E. [see also Protonotariou-Deïlaki] (1973) ''Αρχαιότητες καὶ μνημεῖα 'Αργολίδος-Κορινθίας', *Deltion* 28B: 80–122.

(1973–4) ''Ανασκαφικαὶ ἐργασίες', *Deltion* 29B: 200–10.

Demakopoulou, K. (1982) *Το μυκηναϊκό ιερό στο Αμυκλαίο και η ΥΕ ΙΙΙΓ περίοδος στη Λακωνία*. Ph.D. dissertation, University of Athens.

Dengate, C. (1988) *The sanctuaries of Apollo in the Peloponnesos*. Ph.D. dissertation, University of Chicago.

Desborough, V. R. d'A. (1952) *Protogeometric pottery*. Oxford.

(1954) 'Mycenae 1939–1953. Part IV: four tombs', *BSA* 49: 258–66.

(1964) *The last Mycenaeans and their successors: an archaeological survey c.1200–c.1000 BC*. Oxford.

(1972) *The Greek Dark Ages*. London.

(1975) 'The end of Mycenaean civilization and the Dark Age: the archaeological background', *CAH* (3rd edition) II.2, 658–77.

Deschamps, J-C. (1982) 'Social identity and relations of power between groups', in H. Tajfel (ed.), *Social identity and intergroup relations*, 85–98. Cambridge.

Deshayes, J. (1966) *Argos: les fouilles de la Deiras*. Paris.

Detienne, M. (1986) *The creation of mythology*. Chicago. (Originally published as *L'invention de la mythologie*. Paris, 1981.)

De Vos, G.A. (1995) 'Ethnic pluralism: conflict and accommodation', in L. Romanucci-Ross and G. De Vos (eds.), *Ethnic identity: creation, conflict and accommodation*, 15–47. Walnut Creek CA.

De Vos, G. A. and Romanucci-Ross, L. (1995) 'Ethnic identity: a psychocultural perspective', in L. Romanucci-Ross and G. De Vos (eds.), *Ethnic identity: creation, conflict and accommodation*, 349–79. Walnut Creek CA.

Diamond, A. (ed.) (1991) *The Victorian achievement of Sir Henry Maine: a centennial reappraisal*. Cambridge.

Dickinson, O. T. P. K. (1992) 'Reflections on Bronze Age Laconia', in J. Sanders (ed.), *ΦΙΛΟΛΑΚΩΝ: Lakonian studies in honour of Hector Catling*, 109–14. London.

Diebold, A. R. (1987) 'Linguistic ways to prehistory', in S. Nacev Skomal and E. C. Polomé (eds.), *Proto-Indo-European: the archaeology of a linguistic problem. Studies in honour of Marija Gimbutas*, 19–71. Washington DC.

Dietrich, B. C. (1975) 'The Dorian Hyacinthia: a survival from the Bronze Age', *Kadmos* 14: 133–42.

Doffey, M-C. (1992) 'Les mythes de fondation des concours néméens', in M. Piérart (ed.), *Polydipsion Argos: Argos de la fin des palais mycéniens à la constitution de l'état classique* (*BCH* Supplement 22), 185–93. Paris.

Dolukhanov, P. (1989) 'Cultural and ethnic processes in prehistory as seen through the evidence of archaeology and related disciplines', in S. Shennan (ed.), *Archaeological approaches to cultural identity*, 267–77. London.

Donlan, W. (1985) 'The social groups of Dark Age Greece', *CP* 80: 293–308.

Dowden, K. (1992) *The uses of Greek mythology*. London.

Drerup, H. (1969) *Griechische Baukunst in geometrischer Zeit*. Göttingen.

Drews, R. (1988) *The coming of the Greeks: Indo-European conquests in the Aegean and the Near East*. Princeton.

Duhoux, Y. (1983) *Introduction aux dialectes grecs anciens: problèmes et méthodes, recueil de textes traduits*. Louvain.

(1988) 'Les éléments grecs non doriens du crétois et la situation dialectale grecque au IIe millénaire', *Cret.Stud* 1: 57–72.

Dumézil, G. (1939) *Mythes et dieux des Germains: essai d'interprétation comparative*. Paris.

Durkheim, E. (1915) *The elementary forms of the religious life: a study in religious sociology*. London. (Originally published as *Les formes élémentaires de la vie religieuse: le système totémique en Australie*. Paris, 1912.)

Eder, B. (1990) 'The Dorian migration: religious consequences in the Argolid', in R. Hägg and G. Nordquist (eds.), *Celebrations of death and divinity in the Bronze Age Argolid*, 207–11. Stockholm.

Edmunds, L. (ed.) (1990) *Approaches to Greek myth*. Baltimore.

Eidheim, H. (1969) 'When ethnic identity is a social stigma', in F. Barth (ed.), *Ethnic groups and boundaries: the social organization of culture difference*, 39–57. London.

Eiteljorg, H. (1980) 'The fast wheel, the multiple-brush compass and Athens as the home of the Protogeometric style', *AJA* 84: 445–52.

Eliot, C. (1967) 'Where did the Alkmaionidai live?', *Historia* 16: 279–86.

Elsner, J. (1992) 'Pausanias: a Greek pilgrim in the Roman world', *P.Pres* 135: 3–29.

Emlyn-Jones, C. J. (1980) *The Ionians and Hellenism: a study of the cultural achievement of early Greek inhabitants of Asia Minor.* London.

Eriksen, T. H. (1993) *Ethnicity and nationalism: anthropological perspectives.* London.

Fagerström, K. (1988) *Greek Iron Age architecture: developments through changing times.* Göteborg.

Faklaris, P. B. (1990) *Αρχαία Κυνουρία: ανθρώπινη δραστηριότητα και περιβάλλο* (*Deltion* Supplement 43). Athens.

(1994) 'Aegae: determining the site of the first capital of the Macedonians', *AJA* 98: 609–16.

Fandetti, D. and Gelfand, D. (1983) 'Middle class white ethnics in suburbia: a study of Italian-Americans', in W. McCready (ed.), *Culture, ethnicity and identity*, 111–26. New York.

Faraklas, N. (1972) *Τροιζηνία, Καλαύρεια, Μέθανα* (Ancient Greek Cities 10). Athens.

Farnell, L. R. (1921) *Greek hero cults and ideas of immortality.* Oxford.

Fernández Alvarez, M. P. (1981) *El Argolico occidental y oriental en las inscripciones de los siglos VII, VI y V a.C.* Salamanca.

Finley, M. I. (1968) *A history of Sicily: ancient Sicily to the Arab conquest.* London.

(1977 [1954]) *The world of Odysseus* (2nd edition). London.

(1981 [1970]) *Early Greece: the Bronze and Archaic ages* (2nd edition). New York.

(1986 [1975]) *The use and abuse of history* (2nd edition). London.

Fischer, D. (1989) *Albion's seed: four British folkways in America.* Oxford.

Fishman, J. (1977) 'Language and ethnicity', in H. Giles (ed.), *Language, ethnicity and intergroup relations*, 15–57. London.

(1983) 'Language and ethnicity in bilingual education', in W. McCready (ed.), *Culture, ethnicity and identity: current issues in research*, 127–37. New York.

Foley, A. (1988) *The Argolid 800–600 BC: an archaeological survey.* Göteborg.

Foltiny, S. (1961) 'Athens and the east Hallstatt region: cultural interrelations at the dawn of the Iron Age', *AJA* 65: 283–97.

Forrest, W. G. (1960) 'Themistocles and Argos', *CQ* 10: 221–41.

(1986) 'Greece: the history of the archaic period', in J. Boardman, J. Griffin and O. Murray (eds.), *The Oxford history of the classical world*, 19–49. Oxford.

Forsen, J. (1992) *The twilight of the Early Helladics: a study of the disturbances in east-central and southern Greece towards the end of the Early Bronze Age.* Jonsered.

Forsythe, D. (1989) 'German identity and the problem of history', in E. Tonkin, M. McDonald and M. Chapman (eds.), *History and ethnicity*, 137–56. London.

Fossey, J. (1980) 'La liste des rois argiens: première partie', in *Mélanges d'études anciennes offerts à Maurice Lebel*, 57–75. St-Jean-Chrysostôme.

(1989) 'Πολιτικο-θρησκευτική θέσις της Αργολικής Ασινής κατά την υστερογεωμετρικήν εποχήν', *Peloponnesiaka* Supplement 14: 57–63.

Fraser, C. (1978) 'Small groups, 1: structure and leadership', in H. Tajfel and C. Fraser (eds.), *Introducing social psychology*, 176–200. Harmondsworth.

Frickenhaus, A., Müller, W. and Oelmann, F. (1912) *Tiryns* I. Athens.

Frödin, O. and Persson, A. (1938) *Asine: results of the Swedish excavations, 1922–1930.* Stockholm.

Fustel de Coulanges, N. D. (1893) *Questions historiques.* Paris.

Bibliography

(1980) *The ancient city* (with a foreword by A. Momigliano and S. Humphreys). Baltimore. (Originally published as *La cité antique*. Paris, 1864.)

Gardner, A. E. (1888) *Naukratis* II. London.

Gardner, P. (1887) *Catalogue of Greek coins: Peloponnesus*. London.

Geary, P. (1983) 'Ethnic identity as a situational construct in the early Middle Ages', *MAGW* 113: 15–26.

Geertz, C. (1973) *The interpretation of cultures*. New York.

Gellner, E. (1983) *Nations and nationalism*. Oxford.

(1987) *Culture, identity and politics*. Cambridge.

Giles, H. (1979) 'Ethnicity markers in speech', in K. Scherer and H. Giles (eds.), *Social markers in speech*, 251–289. Cambridge.

Giles, H., Bourhis, R. and Taylor, D. (1977) 'Towards a theory of language in ethnic group relations', in H. Giles (ed.), *Language, ethnicity and intergroup relations*, 307–348. London.

Gilliéron, J. (1919) *La faillite de l' étymologie phonétique*. Paris.

Gilliland, M. K. (1995) 'Nationalism and ethnogenesis in the former Yugoslavia', in L. Romanucci-Ross and G. A. De Vos (eds.), *Ethnic identity: creation, conflict and accommodation*, 197–221. Walnut Creek CA.

Glazer, N. and Moynihan, D. (1975) 'Introduction', in N. Glazer and D. Moynihan (eds.), *Ethnicity: theory and experience*, 1–26. Cambridge MA.

Gordon, M. (1975) 'Toward a general theory of racial and ethnic group relations', in N. Glazer and D. Moynihan (eds.), *Ethnicity: theory and experience*, 84–110. Cambridge MA.

Green, P. (1982) 'The royal tombs of Vergina: a historical analysis', in W. Adams and E. Borza (eds.), *Philip II, Alexander the Great and the Macedonian heritage*, 129–51. Lanham MD.

(1989) *Classical bearings: interpreting ancient history and culture*. London.

Greene, V. (1978) 'Old ethnic stereotypes and present-day white ethnics', *Eth* 5: 328–50.

Guarducci, M. (1987) *L'epigrafia greca dalle origini al tardo impero*. Rome.

Haaland, G. (1969) 'Economic determinants in ethnic processes', in F. Barth (ed.), *Ethnic groups and boundaries: the social organization of culture difference*, 58–73. London.

Haarmann, H. (1986) *Language in ethnicity: a view of basic ecological relations*. Berlin.

Habicht, C. (1985) *Pausanias' guide to ancient Greece*. Berkeley.

Hägg, R. (1965) 'Geometrische Gräber von Asine'. *Op Ath* 6: 117–38.

(1974) *Die Gräber der Argolis in submykenischer, protogeometrischer und geometrischer Zeit. I: Lage und Form der Gräber*. Uppsala.

(1980) 'Some aspects of the burial customs of the Argolid in the Dark Ages', *AAA* 13: 119–26.

(1982) 'Zur Stadtwerdung des dorischen Argos', in D. Papenfuss and V. Strocka (eds.), *Palast und Hütte: Beiträge zum Bauen und Wohnen im Altertum*, 297–307. Mainz-am-Rhein.

(1983) 'Funerary meals in the Geometric necropolis at Asine?', in R. Hägg (ed.), *The Greek renaissance of the eighth century BC: tradition and innovation*, 189–94. Stockholm.

(1987) 'Submycenaean cremation burials in the Argolid?', in R. Laffineur (ed.), *Thanatos: les coutumes funéraires en Egée à l'age du bronze*, 207–11. Liège.

(1990) 'Argos and its neighbours: regional variations in the burial customs of the Protogeometric and Geometric periods'. Paper delivered to the 1990 Argos Conference, Athens (*BCH* Supplement, forthcoming).

(1992) 'Geometric sanctuaries in the Argolid', in M. Piérart (ed.), *Polydipsion Argos: Argos de la fin des palais mycéniens à la constitution de l'état classique* (*BCH* Supplement 22), 9–35. Paris.

198

Hainsworth, J. B. (1967) 'Greek views of Greek dialectology', *TPS* 65: 62–76.

(1982) 'The Greek language and the historical dialects', *CAH* (2nd edition) III.1, 850–65.

Haley, J. and Blegen, C. W. (1928) 'The coming of the Greeks', *AJA* 32: 141–54.

Hall, E. (1989) *Inventing the barbarian: Greek self-definition through tragedy.* Oxford.

(1992) 'When is a myth not a myth? Bernal's "Ancient Model"', *Areth* 25: 181–201.

Hall, J. M. (1990) 'Black Athena: a sheep in wolf's clothing?', *JMA* 3: 247–54.

(1991) 'Practising postprocessualism? Classics and archaeological theory', *ARC* 10: 155–63.

(1993) *Ethnic identity in the Argolid, 900–600 BC.* Ph.D. dissertation, University of Cambridge.

(1995a) 'Approaches to ethnicity in the Early Iron Age of Greece', in N. Spencer (ed.), *Time, tradition and society in Greek archaeology: bridging the 'Great Divide'*, 6–17. London.

(1995b) 'How Argive was the 'Argive' Heraion: the political and cultic geography of the Argive Plain, 900–400 BC', *AJA* 99: 577–613.

(1996) 'Alternative responses within *polis* formation: Argos, Mykenai and Tiryns', in H. Damgaard Andersen et al. (eds.) *Urbanization in the Mediterranean in the 9th to 6th Centuries BC (Act.Hyp.* 7) 89–109. Copenhagen.

(forthcoming) 'Heroes, Hera and Herakleidai in the Argive plain', in R. Hägg (ed.), *Peloponnesian sanctuaries and cults.*

Hammond, N. G. (1975) 'The end of the Mycenaean civilization and the Dark Ages: the literary tradition for the migrations', *CAH* (3rd edition) II.2, 678–712.

(1976) *Migrations and invasions in Greece and adjacent areas.* Park Ridge NJ.

(1994) 'Literary evidence for Macedonian speech', *Historia* 43: 131–42.

Hamp, E. P. (1991) 'Albanian', in J. Gvozdanović (ed.), *Indo-European numerals*, 835–922. Berlin and New York.

(1992) 'On misusing similarity', in G. W. Davies and G. K. Iverson (eds.), *Explanation in historical linguistics*, 95–103. Amsterdam and Philadelphia.

Harrison, J. E. (1912) *Themis: a study of the social origins of Greek religion.* Cambridge.

Hartog, F. (1988a) *Le XIXᵉ siècle et l'histoire: le cas Fustel de Coulanges.* Paris.

(1988b) *The mirror of Herodotus: the representation of the other in the writing of history.* Berkeley. (Originally published as *Le miroir d'Hérodote: essai sur la représentation de l'autre.* Paris, 1980).

Harvey, D. (1994) 'Lacomica: Aristophanes and the Spartans', in A. Powell and S. Hodkinson (eds.), *The shadow of Sparta*, 35–58. London.

Herman, G. (1987) *Ritualised friendship and the Greek city.* Cambridge.

Herrmann, H-V. (1980) 'Pelops in Olympia', in $\Sigma THAH \cdot \tau \acute{o}\mu o\varsigma\ \epsilon\iota\varsigma\ \mu\nu\acute{\eta}\mu\eta\nu\ N\iota\kappa o\lambda\acute{a}o\upsilon\ K o\nu\tau o\lambda\epsilon\acute{o}\nu\tau o\varsigma$, 59–74. Athens.

Herzfeld, M. (1982) *Ours once more: folklore, ideology and the making of modern Greece.* Austin.

(1987) *Anthropology through the looking glass: critical ethnography in the margins of Europe.* Cambridge.

Heubeck, A., West, S. and Hainsworth, J. B. (1988) *A commentary on Homer's Odyssey* I. Oxford.

Highet, G. (1949) *The classical tradition: Greek and Roman influences on western literature.* New York and London.

Hiller, S. (1985) 'E' esistita una cultura dorica nella tarda età del bronzo? Il problema delle testimonianze archeologiche', in D. Musti (ed.), *Le origini dei Greci: Dori e mondo egeo*, 135–69. Rome.

Hobsbawm, E. (1992a) 'Ethnicity and nationalism in Europe today', *AT* 8: 3–8.

(1992b [1990]) *Nations and nationalism since 1780: programme, myth, reality* (2nd edition). Cambridge.

Hock, H. (1988) 'Historical implications of a dialectological approach to convergence', in J. Fisiak (ed.), *Historical dialectology: regional and social trends in linguistics*, 283–328. Berlin.

Höckmann, O. (1980) 'Lanze und Speer im spätmykenischen und mykenischen Griechenland', *RGZM* 27: 13–158.

Hodder, I. (1978) 'Simple correlations between material culture and society: a review', in I. Hodder (ed.), *The spatial organization of culture*, 3–24. London.

(1982) *The present past*. London.

(1987) 'The contribution of the long-term', in I. Hodder (ed.), *Archaeology as long-term history*, 1–8. Cambridge.

(1990) 'Style as historical quality', in M. Conkey and C. Hastorf (eds.), *The uses of style in archaeology*, 44–51. Cambridge.

(1991 [1986]) *Reading the past: current approaches to interpretation in archaeology* (2nd edition). Cambridge.

Hogarth, D. G. (1898–99) Excavations at Naukratis. *A*: site and buildings. *BSA* 5: 26–41.

Holloway, R. R. (1994) *The archaeology of early Rome and Latium*. London.

Hood, M. S. F. (1967) *The home of the heroes: the Aegean before the Greeks*. London.

Hooker, J. T. (1979) 'New reflexions on the Dorian invasion', *Klio* 61: 353–60.

(1980) *The ancient Spartans*. London.

(1989) 'Spartan propaganda', in A. Powell (ed.), *Classical Sparta: techniques behind her success*, 122–41. London.

Hopkins, K. (1983) *Death and renewal*. Cambridge.

Hornblower, S. (1991a) *A commentary on Thucydides* I. Oxford.

(1991b [1983]) *The Greek world 479–323 BC* (2nd edition). London.

Horowitz, D. (1975) 'Ethnic identity', in N. Glazer and D. Moynihan (eds.), *Ethnicity: theory and experience*, 111–40. Cambridge MA.

(1985) *Ethnic groups in conflict*. Berkeley.

Humboldt, W. von (1903) *Wilhelm von Humboldts gesammelte Schriften* I. Berlin.

Humphreys, S. C. (1978) *Anthropology and the Greeks*. London.

Huntington, R. and Metcalf, P. (1979) *Celebrations of death: the anthropology of mortuary ritual*. Cambridge.

Huxley, G. L. (1969) *Greek epic poetry*. London.

Iakovidis, S. (1986) 'Destruction horizons at Late Bronze Age Mycenae'. in $Φιλία$ $ἔπη$ $εἰς$ $Γ.$ $Ε.$ $Μυλωνᾶν$ I, 233–60. Athens.

Issacs, H. (1975) 'Basic group identity: the idols of the tribe', in N. Glazer and D. Moynihan (eds.), *Ethnicity: theory and experience*, 29–52. Cambridge MA.

Jacob-Felsch, M. (1988) 'Compass-drawn concentric circles in vase painting. A problem of relative chronology at the end of the Bronze Age', in E. B. French and K. A. Wardle (eds.), *Problems in Greek prehistory. Papers presented at the Centenary Conference of the British School of Archaeology at Athens, Manchester April 1986*, 193–99. Bristol.

Jaeger, W. (1933) *Paideia: die Formung des griechischen Menschen*. Berlin.

Jahoda, G. (1978) 'Cross-cultural perspectives', in H. Tajfel and C. Fraser (eds.), *Introducing social psychology*, 76–95. Harmondsworth.

James, P. et al. (1991) *Centuries of darkness*. London.

Jameson, M. H. (1969) 'Excavations at Porto Cheli and vicinity, preliminary report I: Halieis, 1962–1968', *Hesperia* 38: 311–42.

(1972) 'Excavations at Porto Cheli, excavations at Halieis, final report', *Deltion* 27B: 233–36.

(1973–74) 'Excavations at Halieis (Porto Cheli), 1973', *Deltion* 29B: 261–64.

(1974) 'A treasury of Athena in the Argolid (*IG* IV, 554)', in D. Bradeen and M. McGregor (eds.), *ΦΟΡΟΣ – a tribute to B.D. Meritt*, 67–75. Locust Valley NY.

(1980) 'Apollo Lykeios in Athens', *Archaiognosia* 1: 213–36.

(1990) 'Perseus, the hero of Mykenai', in R. Hägg and G. Nordquist (eds.), *Celebrations of death and divinity in the Bronze Age Argolid*, 213–23. Stockholm.

Jameson, M. H., Runnels, C. and Van Andel, T. (1995) *A Greek countryside: the Southern Argolid from prehistory to present day.* Stanford.

Jantzen, U. (ed.) (1975) *Führer durch Tiryns von den Mitarbeitern der Grabung.* Athens.

Jardé, A. (1926) *The formation of the Greek people.* New York.

Jeffery, L.H. (1976) *Archaic Greece: the city states c.700–500 BC.* London.

(1990 [1961]) *The local scripts of archaic Greece: a study of the origin of the Greek alphabet and its development from the eighth to the fifth centuries BC.* (2nd edition, corrected and augmented by A.W. Johnston.) Oxford.

Johnston, A. W. (1983) 'The extent and use of literacy: the archaeological evidence', in R. Hägg (ed.), *The Greek renaissance of the eighth century BC: tradition and innovation*, 63–68. Stockholm.

Jones, N. F. (1980) 'The order of the Dorian *phylai*', *CP* 75: 197–215.

(1987) *Public organization in ancient Greece: a documentary study.* Philadelphia.

Jost, M. (1992) 'La légende de Mélampous en Argolide et dans le Péloponnèse', in M. Piérart (ed.), *Polydipsion Argos: Argos de la fin des palais mycéniens à la constitution de l'état classique (BCH* Supplement 22), 173–84. Paris.

Just, R. (1989) 'Triumph of the ethnos', in E. Tonkin, M. McDonald and M. Chapman (eds.), *History and ethnicity*, 71–88. London.

Karpat, K. (1985) 'The ethnicity problem in a multi-ethnic anational Islamic state; continuity and recasting of ethnic identity in the Ottoman state', in P. Brass (ed.), *Ethnic groups and the state*, 94–114. London.

Kavvadias, P. (1900) *Τὸ ἱερὸν τοῦ Ἀσκληπιοῦ ἐν Ἐπιδαύρῳ.* Athens.

Kearsley, R. (1989) *The pendent semi-circle skyphos: a study of its development and chronology and an examination of it as evidence for Euboean activity at Al Mina (BICS* Supplement 44). London.

Kelly, T. (1966) 'The Calaurian amphictiony', *AJA* 70: 113–21.

(1967) 'The Argive Destruction of Asine', *Historia* 16: 422–31.

(1976) *A history of Argos to 500 BC.* Minneapolis.

Keyes, C. (1976) 'Towards a new formulation of the concept of the ethnic group', *Eth* 3: 202–13.

(1995) 'Who are the Tai? Reflections on the invention of identities', in L. Romanucci-Ross and G. A. De Vos (eds.), *Ethnic identity: creation, conflict and accommodation*, 136–60. Walnut Creek CA.

Kilian, K. (1978) 'Nordwestgriechische Keramik aus der Argolis und ihre Entsprechungen in der Subapennin-facies', in *Atti della XX Riunione Scientifica dell' Istituto Italiano di Preistoria e Protostoria in Basilicata 1976*, 311–20. Florence.

(1980) 'Zum Ende der mykenischen Epoche in der Argolis', *RGZM* 27: 166–95.

(1981) 'Ausgrabungen in Tiryns, 1978, 1979', *AA*, 149–94.

(1981–82) Ἱστορικὴ ἐξέλιξη τῆς Πελοποννήσου κατὰ τὰ τέλη τῆς μυκηναϊκῆς ἐποχῆς', *Peloponnesiaka* Supplement 8.1: 155–59.

(1985) 'La caduta dei palazzi micenei continentali: aspetti archeologici', in D. Musti (ed.), *Le origini dei Greci: Dori e mondo egeo*, 73–115. Rome.

(1987–8) Ἀρχαιολογία καθόδου τῶν Δωριέων', *Peloponnesiaka* Supplement 13.1: 148–58.

Kirchhoff, A. (1877 [1863]) *Studien zur Geschichte des griechischen Alphabets* (3rd edition). Berlin.

Kirk, G. (1970) *Myth: its meaning and functions in ancient and other cultures*. Berkeley and Los Angeles.

Kirsten, E. (1959) *Die griechischen Landschaften* III.1: *Der Peloponnes*. Frankfurt.

Kobyliansky, E. (1983) 'Changes in cephalic morphology of Israelis due to migration', *JHE* 12: 779–86.

Koerner, R. (1985) 'Tiryns als Beispiel einer frühen dorischen Polis', *Klio* 67: 452–57.

Kossinna, G. (1902) 'Die indogermanische Frage archäologisch beantwortet', *ZE* 34: 161–222.

Koster, H. (1977) *The ecology of pastoralism in relation to changing patterns of land use in the northeast Peloponnese*. Ph.D. dissertation, University of Pennsylvania.

Kraiker, W. and Kübler, K. (1939) *Kerameikos. Ergebnisse der Ausgrabungen* X: *die Nekropolen des 12. bis 10. Jahrhunderts*. Berlin.

Kretschmer, P. (1909) 'Zur Geschichte der griechischen Dialekte', *Glotta* 1: 1–59.

Kritzas, C. (1972) Ἀρχαιότητες καὶ μνημεῖα Ἀργολιδοκορινθίας', *Deltion* 27B: 192–219.

(1973) Ἄργος', *Deltion* 28B: 122–35.

(1973–74) Ἀνασκαφικαὶ ἐργασίαι', *Deltion* 29B: 212–49.

Kunze, E. (1950) *Olympische Forschungen* II: *archaische Schildbänder, ein Beitrag zur frühgriechischen Bildgeschichte und Sagenüberlieferung*. Berlin.

Kuruniotis, K. (1901) 'Porossculpturen aus Mykene', *JDAI* 16: 18–22.

Lambrinoudakis, V. (1975) Ἱερὸν Μαλεάτου Ἀπόλλωνος εἰς Ἐπίδαυρον', *Praktika*, 162–75.

(1978–79) 'Σχέσεις Ἐπιδαύρου καὶ Κορίνθου ὑπὸ τὸ φῶς τῶν ἀνασκαφῶν', *Peloponnesiaka* Supplement 14: 28–36.

Leach, E. (1954) *Political systems of Highland Burma*. London.

(1977) 'A view from the bridge', in M. Spriggs (ed.), *Archaeology and anthropology* (*BAR* Supplementary Series 19), 161–76.

Legrand, P. (1893) 'Inscriptions de Trézène', *BCH* 17: 84–121.

(1905) 'Antiquités de Trézène', *BCH* 29: 269–318.

Lehmann, H. (1937) *Argolis* I: *Landeskunde der Ebene von Argos und ihrer Randgebiete*. Athens.

Lehmann, W. P. (1967) *A reader in nineteenth-century historical Indo-European linguistics*. Bloomington and London.

Lejeune, M. (1972 [1946]) *Phonétique historique du mycénien et du grec ancien* (3rd edition). Paris.

Lévi-Strauss, C. (1985) *The view from afar*. Oxford. (Originally published as *Le regard éloigné*. Paris, 1983.)

Lloyd, C. (1986) *Explanation in social history*. Oxford.

Lolling, H. (1880) *Das Kuppelgrab bei Menidi*. Athens.

López Eire, A. (1978) 'El retorno de los Heraclidas', *Zephyrus* 28–29: 287–97.

Loraux, N. (1986) *The invention of Athens: the funeral oration in the classical city*. London. (Originally published as *L'invention d'Athènes: histoire de l' oraison funèbre dans la 'cité classique'*. Paris, 1981.)

(1993) *The children of Athena: Athenian ideas about citizenship and the division between the sexes*. Princeton. (Originally published as *Les enfants d'Athèna: idées athéniennes sur la citoyenneté et la division des sexes*. Paris, 1984.)

Löschcke, G. (1878) 'Stele aus Amyklae', *AM* 3: 164–71.

Macdonald, W. (1990) 'Investigating style: an exploratory analysis of some Plains burials', in M. Conkey and C. Hastorf (eds.), *The uses of style in archaeology*, 52–60. Cambridge.

Malkin, I. (1994) *Myth and territory in the Spartan Mediterranean*. Cambridge.

Marchetti, P. (1993) 'Recherches sur les mythes et la topographie d' Argos, I: Hermès et Aphrodite', *BCH* 117: 211–23.

Marinatos, S. (1953) 'Περὶ τοὺς νέους βασιλικοὺς τάφους τῶν Μυκηνῶν', in *Γέρας Ἀντωνίου Κεραμοπούλλου*, 54–88. Athens.

Marrou, H. (1956) *A history of education in antiquity*. London. (Originally published as *Histoire de l' éducation dans l' antiquité*. Paris, 1948.)

Martens, J. (1989) 'The Vandals: myths and facts about a Germanic tribe of the first half of the 1st millennium AD', in S. Shennan (ed.), *Archaeological approaches to cultural identity*, 57–65. London.

Mattingly, H. (1982) 'The Athena temple reconsidered', *AJA* 86: 381–85.

(1992) 'Epigraphy and the Athenian empire', *Historia* 41: 129–38.

Mazarakis-Ainian, A. (1987) 'Geometric Eretria', *AK* 30: 3–24.

(1988) 'Early Greek temples: their origin and function', in R. Hägg, N. Marinatos and G. Nordquist (eds.), *Early Greek cult practice*, 105–19. Stockholm.

McAllister, M. (1969) 'A temple at Hermione', *Hesperia* 38: 169–85.

McDonald, W. and Thomas, C. G. (1990 [1967]) *Progress into the past: the rediscovery of Mycenaean civilization* (2nd edition). Bloomington.

McGuire, R. (1982) 'The study of ethnicity in historical archaeology', *JAA* 1: 159–78.

Meillet, A. (1965 [1913]) *Aperçu d'une histoire de la langue grecque* (7th edition). Paris.

Mele, A. (1995) 'Tradizioni eroiche e colonizzazione greca: le colonie achee', in A. S. Marino (ed.), *L'incidenza dell'antico. Studi in memoria di Ettore Lepore*, 427–50. Naples.

Méndez Dosuna, J. (1985) *Los dialectos del Noroeste. Gramática y estudio dialectal*. Salamanca.

Mertens, D. (1976) 'Zur archaischen Architektur der achaïschen Kolonien in Unteritalien', in U. Jantzen (ed.), *Neue Forschungen in griechischen Heiligtümern*, 167–96. Tübingen.

(1990) 'Some principal features of West Greek colonial architecture', in J-P. Descoeudres (ed.), *Greek colonists and native populations*, 373–83. Oxford.

Milroy, J. (1981) *Regional accents of English: Belfast*. Belfast.

(1992) *Linguistic variation and change: on the historical sociolinguistics of English*. Oxford.

Moerman, M. (1965) 'Who are the Lue? Ethnic identification in a complex civilization', *Am.Anth* 67: 1215–29.

Moggi, M. (1974) 'I sinecismi e le annessioni territoriali di Argo nel V secolo a.C.', *ASNSP* 4: 1249–63.

Montanari, E. (1981) *Il mito dell' autoctonia: linee di una dinamica mitico-politica ateniese*. Rome.

Moralejo Alvarez, J. J. (1977) 'Los Dorios: su migracion y su dialecto', *Emerita* 45: 243–67.

Morgan, C. (1990) *Athletes and oracles: the transformation of Olympia and Delphi in the eighth century BC*. Cambridge.

(1991) 'Ethnicity and early Greek states: historical and material perspectives', *PCPS* 37: 131–63.

(1993) 'The origins of pan-Hellenism', in N. Marinatos and R. Hägg (eds.), *Greek sanctuaries: new approaches*, 18–44. London.

(1994) 'The evolution of a sacral 'landscape': Isthmia, Perachora, and the early Corinthian state', in S. E. Alcock and R.Osborne (eds.), *Placing the gods: sanctuaries and sacred space in ancient Greece*, 105–42. Oxford.

Morgan, C. and Hall, J. M. (1996) 'Achaian poleis and Achaian colonisation', in M. H. Hansen (ed.), *Introduction to an inventory of poleis. Acts of the Copenhagen Polis Centre 3*, 164–232. Copenhagen.

Morgan, C. and Whitelaw, T. (1991) 'Pots and politics: ceramic evidence for the rise of the Argive state', *AJA* 95: 79–108.

Morpurgo Davies, A. (1985) 'Mycenaean and Greek language', in A. Morpurgo Davies and Y. Duhoux (eds), *Linear B: a 1984 survey*, 75–125. Louvain-la-neuve.

(1986) 'Karl Brugmann and late nineteenth-century linguistics', in T. Bynon and F. R. Palmer (eds.), *Studies in the history of western linguistics in honour of R. H. Robins*, 150–71. Cambridge.

(1987) 'The Greek notion of dialect', *Verbum* 10: 7–28.

Morris, I. (1986a) 'Gift and commodity in archaic Greece', *Man* 21: 1–17.

(1986b) 'The use and abuse of Homer', *Cl.Ant* 5: 81–138.

(1987) *Burial and ancient society: the rise of the Greek city-state.* Cambridge.

(1988) 'Tomb cult and the 'Greek renaissance': the past in the present in the 8th century BC', *Ant* 62: 750–61.

(1992) *Death-ritual and social structure in classical antiquity.* Cambridge.

Morris, S. P. (1990) 'Greece and the Levant', *JMA* 3: 57–66.

Mountjoy, P. (1988) 'LHIIIC Late versus Submycenaean. The Kerameikos Pompeion cemetery reviewed', *JDAI* 103: 1–37.

Müller, K. O. (1830) *The history and antiquities of the Doric race.* Oxford.

(1844 [1824]) *Die Dorier* (2nd edition) (*Geschichten hellenischer Stämme und Städte* II and III). Breslau.

Müller, K. (1930) *Tiryns* III. Augsburg.

Muhly, J. (1979) 'On the shaft graves at Mycenae', in M. Powell and R. Sack (eds.), *Studies in honour of Tom B. Jones (Alter Orient und Altes Testament* 203), 311–23. Neukirchen-Vluyn.

Murray, O. (1993 [1980]) *Early Greece* (2nd edition). London.

Musti, D. (1985a) 'Introduzione', in D. Musti (ed.), *Le origini dei Greci: Dori e mondo egeo*, vii-xxv. Rome.

(1985b) 'Continuità e discontinuità tra Achei e Dori nelle tradizioni storiche', in D. Musti (ed.), *Le origini dei Greci: Dori e mondo egeo*, 37–71. Rome.

(1990 [1989]) *Storia greca: linee di sviluppo dall'età micenea all'età romana* (2nd edition). Rome.

(1991) 'Linee di sviluppo istituzionale e territoriale tra miceneo e alto arcaismo', in D. Musti et al (eds.), *La transizione dal miceneo all'alto arcaismo: dal palazzo alla città*, 15–34. Rome.

Musti, D. and Torelli, M. (1986) *Pausania: guida della Grecia* II. Rome and Milan.

Mylonas, G. (1964) ''Ανασκαφή Μυκηνών', *Praktika*, 68–77.

(1965) ''Ανασκαφή Μυκηνών', *Praktika*, 85–96.

(1966) ''Ανασκαφή Μυκηνών', *Praktika*, 103–14.

Myres, J. L. (1930) *Who were the Greeks?* Berkeley.

Nagel, J. (1980) 'The conditions of ethnic separatism: the Kurds in Turkey, Iran and Iraq', *Eth* 7: 279–97.

Nagy, G. (1987) 'The Indo-European heritage of tribal organization: evidence from the Greek *polis*', in S. Nacev Skomal and E. C. Polomé (eds.), *Proto-Indo-European: the archaeology of a linguistic problem. Studies in honour of Marija Gimbutas*, 245–66. Washington DC.

Naveh, J. (1973) 'Some epigraphic considerations on the antiquity of the Greek alphabet', *AJA* 77: 1–8.

Neel, J. (1970) 'Lessons from a 'primitive' people', *Science* 170: 815–22.

Nilsson, M. P. (1950 [1927]) *The Minoan-Mycenaean religion and its survival in Greek religion* (2nd edition). Lund.

(1951) *Cults, myths, oracles and politics in ancient Greece*. Lund.

(1972 [1932]) *The Mycenaean origin of Greek mythology* (2nd edition). Berkeley and Los Angeles.

Nippel, W. (1990) *Griechen, Barbaren und 'Wilde': alte Geschichte und Sozialanthropologie*. Frankfurt.

Nixon, I. (1968) *The rise of the Dorians*. Puckeridge.

O'Brien, J. V. (1993) *The transformation of Hera: a study of ritual, hero and the goddess in the 'Iliad'*. Lanham MD.

Osborn, A. (1989) 'Multiculturalism in the eastern Andes', in S. Shennan (ed.), *Archaeological approaches to cultural identity*, 141–56. London.

O'Shea, J. (1981) 'Social configurations and the archaeological study of mortuary practices: a case study', in R. Chapman, I. Kinnes and K. Randsborg (eds.), *The archaeology of death*, 39–52. Cambridge.

(1984) *Mortuary variability: an archaeological investigation*. Orlando.

Osthoff, H. and Brugmann, K. (1878) 'Vorwort', *Morph. Unt* 1: iii-xx.

Overing, J. (1985) 'Introduction', in J. Overing (ed.), *Reason and morality*, 1–28. London.

Paidoussis, M. and Sbarounis, C. N. (1975) 'A study of cremated bones from the cemetery of Perati (LHIIIC)', *Op.Ath* 11: 129–60.

Palmer, L. R. (1980) *The Greek language*. London and Boston.

Papachristodoulou, I. (1968) ''Αργολίς', *Deltion* 23B: 127–33.

Papadimitriou, A. (1988) 'Bericht zur früheisenzeitlichen Keramik aus der Unterburg von Tiryns. Ausgrabungen in Tiryns 1982/83', *AA*, 227–43.

Papadimitriou, I. (1949) 'Le sanctuaire d'Apollon Maléatas à Epidaure', *BCH* 73: 361–83.

(1953) ''Ανασκαφαὶ ἐν Μυκήναις', *Praktika*, 205–37.

Papadopoulos, T. J. (1979) *Mycenaean Achaea*. Göteborg.

Paraskevaidou, H. (1991) 'The name of the Pelasgians', in D. Musti et al. (eds.), *La transizione dal miceneo all'alto arcaismo: dal palazzo alla città*, 281–83. Rome.

Pariente, A. (1992) 'Le monument argien des "sept contre Thèbes"', in M. Piérart (ed.), *Polydipsion Argos: Argos de la fin des palais mycéniens à la constitution de l'état classique (BCH* Supplement 22), 195–229. Paris.

Parke, H. W. (1967) *The oracles of Zeus*. Oxford.

Parker, R. (1987) 'Myths of early Athens', in J. Bremmer (ed.), *Interpretations of Greek mythology*, 187–214. London.

(1989) 'Spartan religion', in A. Powell (ed.), *Classical Sparta: techniques behind her success*, 142–72. London.

Bibliography

Parker, V. (1995) 'Zur Datierung der dorischen Wanderung', *Mus.Helv* 52: 130–54.

Parker Pearson, M. (1982) 'Mortuary practices, society and ideology: an ethnoarchaeological study', in I. Hodder (ed.), *Symbolic and structural archaeology*, 99–113. Cambridge.

Parkin, F. (1979) *Marxism and class theory: a bourgeois critique*. London.

Parsons, T. (1975) 'Some theoretical considerations on the nature and trends of change of ethnicity', in N. Glazer and D. Moynihan (eds.), *Ethnicity: theory and experience*, 53–83. Cambridge MA.

Patterson, O. (1975) 'Context and choice in ethnic allegiance: a theoretical framework and Caribbean case study', in N. Glazer and D. Moynihan (eds.), *Ethnicity: theory and experience*, 305–49. Cambridge MA.

Peek, W. (1941) 'Heilige Gesetze', *AM* 66: 171–217.

Persson, A. (1931) *The royal tombs at Dendra near Midea*. Lund.

Petersen, W. (1975) 'On the subnations of western Europe', in N. Glazer and D. Moynihan (eds.), *Ethnicity: theory and experience*, 177–208. Cambridge MA.

Petrie, W. M. F. (1886) *Naukratis* I. London.

Pettersson, M. (1992) *Cults of Apollo at Sparta: the Hyakinthia, the Gymnopaidiai and the Karneia*. Stockholm.

Pfaff, C. (1992) *The Argive Heraion: the architecture of the Classical temple of Hera*. Ph.D. dissertation, New York University.

Philadelpheus, A. (1909) 'Ἀνασκαφαὶ ἐν Ἑρμιονίδι', *Praktika*, 172–84.

Piérart, M. (1982) 'Deux notes sur l'itinéraire argien de Pausanias', *BCH* 106: 139–52.

(1983) 'L'itinéraire argien de Pausanias', *Rev.Arch*, 175–78.

(1985) 'Le tradizioni epiche e il loro rapporto con la questione dorica: Argo e l'Argolide', in D. Musti (ed.), *Le origini dei Greci: Dori e mondo egeo*, 277–92. Rome.

(1990) 'L'itinéraire de Pausanias à Argos'. Paper delivered to the 1990 Argos Conference, Athens. (*BCH* Supplement, forthcoming).

(1991) 'Aspects de la transition en Argolide', in D. Musti et al. (eds.), *La transizione dal miceneo all'alto arcaismo: dal palazzo alla città*, 133–44. Rome.

(1992) '"Argos assoiffée" et "Argos riche en cavales": provinces culturelles à l'époque proto-historique', in M. Piérart (ed.), *Polydipsion Argos: Argos de la fin des palais mycéniens à la constitution de l'état classique* (*BCH* Supplement 22), 119–55. Paris.

Piérart, M. and Thalmann, J-P. (1987) 'Argos, agora', *BCH* 111: 585–91.

Piggot, S. (1957) *Approach to archaeology*. London.

Pisani, V. (1955) 'Die Entzifferung der ägäische linear B Schrift und die griechischen Dialekte', *Rh.M* 98: 1–18.

Pleiner, R. (1969) *Iron working in ancient Greece*. Prague.

Plommer, H. (1977) 'Shadowy Megara', *JHS* 97: 75–88.

(1984) 'The old platform in the Argive Heraion', *JHS* 104: 183–84.

Podlecki, A. J. (1971) 'Stesichoreia', *Athenaeum* 49: 313–27.

Polignac, F. de (1995) *Cults, territory and the origins of the Greek city-state*. Chicago. (Originally published as *La naissance de la cité grecque*. Paris, 1984.)

Popham, M. (1994) 'Precolonization: early Greek contact with the east', in G. R. Tsetskhladze and F. de Angelis (eds.), *The archaeology of Greek colonisation: essays dedicated to Sir John Boardman*, 11–34. Oxford.

Popham, M., Sackett, H. and Themelis, P. (eds.), (1980) *Lefkandi* I: *the Iron Age*. (*BSA* Supplementary Volume 11). London.

Porzig, W. (1954) 'Sprachgeographie Untersuchungen zu den griechischen Dialekten', *IF* 61: 147–69.

Pötscher, W. (1961) 'Hera und Heros', *Rh.M* 104: 302–55.

(1987) *Hera: eine Strukturanalyse im Vergleich mit Athena*. Darmstadt.

Pouilloux, J. and Roux, G. (1963) *Énigmes à Delphes*. Paris.

Protonotariou-Deïlaki, E. [see also under Deïlaki] (1963) 'Ἀνασκαφή εἰς Προφήτην Ἠλίαν τῆς κοινότητος Ἀδριάνου', *Deltion* 18B: 65–66.

(1970) 'Ἀρχαιότητες καὶ μνημεῖα Ἀργολιδοκορινθίας', *Deltion* 25B: 154–58.

(1980) *Οἱ τύμβοι τοῦ Ἄργου*. Ph.D. dissertation, University of Athens.

(1982) 'Ἀπό το Ἄργος τοῦ 8ου και 7ου αἰώνα', *A.S.Atene* 60: 33–48.

Rawson, E. (1991 [1969]) *The Spartan tradition in European thought* (2nd edition). Oxford.

Reber, K. (1991) *Untersuchungen zur handgemachten Keramik Griechenlands in der submykenischen, protogeometrischen und der geometrischen Zeit*. Jonsered.

Renfrew, A. C. (1984) *Approaches to social archaeology*. Edinburgh.

(1987) *Archaeology and language: the puzzle of Indo-European origins*. London.

Richter, G. (1949) *Archaic Greek art against its historical background*. New York.

Ridgway, D. (1992) *The first western Greeks*. Cambridge. (Originally published as *L' alba della Magna Grecia*. Milan, 1984.)

Risch, E. (1966) 'Les différences dialectales dans le mycénien', in L. Palmer and J. Chadwick (eds.), *Proceedings of the Cambridge Colloquium on Mycenaean Studies*, 150–57. Cambridge.

(1985) 'La posizione del dialetto dorico', in D. Musti (ed.), *Le origini dei Greci: Dori e mondo egeo*, 13–35. Rome.

(1991) 'La contribution de la langue mycénienne au problème de la transition du palais à la cité', in D. Musti et al. (eds.), *La transizione dal miceneo all'alto arcaismo: dal palazzo alla città*, 231–40. Rome.

Robertson, N. (1980) 'The Dorian migration and Corinthian ritual', *CP* 75: 1–22.

Roes, A. (1953) 'Fragments de poterie géométriques trouvés sur les citadelles d'Argos', *BCH* 77: 90–104.

Romaine, S. (1994) *Language in society: an introduction to sociolinguistics*. Oxford.

Romeo, R. (1981) *Italia mille anni: dall'età feudale all'Italia moderna ed europea*. Florence.

Rosivach, V. J. (1987) 'Autochthony and the Athenians', *CQ* 37: 294–306.

Roussel, D. (1976) *Tribu et cité: études sur les groupes sociaux dans les cités grecques aux époques archaïque et classique*. Paris.

Roux, G. (1953) 'Autel à triglyphes bas trouvé sur l'agora d'Argos', *BCH* 77: 116–23.

(1957) 'Le sanctuaire argien d'Apollon pythéen', *REG* 70: 474–87.

Rubinsohn, Z. (1975) 'The Dorian invasion again', *PP* 30: 105–31.

Ruijgh, C. J. (1986) 'Review of M.P. Fernández Alvarez, *El Argolico occidental y oriental*', *Mnem* 39: 452–59.

(1989) 'Review of J. Méndez Dosuna, *Los dialectos del Noroeste*', *Mnem* 42: 155–63.

Ruipérez, M. S. (1972) 'Le dialecte mycénien', in M. S. Ruipérez (ed.), *Acta Mycenaea* I, 136–69. Salamanca.

Rupp, D. (1976) 'The altars of Zeus and Hera on Mt Arachnaion in the Argeia, Greece', *JFA* 3: 261–68.

(1983) 'Reflections on the development of altars in the eighth century BC', in R. Hägg (ed.), *The Greek renaissance of the eighth century BC: tradition and innovation*, 101–07. Stockholm.

Bibliography

Rutter, J. B. (1975) 'Ceramic evidence for northern intruders in southern Greece at the beginning of the Late Helladic IIIC period', *AJA* 79: 17–32.

(1990) 'Some comments on interpreting the dark-surfaced handmade burnished pottery of the 13th and 12th century BC Aegean', *JMA* 3: 29–49.

Sacconi, A. (1991) 'I sistemi grafici del mondo egeo tra la fine del II e l'inizio del I millennio a.C.', in D. Musti et al. (eds.), *La transizione dal miceneo all'alto arcaismo: dal palazzo alla città*, 43–52. Rome.

Sackett, J. (1977) 'The meaning of style in archaeology', *Am.Ant* 42: 369–80.

(1990) 'Style and ethnicity in archaeology: the case for isochrestism', in M. Conkey and C. Hastorf (eds.), *The uses of style in archaeology*, 32–43. Cambridge.

Säflund, G. (1965) *Excavations at Berbati, 1936–1937*. Stockholm.

Said, E. (1978) *Orientalism*. New York.

Sakellariou, M. B. (1977) *Peuples préhelléniques d'origine indo-européenne*. Athens.

(1980) *Les Proto-Grecs*. Athens.

(1989) *The polis-state: definition and origin*. Athens.

(1990) *Between memory and oblivion: the transmission of early Greek historical traditions*. Athens.

Salmon, J. B. (1984) *Wealthy Corinth: a history of the city to 338 BC*. Oxford.

Salo, M. (1979) 'Gypsy ethnicity: implications of native categories and interaction for ethnic classification', *Eth* 6: 73–96.

Salviat, F. (1965) 'L' offrande argienne de l'hémicycle des rois à Delphes et l'Héraklès béotien', *BCH* 89: 307–14.

Sarna, J. (1978) 'From immigrants to ethnics: toward a new theory of "ethnicization"', *Eth* 5: 370–78.

Saville-Troike, M. (1989 [1982]) *The ethnography of communication: an introduction* (2nd edition). Oxford.

Schermerhorn, R. (1974) 'Ethnicity in the perspective of the sociology of knowledge', *Eth* 1: 1–14.

Schlegel, F. von (1808) *Über die Sprache und Weisheit der Indier*. Heidelberg.

Schleicher, A. (1863) *Die darwinische Theorie und die Sprachwissenschaft*, Weimar.

Schliemann, H. (1886) *Tiryns: the prehistoric palace of the kings of Tiryns*. London.

Schmidt, J. (1872) *Die Verwandtschaftsverhältnisse der indogermanischen Sprachen*. Weimar.

Schnapp-Gourbeillon, A. (1979) 'Le mythe dorien', *AION (ASA)* 1: 1–11.

(1986) 'L'invasion dorienne a-t-elle eu lieu?', in C. Mossé (ed.), *La Grèce ancienne*, 43–57. Paris.

Schumacher, R. W. M. (1993) 'Three related sanctuaries of Poseidon: Geraistos, Kalaureia and Tainaron', in N. Marinatos and R. Hägg (eds.), *Greek sanctuaries: new approaches*, 62–87. London.

Segal, C. P. (1962) 'The Phaeacians and the symbolism of Odysseus' return', *Arion* 1: 17–63.

Shanks, M. and Tilley, C. (1987a) *Social theory and archaeology*. Cambridge.

(1987b) *Reconstructing archaeology: theory and practice*. Cambridge.

Shaw, J. (1989) 'Phoenicians in southern Crete', *AJA* 93: 165–83.

Shennan, S. (1989) 'Introduction', in S. Shennan (ed.), *Archaeological approaches to cultural identity*, 1–32. London.

Silverman, E. (1990) 'Clifford Geertz: towards a more 'thick' understanding?', in C. Tilley (ed.), *Reading material culture*, 121–59. Oxford.

Simić, A. (1991) 'Obstacles to the development of a Yugoslav national consciousness: ethnic identity and folk culture in the Balkans', *JMS* 1: 18–36.

208

Sinn, U. (1994) 'Apollon und die Kentauromachie im Westgiebel des Zeustempels in Olympia: die Wettkampfstätte als Forum der griechischen Diplomatie nach den Persekrieger', *AA*, 582–602.

Siriopoulos, K. (1989) 'Το Άργος κατά τους υστερομυκηναϊκούς και μεταμυκήναϊκούς χρονούς και η εγκατάστασις των Δωριέων εις αυτό', *Peloponnesiaka* Supplement 14: 321–38.

Skeat, T. (1934) *The Dorians in archaeology.* London.

Small, D. B. (1990) 'Handmade burnished ware and prehistoric Aegean economics: an argument for indigenous appearance', *JMA* 3: 3–25.

Smith, A. D. (1986) *The ethnic origins of nations.* Oxford.

Snodgrass, A. M. (1965) 'Barbarian Europe and Early Iron Age Greece', *PPS* 31: 229–40.

(1967) *Arms and armour of the Greeks.* London.

(1971) *The Dark Age of Greece: an archaeological survey of the eleventh to the eighth centuries BC.* Edinburgh.

(1980a) *Archaic Greece: the age of experiment.* London.

(1980b) 'Iron and early metallurgy in the Mediterranean', in T. A. Wertime and J. D. Muhly (eds.), *The coming of the age of iron*, 335–74. New Haven and London.

(1982a) 'Les origines du culte des héros dans la Grèce antique', in G. Gnoli and J-P. Vernant (eds.), *La mort, les morts dans les sociétés anciennes*, 107–19. Paris and Cambridge.

(1982b) 'Cyprus and the beginnings of iron technology in the eastern Mediterranean', in J. D. Muhly, R. Maddin and V. Karageorghis (eds.), *Early metallurgy in Cyprus, 4000–500 BC*, 285–94. Nicosia.

(1987) *An archaeology of Greece: the present state and future scope of a discipline.* Berkeley.

(1988) 'The archaeology of the hero', *AION (ASA)* 10: 19–26.

(1994) 'The nature and standing of the early western colonies', in G. R. Tsetskhladze and F. de Angelis (eds.), *The archaeology of Greek colonisation: essays dedicated to Sir John Boardman*, 1–10. Oxford.

Spawforth, A. and Walker, S. (1986) 'The world of the Panhellenion II: three Dorian cities', *JRS* 76: 88–105.

Starr, C. G. (1962) *The origins of Greek civilization, 1100–650 BC.* London.

Stoddart, S. and Whitley, A.J. (1988) 'The social context of literacy in Archaic Greece and Etruria', *Ant* 62: 761–72.

Ström, I. (1988) 'The early sanctuary of the Argive Heraion and its external relations (8th-early 6th centuries). The monumental architecture', *Act.Arch* 59: 173–203.

(1992) 'Evidence from the sanctuaries', in G. Kopcke and I. Tokumaru (eds.), *Greece between east and west: 10th-8th centuries BC*, 46–60. Mainz.

(1995) 'The early sanctuary of the Argive Heraion and its external relations (8th-early 6th centuries). The Greek Geometric bronzes', *PDIA* 1: 37–127.

Stroud, R. S. (1968) 'Tribal boundary markers from Corinth', *CSCA* 1: 233–42.

Stubbings, F. H. (1975) 'The recession of Mycenaean civilization', *CAH* (3rd edition) II.2, 338–58.

Sznycer, M. (1979) 'L' inscription phénicienne de Tekke, près de Cnossus', *Kadmos* 18: 89–93.

Tajfel, H. (1978) 'Intergroup behaviour, 2: group perspectives', in H. Tajfel and C. Fraser (eds.), *Introducing social psychology*, 423–46. Harmondsworth.

(1982) 'Introduction', in H. Tajfel (ed.), *Social identity and intergroup relations*, 1–11. Cambridge.

Tambiah, S. J. (1989) 'Ethnic conflict in the world today', *Am.Eth* 16: 335–49.

Taylor, D., Bassili, J. and Aboud, F. (1973) 'Dimensions of ethnic identity: an example from Québec', *JSP* 89: 185–92.

Thomas, C. G. (1978) 'A Dorian invasion? The early literary evidence', *SMEA* 19: 77–87.

Thomas, R. (1989) *Oral tradition and written record in classical Athens*. Cambridge.

Thompson, B. (1983) 'Social ties and ethnic settlement patterns', in W. McCready (ed.), *Culture, ethnicity and identity: current issues in research*, 341–60. New York.

Thumb, A. (1932 [1909]) *Handbuch der griechischen Dialekte* I (2nd edition, expanded by E. Kieckers). Heidelberg.

Tigerstedt, E. N. (1965) *The legend of Sparta in classical antiquity* I. Stockholm, Göteborg and Uppsala.

Tomlinson, R. A. (1972) *Argos and the Argolid from the end of the Bronze Age to the Roman Occupation*. London.

(1983) *Epidauros*. Austin.

Tonkin, E., McDonald, M. and Chapman, M. (1989) 'Introduction', in E. Tonkin et al. (eds.), *History and ethnicity*, 1–21. London.

Touchais, G. (1980) 'Chronique des fouilles et découvertes archéologiques en Grèce en 1979', *BCH* 104: 581–755.

Trigger, B. (1980) *Gordon Childe: revolutions in archaeology*. London.

Trudgill, P. (1983) *On dialect: social and geographical perspectives*. Oxford.

(1986) *Dialects in contact*. Oxford.

(1992) *The dialects of England*. Oxford.

Trudgill, P. and Tzavaras, G. (1977) 'Why Albanian Greeks are not Albanians: language shift in Attica and Biotia', in H. Giles (ed.), *Language, ethnicity and intergroup relations*, 171–84. London.

Tsountas, C. and Manatt, J. I. (1897) *The Mycenaean age: a study of the monuments and culture of pre-Homeric Greece*. London.

Turner, J. (1982) 'Towards a cognitive redefinition of the social group', in H. Tajfel (ed.), *Social identity and intergroup relations*, 15–40. Cambridge.

Ucko, P. (1969) 'Ethnography and archaeological interpretation of funerary remains', *WA* 1: 262–80.

Van Andel, T. and Runnels, C. (1987) *Beyond the acropolis: a rural Greek past*. Stanford.

Van den Berghe, P. (1976) 'Ethnic pluralism in industrial societies: a special case?', *Eth* 3: 242–55.

Van Effenterre, H. (1985) 'Il problema delle istituzioni doriche', in D. Musti (ed.), *Le origini dei Greci: Dori e mondo egeo*, 293–312. Rome.

(1991) 'Diversité dialectale de la Crète', in C. Brixhe (ed.), *Sur la Crète antique: histoire, écritures, langues*, 79–83. Nancy.

Vanschoonwinkel, J. (1991) *L'Égée et la Méditerranée orientale à la fin du IIe millénaire: temoignages archéologiques et sources écrites*. Louvain-la-Neuve and Providence RI.

Vansina, J. (1985) *Oral tradition as history*. Madison.

Van Soesbergen, P. G. (1981) 'The coming of the Dorians', *Kadmos* 20: 38–51.

Van Wees, H. (1992) *Status warriors: war, violence and society in Homer and history*. Amsterdam.

Vecoli, R. (1978) 'The coming of age of the Italian Americans: 1945–1974', *Eth* 5: 119–47.

Veit, U. (1989) 'Ethnic concepts in German prehistory: a case study on the relationship between cultural identity and archaeological objectivity', in S. Shennan (ed.), *Archaeological approaches to cultural identity*, 35–56. London.

Verbaarschot, G. (1988) 'Dialect passages and text constitution in Aristophanes' *Acharnians*', *Mnem* 41: 269–75.

Verdelis, N. M. (1958) '*Ο πρωτογεωμετρικὸς ρυθμὸς τῆς Θεσσαλίας.* Athens.

(1962a) '*Ἀνασκαφὴ Μυκηνῶν*', *Praktika*, 57–89.

(1962b) 'A sanctuary at Solygeia', *Archaeology* 15: 184–92.

Verdelis, N., Jameson, M. H. and Papachristodoulou, I. (1975) '*Ἀρχαϊκαὶ ἐπιγραφαὶ ἐξ Τίρυνθος*', *Arch.Eph*, 150–205.

Vernant, J-P. (1980) *Myth and society in ancient Greece.* London. (Originally published as *Mythe et société en Grèce ancienne.* Paris, 1974.)

Veyne, P. (1988) *Did the Greeks believe their myths?* Chicago. (Originally published as *Les Grecs ont-il cru à leurs mythes?* Paris, 1983.)

Vidal-Naquet, P. (1981a) 'Slavery and the rule of women in tradition, myth and utopia', in R. L. Gordon (ed.), *Myth, religion and society*, 187–200. Cambridge.

(1981b) 'Land and sacrifice in the Odyssey: a study of religious and mythical meanings', in R.L. Gordon (ed.), *Myth, religion and society*, 80–94. Cambridge.

Vollgraff, W. (1904) 'Fouilles d'Argos', *BCH* 28: 364–99.

(1907) 'Fouilles d'Argos: la topographie de la ville hellénique', *BCH* 31: 144–84.

(1928) 'Arx Argorum', *Mnem* 56: 315–28.

(1934) 'Une offrande à Enyalios', *BCH* 58: 138–56.

(1956) *Le sanctuaire d'Apollon Pythéen à Argos.* Paris.

Voutsaki, S. (1995) 'Social and political processes in the Mycenaean Argolid: the evidence from the mortuary practices', in R. Laffineur and W-D. Niemeier (eds.), *Politeia: society and state in the Aegean Bronze Age*, 55–66. Liège.

Wace, A. J. B. (1921–23) 'Excavations at Mycenae: Part IX. The tholos tombs', *BSA* 25: 283–396.

(1926) 'Crete and Mycenae', *CAH* (1st edition) II, 431–72.

(1932) *Chamber tombs at Mycenae.* Oxford.

(1939) 'Mycenae, 1939', *JHS* 54: 210–12.

(1949) *Mycenae: an archaeological history and guide.* Princeton.

Wace, A. J. B., Hood, M. S. and Cook, J. M. (1953) 'Mycenae 1939–1952: Part IV. The Epano Phournos tholos tomb', *BSA* 48: 69–83.

Wade, P. (1993) '"Race", nature and culture', *Man* 28: 17–34.

Walberg, G. (1976) 'Northern intruders in Myc IIIC?', *AJA* 80: 186–87.

Waldstein, C. (ed.) (1902) *The Argive Heraeum* I. Boston and New York.

(1905) *The Argive Heraeum* II. Boston and New York.

Wallace, P. and Kase, E. (1978) 'The route of the Dorian invasion', *AAA* 11: 102–107.

Wathelet, P. (1992) 'Argos et l'Argolide dans l'épopée, spécialement dans le *Catalogue des Vaisseaux*', in M. Piérart (ed.), *Polydipsion Argos: Argos de la fin des palais mycéniens à la constitution de l'état classique* (*BCH* Supplement 22), 99–116. Paris.

Weber, M. (1968) *Economy and society* I. New York. [Originally published as *Wirtschaft und Gesellschaft.* Tübingen, 1922].

Wells, B. (1983) *Asine* II: *Results of the excavations east of the acropolis, 1970–1974. Fasc. 4: the Protogeometric period. Part 2: an analysis of the settlement.* Stockholm.

(1987–8) 'Apollo at Asine', *Peloponnesiaka* Supplement 13.2: 349–52.

(1990) 'The Asine sima', *Hesperia* 59: 157–61.

Welter, G. (1941) *Troizen und Kalaureia.* Berlin.

West, M. L. (1969) 'Stesichorus redivivus', *ZPE* 4: 135–49.

(1985) *The Hesiodic Catalogue of Women: its nature, structure and origins.* Oxford.

Wetherell, M. (1982) 'Cross-cultural studies of minimal groups: implications for the social identity theory of intergroup relations', in H. Tajfel (ed.), *Social identity and intergroup relations*, 207–40. Cambridge.

Whitbread, I. K. (1992) 'Petrographic analysis of Barbarian Ware from the Menelaion, Sparta', in J. Sanders (ed.), *ΦΙΛΟΛΑΚΩΝ: Lakonian studies in honour of Hector Catling*, 297–306. London.

White, A. (1978) 'The environment and social behaviour', in H. Tajfel and C. Fraser (eds.), *Introducing social psychology*, 357–79. Harmondsworth.

White, H. (1978) 'Historical text as literary artifact', in R. Canary and H. Kozicki (eds.), *The writing of history*, 41–72. Madison.

Whitley, A. J. (1988) 'Early states and hero cults: a reappraisal', *JHS* 108: 173–82.

(1994) 'The monuments that stood before Marathon: tomb cult and hero cult in Archaic Attica', *AJA* 98: 213–30.

(1995) 'Tomb cult and hero cult: the uses of the past in Archaic Greece', in N. Spencer (ed.), *Time, tradition and society in Greek archaeology: bridging the 'Great Divide'*, 43–63. London.

Wide, S. (1893) *Lakonische Kulte*. Leipzig.

Wide, S. and Kjellberg, L. (1895) 'Ausgrabungen auf Kalaureia', *AM* 20: 267–326.

Wiesner, J. (1938) *Grab und Jenseits: Untersuchungen im ägäischen Raum zur Bronzezeit und frühen Eisenzeit*. Berlin.

Wiessner, P. (1983) 'Style and social information in Kalahari San projectile points', *Am.Ant* 49: 253–76.

(1989) 'Style and changing relations between the individual and society', in I. Hodder (ed.), *The meaning of things: material culture and symbolic expression*, 56–63. London.

(1990) 'Is there a unity to style?', in M. Conkey and C. Hastorf (eds.), *The uses of style in archaeology*, 105–12. Cambridge.

Wilamowitz-Moellendorff, U. von (1893) *Aristoteles und Athen* II. Berlin.

(1959 [1931]) *Der Glaube der Hellenen* I (3rd edition). Basel.

Will, E. (1956) *Doriens et Ioniens: essai sur la valeur du critère ethnique appliqué à l'étude de l'histoire et de la civilisation grecques*. Paris.

Willetts, R. F. (1959) 'The servile interregnum at Argos', *Hermes* 87: 495–506.

Willey, G. and Phillips, P. (1958) *Method and theory in American archaeology*. Chicago.

Williams, C. K. (1982) 'The early urbanization of Corinth', *A.S.Atene* 60: 9–20.

Winter, F. A. (1977) 'An historically derived model for the Dorian invasion', in *Symposium on the Dark Ages in Greece*, 51–59. New York.

Winters, T. F. (1993) 'Kleisthenes and Athenian nomenclature', *JHS* 113: 162–65.

Wittenburg, A. (1984) 'I Dori di K.O. Müller', *ASNSP* 14: 1031–44.

Wobst, M. (1977) 'Stylistic behaviour and information exchange', *MAAP* 61: 317–42.

Wright, J. C. (1982) 'The old temple terrace at the Argive Heraeum and the early cult of Hera in the Argolid', *JHS* 102: 186–201.

Wyatt, W. F. (1970) 'The prehistory of the Greek dialects', *TAPA* 101: 557–632.

Zangger, E. (1991) 'Prehistoric coastal environments in Greece: the vanished landscapes of Dimini Bay and Lake Lerna', *JFA* 18: 1–15.

(1993) *The geoarchaeology of the Argolid (Argolis II)*. Berlin.

(1994) 'The island of Asine: a palaeogeographic reconstruction', *Op.Ath* 20: 221–39.

Index